THE SECRET ROAD
TO WORLD WAR TWO

BOOKS BY PAUL W. BLACKSTOCK

The Strategy of Subversion
Agents of Deceit
The Secret Road to World War Two

PAUL W.
BLACKSTOCK

THE SECRET ROAD TO WORLD WAR TWO

SOVIET VERSUS
WESTERN
INTELLIGENCE
1921-1939

CHICAGO QUADRANGLE BOOKS 1969

For Barbara and Jean

ACKNOWLEDGMENTS

THE RESEARCH for this book was conducted during a sabbatical year (1966–67) in several European cities, mainly Moscow, Munich, London, Brussels, and Paris. I am grateful to the Committee for Productive Research and Scholarship and the Institute of International Studies of the University of South Carolina for financial support.

For the Russian-language sources (mainly Russian Soviet or émigré newspapers and journals) used in the preparation of the manuscript, it was necessary to consult not only the Library of Congress but also major European collections such as the Lenin Library in Moscow, the British Museum, the Munich *Staatsbibliothek,* and the Helsinki University Library. Many collections are incomplete or mutilated. For example, the important "Opperput" articles in *Segodnya* for 1927 in the Helsinki collection were clipped by the Central Investigative Police of Finland, and I am indebted to Mr. Karlevi Ruhala for copies of those missing articles, and to Mr. Aaron Bell for others. I wish to express my thanks to the following of the Institute for the Study of the U.S.S.R. in Munich: Mr. Edward Crowley, Mr. Leon Barat, Mr. Nikolai Galai, and Mrs. Maria Lippert, the chief librarian, whose help was indispensable. Mr. Galai not only read an early draft of the section on the Trust but provided new evidence on the Kutyepov kidnaping. Dr. Helmut Krausnick, director of the *Institut fuer Zeitgeschichte* in Munich, was also helpful with reference to the Tukhachevsky affair.

In London, Mr. Ronald A. Wheateley of the British Foreign Office kindly provided access not only to captured German Foreign Office documents but also to the Smolensk (captured Russian) documents, while Mr. Leopold Labedz, associate editor of *Survey* magazine, was of great assistance. Robin Bruce Lockhart read a first draft of the chapter on Savinkov, Reilly, and Elvengren. Mr. R. G. Allen, superintendent of Readers' Services at the Library of the London School of Economics and Political Science, was most helpful in providing Xerox copies of previously unavailable documents from the Melgunov archive.

In Paris, Mr. P. J. Humbert Droz of *le Contrat Sociale* and Guy Lemannier of *L'Est et Ouest* were most helpful, as was Mr. Alexander de Bilderding of the United States Embassy. Mr. B. Orekhov, editor of *Chasovoi* in Brussels, kindly provided materials on both the Trust and the Tukhachevsky affair. For comment and materials on the Tukhachevsky affair, I also wish to thank Mr. Robert Wolfe and Mr. Phillip Brauer of the National Archives and Records Service in Washington, D.C.

I owe a special debt to Dr. Nikolai Vinogradov of New York City for his review of the section on the Trust episode and the Kutyepov offensive. Dr. Vinogradov and Captain Larionov are the only known survivors of Kutyepov's Combat Organization. Both in reviewing the manuscript and in stripping away the layers of myth surrounding the Trust operation, Dr. Vinogradov's assistance was indispensable. Naturally, I assume full responsibility for errors of fact or interpretation which may yet remain.

For their patience and competence in typing the various drafts of the manuscript, my thanks to Mrs. Cloris A. DeGroot and Mrs. Carole K. Brading. As usual, the helpful cooperation of the Reference and Inter-Library Loan staffs of McKissick Library of the University of South Carolina was welcome.

Finally, I owe a word of appreciation to my wife, Marie Chandler Blackstock, who patiently endured with me the privations of Europe on five dollars a day while typing the first draft of several chapters.

P.W.B.

Columbia, South Carolina
January 1969

AUTHOR'S NOTE

Because of the extensive cast of characters who participate in the historical events described in the pages to follow, a *Dramatis Personae* with brief descriptions is offered as an aid to the reader and will be found at the close of the book, immediately following the Notes.

CONTENTS

INTRODUCTION

A T THE
height of the Cold War in the early 1950's, Senator Joseph
McCarthy, exploiting a wave of anticommunist fear and hysteria, successfully terrorized the State Department and the
U.S. Information Agency, attacked the Pentagon, and even
threatened to "investigate" the Central Intelligence Agency.
McCarthy's irresponsible charges of communist conspiracy and
the employment of "security risks" among military personnel
led to the interrogation of top military and civilian defense
officials in full view of television cameras and nationwide
publicity.

Suppose that in this atmosphere laden with fear and suspicion, the President had called a special top-secret meeting of
both the National Security Council and the Joint Chiefs of
Staff—the nation's highest civilian and military organizations
charged with securing the national interest. At this imaginary
meeting, President Eisenhower gravely announced that the
Federal Bureau of Investigation had uncovered a military plot
not only aimed at overthrowing the United States government
but also linked to a parallel plot by top-ranking Soviet military
leaders to seize power in the U.S.S.R. Having disposed of their
respective civilian governments, the two general staff organizations and their leaders could then join forces and hold the
balance of power in the world.

J. Edgar Hoover, head of the FBI, was then called upon
to present the dossiers with documentary evidence of the plot.
There were two sets of dossiers. The first contained evidence

from confidential FBI files. The second consisted of fifteen
sheets of microfilm copies of correspondence, dating back several years, between American and Soviet officers, plus an
original handwritten letter from one of the top American
officers involved. The top-secret stamps, routing or "buck slips"
attached to the papers, and the signatures and initials appeared
to be absolutely genuine—so much so that those officers present
who had been excluded from the conspiracy were convinced
of their authenticity. In the last days of World War II at the
Allied *Kommandatura* in Berlin, the U.S. officers charged with
the conspiracy had indeed had contacts and exchanged official
correspondence with their Russian counterparts. Even President
Eisenhower, then Supreme Allied Commander in Europe, had
had friendly contacts with Soviet Marshal Georgi Zhukov.
There had also been a secret Clay-Sokolovsky agreement between the U.S. and Soviet commanders in Berlin to return
AWOL soldiers and defectors. J. Edgar Hoover explained that
the FBI had obtained the file of incriminating documents from
a friendly intelligence service in Berlin. In checking on each
item in the foreign dossier, the Bureau had collected a mass of
incriminating evidence from its own and Army Counterintelligence Division files which fully confirmed the existence of
the plot.

Those of the American officers present who were implicated in the alleged plot were stunned into silence. What could
they say without legal counsel? And they could hardly deny
the existence of the correspondence itself and the authenticity
of the signatures, initials, penciled comments, and routing slips.
The meeting broke up in a mixture of subdued murmurs, sidelong glances, and stunned silence as the President, in his capacity as commander in chief of the U.S. armed forces, announced
that he would declare a state of national emergency and proceed
at once with an immediate court-martial of the accused. Within
a week the entire Joint Chiefs of Staff were executed (there
was one reported suicide) and an unprecedented purge of the
armed forces took place, which, it was admitted later, had been
excessive and overstepped the "due process" limits built into the
Military Code. Nevertheless—and this is the key element in the
situation—the evidence presented at the original NSC-JCS meeting was so convincing that the chief executive, who ordered the
executions, never lost the loyalty and trust of those who sur-

vived. The purges took place on the eve of a world war and
had so weakened the U.S. armed forces that they were barely
able to survive the ensuing holocaust. Not until years after the
war were historians able to establish the fact that the incriminating documents acquired in Berlin "from a friendly intelligence source," the documents that were presented at the
dramatic NSC-JCS meeting, were forged. The forgery and
planting of this false evidence had been one of the most successful covert operations in modern history.

Of course, the nightmare fantasy thus briefly outlined did
not materialize, and in the more relaxed political atmosphere
of the mid-1960's, a covert operation with such sweeping historical consequences seems absurdly improbable. But something closely analogous to this imaginary scenario did in fact
take·place in Moscow at an extraordinary session of the Military Soviet attached to the Commissariat of Defense which
lasted for three days, June 1–4, 1937. On June 12 the Moscow
papers announced that Marshal Mikhail Tukhachevsky and
other top military leaders (Uborevich, Yakir, Eideman, Kork,
Primakov, and Putna were named) had been condemned to
death by a special military tribunal and shot like "mad dogs."
The evidence presented earlier at the extraordinary session of
the Moscow Military Soviet consisted of NKVD (Soviet security
police) files and forged German documents. The "documentary
proof" was so convincing that throughout the bloody purges
that ensued, the army was not alienated from the regime, and,
in spite of staggering losses in the first months of the Nazi
invasion, fought back stubbornly to ultimate victory. The incident became known as "the Tukhachevsky affair," after the
name of the principal figure involved, and is related in the final
section of this book. But behind the immediate events leading
up to the liquidation of Tukhachevsky and tens of thousands of
other high-ranking Soviet officers lies an incredibly tangled
web of political intrigue and covert operations of the intelligence agencies of the great powers.

Our trilogy of stories—three strangely interlocking episodes in the battle of Soviet versus Western intelligence agencies
—begins back in 1921–22. Let us briefly review the situation
at that time. England, France, and the United States had
emerged triumphant but badly shaken from World War I only

to face an entirely new set of problems. Their former ally, tsarist Russia, not only had collapsed in the last days of the regime but had been swept away by a great political and social revolution. A weak and confused provisional government had in turn been overthrown in an almost bloodless seizure of power by the Bolsheviks under the brilliant and dynamic leadership of Nikolai Lenin. The old bourgeois order was destroyed and the new Bolshevik regime brazenly declared its intention of carrying the revolution abroad. Indeed, Lenin, Trotsky, and other Old Bolsheviks were convinced that their only chance of survival—of saving the revolution at home, as they put it—lay in spreading brush fires of revolution in western Europe. Events proved them wrong. The Bolsheviks were able not only to survive the challenge of a civil war and bumbling Allied intervention but also to consolidate their regime and to restore their war-torn economy. The Bolshevik regime had passed its baptism of fire, so to speak, and could utilize what Lenin called a much-needed "breathing space." The regime could now turn its attention to the next order of business, the export of revolution, a goal that had been necessarily neglected in the struggle for survival. For this longer-range objective the Bolshevik leaders had already set up the Communist International, or Comintern, in 1919, even before the civil war itself had ended. The Comintern was a worldwide organization of Communist parties pledged not only to carry the torch of revolution, using the conspiratorial techniques of the model Bolshevik party, but also to defend the interests of the Soviet Union as a state. In spite of absurd official denials to the contrary, by the time of its Second Congress in 1921 the Comintern had already proclaimed "the cause of Soviet Russia to be its own cause." With respect to its universal revolutionary aims, a typical Comintern resolution of 1922 declared that "it is the historical mission of the Communist International to be the gravedigger of bourgeois society."

Responsibility for meeting the threat to internal security posed by the existence of Soviet Russia as a revolutionary storm center rested with the security police forces of the Western powers (as with the Federal Bureau of Investigation in the United States today). In spite of some excesses in the "Red Scare" period of the early 1920's, this responsibility was reasonably well discharged. At the same time, the U.S.S.R. became the priority target of the Western intelligence agencies, and a major effort was made to collect as much information as possible about the new Bolshevik regime both from sources remaining within the country and from espionage agents sent in from abroad.

By 1920 the Bolshevik regime was firmly in the saddle. The Cheka, the Soviet security police, had ruthlessly executed thousands of internal "enemies of the people," but there were still some scattered resistance elements left, although they had been driven underground. Moreover, as the civil war ended, about 150,000 so-called White Russians had withdrawn from the Crimea and had resettled in Bulgaria and Yugoslavia under the leadership of General Piotr Nikolayevich Wrangel. A small nucleus of 15,000 to 25,000 of the troops kept up their military training and morale under General Aleksandr Pavlovich Kutyepov and constituted a potential reserve force for paramilitary and counterrevolutionary purposes.

Moreover, there were roughly a million Russian émigrés and refugees who had left during the war and revolution and were scattered in colonies in Berlin, Paris, London, New York, Chicago, and elsewhere. The political attitudes of the émigrés were mixed and ambivalent, although as a rule profoundly nationalistic. Most of them simply accepted the Bolshevik regime as an unpleasant fact of life, turned away from the past, and began the slow process of integrating themselves into their newly adopted lands, learning new languages and building new lives for themselves and their families. A small minority of the émigrés were drawn into the Communist party (75 percent of the CP membership in Chicago in 1920, for example, was of Russian origin). Another minority refused to believe that the Bolshevik regime was anything more than an ugly passing phenomenon which would soon be overthrown in a counterrevolution. Of this group an even smaller faction was dedicated to a restoration of the monarch—like the aristocratic French émigrés scattered abroad after the French Revolution of 1789. These monarchist groups in Paris, Berlin, or Yugoslavia were in occasional touch with like-minded underground groups that had survived extermination by the Cheka inside the U.S.S.R. They also had the sympathy and at times the active support of Western intelligence agencies, since they provided a ready-made pool of intelligence "assets" for collecting information or for political warfare purposes. If, as many people in high places hoped and believed, the Bolshevik regime would sooner or later be overthrown, obviously a major task of the Western intelligence agencies was to keep in close, although necessarily secret, touch with the groups and individuals who would form the nucleus of future government. Quite apart from the political sympathies or preferences of its personnel, this kind of task is by definition a major responsibility of any intelligence agency with respect to the principal powers with which it deals.

On the other side of the fence, inside the U.S.S.R., the Soviet security police and counterintelligence services also had their work cut out for them. Internally they were concerned with keeping the scattered resistance elements left over from the civil war under surveillance and control, exiling them to Siberia, or exterminating them. All three techniques were used. But the underground resistance elements within the U.S.S.R. were also in communication with anti-Bolshevik émigrés abroad, and these in turn were at least potential assets of Western intelligence agencies. Hence, penetrating the Russian émigré groups abroad and keeping them under surveillance automatically became a priority task of Soviet counterintelligence.

Thus the stage was set for the battle of Soviet versus Western intelligence agencies. The first round in this struggle, a major engagement lasting roughly five years, from 1922 to 1927, centered around a Soviet-inspired operation called "the Trust." By means of this skillfully conducted provocation, Soviet intelligence was able to penetrate hostile émigré groups abroad, to deceive the Western intelligence agencies, and to some extent to suppress counterrevolutionary activities directed against the U.S.S.R. from abroad. This was a highly complex and delicate affair involving a large cast of both Soviet and Western characters, including the famous revolutionary terrorist Boris Savinkov and Britain's "master spy," Sidney Reilly, both of whom were deeply involved. On the Soviet side, the real hero of the operation was Aleksandr Aleksandrovich Yakushev, an obscure specialist, not in counterintelligence, but in canals and waterways.

In the continuous subsurface battle of the intelligence services, the individual agent is expendable, like the individual soldier in open military hostilities. Nevertheless, although directed by great, impersonal government bureaucracies, covert operations depend for their ultimate success or failure on the characteristics and capabilities of the individuals involved on the working level. For this reason, the emphasis in the reconstruction of the Trust operation, which makes up the first section of this book, is on the role of the individual agents caught up in the tangled web of plot and counterplot, at the cost to some of them of life itself.

The second section of the book deals with the Soviet war scare in the spring and summer of 1927 as the Trust collapsed and was no longer able to prevent the émigré general Kutyepov's Combat Corps in Paris from sending terrorists into the U.S.S.R. Viewed in retrospect, these strategic-services operations—sporadic bombings and assassinations—add up to no more than a minor tempest in a teapot. But they coincided with the collapse of Soviet efforts to bolshevize China and with a confused and deadly power struggle within the U.S.S.R. During this period of his rise to supreme power, Stalin moved rapidly to eliminate his archrival Trotsky and other opponents. He exploited the occasional bombings and the war scare by accusing the opposition of being linked to White Russian and foreign intelligence agents—a charge that was mechanically repeated a decade later in connection with the Great Purges of the midthirties. As the war scare subsided and Stalin consolidated his power, the OGPU continued its relentless political warfare against the Russian émigrés in Paris.

Although the anti-Soviet operations of the Russian émigrés were secretly and heavily subsidized by Western governments, they ended in failure and have been virtually ignored by Western historians. As a result, Soviet propagandists have preempted the field and have created a distorted image of the émigrés as black reactionaries seeking nothing more than a restoration of the monarchy and a return of the landlords. Émigré military leaders such as Generals Wrangel and Kutyepov have been portrayed as blind dupes of the OGPU and their followers as no more than an armed rabble of "White Guardist" cutthroats and mercenaries. An attempt has been made in the first half of this study to correct this image by letting the facts speak for themselves. A second general objective has been to concentrate on the problems and reactions of real people at the working level of covert operations. Accordingly, whenever fragments of personal notebooks, conversations, or journals have been discovered, they have been quoted extensively in order to let the little men out in "the cold" tell their own story of events as they saw them. Thus an abridged version of Captain Larionov's account of his bombing of the Leningrad Central Party Club is printed for the first time in English.

The third section of the book deals with the golden age of organized murder, kidnaping, and subversion, roughly the decade 1927–37, during which the last of the amateurish terror raids of General Kutyepov's Combat Corps were followed by the professionally organized crimes of the OGPU (renamed the NKVD after 1934). This was the period during which the individual, often free-lance terrorist was replaced by the new "organization man," the paid assassin of the Soviet and later of the Nazi and other intelligence agencies. By the middle of the decade Europe had been politically polarized into left and right extremes, and mass subversion became the order of the day as politically organized bands clashed noisily in the streets. By the eve of World War II the new, professionally manipulated violence reached its logical end point in the Nazi extermination camps on the one hand and in the bloody purges and slave-labor camps of the U.S.S.R. on the other. Against this background the Russian émigré colony in Paris split into politicized factions and its leadership was neutralized with the kidnaping of General Kutyepov and his successor, General Yevgeny Karlovich Miller.

The fourth and final section of the book deals mainly with the Tukhachevsky affair and the onset of the Great Purges, a blood bath without parallel in modern history, in which not only most of the Old Bolshevik political leadership was liquidated but also the ablest of the Red Army commanders, leaving the Soviet armed forces badly crippled as Hitler rose to the apex of his power and, together with Stalin, plunged the world into war. During this period, in addition to the Soviet NKVD, the Nazi security police empire of Himmler and Heydrich played a major role in the Tukhachevsky frame-up.

Thus the battle of the intelligence services, of which only a few episodes are described in this book, played an important role in the tragicomedy of events that led to the breakdown of world order and the Second World War. Most of the British or French agents involved in these covert operations have died, either through natural causes or by design. One by one, the principal Russian émigrés concerned after being entrapped or kidnaped have been liquidated, either out of revenge or because they knew too much. The dead operators from this shadowy world have left almost no memoirs except for Captain Larionov and Mrs. Reilly, who was more an innocent victim than an agent. The principal Soviet figures perished in the purges. On the Nazi side almost all were killed in the war, and the few survivors either have been reluctant to talk or have left a trail of suspect and conflicting testimony. A recent Soviet account of the Trust operation is based in part on original sources, but is designed primarily for propaganda purposes, to restore the tarnished image of the OGPU. The Soviet account is in the form of a historical novel, *Troubled Waters* (*Mertvaya Zyb*, Moscow, 1966), by Lev Nikulin. With regard to the basic history of the operation *from the Soviet point of view* there is no reason to doubt the broad outlines of Nikulin's narrative, although he distorts the role of Edward Staunitz (Opperput), one of the principal OGPU agents, and relies mainly on secondary sources for his sections on the entrapment of Boris Savinkov and Sidney Reilly.

In a sense the story of the Trust has become a firmly entrenched historical myth or legend, to which Western accounts have also contributed their share of exaggerations, so that all sources must be used with caution. Although in some cases it is still impossible to strip the layers of legend from the core of reality beneath, nevertheless, even as a fable the story of the Trust operation is important for the lessons to be drawn from it and for the insights it provides into the methods of the OGPU or of any other security police or counterintelligence agency.

Marshal Tukhachevsky and many others have since been "rehabilitated" and restored to their rightful place of honor in Soviet history. But the inside story of the Tukhachevsky affair is still very sensitive, and the official Soviet biographies of Tukhachevsky rely exclusively on contradictory German sources in sketching in the last days of the Marshal. Nevertheless, with a "logic of the situation" approach and some acquaintance with intelligence operations, it is possible to interpret the evidence available and reconstruct the episodes treated in this book with some approximation to the reality of the historical past.

PART 1
THE TRUST

1

YAKUSHEV: The Recruitment, Care, and Feeding of a Double Agent

T HE TIME
is January 1922. The place, the dining room of a huge five-story town house in the heart of Moscow, a former mansion occupying one entire side of Lubyanka Square. For a time during the war the building had housed an insurance company, but when the Bolsheviks moved the capital from Petrograd to Moscow, it was converted into the headquarters of the dread Cheka, "the All-Russian Extraordinary Commission for combating counterrevolution and sabotage." From here Feliks Dzerzhinsky, aided by seven other commissars and a staff of about 120, directed the famous Red Terror of September 1918. "The Cheka," one of its members explained at the time, "does not judge, it strikes." Some 800 high tsarist officials were summarily executed in Petrograd alone, 512 during the single night of September 7.[1] Obviously, many of those executed were not guilty, but as Dzerzhinsky declared in a press interview: "The Cheka must defend the revolution and conquer the enemy even if its sword falls occasionally on the heads of the innocent." [2] Dzerzhinsky's opponents soon called him the Inquisitor, or the Red Torquemada, but a year later, in a speech to the Second All-Russian Congress of Soviets, Lenin supported him and his methods by declaring that "both terror and the Cheka are absolutely indispensable." [3]

By 1921 the worst of the Terror was over. In March of that year Lenin had introduced the NEP, the "New Economic

Policy," which restored a measure of private initiative in retail trade and light industry, and which was designed to provide a "breathing space," a respite from the havoc of War Communism and revolution. By January 1922, when Dzerzhinsky gathered his principal lieutenants around him in the dining room of the Lubyanka, organized political opposition to the Bolshevik regime had been largely crushed or driven underground. However, as Dzerzhinsky explained in his briefing, both intelligence reports from· abroad and internal Cheka reports indicated the existence of an underground counterrevolutionary organization, the MOCR (Monarchist Organization of Central Russia), with its center in Moscow and branches in Petrograd, Nizhni Novgorod, Kiev, Rostov-on-the-Don, and the north Caucasus. The MOCR had established direct contact with White Russian émigré centers abroad, and with their help was preparing an internal uprising against the Soviet regime. Dzerzhinsky had presented a report on the MOCR to the Party Central Committee and had been directed not to arrest known members of the organization, but to attempt to penetrate it, to discover its leaders, its staff, its methods, its communications links abroad, and if possible to bring it under covert control. An important part of the task was to obtain control of the MOCR's courier system and to establish "windows" on the frontier through which agents could be sent abroad to infiltrate White Russian émigré organizations in Berlin, Paris, London, and other bourgeois capitals.[4] The Cheka, which had understandably acquired a very unsavory reputation, was soon to be abolished and its functions taken over in February 1922 by the same staff with a new title, the State Political Administration (*Gosudarstvennoe Politicheskoe Upravlenie,* or GPU), which in turn became the OGPU (Unified State Political Administration) in November 1923. Continuity was assured by the fact that Dzerzhinsky headed all three organizations, ably assisted by his deputy, Vyacheslav Rudolfovich Menzhinsky, who took over when his chief died on July 20, 1926, during the last year of the Trust. (Because some of the dates cannot be verified, and for the sake of uniformity, the designation OGPU will be used throughout the text of this narrative, although with some loss of accuracy.) [5]

Since, in turn, the White Russian émigré groups abroad were supported by French, British, and later German intelli-

gencc or security agencies, with this directive of the Central
Committee the postwar battle of the intelligence services was
officially joined. This deadly, confused, and uncertain struggle
continued over the next two decades, although it was only
rarely visible beneath the surface of historical events which led
directly to World War II. The struggle was marked by all the
hallmarks of covert operations—penetration, subversion, defection and redefection, fraud, forgery, kidnaping, and assassination. These operations directly affected the military estimates
of the great powers, and culminated in the disastrous purge of
the Soviet armed forces in 1937–38. The purge so weakened
the Red Army that after the Nazi onslaught Stalin complained
bitterly in a top-secret telegram to his field army commands
that "unfortunately firm and steady commanders and commissars are not very numerous in our ranks." [6]

As Dzerzhinsky continued his briefing on the MOCR, he
could hardly foresee that this first major counterintelligence
operation of the OGPU would be crowned with success, and
that after his death in 1926 the site of the OGPU headquarters
would be renamed Dzerzhinsky Square in his honor. In answer
to his own rhetorical question, "What should we do?," he observed that what was needed was someone well known in Moscow for his monarchist convictions who might be able to penetrate the MOCR, become one of its political leaders, and then
work within it in the interests of the OGPU and the Soviet
regime. Fortunately, the security police knew an individual who
was a likely candidate for the job if he could be persuaded to
cooperate.

The prospective double agent had already been arrested
and held incommunicado by the OGPU in the "inner prison"
(a maze of interior rooms in the rambling old mansion on
Lubyanka Square) since November 22. His name was Aleksandr Aleksandrovich Yakushev. According to his first deposition, he was forty-five years old at the time of his arrest, was
married, and had three children. A well-known specialist in
water transport, he had held a "solid position" in the Ministry
of Navigable Waterways under the tsarist regime, but due to his
strong monarchist convictions had refused the offer of a similar
post in the Provisional Government set up after the February
1917 Revolution. However, he had since been employed by the
Soviet regime as a consultant on water-transport problems. Al-

though he belonged to no political party, he described himself as a "Russian nationalist and monarchist." He admitted to having taken part in organizing a mutinous uprising in Petrograd in 1919, which the Cheka had speedily crushed. He had gone to Sweden on official business during the first week in November, had returned on the twenty-second, and was arrested just as he was leaving for Irkutsk on another assignment. He emphasized that both before and after the Revolution he had been and remained a Russian nationalist and monarchist. He disavowed any current counterrevolutionary activity and refused to name or implicate any of his friends or acquaintances.

Dzerzhinsky continued briefing the other Chekists present at the meeting: Abram A. Slutsky (alias Artuzov), Roman Aleksandrovich Pillar, and Viktor Stanislavovich Kiakovsky. Yakushev had been under surveillance for some time and the OGPU had collected a substantial dossier on him. The suspect had an early record of sabotage, which he had freely admitted. But, Dzerzhinsky noted, as an individual who placed "Russian national interests above everything," Yakushev had opposed the Allied intervention. In spite of his strong monarchist convictions, he disapproved of terrorism and other methods of his fellow conspirators, including espionage for the Entente powers. Yakushev was undoubtedly a leading member of the political council of the MOCR, but he refused to admit it or to name any of his colleagues. His arrest had not been announced and would be kept secret. If he could be won over and persuaded to work for the OGPU as a double agent, he might be the missing key by which the OGPU could gain access to the MOCR and its affiliates among the White Russian émigrés abroad. Everything depended on whether Yakushev could be won over and persuaded to play what would admittedly be a very difficult and dangerous role, one that required courage, ingenuity, and the ability to hold up under pressure.

The importance that Dzerzhinsky attached to winning over Yakushev is shown by the high-powered task force that went to work on the prisoner during the next two months. The team included Artuzov, Pillar, and Kiakovsky, three of the ablest and toughest OGPU commissars. A. A. Artuzov, who had prepared Yakushev's dossier, was a short, gray-haired man with a small mustache and goatee. Of Italian origin, Artuzov had come to Russia from Genoa in 1917, and for a while taught

French in a girls' school. A music lover and model family man, he rose rapidly in the ranks of the OGPU. At the time of Yakushev's arrest in November 1921, Artuzov was chief of the counterintelligence department (KRO) of the OGPU, and thus was directly in charge of the case.

A former Baltic baron, Roman Aleksandrovich Pillar von Pilhau had been arrested by the tsarist police before the revolution. In filling out his questionnaire, opposite the blank for "Profession" he had written "Revolutionary." He joined the Bolshevik party in 1918 and later became one of Dzerzhinsky's most able and trusted lieutenants. Pillar played an active role not only in the Yakushev case but also later in the capture of the British agents Sidney Reilly and Boris Savinkov.

Viktor Stanislavovich Kiakovsky was a Pole whose family name was Viktor Stetskevich. During the brief Polish-Soviet war of 1920–21 he had operated behind the Soviet lines as one of Poland's most daring agents. After Kiakovsky's arrest, Dzerzhinsky, who was himself Polish-born, persuaded him to work for the Cheka under various aliases: Kosinov, Kosinsky, Kolesnikov. In addition to his role in the Yakushev case, he worked as an OGPU counterintelligence agent in the Soviet legations in Riga, Latvia, and Helsinki, and in 1926, under the alias Petrovsky, took part in the Moscow kidnaping of the Estonian minister to the U.S.S.R., Ado Birk.[7] He was murdered by a religious fanatic in Mongolia in 1932.

For the next two months Artuzov, Pillar, and Kiakovsky took turns at interrogating Yakushev. Occasionally, at dramatic moments in the process of breaking their subject down, they were ably assisted by Dzerzhinsky himself. According to a semi-official Soviet account, the seemingly endless interrogations were conducted quietly, in a detached, almost sympathetic manner, without recourse to the brutal mistreatment and torture that were used during the earlier Red Terror and later during the Great Purge trials.[8] According to a Western source, Yakushev and a fellow prisoner

> were subjected to some of the Cheka's more effective methods of persuasion. Thus, they were made to witness a few mass executions . . . something which none of those exposed to it were ever able to survive without breaking. After that they were themselves several times taken out to be shot, only to be

dragged back to their cells at the last minute, supposedly under a temporary reprieve.[9]

This traditional Russian technique of manipulative persuasion dates back to the tsarist regime (Dostoevsky was put through the ordeal of a mock execution by the Okhrana, the tsarist secret police). But it is doubtful that the OGPU used such methods on Yakushev, who, once he had been persuaded to work with them, served his new masters faithfully for years at considerable personal risk when he could easily have defected during his many trips to London, Paris, Berlin, and other émigré centers abroad.

In persuading Yakushev, a defiant, convinced monarchist, to work for them, the OGPU commissars were faced with the basic problem of subversion: how to undermine the loyalties of the individual subject, detach them from the symbols and institutions (the Tsar and the MOCR) with which those loyalties had been associated, and gradually restructure them to serve the interests of the Soviet regime. Fortunately, Artuzov and his colleagues held a trump card—one that later proved to be a decisive psychological factor—in the circumstances surrounding Yakushev's arrest.

Like most Moscow families then and now, the Yakushevs lived in a multiple-family dwelling. One of those who shared their quarters was a middle-aged woman, Barbara Nikolayevna Strashkevich. Barbara, Yakushev later told his interrogators, was a good soprano. He himself was a basso, and they often sang duets together, so naturally they were old friends. (They had even been intimate friends, he admitted under further pressure.) Furthermore, Barbara Strashkevich was the aunt of one of Yakushev's boyhood friends, Yuri A. Artamonov. The two young men had attended the famous imperial lycée in St. Petersburg together, and the OGPU files included a graduation photograph of them dated 1907. After the revolution, Artamonov, a tsarist army officer, had served in Kiev under the hetman Skoropadsky, the head of a German-sponsored puppet government in the Ukraine which lasted from April 1918 until the German military collapse in November. With the collapse of the ephemeral Skoropadsky government, Artamonov had fled abroad, and at the time of Yakushev's arrest (November 22, 1921) was working as a translator in the passport office of the

British embassy in Reval, Estonia.[10] In Reval, Artamonov was active in Russian émigré circles supported by British intelligence. At that time the two Baltic "windows," Riga and Reval, were major Western sources of intelligence on Soviet affairs, and since 1920 formal collaboration between the American and British intelligence services had been established in Riga, and presumably in Reval as well.[11]

Before leaving on his ill-starred official journey to Sweden and Norway, Yakushev had agreed, as a favor to an old friend, to visit Barbara Strashkevich's nephew Yuri Artamonov in Reval, and deliver for her a simple, two-word personal message: "Alive, well."

All these facts were well known to Yakushev's OGPU interrogators when he wrote his first, defiant deposition in which he denied any counterrevolutionary connections and flatly refused to name any associates. But Yakushev did not know that he had been under close surveillance, and his ignorance of his real situation accounted for his self-assurance. It also provided the OGPU with the means of breaking him down. In a dramatic scene during one of the interrogations, Artuzov and Pillar confronted Yakushev with Barbara Strashkevich, and he was forced to admit that he had delivered a message from her to Artamonov, whom he knew to be an "enemy of the Soviet state" and a British intelligence agent. He was also forced to confess that Captain Vsyevolod Ivanovich Shchelgachev was with Artamonov at their meeting in Reval, and that he knew Shchelgachev was an intelligence officer serving General Wrangel, the commander of the émigré forces that had sought refuge in Yugoslavia at the end of the civil war.

Yakushev fully realized that with these incriminating admissions he had virtually sealed his own death warrant. Then came the agonizing questions that enabled the OGPU to play its trump card: How had they found out about the meeting? Who had betrayed him? Certainly neither Shchelgachev nor Artamonov, who were sworn enemies of the Soviets! This was the moment his interrogators had been waiting for, and Pillar, who held in his hands a letter, named Yuri Artamonov, Yakushev's boyhood friend, as his betrayer. Pillar showed him the salutation, "Dear Kyril," and the signature, "Yours, Yuri." The envelope was inscribed, "To Prince Kyril Shirinsky-Shikhmatov, Kurfürstendamm 16, Berlin, from Yuri A. Artamonov." Then

Pillar read extracts from the letter, which was obviously a full report on Yakushev, his importance as a leader of the MOCR, his views and convictions as he had expressed them during his November 21 meeting with Artamonov and Shchelgachev.

At this point Dzerzhinsky himself entered the room and began the process of winning Yakushev over. His approach was indirect, but, given Yakushev's traumatic state, highly persuasive. The OGPU knew everything about him. Their agents in Berlin had intercepted the letter. Yakushev should realize that he was dealing with "serious people" and a powerful organization, not with juvenile delinquents who played at conspiracy and, from safe positions abroad, gambled with the lives of their friends. In spite of his record, the Soviets had given him work, as they had to many other specialists who were needed to transform the old Russia into the world's first socialist state. And in return, he, Yakushev, had used his position as a cover for plotting a counterrevolutionary conspiracy! His only hope of obtaining clemency was to rewrite his deposition and to make a full breast of everything, a full recognition of his guilt and his crimes.

The next day Yakushev wrote a full confession, ending it with the words "If I am allowed to live, I shall never again take part in any kind of political activity. A. Yakushev."

Actually, Yakushev had not been "betrayed" by his émigré friends, but Artamonov's irresponsibility in handling the report was, in Talleyrand's famous phrase, "worse than a crime—it was a blunder." The psychological effect on Yakushev of this amateurish bungling was the same as if he had been deliberately betrayed. Although he was probably unaware of it in his state of shock at the time, Yakushev's loyalties to the émigré cause had already been undermined. In the sequel, events themselves served to restructure his loyalties and ultimately to attach them to the Soviet cause, which he was soon to serve. Actually Yakushev had much to confess, unlike later OGPU victims (including most of the Old Bolsheviks) who were forced to admit to all kinds of imaginary counterrevolutionary crimes. How much did the OGPU know about the MOCR, with which Yakushev was affiliated at the time of his interrogation? Not much more than the fact of its existence, so far as can be surmised from the Soviet account. However, documents taken from a Russian courier in Reval (presumably by a Western intelligence agency) indicate that it was a modest but active organization which was already corresponding with émigrés in Berlin before Yakushev's arrest during the last week in November 1922. By that time the MOCR had been in existence for over a year, although precisely when Yakushev became associated with it is not known. An intercepted letter tells how it got started:

> Early in November 1921 rumors about the work of Russian monarchists abroad circulated among monarchist circles in Moscow and aroused lively interest. Groups which had been demoralized, scattered, and almost exterminated by the Terror came alive again as a fresh influx of young monarchists, for the most part former officers, joined the ranks. . . . The most active elements centered around Boyar Vasily, the present [May 1922] Supreme Emissary. But there was still no organization on the first of December. For a while the organization was anonymous and without any definite structure, but manifested feverish activity. They took stock of themselves and established liaison with the monarchists in Petrograd.
>
> . . . January and the first half of February [1922] were spent in making contact with monarchists in the provinces, sending out feelers to small groups in Rostov, Yaroslavl, Smolensk, Tveri, and among the Don Cossacks. The idea occurred of calling a convention of the strongest and most active groups of monarchists. The second half of February was taken up with preparations for the convention, which began on the first of March. . . . Ten members attended from the Moscow organization and eleven from the provinces. Some of those who were invited but unable to attend sent written reports of their local activities and their views on future possibilities of fighting the Bolsheviks. Following the report of the group initiating the convention, the delegates declared themselves to be the Constituent Assembly of the MOCR.[12]

The head of the organization, General A. M. Zayonchovsky, was given the exalted title of Supreme Emissary and later used the cover name of Boyar Vasily or Verkhovsky in correspondence abroad.[13] A Political Council of five members and a chief of staff and his deputy were appointed. The military members of the organization were organized into three ranks with 280 men in Moscow and the rest in provincial groups. Total membership was estimated at 400, a modest but vigorous beginning.

Liaison with Berlin émigrés was soon established through Yakushev's friend Artamonov, who received letters in Reval and forwarded them to leaders of the VMC, the Supreme Monarchist Council. During the first year of its existence the Moscow organization regarded itself as subordinate to the Berlin council, from which it sought financial support in a series of increasingly disillusioned letters as no funds were forthcoming. One of the most bitterly disappointed members of the MOCR was Yakushev, who was well known for his "anti-émigré" views, but nevertheless was nominated to attend a monarchist convention scheduled to take place in Paris the following year.[14] Yakushev was named to represent the MOCR presumably because his government position as a consultant for navigation and waterways made it possible for him to obtain an exit visa, denied to all but a few privileged Soviet citizens for official travel abroad. His ill-fated meeting with Artamonov and Shchelgachev in Reval shortly before his arrest in November 1922 was apparently the first face-to-face contact between the Moscow monarchists and those abroad.

Having obtained a full confession from Yakushev, the OGPU left him to brood on his ultimate fate and to nurse his resentment at having been betrayed by his émigré contacts. Another week or two went by. Then, toward the end of February, he was summoned to the main office for a final session with Artuzov. Yakushev was informed that his confession was accepted and that the OGPU respected him as a man of principle, a patriot whose mistaken monarchist convictions were due to his class origin and upbringing. He had recognized his mistakes and had sworn not to take part in further political intrigue. The OGPU would wait and see. Meanwhile, he was free to return to his government post, where he could again serve his native land. There was only one condition attached to his release: he was to say nothing of his arrest to anyone, not even to his wife and family. Some weeks previously his wife had received a telegram from Irkutsk stating that he was hospitalized with a severe case of typhus. His travel orders had been properly stamped to show his arrival and return, so that his cover story was entirely credible. Artuzov then handed him his identity papers and a

pass to permit him to leave the building. Overcome with amazement and gratitude for his unexpected release, Yakushev stag-
gered out of the grim OGPU headquarters on Lubyanka Square
thinking himself a free man at last.

Yakushev was overjoyed to return to his family and his
government post, but without realizing it, in accepting the conditions set down for his release, he was already a *de facto*
agent of the OGPU, with Artuzov as his case officer. Psychologically and operationally, Artuzov could easily predict what
would happen to his pigeon after his release from the Lubyanka.
Yakushev had sworn to renounce all political intrigue. But he
was in fact a member of the Political Council of the underground MOCR. After his "return from Irkutsk," other members
of the organization would inevitably contact him. Yakushev
would then be placed between the hammer and the anvil.
Knowing he was under surveillance, he would report these contacts to the OGPU for his own protection. But he was also too
high up in the MOCR to leave the organization cold without
arousing the suspicion that he had "sold out to the interests,"
in which case he might well be murdered. Faced with this
dilemma, Yakushev would then turn to the OGPU for further
advice and instructions.

Within a month this pattern of events unfolded according
to plan. Sometime in April Yakushev returned to the Lubyanka
for advice and Dzerzhinsky himself made a final maneuver to
win him over. The OGPU sympathized with Yakushev's difficult
position and was obligated to help him. But how? One solution
would be to find him a position in one of the provinces remote
from Moscow, but this would be very inconvenient, and such
a sudden break would look suspicious. If Yakushev really
wanted to serve his country, he would do better to remain at his
post in Moscow and continue to work within the MOCR as an
agent of the OGPU. This role, as he well knew, would also be
dangerous, but they would provide him every possible protection. From his leading position within the MOCR he could help
channel its activities away from senseless acts of terrorism,
which he disapproved of in principle anyway. He could also
help block its espionage for the allied powers, activities which,
as a patriot, he had always rejected in principle. As for his
monarchist émigré friends abroad, he already knew what they
were worth from his one experience with them. Yakushev could

go home and think it over. There was no need to hurry; they would wait for his decision.

The OGPU did not have to wait long. After his first few clandestine contacts with Staunitz, Rtishchev, and other members of the monarchist underground, Yakushev wrote Dzerzhinsky a note saying that he (Yakushev) could no longer straddle the fence. He was casting his lot with the OGPU and wanted to know what line he should take at a clandestine meeting of the Political Council and "action group" (sabotage, bank robbery, etc.) of the MOCR which was scheduled to take place in the near future. In response to his overture, Yakushev was asked to attend a planning conference at the Lubyanka and was accepted as a new member of the OGPU task force that included Artuzov, Pillar, and Kiakovsky. At this meeting Dzerzhinsky explained that with Yakushev's aid the MOCR could be transformed and brought under OGPU control. To keep up with the changing times (Lenin's New Economic Policy was then in full swing), it would be renamed and given a commercial cover, the Moscow Municipal Credit Association—the Trust, as it later came to be known abroad. Posing as "Nepmen," OGPU agents could easily be brought into the organization. As a political leader of the MOCR, Yakushev should use his influence to prevent acts of terror, sabotage, and "expropriations" (a euphemism for bank robbery and theft, methods the Bolsheviks themselves had formerly used to raise money before the revolution). He should take the line that such *terakts* (as they were called in the jargon of the underground) were dangerous and would bring the OGPU into the act, thus risking everything—two undeniable arguments. It would be much safer and more profitable to raise money by obtaining donations to the cause from émigré groups abroad, with whom Yakushev had already made the first person-to-person contact in Reval, which he would soon visit again.

With this first staff meeting the Trust was born.

From an analytical point of view, the OGPU handling of Yakushev is a classic illustration of the successful recruitment or early care and feeding of a double agent. The operation was brilliantly conducted and merits professional admiration. By way of qualification, however, it should be noted that almost all the ingredients for successful subversion were present from the outset. First, there was the inexcusable security break that led to the arrest of the prospective recruit, and which later convinced him that he had been betrayed by his colleagues. Second, the individual himself was a person of strong moral convictions and a genuine patriotism of sorts, for which he had already taken great risks. Once his value structure and loyalties were reoriented, he could be relied upon to serve a new cause faithfully, motivated less by personal gain than by conscious or unconscious gratitude that his life had been spared, and by the conviction that he was serving the best interests of his native land. Given these favorable conditions, it required only a little imagination and psychological grasp of the situation to establish the scenario and let the subsequent events follow their clearly predictable course.

2
OPERATIONS AT HOME
AND LIAISON
ABROAD

Having recruited Aleksandr Aleksandrovich Yakushev, a political leader of the underground MOCR (the Monarchist Organization of Central Russia), in April 1922, the Soviet secret police had to move quickly in order to develop the operational potential that this lucky penetration presented. The first step was to obtain control over all liaison and communications of the organization with the outside world in order to use these channels later for penetrating émigré groups abroad.

As the weeks went by after Yakushev's arrest, Yuri Artamonov was naturally concerned at having lost contact with him. If Yakushev had been arrested, other arrests could be expected, but there was no evidence that any had taken place.

Under these circumstances Artamonov was surprised late one evening by the arrival at his quarters in Reval of a total stranger instead of Captain Vsyevolod Ivanovich Shchelgachev, whom he had been expecting. By way of introducing himself, the unexpected guest handed him a note from Artamonov's aunt, Barbara Strashkevich, in Moscow. His aunt wrote that her note would be delivered to him by Pavel Petrovich Kolesnikov, a government economist who had done her a number of favors, and that, thank God, all was well with her in Moscow. Kolesnikov brought news of Yakushev, he said.

About this time, Captain Shchelgachev arrived, and drinks were served to give the stranger a real Russian welcome and to celebrate the renewed contact with Yakushev and the MOCR. After a few drinks, with the typical reaction of a counterintelligence agent, Shchelgachev accused Kolesnikov of being a "plant," and challenged him to prove that he was from Moscow. It was a tense moment. Coolly, Kolesnikov asked for a penknife, slit open the cover of a notebook he was carrying, and pulled out a small piece of linen on which a letter was enciphered. The key, Kolesnikov explained, would be found on page 86 of Otto Weininger's *Sex and Character* on Artamonov's bookshelf. While Shchelgachev spent the next half-hour deciphering the message from Yakushev and the MOCR, Kolesnikov explained that Yakushev had nearly died of typhus in Irkutsk, but that he was well again, and hoped to establish close connections with émigré organizations abroad through Reval; that until a regular courier system could be set up he would use the Estonian diplomatic pouch. The message, when deciphered, confirmed what Kolesnikov had said, but any further business was postponed until morning, when they would all be sober, since by then the vodka and the excitement of the occasion had become almost too much for them.

After the meeting the next day, Kolesnikov—or Kiakovsky, as he was also known—returned to Moscow and reported on the success of his mission to his OGPU colleagues. So far as the outside world was concerned, the Trust had replaced the MOCR, had established its first contact abroad, and had successfully deceived not only British intelligence in the person of Artamonov, but also a highly suspicious counterintelligence agent of General Wrangel's forces, Captain Shchelgachev.[1]

This was the first of many successful missions of OGPU Commissar Viktor Stanislavovich Kiakovsky, who with A. A. Artuzov, Roman Aleksandrovich Pillar, and Aleksandr Aleksandrovich Yakushev got the Trust operation off to a good start. Artuzov and Pillar had worked out a cover story for Kiakovsky, according to which he represented himself as the former tsarist lieutenant Kolesnikov, who had been convicted by the Communists of robbery during the civil war, but had managed to conceal his past and was now working for the Soviets as an economist.

Kiakovsky undoubtedly played the scene well. But, as in so many of the later achievements of the Trust, the success of this ploy was almost assured from the outset by the defection

of Yakushev, who had provided the inside knowledge of the cipher key. This was the one top-secret element that immediately removed any suspicions about the unknown visitor.

In the report on his mission to Reval Kiakovsky wrote that Artamonov and Shchelgachev had spoken freely and in critical terms about the key émigré organization in Berlin, the VMC, or Supreme Monarchist Council, led by Nikolai Yevgenevich Markov, a former member of the Russian *Duma,* and Prince Yuri Aleksevich Shirinsky-Shikhmatov (to whose son, Kyril, Artamonov had written the fatal letter that had betrayed Yakushev). They had praised Yakushev highly as the logical person to coordinate the activities of the Moscow and Berlin groups and indicated that the Supreme Council in Berlin would like to take the MOCR over and to direct its anti-Soviet activities.[2]

Communications between Reval and the Trust were set up as follows: An innocuous postcard would be sent by regular mail to Yakushev. After receiving the card he was to call Roman Gustavovich Birk, the press attaché at the Estonian legation, saying: "Dr. Lyubsky has asked about your health." Birk would reply, "My leg doesn't bother me, thanks, but I want to make an appointment for a massage," naming the day and the hour. The meetings were to take place at the Art Theater on Arbat Street, at which time Birk and Yakushev (or another Trust representative) would exchange letters or packages. Artamonov gave Kolesnikov a copy of the book *The Last Days of the Last Emperor,* indicating the page number for the cipher to be used.

There was nothing technically wrong with these familiar "chatterbox code" arrangements for establishing liaison between Western intelligence agencies in Reval and the underground Trust organization in Moscow. However, neither Artamonov and Shchelgachev nor the intelligence agencies they served could foresee that by another stroke of good fortune, Roman Birk, the pivot man in their chain of communications, was soon to fall into OGPU hands, a second defection that greatly facilitated the successful launching of the Trust. Western intelligence services had already been duped into accepting Kiakovsky, an OGPU commissar, masquerading as Lieutenant Kolesnikov, as a courier for the Trust. They were soon to be doubly deceived by Roman Birk.

Roman Birk: A Red Sheep Returns to the Fold

Roman Gustavovich Birk, the press attaché in the Estonian embassy in Moscow, was the nephew of Ado Birk, Estonian minister to the U.S.S.R. who was later kidnaped and became the victim of a complicated OGPU plot which has still not been satisfactorily explained.[3]

After the October Revolution in Russia, Bolshevik regimes had been proclaimed in the Baltic states, only to be swept away by the advancing German armies. After the German surrender in 1918, civil war broke out in Estonia, in which local Communist and Red Army troops took part. But order was soon restored, and by the second of February 1920 a nonsocialist, democratic government signed a treaty of peace with the U.S.S.R. and diplomatic relations were established, as "the Soviet regime needed a neutral, yet not unfriendly, port and clearing house through which trade might pass. Tallin, the Estonian capital, was well suited for the purpose."[4] It was also admirably suited for espionage purposes. Reval (renamed Tallin) was an ideal listening post for Western intelligence services, and it soon became a window through which the OGPU also passed its agents who operated the Trust.

During the confused hostilities of the war and civil war period, Roman Birk had served as a Red Army intelligence officer in Estonia. As the Red Army forces retreated, two of his companions were killed, and he had sought refuge in a farmhouse, burning his identity papers and disguising himself as a farm hand. Later, after order was restored, he had used his uncle's influence to get into the Estonian diplomatic service and was posted as press attaché to Moscow. He had concealed his Communist–Red Army past from his uncle and, needless to say, from the Estonian government; otherwise he would not have been given a security clearance and hired for the job. If his past were exposed he faced immediate dismissal, or worse. One of his colleagues, Kingisepp, had recently been unmasked and summarily executed by a military court-martial.

Under these already difficult circumstances, Birk was called into the office of the Estonian military attaché, Major Lauritz, and was told that, while retaining his nominal position as press attaché for cover, he was being assigned to a secret liaison mission, which, if carried out successfully, would further his diplomatic career. (This assignment took place shortly after the OGPU had established contact in Reval through Kiakovsky's visit to Artamonov and Captain Shchelgachev.) He could expect a telephone call from a "Doctor Lyubsky" and was to set up a date for a "massage," the chatterbox-code name for a rendezvous that would take place during the last run of the current film at the Art Theater on Arbat Street. ("Lyubsky" was a cover name used by Rtishchev, the head of the Trust's political council.) His contact would be carrying a green scarf and would deliver a package. He was to arrange a second rendezvous and ask to meet one of the leaders of the man's organization.

Birk's appointment for a "massage" took place at the Art Theater as scheduled. He arrived early and easily recognized a stranger who approached him, carrying a green scarf. The contact introduced himself to Birk as Kolesnikov, and arranged a second meeting at a safe house on Serebrany Street. Lauritz, the military attaché, was delighted. He prepared a list of questions—intelligence requirements—which Birk was to deliver to his contact at their next meeting at the safe house on Serebrany Street.

Toward the end of April 1922, sometime between his first and second meetings with representatives of the Trust in Moscow, Roman Birk was deeply disturbed—and with reason. All over Estonia his former Communist friends, who had gone underground, were being hunted down by the Estonian security police, arrested, interrogated, and shot. If under torture one of them named him as a former Red Army intelligence officer, he too was finished. Moreover, as a former Communist he was revolted by his present assignment and by Major Lauritz, his new boss, who for all practical purposes was a British intelligence agent—all in all, a very unpleasant situation.

It was a late spring that year. Birk was standing on a bridge over the Moscow River, moodily watching the ice floes breaking up below, when a military figure passing by suddenly stopped and greeted him. It was August Ivanovich Kork, the Red Army commander with whom he had served in Estonia, and who assumed that he had been killed. Kork had since commanded the Sixth Red Army against the White Russian forces of General Wrangel in the autumn of 1920, and was then head of the Kharkhov Military District. The two exchanged reminiscences, and in a moment of candor Roman Birk shamefacedly explained his present precarious position and his ambivalent feelings. Kork listened sympathetically and told him that if he should decide to defect to the Soviet side, he would support him as he would any former comrade at arms, and gave him a telephone number to call, just in case. The two shook hands and parted.

The next day Major Lauritz handed Birk the list of questions he was supposed to deliver to his Trust contact at their next meeting at the Serebrany Street address. Birk did not touch his lunch, feigning a severe toothache, and left work early for an alleged dental appointment. Near his dentist's office was a public telephone. He called the number Kork had given him, using the Red Army commander's name, and asked for an appointment. To his amazement, he was told to keep the appointment previously set up for him by Kolesnikov at the Serebrany Street house. The next day when he arrived there, Kolesnikov introduced him to Commissar Artuzov of the OGPU, who had answered his telephone call. Commander Kork had given Birk Artuzov's telephone number, and had told the latter about their chance meeting, playing a hunch that one of their lost sheep was ready to return to the fold. When Birk arrived at the rendezvous, the scenario was already set for him. According to a recent Soviet account of the meeting, Birk volunteered his services. But the OGPU could easily have persuaded him to work for them by the simple threat of exposing his previous Red Army service to the Estonian police. In any case, Roman Birk was back at the old stand again, working for Soviet intelligence, this time as a double agent under Major Lauritz, the Estonian military attaché, with the assigned task of liaison agent with the Trust, precisely the position in which he could render the most valuable service to the OGPU over the next few years.[5]

Commander Kork had done the OGPU a considerable favor. He had precipitated Birk's decision to defect and had made it physically easy (and secure) for him to return to his former allegiance. Kork had no way of knowing then that both he and Artuzov would be among the first to perish in the Red Army and political purges of 1937–38 as a result of an insidious plot carefully spun in the recesses of the OGPU headquarters on Lubyanka Square.

Take-over and Passive Ideology

By a stroke of good fortune the OGPU had won over an active, intelligent, and respected member of the monarchist organization in Moscow and had also assured its control over all communications with émigré groups in the Baltic states and Berlin. An excellent start had been made toward converting the MOCR (now known as the Trust) into a means of observing and controlling counterrevolutionary activity both at home and abroad. The MOCR was, of course, a conspiratorial organization made up, for security reasons, of small groups or cells, each taking orders from either the Political Council or the military staff at the second echelon, who in turn took orders from the "Supreme Emissary," General A. M. Zayonchovsky. With such command channels two steps were necessary for the OGPU to obtain covert control over the organization, now that Yakushev had become an OGPU agent. The first was to win over or neutralize General Zayonchovsky, and the second was to secure a place for their agent on the Political Council of the organization, a move that would be facilitated by the General's cooperation. The OGPU reportedly forced General Zayonchovsky to cooperate by the simple expedient of threatening the life of his wife and daughter.[6] The General was known and respected as the founder of the Monarchist Union, and as "Boyar Vasily" frequently signed the correspondence between the MOCR and the VMC (Supreme Monarchist Council) in Berlin throughout the year 1922 and up to mid-February 1923.[7]

Zayonchovsky presided over a second underground convention of the MOCR and apparently used his influence to advance Yakushev to a position on the Political Council of the organization, from which he could influence its tactical decisions. In a letter dated September 12, 1922, the VMC in Berlin was invited to send a representative to the underground convention, but failed to do so. Finding a volunteer willing to risk his life to attend a secret meeting of that many people (thirty-five delegates were expected) right under the nose of the OGPU was understandably difficult. It was much easier to wait for an emissary (Yakushev) to arrive in Berlin. Whatever the exact date, the MOCR convention took place before Yakushev's first trip to Berlin in mid-November 1922.[8]

To summarize, within the first six months of the Trust operation the OGPU had considerably advanced the position of Yakushev, its "defector in place," within the organization until he was expected abroad, and had gained firm control over all organized monarchist communications with the Moscow group. Second, it also seems clear that the OGPU had secured the cooperation of the founder of the MOCR, General Zayonchovsky, who henceforth was in fact reduced to a mere figurehead, obviously under adequate control—the threat hanging over his wife and daughter.[9] Unknown to the lower echelon groups within the Trust, the OGPU had thus seized the "commanding heights" of the organization and achieved covert control.

But while security police may penetrate an organization and exert influence over its present and future actions, it is of course powerless to reshape the past. It should be emphasized again that much had happened during the first year's existence of the MOCR before it was taken over by the OGPU. By then the organization had its own ideology and tactics, and had carried on an extensive exchange of ideas by correspondence with the émigré movement abroad, as represented by the VMC, the Supreme Monarchist Council.[10]

During the first year and a half of its existence the MOCR sought not only financial aid (in which it was badly disappointed), but also ideological advice and encouragement from the VMC in Berlin as the realization dawned that the old slogan "God, Tsar, and Fatherland" was inadequate to rally popular support under the radically changed conditions of Bolshevik rule. While Markov was the titular head of the Monarchist Council, Prince Yuri A. Shirinsky-Shikhmatov was its ideologist. As early as March 15, 1921 (when the MOCR was just getting organized), he published an article, "Our Tasks," which was anti-interventionist, and anti-Western as well. A typical pronouncement clearly prefigures the Trust line later developed by Yakushev:

> A popular movement is not created by individuals, it takes place spontaneously—all that is needed is to know how to exploit it . . . Above all we need to understand and imbue our minds with the conviction that our real work is *inside* Russia.[11]

The curious concept of a future "Soviet monarchy" is put forward in a later article (May 28, 1921) as "the only path of complete liberation of Russia . . . from the yoke of Western culture." This kind of confused mixture of passive, Slavophile, and noninterventionist ideas was worked into "program material" when Yakushev visited Berlin in December 1922 and was later published in the Berlin monarchist journals.[12] The myth thus developed that the OGPU, through the Trust, successfully paralyzed all counterrevolutionary activity. Actually the Trust, as such, merely added the finishing stroke to self-imposed paralysis, so far as the top leadership of the Berlin monarchists was concerned. The younger men associated with the Monarchist Council were soon disgusted with the inactivity of its top leadership, and suggested that the Trust should turn elsewhere—to Generals Wrangel and Kutyepov—for assistance. In any case, by early 1924 the VMC broke with the Trust, refusing to accept its leadership and control. The OGPU in the meantime had set up a separate operation (using some Trust personnel) to penetrate and exploit the so-called "Eurasian" ideological movement which had attracted the younger, more militant monarchists associated with the VMC.

Innocents Abroad: The Early Trust Missions to Berlin, Paris, and Yugoslavia

By the summer of 1922 at the latest the Trust had established regular liaison with the British intelligence service's listening post in Reval (Tallin), Estonia. Thanks to Artamonov's enthusiastic reports from the Reval station, the Russian émigré organization in Berlin, the Supreme Monarchist Council, was anxious to meet Yakushev, who before his arrest and subversion by the OGPU had been selected to represent the MOCR. He had been invited to attend the second monarchist convention, held in Paris, November 16–22, 1922, as an MOCR delegate, but was unable to leave Moscow until November 18.[13] His commercial cover was firmly established, since the Trust was known officially abroad as the Moscow Municipal Credit Association. The ostensible reason for his journey—a visit to the Königsberg trade fair—would not arouse undue suspicion. (In those days Western security police regarded practically every traveling Soviet official as an agent of OGPU—not without reason.) The OGPU was also anxious to establish liaison with General Wrangel's forces, for they were the only émigré elements with organized military capabilities.

After his defeat in the civil war in the fall of 1920, the ablest of the White Russian commanders, General Piotr Nikolayevich Wrangel, had managed to withdraw his forces and sympathizers (about 145,000 men, women, and children) to the Gallipoli Peninsula in Greece. After a year of incredible hardship they were resettled in Bulgaria and Yugoslavia, where Wrangel set up his headquarters, with General Aleksandr Pavlovich Kutyepov as second in command. Before leaving on his mission Yakushev made prior arrangements to renew his acquaintance with Artamonov, who came from Reval to meet him during a few hours' stopover in Riga, Latvia. Artamonov brought along a young man, Arapov, a former tsarist horseguardsman and General Wrangel's nephew. The three traveled on to Berlin that evening, arriving on or about November 18, 1922.[14]

Yakushev's first meetings in Berlin were with the "old guard" émigrés, many of them former landowners, industrialists, and high officials of the tsarist regime. Yakushev had known some of these men personally in the old days before the revolution. On December 8, Nikolai Yevgenevich Markov arrived from Paris, following the second monarchist convention. He came as a representative of the Grand Duke Nikolai, and was very favorably impressed by the Trust envoy from Moscow. At a full-dress gathering Yakushev told his aristocratic audience what they wanted to hear: that, led by the Trust, there was a powerful monarchist underground movement in Russia which was preparing to seize power, and that the Soviet regime would not last more than two years. Fired with enthusiasm by Yakushev's hopeful forecast, the émigrés told him that if there were a renewed Allied intervention, they could supply fifty thousand to sixty thousand White Russian troops and three thousand or four thousand foreign volunteers, which would assure the success of their cause, the restoration of the Empire.

Yakushev soon discovered that there was considerable friction between members of the older generation, such as Markov, at the head of the Supreme Monarchist Council, and the younger officers who, like Arapov, represented General Wrangel's forces. Unknown to the older group, Arapov,

Wrangel's nephew, arranged a secret meeting with the General's representative in Berlin, Colonel von Lampe. Von Lampe stated that Russia's salvation lay with these younger militant forces in Yugoslavia, not with the superannuated aristocrats of the VMC in Berlin. Through Colonel von Lampe, Yakushev was introduced to General Klimovich, the head of Wrangel's counterintelligence and security service and a former tsarist police director. Klimovich informed him that while Wrangel's forces were not yet combat-ready, they had been able to infiltrate agents into the U.S.S.R., and were developing their own underground and security techniques. Yakushev promised to give them both a special briefing on his next trip, and returned to Moscow to report on the success of his mission.

For the next six months the OGPU concentrated on the internal security or police aspects of the MOCR. Internally the problem was to keep terrorist members of the group under surveillance and control. Yakushev used his leading position in the organization's Political Council to take a firm stand against *terakts* such as the assassination in Lausanne, Switzerland, in April 1923 of Soviet Ambassador Vatslav Vorovsky by the White Russian fanatic Konrady.[15]

In order to check on Yakushev and to have two independent sources of information, the OGPU also planted one of its agents, Aleksei Zubov, in the MOCR. A young Red Army officer who had taken part in the civil war and later in the suppression of the Basmachi revolt in Soviet Turkestan, Zubov posed as a student terrorist. His father had supposedly been killed in the Kronstadt rebellion by the Bolshevik forces under Tukhachevsky. When Yakushev ran into him by chance at the Lubyanka, he first thought that Zubov had been arrested, but the situation was soon clarified, and Zubov was then put under Yakushev's orders. Later he was to lose his life on the job in a bloody episode that backfired. (See Chapter 5, below.)

For the most part the OGPU, thanks to Yakushev's influence, was able to keep terrorists who drifted in and out of the MOCR in Moscow under surveillance and control or to eliminate them. One such individual committed suicide. But it was far less successful in preventing sporadic acts of violence in the provinces and abroad. On February 5, 1926, the Soviet diplomatic couriers Teodor Hette and Yugann Makhmastal were fired upon while traveling through Latvia. Hette was killed in the attack and Makhamstal was seriously injured, although he saved the diplomatic pouch from being violated.[16]

In August 1923 Yakushev's second liaison mission abroad, during which he used a false passport and the alias Fedorov, took him first to Berlin and then to Paris. As he had promised earlier, on August 7 he gave a special briefing in Berlin to Colonel von Lampe, General Klimovich, Wrangel's counterintelligence chief, and Vasily Vitalevich Shulgin, a leading civilian in General Wrangel's entourage who later made a fantastic trip to the U.S.S.R. as a special guest of the Trust. Chebishev, Wrangel's political consultant and civil-affairs officer, was also present. The report lasted about two hours.[17] When Yakushev had finished, General Klimovich asked the crucial question: How could such a broad-based underground organization as the MOCR escape the surveillance of the OGPU, with which all present at the meeting had had such bitter experience?

Yakushev had anticipated this kind of challenge, and in reply took the line that he and his colleagues, like the cat in the Krilov fable, had learned a great deal about conspiracy the hard way. Having penetrated all agencies of the Soviet government, they were capable of warding off a blow from any direction. They had established supporting links with friendly intelligence agencies, and had already set up a clandestine border-crossing point near Reval. In a word, seated in Berlin, his audience had only the vaguest picture of what was happening in Moscow, or anywhere else in Russia.

As the door closed behind Yakushev a heated discussion broke out. Chebishev stated flatly that Yakushev was a dangerous type and the Trust was a "mystification"—an OGPU provocation. Then, according to the Soviet account of the discussion, Wrangel's representatives, Von Lampe and Klimovich, argued that both the Poles and the British accepted the fact that there was a powerful underground organization in Russia, and that their own agents, in spite of the OGPU, had also been able to penetrate the U.S.S.R. Shulgin, who apparently did not wish to take either side of the argument, was silent.[18] According to Von Lampe, the only living survivor, both he and Klimovich agreed with Chebishev and were categorically opposed to taking Yakushev into their confidence.[19]

Yakushev remained a second week in Berlin, working on ideological and propaganda material with Prince Yuri Shirinsky-Shikhmatov at the top level of the VMC and meeting frequently with Wrangel's nephew Arapov and other young monarchist officers. Arapov, who believed wholeheartedly in the Trust and was an enthusiastic supporter of Yakushev, undoubtedly wrote a glowing letter to his uncle in Yugoslavia.

During his second week in Berlin Yakushev played the VMC and the Wrangel factions against each other and believed that he had successfully hoodwinked both of them. From Markov of the VMC group he obtained letters of recommendation to Prince Obolensky and Count Hendrikov in Paris, who were close to the Grand Duke Nikolai. From Von Lampe he obtained letters to Wrangel's representatives in Paris, General Kholmsen and General Miller. What Yakushev did not know was that at the same time Von Lampe had written confidential letters to the two generals in Paris warning them that the Trust was an OGPU provocation and that Yakushev should be handled with caution.[20] On August 23, 1923, he left for Paris via Wiesbaden and Frankfurt in an automobile driven by Arapov.

In Paris as in Berlin, Yakushev undoubtedly pleaded the Trust line: The émigrés should go slowly, conserve their strength and train troops for the day of restoration, rather than waste their energies in senseless acts of terror. Above all, they should wait until the Soviet regime was ready to collapse from within, avoiding the fatal error of a premature attack which would risk everything. Moreover, restoration of the monarchy would ultimately depend on the internal support of a powerful monarchist party, which the Trust represented. The future government should be made up mainly of those who struggled for it inside Russia, and who had lived there throughout the difficult years.

Before leaving Paris Yakushev also set up regular liaison channels with General Wrangel's representatives there. Correspondence was to be handled by General Kholmsen. Arapov, Wrangel's nephew, would perform the same function and represent the Trust in Berlin.[21] Artamonov, who had previously established the link with British intelligence in Reval, Estonia, had in the meantime moved to Warsaw, where, using the alias Lipsky, he provided liaison with Polish G-2 (and presumably continued to report to his British intelligence contacts as well).[22]

Although there is no mention of this in the Soviet account, there is little doubt that during the summer of 1923 Yakushev

was frequently in touch with General Kutyepov, who had previously served as Wrangel's second in command. At that time
Kutyepov had left Yugoslavia for Paris, where he was loosely
attached to the Grand Duke Nikolai but had not yet taken up
his new official duties. (He was not put in charge of political
work, including covert operations, until March 1924.) Since
he had no official ties, his meetings with Yakushev were quite
open. Like almost everyone else, Kutyepov was at first favorably
impressed with him, although he was suspicious of the Trust
from the outset.[23]

Yakushev's first two missions abroad had been successful
in establishing friendly contacts with the older generation of
monarchist politicians and enthusiastic young liaison officers in
Berlin and Paris. He had also met General Kutyepov on several
occasions. However, Yakushev was a civilian with no military
background or stature. Dzerzshinsky and the OGPU task force
operating the Trust (Artuzov, Pillar, and Kiakovsky) decided
that they needed an impressive military personality for liaison
with General Wrangel and the émigré military forces. Former
Lieutenant General Nikolai Mikhailovich Potapov, who had
known Wrangel at the tsarist General Staff College, was recruited to play the fictional role of "chief of staff" for the Trust,
and to contact his former comrade at arms.[24]

On October 19, 1923, Yakushev and General Potapov
traveled together to Warsaw, crossing the Soviet border at a
clandestine transfer point, a new window which the Trust had
recently set up with the help of Polish intelligence. They were
met in Warsaw by Colonel Bayer of the Polish General Staff.
Artamonov (alias Lipsky) was able to provide them with much
useful advance information for the political and military conferences that took place during the next month. Anti-Soviet
guerrillas had formerly been active in the forests along the
border, and the Polish General Staff continued to use individual
survivors of these earlier operations for intelligence-collection
purposes. General Potapov obtained a formal agreement from
the Poles that any "initiatives" for subversive action would
come from the Trust, with the Poles and Allied forces in supporting roles. (This agreement in effect gave the Trust a built-in
veto on any diversionary action, which was their main objective.) On November 22 Yakushev returned to Moscow, while
Potapov continued his liaison mission, going first to Paris and

then to General Wrangel's headquarters in Sremski Karlovci in Yugoslavia.[25]

In Paris Potapov met with the émigré generals Miller and Kholmsen and with Wrangel's counterintelligence chief, Klimovich, whom he had known slightly when Klimovich had been director of a tsarist police department. Kholmsen and Klimovich then traveled with Potapov to Wrangel's staff headquarters in the Yugoslav village of Sremski Karlovci, where the military talks continued. Two months earlier, on September 1, 1923, Wrangel had announced the creation of the Russian Armed Services Union, or ROVS (Rossiski Obshche-Voinsky Soyuz), which was designed to absorb into its ranks most ex-tsarist and White Rusian army veterans. Wrangel informed Potapov that the hard core of his forces consisted of General Kutyepov's Combat Corps, two divisions (15,000 men) of trained, disciplined veterans, most of whom had originally been evacuated to the Gallipoli Peninsula in the fall of 1920. Half of Kutyepov's troops were officers, and the corps could be expanded to four divisions for combat operations. Future liaison with the Trust would be handled by General Klimovich, who returned with Potapov and Miller to Paris. According to the Soviet account, during the return trip Potapov was told that Chebishev, Wrangel's minister of internal affairs, still believed that the Trust was an OGPU provocation and opposed collaboration with it.[26] What he was *not* told was that his traveling companion, General Klimovich, who was to handle all liaison between Wrangel and the Trust, felt the same way. Two can play the game of deception as well as one, and it is clear that General Potapov's mission resulted in no more than friendly liaison and contact with a former classmate at the Imperial General Staff College. Not a single agent was later sent into Russia from Wrangel's forces through Trust channels. Quite the contrary; as in the past, they wisely preferred their own. For example, General Ulagai and his four brothers, two in the U.S.S.R., had organized armed resistance groups in the northern Caucasus. They lost a courier, a Cossack officer, to the OGPU after his arrest in Armavir, but one of their agents crossed the Turkish border and penetrated as far as Sochi.[27] Later, in December 1926, Ulagai told Yakushev that while he personally believed him, he would continue to work alone.[28]

Meanwhile, considerable friction developed between Gen-

erals Wrangel and Kutyepov, who had already moved to Paris.
In March 1924, at the request of the Grand Duke Nikolai,
Kutyepov officially took charge of all "political work"—meaning
covert operations—for the émigré forces. It was here in Paris
that he began the selection and training of his so-called Combat
Corps for the purpose of espionage, subversion, and later terrorist diversions inside the U.S.S.R.

This was an important development. Infantry General
Aleksandr Pavlovich Kutyepov represented the tsarist combat
officer at his best. With a reputation for personal integrity and
great physical courage, he had emerged from World War I at
the age of thirty-six as one of the outstanding regimental commanders in the Imperial Guards. Casting his lot with the White
forces in the civil war, he rose to the position of Wrangel's
second in command. In the dark days of defeat and withdrawal,
first to the Gallipoli Peninsula and then to Bulgaria and Yugoslavia, it was Kutyepov's unflagging energy and faith in the
cause which kept up the morale of the White troops and their
soldierly appearance. He was first and foremost a combat officer
in the best but also the narrowest sense of the word; that is, he
had had little or no experience in staff or intelligence work.
Like many other combat officers, he was inclined to oversim-
plify complex political problems and to look for military solu-
tions to them. Thus, when in March 1924 Kutyepov took
charge of all covert operations inside Russia, the OGPU correctly estimated that this would probably mean an intensification of direct action—assassinations, bombings, etc.—precisely
what the Trust wished to suppress and control.[29]

For fifty years Soviet propaganda has portrayed the goals
of such émigré leaders as Wrangel and Kutyepov in oversim-
plified terms as "a restoration of the overthrown monarchical
regime," and a return to the former rule of bureaucrats and
"black hundreds" and landlords. The image is false, so far as
Wrangel is concerned. Although he was personally a conservative, Wrangel clearly intended to submit the question of the
nature of the central government to popular decision: "If they
want a king, Russia will be a monarchy; if they think a republic
will be most useful to them, we shall have a republic." [30] It is
also false with respect to Kutyepov, who regarded the idea of
a restoration of the landowners as "dangerous nonsense" and
for this reason incurred the enmity of the right-wing monarchists

among the émigrés.[31] Like Wrangel, he was primarily interested in the liberation of Russia, not in the form of government that would follow overthrow of the Bolshevik regime: "I may be a monarchist, but I swear on the cross that I would defend to my last drop of blood any republic which liberates Russia from the Bolsheviks and frees the Russian people. I would fight with weapons in hand against any infringement of the powers of such a government." [32]

Anti-Soviet Resistance—The Zakharchenko-Radkovich Missions to Moscow

In the fall of 1922 General Kutyepov was still serving as second in command of the White Russian forces in Yugoslavia under Wrangel. Kutyepov had brought with him from the Gallipoli encampment a daring young couple who volunteered to undertake the first émigré intelligence mission inside the U.S.S.R. They were Maria Vladislavovna Zakharchenko and her common-law second husband, Georgi Nikolayevich Radkovich.

Maria, who was so close to Kutyepov that she was mistakenly regarded as his niece, was born a soldier in every respect except her sex. Even before the war she had been a well-known figure in St. Petersburg military circles. She had volunteered as a private for front-line duty in World War I and not only had been commissioned as an officer but also had been decorated with the Georgian Cross. Zakharchenko, her first husband, had been killed in the civil war, in which she also fought as a volunteer under General Denikin.

A captain who served in the First Cavalry Regiment in Denikin's army later wrote that Maria produced a remarkable impression wherever she served:

> There was nothing feminine about her external appearance. She was slight in figure, slender with a drawn face. When she rode on numerous mounted patrols only her name —Maria Vladislavovna—distinguished her from the other soldiers. In battle, under fire, she was courageous, never "bending low" [to take cover] . . . I never saw her dressed in civilian clothes, but imagine that she must have looked like an "English governess." I can readily believe that she was capable of . . . [any] heroic deed.[33]

Another colleague who knew Maria later as a dedicated counterrevolutionary writes: "I regard Maria Vladislavovna as by all odds the most remarkable woman produced by the Russian counterrevolution: there will never be another like her." [34]

Little is known about Georgi Radkovich except that among his fellow officers he had the reputation of being a daring intelligence officer. He also impressed Western observers as being overshadowed by the dominating personality of his wife.

Both Maria and Georgi shared with General Kutyepov the conviction that counterrevolutionary operations against the U.S.S.R. were unthinkable without first acquiring an intimate knowledge of the target regime. As the White forces withdrew in defeat and disorder at the end of the civil war, they had not been able to leave behind any organized networks of informants; these would have to be built up from scratch. Unlike the major powers, the émigrés had no representatives in the U.S.S.R. to gather information—a difficult and dangerous job at best, since even Western diplomats were under close and constant surveillance by the omnipresent Soviet security police.

Having decided to undertake their extended intelligence mission, the Radkoviches found that they had all kinds of obstacles to surmount. Their funds, which were provided by General Kutyepov, were extremely limited, barely enough for survival, and such problems as obtaining false passports and guides to an illegal crossing point (presumably on the Polish-Soviet border) were not easy to solve without money. Anyone less determined would have abandoned the project in the preparatory stages, which dragged on for several agonizing months. They finally arrived at the Soviet border one cold autumn evening, and Georgi Radkovich later described their mission as follows:

> The smuggler decided not to cross the border himself, and merely indicated our route by the stars and by the glow of light reflected in the night sky from a big city. We moved forward silently and stealthily as if we were making our way through a barbed-wire barrier on a wartime intelligence patrol.
>
> When we had passed through a band of bushes, in front of us stretched an endless swamp where we sank up to our knees and a long backwater which was ice-cold and waist-

deep. We were occasionally startled when a flight of ducks
would noisily take off from either side of us. Fast-moving
clouds hid the stars, and everything was plunged into an
impenetrable darkness and gloom. From nine in the evening
until three in the morning our path led us through that
dreadful swamp. . . .

Sometime before dawn we crossed a deep river and after
penetrating into the bushes on the other side we slept as
if dead. We were awakened by an agonizing cold—everything around us was covered with hoarfrost. We were another
day and half a night en route. We spent the second night
in an open shed and found shelter only on the third.

Georgi and Maria successfully avoided detection and traveled all over Russia in freightcars equipped with a stove, visiting
the villages as well as the big cities and eagerly observing the
new life unfolding around them. As a result of their first intelligence mission, both agents drew somber and disturbing conclusions with respect to future operations in Russia. After
returning Radkovich observed:

In order to work there, in order to achieve any of our
objectives, we must live in Russia ourselves. We must transform ourselves from émigrés into Russian citizens. There is
no other solution for us. Without our own bases inside Russia
any kind of work is unthinkable. At present Russia is deaf
and dumb. Any contact with the population—at least during
the first stage of our work—is out of the question. The
Russians are no longer themselves. They are tired and
totally preoccupied with personal affairs, with the struggle
for a crust of bread. In Russia there is neither faith nor
trust. In the provinces, where the fighting was most intense
and the people were most heavily engaged in it, there are
still resisting elements. But in the big cities where we must
live all that is left are the dispirited Russian inhabitants who
have accepted their fate and Soviet power. We certainly
can't ally ourselves with them. We can rely only on ourselves.
We must place our people there and all of us must dig a
place for ourselves in Soviet life. That is our first task.

"But how can we do this?" Radkovich asked, and, in reply
to his own question, answered despondently: "It's almost hopeless. We need enormous funds and many connections. Where

can we find them? Who will help us?" Then with a toss of his head he added: "But only the first steps seem hopeless—it's always like that." [35]

While Maria and Georgi Radkovich were enduring the hardships of their first intelligence mission in the U.S.S.R., the OGPU was setting up the Trust, and Yakushev, their principal liaison man abroad, had made his first exploratory visit to Berlin and Paris. The Radkoviches returned from their difficult and disappointing trip about the time of Yakushev's second visit to Paris in the summer of 1923. Both Maria and Georgi were favorably impressed by the talented and persuasive OGPU envoy. In fact, according to the only surviving source who knew personally the characters involved:

> It was due to [their] insistence that General Kutyepov saw Yakushev rather frequently during the summer of 1923. These meetings led to the second trip of Zakharchenko and Radkovich to the U.S.S.R. under auspices of an "internal Russian monarchist organization" [the Trust]. However, it can be stated categorically that both of them [the Radkoviches] and Kutyepov were fully aware of the character of the organization.[36]

Before leaving on their second mission, Radkovich was highly suspicious of the ease with which Yakushev made all the necessary arrangements. He observed:

> At that time, a year ago, Maria Vladislavovna and I were unable to obtain the necessary administrative decisions or visas for the trip. This year, with the help of Yakushev's connections, everything was approved and set up within a few days, and the journey itself will take place in comfort of which we couldn't have dreamed.
> The most striking thing about these operations are Yakushev's extensive contacts with foreigners. It is possible that an underground organization might be able to organize something inside Russia, but it is hard to believe. . . . It is even more astonishing that any Russian national underground organization, much less a monarchist one, should have such extensive contacts with neighboring governments. Why, all the states which have been "liberated" from Russia are presently steeped in chauvinism and hatred of everything Russian! How is it that such governments, which without exception have been hostile to legal monarchist émigrés, should be so

favorably inclined to underground monarchists? . . . All this would make more sense if the underground organization in the U.S.S.R. were Socialist Revolutionary: the SR's may still have some remnants of their former conspiratorial organizations, and they have contacts with the Western democrats.[37]

It is clear from such comments that Maria Zakharchenko and Georgi Radkovich suspected that the Trust was a provocation. But it was the only channel open to them for a return to the U.S.S.R. so that they could gather intelligence on the real situation inside the country. General Kutyepov lacked both the financial means and the connections to sponsor a second mission. He was also aware of the dangers if the Trust were in fact controlled by the OGPU. Nevertheless, like Maria and Georgi Radkovich, he obviously felt that the chance to establish an operating base inside the U.S.S.R. was worth the calculated risk involved. He approved their second mission, which began under circumstances vastly different from the first. Maria later described them as follows:

> This time we went with a guide—one of our new friends from over there. Actually it was more like a pleasant walk than a field march, and Georgi and I frequently compared it with our trip of the year before.
>
> Our guide produced a very favorable impression on us. He was courteous, very taciturn, extremely tactful, and was obviously a highly experienced "pathfinder." He was so familiar with the area through which we traveled that it seemed to me at the time that we did not lose a single kilometer in moving to a given point as planned.
>
> "He's some guy!" Georgi said to me in a low voice when we were somewhat separated from our guide. "He must be an officer: you can sense the discipline. But what do you think: is he one of us or one of them? Should we embrace him or shoot him?"
>
> After twenty hours of continuous marching we were approaching the town of C . . . before dawn of the following day. When we arrived at the outskirts of the sleeping town our guide asked us to follow him at a considerable distance but not to lose sight of him. The town was asleep and empty. At first Georgi and I walked on the planked sidewalk, but we were frightened by the noise of our footsteps in the silence and quickly stepped into the street.
>
> Suddenly our guide stopped at a side street in front of

a small, plain house. He knocked and someone opened the door for him. He said something and gestured to us to come out from behind the picket fence where we had quickly hidden ourselves. We approached. Judging by a small, half-obliterated signboard on which was sketched a boot, and which was attached to the gatepost, this was the shoemaker's house. In the back of a small courtyard stood an even more ramshackle outbuilding, to which our thoughtful guide brought us.

For half an hour we quietly drank tea, restraining ourselves from making any observations about our first impressions. Our guide brought us the tea and simple cots on which to sleep. He wished us a good night's rest and said he would see us in the morning. As he closed the door he indicated how we should knock, and asked us not to go out in the yard.

We were left alone in the half-light of dawn. We sat down in silence, looking around us. It would be difficult to imagine now all the thoughts that swirled through our heads that morning.

What should we expect next? What did we actually know about the new organization, about our new friends? Or were they our friends? So far there had been nothing but talk and mystification.

"In any case, it's quiet here in the woods," Georgi said, suddenly breaking our long silence. "The walk was all right, and how about the tea? Not bad, eh?"

In spite of being dead tired, we slept our usual half sleep as if we were still on the march.

At ten o'clock our guide came, brought us more tea and food, and said that we would not be able to continue our trip until the train for Mogilev left that evening at eleven P.M.

"I hope everything is all right," he added as he left.

The agonizing day dragged on. From the window of the house we saw the usual peaceful scene presented by any God-forsaken little town in Russia: beyond the gate, an occasional pedestrian walked along the street; every once in a while the gloomy, elderly shoemaker passed through the courtyard.

We decided to take our bearings. We had to try to clarify our situation, but how? We racked our brains over how to do it.

"We ought to question the inhabitants," Georgi Niko-layevich suggested.

Suddenly the idea struck me—go find the shoemaker!

"Not bad," Georgi agreed.

As it was getting dark I slipped out of the passageway into the courtyard and looked carefully around. A little shed stood in the shadow of the side wall. It seemed to me that it would not be difficult to slip out through the back yard into a street running parallel to ours. I quickly ducked through the half-broken fence around the neighbor's yard and soon found myself in the street. At the gate of one of the adjacent houses an elderly woman was standing with a child in her arms.

I asked her where I could buy some stationery and envelopes.

"Why, who are you?"

"I'm a schoolteacher. I just got here today and still don't know my way around."

"There's a shop close by—over that way."

"You don't happen to know a shoemaker? I've got to have my shoes repaired."

"I wouldn't know. I don't live here."

I walked on until I ran into a patch of light on the planked sidewalk coming from the tobacco shop. I entered and asked for paper and envelopes. The proprietor, a gray-haired old man, looked me over intently and silently pulled from a drawer a yellowish sheet of letter paper and a flabby envelope.

"I've been looking all day, and haven't been able to find a room," I said as I put away my wretched, unnecessary purchase. "I'm worn out. Do you know where I could find one? I'm the new schoolteacher—just arrived today."

"A room?" the old man asked. "That's difficult. You'll have to go to the local Soviet."

"But I've already been there. They gave me a requisition for a room which was filthy, so I decided to look for one myself, hoping to find one a little cleaner."

"That's difficult," the tobacconist insisted. "Without the Soviet's approval, it's forbidden."

"I'm willing to pay for it."

"I don't know of any. There are no rooms now."

"Well, another thing. Do you know where I can find a shoemaker? My shoes are all torn," I said, lifting one foot to show him, "and I've got to get them repaired. I'm ashamed to go to school with them like that."

"Ach, there's no reason to be ashamed," the old man

replied dryly and unpleasantly. "Everybody's shoes are like that. Besides, it's late. You can get them repaired tomorrow at the marketplace."

"But some woman told me that there is a shoemaker not far from here on a neighboring street—only I don't know where, and tomorrow morning I have school."

"Around here? I don't know of any. There used to be a shoemaker by the name of Khaimov near here, but they recently moved him away. The police took over his house. He now has a workshop at the marketplace and can fix your shoes there."

"Well, thanks a lot, anyway. How difficult everything is these days!" The remark slipped out unintentionally.

"Of course it's difficult. Everything's difficult."

I cautiously returned to the outbuilding.

The seeds of doubt had been planted: we were prisoners in "their" hands.[38]

According to the Soviet account of the second Zakharchenko-Radkovich intelligence mission, something went wrong with Trust channels after the initial smooth border crossing. The "Cousins," as they were nicknamed by the OGPU, lost their way after traveling as far as Pskov. They were supposed to report in Moscow, not to Yakushev (who had already left for Warsaw and Paris with General Potapov), but to another member of the organization, Edward Ottovich Staunitz, also known as Opperput. They were long overdue when they suddenly turned up in Moscow late one evening at Staunitz' quarters.

Staunitz, who played a role in the Trust second in importance only to that of Yakushev, had a long record of conspiracy and treachery in the service of first the Cheka and then the OGPU. According to Chebishev, Wrangel's political adviser, Staunitz was born a Latvian with the family name Upenish. In 1918 he took part in the shooting of White officers during the Red (Cheka) Terror in St. Petersburg and Kronstadt. In 1920 he had belonged to an anti-Bolshevik organization in Leningrad known as the Tagantsev group, after its leader. At that time Staunitz used the alias Savelev before betraying the group to the Cheka. He also helped betray the so-called Union for the Defense of Fatherland and Freedom, organized by the former Socialist Revolutionary terrorist Boris Savinkov as an anti-Bolshevik force in 1918. Upenish also used the aliases Kasatkin-

Ring and Selyaninov, as well as Staunitz and Opperput.[39] During the first months of the Bolshevik regime he had belonged to underground groups in Moscow controlled by Captain Sidney George Reilly of British intelligence.[40] It was only natural, then, that he should turn up again as Opperput in Berlin in 1922, working for both Reilly and Savinkov until he was sent on a mission into the U.S.S.R. and walked into a trap set by the OGPU in Minsk.[41] According to the Soviet account, he "escaped by a miracle." He had a wife and two children and had been living by his wits in various black-market business enterprises when he became associated with the Trust. According to Staunitz' own story, he had shared a prison cell in the Lubyanka with Yakushev and was recruited for work in the Trust at the same time as his boss. In addition to leading a cell of seven members, acting as code clerk, and working with the Eurasian faction of the Trust, Staunitz was apparently allowed considerable leeway in his black-market activities—a commercial cover frequently used by intelligence agencies. When he took charge of Georgi Radkovich and Maria Zakharchenko as they arrived late that night in Moscow, he might have had less enthusiasm for his job if he had known that he would eventually become captivated by Maria, and that the two ill-starred lovers would die an untimely death together.

"Operational Theater" in Moscow

With the arrival in Moscow of Maria Zakharchenko and Georgi Radkovich there began one of the longest and most remarkable deceptions in modern intelligence history. The OGPU did not know that the Cousins suspected the Trust from the outset. Maria had communicated her suspicions to General Kutyepov during a brief visit to Paris in December 1923. A few months later, in the spring of 1924, the Grand Duke Nikolai put Kutyepov in charge of all political work—meaning covert operations—which increased the importance to the OGPU of the Cousins. They represented a direct channel of communication to Paris, a means of penetrating into the highest émigré circles and hopefully of collecting intelligence on enemy intentions and capabilities.

For three years the OGPU task force in charge of the Trust devised all kinds of credible scenarios and kept the Cousins busy in plausible but make-believe conspiratorial activity. For their part the Radkoviches had to play along with this phony activity without revealing their suspicions, for they were totally at the mercy of the OGPU and could have been liquidated at any moment. The nervous strain of such a double life was almost unbearable.

The story of this reciprocal double deception is an engrossing chapter in the battle of the intelligence services. To those unfamiliar with conspiratorial techniques and organization, it seems an incredible achievement in what today might be called "operational theater." However, it is clear from the long history of successful tsarist police provocations that, by definition, the conditions of conspiratorial activity lend themselves readily to deception. Not only Maria and her husband, but also the regular bona fide members of the MOCR—a cast of at least fifty persons—were familiar with the traditions and ground rules of underground organizations which Dostoevsky had portrayed so graphically in his novel *The Possessed*. They accepted without question the fact that for the sake of security the MOCR had to be compartmentalized into small conspiratorial groups or cells operating independently of each other under the leadership of the "initiated few" at the top, which of course meant Generals Zayonchovsky and Potapov, Yakushev, Staunitz, Zubov (a Red Army officer assigned to the task of controlling the Cousins), and other double agents of the OGPU. Each member of the underground also accepted the need for iron discipline and blind obedience to the leadership of the organization. Thus Yakushev, as a leader of the Trust's Political Council with important contacts abroad, was able to impose a ban on such *terakts* as bank robbery and assassination, and in general to control the tempo and character of the organization's "revolutionary" activities, at least in Moscow. Yakushev soon realized that in Maria, a dedicated terrorist, they had a tigress on their hands, one who would eventually break loose, but who meanwhile had to be indulged since she represented their only confidential access to General Kutyepov.

At the outset each of the Cousins was provided with false identity papers (Maria assuming the family name of Berezovska and her husband that of Karpov) and inconspicuous non-Western clothes. Since under Lenin's New Economic Policy small shopkeepers had reappeared everywhere, they were given a stall at the central market, where, under cover of selling sugar,

they handled mail and packages for the Trust to and from
Warsaw, Berlin, and Paris.

Controlled Terror

One of General Kutyepov's first projects after taking
charge of covert operations for the Grand Duke Nikolai was to
send into the U.S.S.R. through Trust channels three agents
who were to contact and work with Maria Zakharchenko and
Georgi Radkovich in Moscow. However, according to the Soviet
account, the three of them—Aleksandr A. Shorin, Colonel Ivan
Mikhailovich Sussalin, and one Korinsky—at first were placed
in Leningrad to keep them away from Maria and Georgi and
under the direct surveillance of Pillar, one of the OGPU task
force in charge of the Trust.[42] Both Kutyepov and Wrangel
also sent in other agents without Trust approval, such as the
terrorist Kizyakov, who was sent to Moscow.[43] Two of Wrangel's agents who went in outside Trust channels, Colonel Zhu-
kovsky and Naval Cadet Burkhzhovsky, were quickly captured
by the OGPU and liquidated.[44]

Apparently Colonel Sussalin was later transferred to Moscow, because Maria Zakharchenko spoke of knowing him there.
She stated that one fine day, after hinting darkly that he was
going to find out the truth about the Trust, he went out for a
walk and never returned. When she inquired as to his whereabouts she was told that a Bulgarian Communist who recognized him on the street had denounced him to the OGPU, which
had shot him before the Trust could intervene to save him.[45] A
much more likely explanation of what happened to Sussalin
can be deduced from a Soviet source. According to the latter,
Sussalin told the OGPU agent Pillar that he was a double agent
for the Sûreté, the French Secret Police, and knew the names
of French intelligence agents who had infiltrated the Soviet
embassy in Paris.[46] Since he was later listed by the Soviet newspaper *Izvestia* (June 9, 1927) as having been shot by the OGPU,
it is probable that Sussalin was kept in the inner prison of the
Lubyanka and tortured to extract this valuable counterintelligence information before he was liquidated.

To the uninitiated it may seem incredible that General
Kutyepov would send in agents through Trust channels knowing they were suspect. But not to do so involved even higher
risks and threatened the security of Maria Zakharchenko and

Georgi Radkovich. During the winter of 1924 General Kutyepov told Melgunov, the editor of the Paris émigré newspaper
Borba za Rossiu, that he suspected the Trust:

> Among the arguments on which he based his distrust
> of the Moscow organization he emphasized the fact of its
> unimpeded existence over the course of several years during
> which it had carried on markedly active liaison abroad. If
> one took into consideration the internal Russian obstacles,
> such activity, he said, could only be explained by the active
> connivance of the Communist authorities.[47]

Given these circumstances, it may be assumed that Kutyepov finally consented to severely limited cooperation with the
Trust because he believed it would be advantageous in the
struggle in which he ultimately lost his life.[48]

Before leaving on a covert operational mission to Russia
during which he contacted the Trust, one of Kutyepov's agents
was briefed as follows:

> We do not have enough facts to prove that the "Trust"
> is an organization of *provocateurs,* but you should know that,
> as appears to be the case in every counterrevolutionary
> organization, the chances are fifty-fifty that there are OGPU
> agents in it already or there will be. It is impossible to work
> inside the U.S.S.R. without risks—great risks—and you should
> know what you are getting into.

After this frank warning the agent writes that he, and
others like him, were assigned two objectives: "(1) they should
try in every possible way to check on the Trust in order to
determine to what extent it was controlled by the OGPU, and
(2) while working in contact with the Trust, they should by no
means reveal all their tasks, but should keep part of their operations secret from all Trust agents." [49]

How many of their operations Kutyepov's agents were able
to keep secret from the Trust we do not know. Surprisingly
enough, certain *terakts* were apparently conducted under OGPU
surveillance and control, presumably to add an element of
realism to the fake activity with which Maria Zakharchenko and
Georgi Radkovich were kept preoccupied. According to
Staunitz' testimony, the task force or "special group" in charge
of the Trust used the organization secretly to purge certain
OGPU agents who were considered unreliable or who had out-

lived their usefulness. These men were quietly murdered by or with the help of Radkovich and other of General Kutyepov's agents, thus satisfying Maria Zakharchenko's insistent demands for "action." At first Maria and Georgi believed that they had discovered sincerely anti-Bolshevik people within the Trust ranks who would cooperate with them in their resistance work. Later they realized that they were being exploited by the OGPU as executioners. They continued to cooperate, however, because not to do so would have been dangerous, and in any case some of the Chekists thus liquidated were notorious for their cruelty, such as Naimsky in Petrograd, Orlov in Moscow, Turov-Ginsburg in the Moscow suburbs, and Opansky, the OGPU deputy chief in Minsk.[50]

In March 1924 the Grand Duke Nikolai had put General Kutyepov in charge of covert operations, and a small but steady stream of agents had been sent into the U.S.S.R. on intelligence-collecting and other missions. Some had collaborated with the Cousins in terrorist acts carried out under Trust surveillance. Naturally the OGPU watched all these developments with great interest, and by the fall of 1924 decided to send the Trust liaison agents Yakushev and General Potapov on a special fact-finding mission to Paris. Presumably such a mission was necessary due to the lack of detailed information on émigré plans and intentions in the correspondence between the Trust and Paris. That Kutyepov carefully avoided revealing anything important in such correspondence followed naturally from his well-founded suspicions that the Trust was an OGPU provocation.

Ostensibly the purpose of this, the second Yakushev-Potapov mission to Paris, was to raise funds for underground work inside Russia. According to the Soviet account, the two Trust representatives left Moscow in October 1924, crossing the border illegally at a Polish window near Wilno.[51] Soon after their arrival in Paris they visited General Kutyepov and insisted on meeting the Grand Duke Nikolai. A surviving member of the General's Combat Corps has told how the meeting came about:

> Kutyepov advanced all kinds of reasons why such a meeting would be impossible, since he well knew that it would give the two *agents provocateurs* great prestige with their Chekist superiors. (Like other agents recruited from the

former tsarist elite, the two emissaries had never been fully
trusted within the OGPU.) Kutyepov also figured that a meeting of Yakushev and Potapov with the Grand Duke would
constitute a special mark of approval indicating that these
agents had won the confidence of the leaders of the White
movement.

In spite of General Kutyepov's opposition, Yakushev,
and especially Potapov, persisted in demanding an audience
with the Grand Duke, advancing among many reasons the
argument that refusal would be interpreted as evidence of a
lack of faith in the Trust. Kutyepov understood that if these
agents returned without having obtained an audience with
the Grand Duke, the entire group in Moscow might suffer
the same fate as [Colonel] Sussalin [who had disappeared
without a trace].

Kutyepov then briefed the Grand Duke on all aspects
of the situation as it had developed, leaving him with the
difficult decision as to whether to meet the agents.

The Grand Duke decided to receive them. This is the
true story of how the meeting came about, although General
Kutyepov never revealed the details of what took place at it.[52]

According to the Soviet account, in their search for funds
(the ostensible purpose of their mission), Yakushev and Potapov also visited the former tsarist prime minister Kokovtsov,
who was in charge of émigré finances. Potapov stated flatly that
it would cost $25 million to finance preparations for a revolu-
tion in Russia, and that no results could be expected for at least
six months after the receipt of the money. This, the Trust representatives admitted, was perhaps too much to expect at once,
but meanwhile an advance of $10 million would help. In later
conversations with Kokovtsov (whom Yakushev discovered was
well informed about Soviet affairs), there was some talk of
raising money from businessmen sympathetic to the monarchist
cause, but apparently nothing substantial ever came of it. They
returned to Moscow on November 15, 1924, without having
obtained any funds and with very little new information, although Yakushev's prestige was undoubtedly enhanced by
the audience with the Grand Duke Nikolai.[53]

Maria Zakharchenko Visits Paris: The Crest of the Wave

After a few months' residence in the center of the city,
where they operated a sugar concession in the central market

for cover, Maria Zakharchenko and Georgi Radkovich were moved to a *dacha* (summer cottage) in the suburbs. They were told that a wave of OGPU arrests was expected and that the move to the new quarters was for their own security. Maria was soon bored with her duties as postmaster and bookkeeper for the Trust, and in her talks with Yakushev pleaded for more direct action—the use of terror. As events later showed, Maria preferred throwing bombs to keeping books. She complained that the Trust was wasting its time with the Polish intelligence service, the superannuated émigrés in Berlin, and even with General Wrangel. What was needed was a close working relationship with General Kutyepov in Paris. She pleaded with Yakushev to travel to Paris with her for that purpose. After setting up another window on the Finnish border, Yakushev finally consented (with OGPU approval), and the two arrived in Paris on July 6, 1925.

Before leaving for Paris Yakushev was briefed on his mission by Artuzov, one of the OGPU task force operating the Trust: General Kutyepov had placed representatives in Germany, Czechoslovakia, Poland, and Finland. His Combat Corps had been able to send agents into Russia outside Trust channels, and thus beyond its control. The activist group in Leningrad, which had been linked to both the old MOCR and Kutyepov's organization, had in fact got out of hand and had recently been liquidated by the OGPU. The number of men lost in this action would undoubtedly give Kutyepov some second thoughts as to the usefulness of the Trust, with which he had thus far refused to cooperate. Perhaps under the changed circumstances, they would have better luck this time.[54]

On the surface, at least so Yakushev's report indicates, the mission to Paris was successful. Kutyepov agreed to represent the Trust in Paris and to cooperate fully with it, sending his warmest greetings to General Zayonchovsky (the founder of the original MOCR and still titular head of the Trust) and to General Potapov.

Yakushev arranged with General Kholmsen and General von Monkewitz to use Sabaneyev's *History of Russian Music* as a cipher for further secret communications. Monkewitz, formerly with Wrangel's intelligence staff, had followed General Kutyepov to Paris.[55] A year and a half later, in November 1926, General Monkewitz disappeared without a trace from his Paris apartment, leaving a suicide note to the effect that he had chosen "this way" of ending his life in order to spare his family the funeral expenses. Shortly thereafter rumors circulated in the Paris press that he had defected to the U.S.S.R. and had in fact been an OGPU agent for years. A controversy over the case has raged ever since. A former member of Kutyepov's Combat Corps stoutly maintains that Monkewitz had nothing to do with the Trust or Kutyepov's Soviet affairs,[56] whereas others, such as Melgunov, write that Monkewitz was an OGPU agent and that Yakushev had been warned about him during his first visit to Paris.[57] The evidence pro and con is entirely circumstantial, and judgment should certainly be suspended.[58]

After Maria Zakharchenko and Yakushev returned to Moscow, the Radkoviches were transferred to Leningrad so that they could cross the Finnish border more easily (at a new window in Sestroretsk province) and carry on liaison work with various intelligence agencies in Helsinki.

Indeed, since the beginning of the year (1925), presumably to relieve Maria's boredom and to give her a sense of participation in more important tasks than handling the Trust correspondence, both she and her husband had been sent on frequent trips to Helsinki and Reval.[59] They had successfully cultivated contacts with the Finnish intelligence service (which made it possible to set up the illegal border-crossing window) and had won the confidence of the British intelligence service attached to the consulate in Reval. The Trust was apparently at the peak of its prestige. But there is an old Arabic proverb that warns, "By the time the new house is finished, death has already knocked at the door."

A year earlier the Monarchist Council in Berlin had broken with the Trust, refusing to take orders from the MOCR in Moscow. Klimovich, General Wrangel's counterintelligence expert, and Chebishev, his minister of internal affairs, also had serious reservations. Among the Western intelligence services, however, the British and especially the Poles regarded the Trust as a bona fide resistance organization. That confidence was badly shaken when two of the U.S.S.R.'s most implacable enemies, Boris Savinkov and Sidney Reilly, were lured back separately into Russia by OGPU agents and liquidated. These two sensational affairs marked the beginning of the end of what until that point had been a brilliantly conducted operation.

3

SAVINKOV, ELVENGREN,
AND REILLY

Promise me that whatever happens you will never go to Russia. Even if I write asking you to come to me there, you must never go. . . . There are two or three people during whose lifetime the Bolsheviks will never sleep at peace. General Kutyepov is one. Then there is Boris Savinkov. There are two or three others. The Bolsheviks will get them back into Russia if they can, and then . . . !' Sidney spread out his hands in an expressive gesture." [1]

These clairvoyant words of warning were spoken by Sidney Reilly to his third wife, an attractive South American actress, Pepita Bobadilla, in London during the summer of 1923. He did not need to add that, along with the names of Savinkov and Kutyepov, his own figured high on the list of the OGPU's "ten most wanted" enemies. Four years later (after Reilly and Savinkov had been disposed of) the OGPU executed a selected group of twenty victims. Georgi Elvengren's name was second on the list. Savinkov and Reilly have attracted much attention and have been the subject of hundreds of articles.[2] Elvengren, the little man out in "the cold," who worked closely for a while with both of them, is virtually unknown. Only the fact that he gave the OGPU a detailed and extraordinarily frank confession has saved him from oblivion. The Soviet authorities later used it—with Reilly's "testimonial"—for propaganda purposes.[3] Otherwise his biography would have remained permanently buried in the Lubyanka archives.

Savinkov and Elvengren were captured by the OGPU independently of the Trust operation. Nevertheless, the tremendous publicity connected with the Savinkov affair undoubtedly cast a certain shadow over the Trust as well, and the two cases were inevitably linked because of the close collaboration between Savinkov and Reilly in various covert operations over a period of several years. The two first met in 1919 in Paris, where Reilly gave intelligence briefings on the Russian situation to British representatives at the World Peace Conference.[4] (He had just returned at the end of March from a mission to Odessa.) At that time the civil war was still raging in the U.S.S.R. Savinkov, with the self-proclaimed rank of general, represented various White Russian military leaders in turn— Kolchak, Denikin, Wrangel—and was regarded as a renegade by his former Socialist Revolutionary comrades.[5]

Boris Savinkov, the best known of the Russian terrorists, was a sinister, controversial character with a magnetic personality to which it was impossible to be indifferent. His outward physical appearance was unattractive; he was slightly built, balding, a heavy smoker, and a morphine addict.[6] Nevertheless, he was able to inspire blind faith and devotion among his Socialist Revolutionary comrades and assassins, who willingly died for the cause as they carried out his orders. Captain George Hill, the British intelligence agent (I.K. 8) who worked closely with Savinkov for some months after the Bolshevik seizure of power in 1917, writes:

> It was at this period that I came really to know him. He was a short, dark man, whose penetrating eyes certainly had hypnotic qualities. In the days of the Tsar he had organized the Terrorist section and had personally planned and carried through nineteen successful political assassinations. He had never actually done the killing himself, not because he was afraid for his own skin, but because he recognized that he was the brain of the group and therefore should not expose himself unless it was essential. Accordingly he always took up the second position, so that in the event of failure in the first instance he would be ready to hurl the second bomb or fire the fatal shot.
>
> His pen name was Ropshin, and when not organizing assassinations he wrote many articles and a number of books of note. His best-known works are "The Pale Horse," deal-

ing with the assassination of a Governor-General in the Tsar's days, and "The Black Horse," covering the period after the war when he was fighting the Bolsheviks from Poland. . . .

I never liked Boris Savinkov. My distrust of him was a matter of frequent contention between myself and Sidney Reilly, who had a blind belief in the man and spent a fortune in helping him to fight Bolshevism.[7]

Like Elvengren and Reilly, Savinkov, whatever one may think of his politics or character, was a born conspirator. In this regard Winston Churchill, who devoted a chapter of his book *Great Contemporaries* to Savinkov, writes:

Boris Savinkov's whole life has been spent in conspiracy. Without religion as the churches teach it; without morals as men prescribe them; without home or country; without wife or child, or kith or kin; without friend; without fear; hunter and hunted; implacable, unconquerable, alone. Yet he had found his consolation. His being was organized upon a theme. His life was devoted to a cause. That cause was the freedom of the Russian people. In that cause there was nothing he would not dare or endure. He had not even the stimulus of fanaticism. He was that extraordinary product—a Terrorist for moderate aims. A reasonable and enlightened policy— the Parliamentary system of England, the land tenure of France, freedom, toleration and goodwill—to be achieved whenever necessary by dynamite at the risk of death. No disguise could baffle his clear-cut perceptions. The form of government might be revolutionized; the top might become the bottom and the bottom the top; the meaning of words, the association of ideas, the roles of individuals, the semblance of things might be changed out of all recognition without deceiving him. His instinct was sure; his course was unchanging. However winds might veer or currents shift, he always knew the port for which he was making; he always steered by the same star, and that star was red.

During the first part of his life he waged war, often singlehanded, he fought the Bolshevik Revolution. The Czar and Lenin seemed to him the same thing expressed in different terms, the same tyranny in different trappings, the same barrier in the path of Russian freedom. Against that barrier of bayonets, police, spies, gaolers, and executioners he strove unceasingly. A hard fate, an inescapable destiny, a fearful doom! All would have been spared him had he been born in Britain, in France, in the United States, in Scandinavia, in Switzerland. A hundred happy careers lay open. But born in Russia with such a mind and such a will, his life was a torment rising in crescendo to a death in torture. Amid these miseries, perils and crimes he displayed the wisdom of a statesman, the qualities of a commander, the courage of a hero, and the endurance of a martyr.[8]

According to Somerset Maugham, who regarded him as the most remarkable man he had ever met, Savinkov once declared: " 'Between me and Lenin, it's a war to the death. One of these days he will put me with my back to the wall and shoot me, or I shall put him with his back to the wall and shoot him. One thing I can tell you is that I shall never run away' . . ." [9]

Lenin died on January 21, 1924, but his security police chief, Dzerzhinsky, remained at his post. Less than a year and a half later, had he lived, Lenin would have been pleased by a letter written by Savinkov from the inner prison of the Lubyanka in which he requested: "Either shoot me or give me the opportunity to work . . . I cannot endure this half-and-half existence . . . of merely lingering in the prison and becoming one of its denizens." The letter was not published in the Soviet papers until after the OGPU had announced that Savinkov's body had been found crushed on the flagstone courtyard of the Lubyanka beneath the apartment in which he had been held prisoner.[10] Winston Churchill later observed that whether Savinkov was shot in prison or committed suicide is uncertain and unimportant because:

> They had destroyed him body and soul. They had reduced his life's effort to a meaningless grimace, had made him insult his cause and fouled his memory forever. Yet when all is said and done, and with all the stains and tarnishes there be, few men tried more, gave more, dared more and suffered more for the Russian people.[11]

In writing about Savinkov, Churchill had unwittingly written the epitaph of thousands who were later to perish in the Great Purges of the mid-1930's when the Old Bolshevik elite was destroyed after spectacular show trials for which Savinkov's trial set a precedent. However, few of those who later perished in the purges were able to address the courts they faced with Savinkov's ringing words: "I am not afraid to die . . . I know your sentence already, but I do not care. I am Savinkov, who always played on death's doorstep; Boris Savinkov, Revolutionary and friend of Revolutionaries, now to be judged by your Revolutionary court." [12]

After the Socialist Revolutionary party—the SR for short —turned to active opposition against the Bolsheviks in the spring of 1918, Savinkov with French and British financial aid had organized the so-called Union for the Defense of Fatherland and Freedom. Savinkov hoped the Union would match the exploits of his famous Combat Organization of the old antitsarist days. With several thousand anti-Bolshevik troops, Savinkov's Union attacked and seized Yaroslavl, a town a few hundred miles north of Moscow. The attack was intended to coincide with the Allied landings at Archangel, which were delayed a fortnight, and after valiant fighting the town was recaptured by the Bolsheviks. [13] With an estimated membership of five thousand anticommunist ex-tsarist officers, Savinkov's Union soon established branches in the neighboring Baltic states, where it undoubtedly had the covert support of Western intelligence agencies. It was in this connection that Georgi Elvengren, who already had a two-year record of anticommunist intrigue, came into first contact with Savinkov as his official "representative" in Finland.

At that time Georgi Yevgenevich Elvengren (alias Georgiev, Georgievsky, and Yurievsky) was living in Brende, a suburb of Helsinki, with his family and two technical assistants who helped him in his conspiratorial work with a counter-revolutionary organization in Leningrad led by a certain Tagantsev and known as the PVO (Petrograd Combat Organization). As Savinkov's representative, Elvengren later testified:

> I established more or less regular relations with Savinkov by correspondence. From time to time I regularly sent him information, intelligence summaries and reports on the situation and activities of other Russian organizations as well as bulletins from the Finnish and Russian press on political questions. I sent my packages to Warsaw through the military attaché of the Polish embassy in Helsinki via the diplomatic pouch. In turn I periodically received from Savinkov his summaries and all kinds of literature for distribution.
>
> My connection with Savinkov was known among the Russian monarchist groups in Finland, but I worked that

channel entirely alone and rarely referred to it, since in most cases mentioning Savinkov's name among the monarchists was counterproductive.[14]

Savinkov soon discovered that his Union of ex-tsarist officers, who were united only by hatred of the Bolshevik regime, lacked the fighting spirit of his former SR Combat Organization, dedicated to the overthrow of tsarism by the selective use of terror. In his many discussions of terrorist tactics with Captain Hill, Savinkov explained that in tsarist days it was relatively easy to mold the "simple people" with whom he worked into fanatics: "It was easy to instill the idea into their heads that they were carrying out a divine purpose by murdering representatives of the oppressors." After the revolution, however, although the so-called White Russians, the officers of the imperial army, hated the Bolsheviks, it was very difficult to mold them into effective terrorists: "From childhood they had been taught that murder was a sin and a crime; to kill anyone in cold blood was anathema to them. No matter how gallant and brave they were . . . [they] could not bring themselves even for the good of their country to become assassins." [15]

Under the changed circumstances which followed the revolution the former "executioner" found that his relationship to the SR party deteriorated rapidly. As a former admirer and colleague summarized the situation:

> Savinkov's position was really unpleasant . . . To the party he became an antagonist, tolerated out of generosity. The "Organization" left him. No one had a job for him. . . .
> Savinkov was not taken into the SR government in Samara, and he immediately began to intrigue against it. The nonparty "Directory" which followed was naïve enough to send him abroad on a trumped-up "mission" so that he could not "meddle" with its work in Siberia. Savinkov left for Shanghai by boat. During his crossing Kolchak's revolt broke out.[16]

We have previously noted that "General" Savinkov fought the rest of the civil war in the salons of Paris as a representative of one military leader after another, until with the defeat of the White armies he wound up organizing paramilitary forces in Poland with support from the Polish government.

In the confusion of the civil war, in the spring of 1920 the Poles under General Pilsudski had swept into Russia and had taken Kiev, only to be pushed back in a counteroffensive led by General Mikhail Tukhachevsky, who led the Red Army to the gates of Warsaw but failed to take the Polish capital during the summer. By October an armistice had been signed.[17] But with General Pilsudski's material support, Savinkov organized a force of "eight thousand Ukrainian anti-Soviet rebels who hid in the forests . . . to strike at the rear of the Twelfth. . . ." [18]

As is so often the case, many of these so-called guerrillas were in reality little more than bandits, "who could hardly be dignified with the term of counterrevolutionaries. The initial idealism of the White movement was beginning to become corrupted by despair." [19]

It was also being corrupted at the center as well. Not unexpectedly Elvengren at his secure little post in Helsinki again represented Savinkov, this time in the service of Savinkov's "Russian Political Committee in Poland." Elvengren tells how during one of his trips to Warsaw he saw how the fraudulent "Warsaw Document" was produced. According to his account, Savinkov's forces under the "Committee" were divided into two groups, the army of Balakhovich and the "Third Russian Army" of Peremykin. Relations between the two had deteriorated almost to the point of an open break. News of this situation could not be kept secret either in Poland or in the West. Savinkov's position was thus threatened and his policy suspect. To restore confidence he hit upon the idea of having a manifesto published in support of his policies. The document would then be signed by the two rival military forces as well as by a large number of other organizations, real or imaginary. Elvengren composed a rough draft of the manifesto, which he coordinated with Dickhoff-Dehrenthal, Savinkov's lieutenant. Then at a meeting in the Hotel Bristol a finished copy was typed up, and each of the several persons present signed as if he were commandant of "all forces in northern Russia," etc. The "Warsaw Document" was then published in Savinkov's organ *Za Svobodu* ("For Freedom") and later picked up by other émigré newspapers.[20]

When in March 1921 the Treaty of Riga put an end to the Soviet-Polish War, Savinkov became an embarrassment to his Polish hosts, and he then moved on to Prague, Czechoslovakia. There, with the aid of General Rudolf Gayda (who had led one of the Czech legions in the civil war), he organized another group of anticommunist terrorists, the so-called Green Guards, who operated for a while in the western Ukraine.[21] When this adventure terminated Savinkov moved on to Paris, where he hoped to obtain support for further anticommunist enterprises. With an émigré population of over 100,000, Paris had become a natural center for British and French intelligence agencies seeking to promote a counterrevolution against the Soviet regime.

Major W. Field-Robinson was head of the Paris office of the British Secret Intelligence Service (S.I.S.) on the Rue Joubert, and had known both Savinkov and Reilly since the days of the Paris Peace Conference.[22] After two years of failure in Poland and Czechoslovakia, however, Savinkov was out of favor with the British, Polish, and French governments, which had formerly provided financial support for his counterrevolutionary undertakings. Elvengren, who had also moved to Paris early in 1922, makes this clear from his later testimony,[23] as does Reilly's biographer, Robin Bruce Lockhart.[24]

As political hopes for mounting a counterrevolution within the U.S.S.R. dwindled, the private individuals and groups who helped finance Elvengren, Savinkov, and Reilly turned naturally to terrorist activity directed against Soviet representatives abroad. One of the first forms of terror to which amateur political-warfare agencies are attracted is assassination, which, as Savinkov noted, is much more easily talked about than planned and executed. The hazards and difficulties of such operations are illustrated by the experience of Elvengren and Savinkov in Paris and Berlin at the time of the Genoa Conference of 1922.

Even before he moved to the French capital, Elvengren had been contacted in Helsinki by a certain Paul Tickston, who represented the *Torgprom,* the Paris-based Commercial and Industrial Association.[25] Tickston was on an intelligence mission, exploring the possibilities of organizing terrorist activity, and discussed two main problems in getting started: (1) the fact that the operation "was so delicate and confidential it could hardly be discussed with anyone," and (2) "that there were so few people in whom one could place enough trust for that sort of thing." [26]

When Elvengren moved to Paris he had several talks with

Tickston, who told him that the *Torgprom* was anxious to organize terrorist activity before the Genoa Conference, and that half a million francs had been set aside for that purpose. He swore Elvengren to secrecy and warned that no political organization would be involved since the work was regarded as entirely apolitical—i.e., as a purely business enterprise. When Elvengren mentioned his friend Savinkov as an experienced terrorist and organizer, he got a negative response. Tickston said that "Savinkov had already approached him for funds for this purpose, but that no one had any confidence in him any longer . . . If they should give him money he might well do nothing more than waste it on one of his political combinations in Poland, or simply gamble it away on the races." [27]

At this point Sidney George Reilly returned to Paris, and soon the three conspirators—Reilly, Savinkov, and Elvengren— joined forces. Financial backers were still reluctant to approve any enterprise in which Savinkov was involved, but finally gave in, presumably because of pressure brought to bear by Reilly, who himself spent a considerable fortune supporting Savinkov out of his own funds.

At a breakfast meeting with Elvengren and Savinkov in a Paris restaurant, Gustav Nobel, one of the *Torgprom* leaders, explained the philosophy of his organization as follows:

> We commercial people are interested in an active struggle against bolshevism, and as we see it now, that means the annihilation of all important leaders of that movement. Inside Russia we are powerless to do anything, but here we can act at will. Political developments and party organizations don't interest us. We're used to looking at things as businessmen. To us only facts are important. You are active and experienced people. We make it possible for you to begin. Accomplish just one deed and your future credit with us will grow at once! [28]

As Soviet leaders traveling on official missions to western Europe usually passed through Berlin, it was decided that the terrorists would locate in the German capital, which was a center of espionage and foreign intrigue. For example, in 1918 during his operations in Moscow and Petrograd, Reilly had been provided with an internal passport by Vladimir Orlov, a former public prosecutor who under an assumed name had

risen to a high position in the Petrograd security police. Forced
to flee the U.S.S.R. later, Orlov had set himself up in the
intelligence and forgery business in Berlin, where he worked
for the British, German, and other intelligence agencies.[29]

Orlov had an extensive collection of biographical intelligence files, including photographs, of important Soviet officials, as well as complete facilities for forging passports, travel
documents, etc. Savinkov already had false identity papers,
and Elvengren was soon provided with a forged Italian passport. Both were lodged by Orlov in a hotel that did not require
identification, and after a whirlwind visit by Reilly (who arrived
from London via Paris by plane, an exciting innovation in
those days), the little group of terrorists was set up in business
with an advance of 80,000 francs from *Torgprom*.[30]

But, as previously noted, political assassinations are more
easily talked about than carried through, not only because of
the extraordinary security precautions taken when important
officials travel abroad, but also because of the breaks of the
game, and the kinds of characters who can be hired as murderers. Elvengren's own description of his group's operations in
Berlin illustrates these problems:

> The following period is rather muddled. I can remember
> only a few episodes other than the fact that we simply spent
> whole days running from bar to bar or from café to café
> meeting each other, assistants and intelligence agents, so that
> my memory of events is blurred except for a few moments.
> I remember that Savinkov was running out of money and
> was constantly writing Paris, where they called him back
> since his incognito was completely exposed and he could do
> nothing but hide most of the time; otherwise he would have
> been arrested. As a result Savinkov returned to Paris and
> I was in charge of bringing all those enterprises to a success-
> ful conclusion. . . . Suddenly I learned that Chicherin was
> supposed to be arriving at a certain railway station. Since
> I didn't have enough time to contact my assistants, I went
> to the station myself, but there I saw nothing but police
> stationed all around. I began to feel uncomfortable—like a
> thief. There was very little time before his arrival, so I had
> a few drinks and took off without having seen anyone except
> a lot of policemen. I soon discovered that part of the Hotel
> Palace on the Potsdammerstrasse had been set apart as
> quarters for Chicherin. A guard was set up to observe the

area, which I checked out, but saw nothing except ministerial automobiles at the hotel where Chicherin was staying. We arranged surveillance by automobile, hoping to be able to follow when Chicherin left and to carry out the terrorist act [assassination], but in vain since Chicherin and his party left in ministerial cars which broke all the city speed limits so that we were unable to follow in our own automobile.

Next I obtained tickets to a meeting of Soviet government officials at which one of the Bolshevik leaders was supposed to give a report, but when I arrived I couldn't find anyone, and couldn't do anything . . .

Having heard that a member of Litvinov's delegation together with Maksim Gorky had taken a loge seat at some theater on Unter den Linden, I also got tickets with the idea of preparing something and, using assistants, set up a watch detail near the theater, but this time we also failed because they left the theater all of a sudden.

Came the departure of the delegation for Genoa. We learned that a special train with saloon cars was being made up at the Potsdammer Station, and we arranged to be able to get our agents on the platform, to which the public was not admitted at the time. Each agent was provided with a foreign passport and an adequate sum of money in case he had to flee. Subsequently we learned that there really was a train with saloon cars on the track filled with low-ranking members of the delegation. General Verkhovsky was seen in one of the cars, but the most important members of the delegation were detained at a dinner at the Foreign Ministry, because of which the train left empty. A short time later Chicherin and other delegation members overtook the train by automobile at one of the nearby stations . . . Thus, essentially, the sad epic ended.[31]

After the series of fiascoes in Berlin, Elvengren spent the next two years in France making contacts with various émigré leaders (he names a score of them, including General Kutyepov), seeking funds and assignments. In the winter of 1925 he was backed by the Swiss lawyer Ober, who two years earlier had directed the assassination of Vorovsky, the Soviet ambassador to Switzerland. With a group of three accomplices Elvengren made a last attempt on Chicherin, who was on leave in the south of France, but again without success. Soviet security was too good, and they were unable to discover the Foreign Minister's exact whereabouts.[32] Some months later, in the summer of 1926, in one of the Moscow railway stations the police arrested a suspicious-looking individual with a Rumanian passport issued to a "merchant" by the name of Pavel Jordan. He was armed with a revolver. Under OGPU interrogation he broke down and admitted his true identity—Georgi Elvengren.[33] Perhaps, as in the old days in Berlin, he had had a few drinks to bolster his courage. But, as in all the other attempts, he failed in this, his last mission.

After the Berlin fiasco Savinkov also settled in Paris, where he was accompanied as always by his lieutenant, Dickhoff-Dehrenthal, and Mrs. Dehrenthal, who was Savinkov's mistress. This *ménage à trois* lived from hand to mouth off funds supplied by Reilly and other private individuals who still hoped to salvage something from Savinkov's anti-Bolshevik undertakings. In 1922 Reilly had introduced Savinkov to Churchill, who saw him as a possible Bonaparte, a future dictator who would seize power when the hated Bolshevik regime collapsed. This would avoid restoration of the tsars, a very unpopular alternative with the postwar democratic regimes that had recently spent so much blood and treasure defeating imperial Germany. Churchill in turn introduced Savinkov to the British Prime Minister, Lloyd George, from whom he was unable to get any support, since at that time Great Britain was liquidating the heritage of the bumbling Allied intervention and seeking trade with the U.S.S.R. Churchill writes:

> Mr. Lloyd George sought information on the Russian situation, and I was authorized to bring Savinkov to Chequers. We motored there together. The scene upon arrival must have been a novel experience for Savinkov. It was Sunday. The Prime Minister was entertaining several leading Free Church divines, and was himself surrounded by a band of Welsh singers who had travelled from their native Principality to do him choral honours. For several hours they sang Welsh hymns in the most beautiful manner. Afterwards we had our talk. I recall only one of its episodes. The Prime Minister argued that revolutions like diseases run a regular course, that the worst was already over in Russia, that the Bolshevik leaders confronted with the responsibilities of actual government would quit their Communistic theories or that they would quarrel among themselves and fall like Robespierre and St. Just, that others weaker or more mod-

erate would succeed them, and that by successive convulsions a more tolerable regime would be established.

"Mr. Prime Minister," said Savinkov in his formal way, "you will permit me the honour of observing that after the fall of the Roman Empire there ensued the Dark Ages." [34]

The Soviet propaganda claim that Lloyd George would have nothing to do with Savinkov "because the English working class firmly said: Hands off Russia!" is too absurd to merit comment.[35]

Like so many other counterrevolutionaries before and since, Savinkov found that one of the two major sources of support—foreign governments—was drying up as a result of policy changes, which to him were inconceivable. The other major source was private enterprise, i.e., ideologically motivated individuals and business groups, such as *Torgprom*. Such groups were interested in immediate action, however, not long-range political contingencies. When he failed to produce results in Berlin during the spring and summer of 1922, Savinkov was thus left in a very unenviable situation. Moreover, although the Russian émigré circles which he then cultivated in Paris recognized his talents, they could not forgive him for the assassination of the Grand Duke Sergei, the Tsar's uncle, his minister of the interior, Von Plehve, and other officials. Reilly's personal funds (he later testified that he had spent between £15,000 and £20,000 on Savinkov's enterprises from 1920 to 1924)[36] were not inexhaustible, and both he and his wife, Pepita Bobadilla, traveled to Paris for consultation with Savinkov before they sailed for New York in July 1923. Mrs. Reilly has described the meeting, which took place in a private apartment of the Chatham Hotel, as follows:

> Savinkoff was a great disappointment to me, though knowing how much my husband admired him and regarded him as the hope of his country, I kept my unfavourable impression to myself. A portly little man strutted in with the most amusing air of self-assurance and self-esteem—a little man with a high brow, a beetle forehead, little eyes and an undershot chin. The little man posed in front of the mantelpiece. Now he gave us a view of one side of his profile, now the other. Now he thrust his hand into his breast in the approved Napoleonic manner, now he flourished it in the air with a theatrical gesture. Every pose was carefully studied so long

that he had passed beyond the stage of taking even a glance at his audience to gauge the measure of its appreciation . . .

The conversation, as Sidney afterwards told me, concerned itself principally with funds. Not only was money badly needed for the counter-revolution, but subscriptions were in urgent request for the keep of Savinkoff, together of course with that of M. and Mme. Dehrenthal. The withdrawal of the support of the French, Czech and Polish Governments had been a serious blow to the cause of counter-revolution. Sidney had already pointed out the danger of exhausting the patience of friendly governments. The feeling was spreading in Europe that, for all the White Russians could do, Bolshevism had come to stay.[37]

During the year the Reillys spent in New York City (July 1923–August 1924), Savinkov established contact with various individuals and scattered remnants of resistance groups inside Russia with whom he had formerly worked. One of these individuals, Colonel Sergei Pavlovsky, had been Savinkov's most trusted lieutenant, a man in whom he placed great trust, and who was also highly regarded by Reilly. According to Soviet sources, however, early in 1924 the OGPU had arrested Pavlovsky, who was broken by familiar police methods and agreed to cooperate in luring Savinkov back into the U.S.S.R. Others arrested were later released but kept under close surveillance.[38]

Other than a subconscious urge to self-destruction, there is still no rational explanation of why an experienced conspirator such as Savinkov walked into the trap set for him by the OGPU. Bruce Lockhart, a British agent in Russia at the time of the revolution who knew him well and had last seen him in a night club in Prague in 1923, has provided perhaps as good an evaluation as any. Even then, Lockhart writes:

> He was a pathetic figure, for whom one couldn't help feeling the deepest sympathy. He had exhausted all his friends and when he later returned to Moscow . . . I was not surprised. Doubtless, behind that tortured brain there was some grandiose scheme of striking a last blow for Russia and carrying out a spectacular *coup d'état*. It was a gambler's throw, but then Savinkov had always played a lone hand . . .[39]

Savinkov had always been a gambler, and reportedly had once lost 15,000 gold rubles of his Socialist Revolutionary party's money in the casino at Monte Carlo.[40] Now, when he was at the end of his rope, it is perhaps not inconceivable that he thought his luck might turn, although, as an old hand at conspiracy, he must have realized that the cards were stacked against him.

In appraising Savinkov's motives one should always consider the tug of Russian nationalism (whether tsarist or Soviet) and a longing to return to his native land at any cost. When questioned later by newsmen, admitted to the Lubyanka, as to why he had returned, he stepped to the window and, pointing to the spires of the Kremlin, replied, "I would rather see those towers from a prison cell than walk freely in the streets of Paris." [41]

Although the exact timing of the events is not clearly established, as the OGPU trap began to close around Savinkov early in the year (1924), he received a letter from Pavlovsky appealing to him to return to Russia to lead a full-scale uprising against the Soviet regime, which was supposedly in a vulnerable position since the death of Lenin in January. According to Winston Churchill, in June 1924 Savinkov also received an invitation to return from Trotsky and Kamenev, both of whom were members of the Soviet Politburo at the time, promising that if he would agree to stand a mock trial, he would be granted an immediate amnesty and be given a responsible position in the Soviet administration.[42] Then in July two Russian couriers, one of them known personally by Savinkov, arrived in Paris with a second letter from Pavlovsky urging him to return as soon as possible. It was in response to this overture that Savinkov had written Reilly (who was then in New York), asking him to return to Paris to consult with him "on a matter of grave importance."

Savinkov was in Italy trying unsuccessfully to raise funds from Mussolini for revolutionary purposes when the Reillys arrived in Paris in July. When he returned empty-handed from his meeting with Mussolini, a dramatic first meeting took place among the Reillys, the two messengers who had brought Pavlovsky's letter, Mr. Dickhoff-Dehrenthal, Savinkov's confidential secretary, Mrs. Dehrenthal, and, of course, Savinkov himself. In her memoirs Mrs. Reilly describes the scene as follows:

> In his letter, which the two men from Moscow had brought, Pavlovsky stated that he had met with an accident, which prevented his coming to see his chief in person: He

begged Savinkov to return to Russia with the two men as his presence was absolutely necessary to the future welfare of the party.

Of the two men, one was known to and trusted by Savinkov, the other was a stranger. The letter was undoubtedly in Pavlovsky's handwriting. When Savinkoff had read out the letter, the eyes of all present—of Savinkov, of the Dehrenthals, of the two messengers—turned automatically to Sidney for his verdict.

"Don't go," said Sidney shortly . . .

His attitude had been throughout, "Have nothing to do with it. It is a provocation." Savinkoff was in doubt, although he trusted Pavlovsky absolutely.

According to Mrs. Reilly's narrative, night after night for the next three weeks the same scene repeated itself, with occasional changes of cast.[43]

Finally, in spite of the repeated warnings or serious misgivings of his friends, Savinkov made his last desperate gamble and on August 10 left for Russia accompanied by the two Moscow emissaries, Pavlov and Fedorov, and Dickhoff-Dehrenthal and his wife. They traveled with false passports and stopped briefly in Berlin and Warsaw to say good-by to old acquaintances.

When, roughly two weeks later (August 29), the Soviet newspaper *Izvestia* printed the news of Savinkov's arrest and trial, his friends in Paris and elsewhere were stunned. Reilly wrote a letter published in the London *Morning Post* in which he angrily declared that the story was a fraud, that "Savinkov was killed when attempting to cross the frontier, and a mock trial, with one of their own agents as chief actor, was staged by the Cheka in Moscow behind closed doors." When the stenographic press reports of the trial were published, with Savinkov's recantation and confession of his previous "errors," Reilly's reaction was bitter in the extreme. In a second letter to the *Post* he wrote:

> Savinkov's treachery [was established] beyond all possibility of doubt . . . He has connived with his captors to deal the heaviest possible blow at the anti-Bolshevik movement, and to provide them with an outstanding political triumph both for internal and external use. By his act, Savinkov has

erased forever his name from the scroll of honor of the anti-Communist movement.

Deeply shaken by what he called the "terrible and inglorious downfall" of his former colleague, Reilly left for New York hoping to sabotage Soviet efforts to obtain credits on the Wall Street market. What seems almost incredible, in retrospect, is that within a year, and under remarkably similar circumstances, Reilly also allowed himself to be lured back into Russia by agents of the Trust, almost as if he were performing some strange ritual of self-immolation.

Thus on the surface the Savinkov affair appears to have been a clear-cut case of entrapment. The OGPU spread its net, Savinkov was caught in it, and, after the familiar tortures, recanted and "confessed," a ritual performed by thousands of other victims during the Great Purges. With complex characters such as Savinkov, however, outward appearances are frequently deceptive. V. L. Burtsev, one of the émigré intellectuals in whom Savinkov confided at the time, has provided what appears to be the most plausible theory in an explanation published in the fall of 1927. Burtsev's account, which he calls "Savinkov's Confession," is the only testimony of any of the émigrés who personally knew the principal figures involved and had considerable insight into their psychology. He writes:

> Toward the end of July 1924 Savinkov paid me an unexpected visit and said: "I am going to Russia and have come to make a full confession to you. I ask only one thing of you: to hear me out to the end."
>
> Savinkov told me that he had a revolutionary organization which was operating inside Russia, that its principal members fully recognized his leadership and would follow him everywhere. They had important connections in the highest Bolshevik ruling and party circles, including even the GPU. They were powerful and could bring about a revolution at the proper moment at will. . . . In the very near future they would be faced with very important political decisions. That is why they had sent for him to come to Russia.
>
> After listening to him I told Savinkov frankly that I would have nothing to do with the plans of his organization, which I thought were fantastic . . . I pointed out to him that the organization was undoubtedly a worn-out provocation and that if it had not yet been scrapped by the Bolsheviks, it was

only because its liquidation did not fit in with the GPU plans.

It was obviously useless to continue our argument about the advisability of his trip to Russia for revolutionary purposes . . . As if accenting every syllable and in the most decisive tone of voice Savinkov said: "My trip to Russia has been decided. I cannot remain abroad. I must go! I cannot fail to go!"

He didn't need to tell me that his personal life had recently become so mixed up as to make a further continuation of his life abroad more difficult than ever, if not impossible. There were not only purely domestic problems but also financial difficulties . . .

As if moved by the sum total of my words and thoughts, Savinkov said: "I am going to Russia in order to die in the struggle against the Bolsheviks. I know that if arrested I can expect only the firing squad. I shall show the people sitting here [and he named a few well-known families] how to die for Russia. My trial and death will be a witness against the Bolsheviks. All will hear my protest."

His words stirred me deeply. I told him that if he seriously thought over his convictions and decision, if he succeeded in carrying it through to the end, then his trial and death would have enormous significance in the history of the struggle with the Bolsheviks.

A few days later Savinkov came to chat with me again and to say his last farewells. We did not talk much about the conditions under which he was leaving Paris and would cross the frontier. I said good-by to Savinkov without much hope of seeing him again anywhere. It seemed to me that only an accident could save him from arrest and consequently from execution.

It was only after Savinkov's arrest, which was not long in coming, that I learned that his departure from Paris took place under much more complicated circumstances than I had imagined based on my conversations with him.

A couple of weeks later my telephone rang. I asked who was calling and heard a voice answer: "I'm Reilly. Do you remember me?"

I answered that I did remember him. (A few years before this I had met him in London and had questioned him about his role in the Lockhart conspiracy. But I had never had anything to do with any of his affairs. I had heard him highly praised by Savinkov.)

"A terrible misfortune has happened," Reilly said to me,

his voice filled with emotion. "You of course understand what I'm talking about. A telegram has come from Russia, but its contents are obviously false. It says that at his trial he went over to the Bolsheviks."

At that we ended our telephone conversation and made an appointment.

Savinkov's trip to Russia had been organized by Pavlov and Fedorov, the two emissaries from Russia who were members of the organization about which Savinkov had talked to me. They had come to Paris more than once. He had known both of them in Warsaw as active anti-Bolsheviks. They had come with letters from one of Savinkov's most important agents, a certain Colonel Pavlovsky, who had previously worked closely with Savinkov in Warsaw. He later returned to Russia and took part in the most hazardous operations against the Bolsheviks, destroying them without mercy in his raids . . . From Russia he kept up a correspondence with Savinkov, who regarded him as one of the most trustworthy and hopeful of his comrades working in Russia . . . At that time no one yet knew that Pavlovsky was already working as an OGPU agent. (He had been arrested and given the choice of death or working for the OGPU.)

. . . During the last days, when, as might be expected, Savinkov was hesitating whether to go or not to go, Pavlov had given him a letter from Pavlovsky in which the latter wrote that they had obtained millions of rubles from a successful "expropriation" (robbery). In his letter Pavlovsky insisted on the necessity of Savinkov's return, since the money could be turned over only to him personally, and to no one else. Pavlovsky himself, in spite of Savinkov's insistent requests, could not come to Paris for a personal conference with him because he had been seriously injured during the robbery and was lying in bed ill with friends near Moscow. At the time everyone believed this story attributed to Pavlovsky.

Pavlov gave Savinkov 2,000 francs from the funds of his organization in Russia for the trip . . . As I had suggested, Savinkov decided not to make the journey alone. His oldest and closest comrade, Dickhoff-Dehrenthal, and the latter's wife went with him . . . Two others also went with them, Pavlov and Fedorov, both GPU agents, and, of course, other Chekists kept them under surveillance from other directions, impatiently awaiting their arrival in Moscow.

At this point precise information on Savinkov's journey

ends, and the fragmentary testimony of more or less reliable
witnesses or the conjectures of other individuals begin. There
is much that is obscure, not understood and problematical
which has been used as source material for the creation of
various Savinkov legends.

When Savinkov and his comrades crossed the border and
arrived in one of the nearby border towns, Pavlov and Fedorov threw away their masks and told him that he was under
arrest. Dehrenthal and his wife were also apprehended.

Moscow was informed of their arrest and three specially
empowered GPU agents came to interrogate him. Savinkov
was informed that an extraordinary tribunal had been named
to try his case without delay, and everyone knew what he
could expect.

It was said that Savinkov took his arrest quietly and
apparently accepted his fate peacefully. However, the GPU
agents from Moscow conducted entirely different conversations with Savinkov than had those who arrested him. They
began by telling Savinkov that they were talking to him as an
old revolutionary and socialist who had mistakenly fought
the Bolsheviks on the side of the Whites. Certainly the Bolsheviks themselves understood that all their experiments in
Russia had ended in total failure, that there was still no communism in the Soviet Union and no hope of creating it in the
near future. Of course, if the monarchists were able to overthrow the regime, they would drive out all Bolsheviks and all
leftist elements, including people like Savinkov himself, and
in Russia, reaction would rule for a long time. Consequently
the salvation of the revolution lay in a common struggle of
both Communists and Socialists against the White movement.
For this reason the authorities needed to recruit democrats
and socialists such as himself, Savinkov. The Bolsheviks
working within the GPU understood this perfectly, but they
were prevented from waging war on the Whites this way by
doctrinaires and scoundrels such as Trotsky and Zinoviev . . .
Therefore a revolutionary like Savinkov ought to side with
them and help them in the struggle. It would be a pity if he
were to be shot. They hoped to be able to save him, but of
course that would depend on his accepting their conditions.
They proposed only one condition: that at the trial he should
openly embrace bolshevism, and in return they would guarantee that the death sentence would be revoked, that he would
simultaneously be granted an amnesty and could join them in
the struggle against Zinoviev. This was the basis of a secret

agreement between Savinkov and the GPU. He was also promised that at his trial the question would not be raised as to why he had returned to Russia. The fact that Dehrenthal and his wife had come with him would be passed over in silence: they would not be brought into the case and everything the GPU knew about the real purpose of Savinkov's trip to Russia would be concealed.

It is difficult to say whether Savinkov believed his seducers from the GPU for even a minute. But obviously he decided that he would try to use them for his own purposes. He had always counted on using the struggle among the Bolsheviks to further his own plans and hoped that in this instance he could successfully use some of the Bolsheviks to fight others.

After his disillusionment abroad with those on whom he had pinned his hopes, Savinkov had been convinced that his comrades working inside Russia could take advantage of the internal power struggle among the Bolsheviks themselves and had based his plans on this concept. And now, isolated in a Bolshevik prison, he decided that this circumstance would make it possible for him to play a major role in this kind of double game. He believed in himself and in his star and hoped that by playing along with the GPU he might realize his grandiose plans. He brought this irrational belief in his own strength to his conversations with the Bolsheviks.

The agreement between Savinkov and the GPU was concluded a few days before the trial. The testimony given by Savinkov and the Dehrenthals has not been published to this day and we do not know what it contains. It most likely consists only of the evidence against Savinkov and the Dehrenthals collected by Pavlovsky, Pavlov, and others.

The Dehrenthals, Savinkov's closest collaborators who shared his aims, are not mentioned in either the statement of charges or the trial record. This obviously proves that an agreement with the GPU was concluded not only by Savinkov, but also by the Dehrenthals. Shortly after their arrest Dehrenthal and his wife were released . . . When they learned that Savinkov had decided to embrace bolshevism, they fully agreed with him.

The Bolsheviks kept their word with Savinkov. He was not sentenced and in prison lived in circumstances not permitted political prisoners in Russia . . . From prison Savinkov carried on correspondence with family and friends, and wrote an open letter to me and Passman. The GPU considered this correspondence of such importance that his letter to me, including his autograph, was published in the Bolshevik newspapers.

The Bolsheviks not only did everything Savinkov expected of them, but also some things which actually were not promised him officially. They did not grant him an amnesty nor did they release him from prison for eight or nine months. He was not amnestied because they did not want to make a common front with him in any struggle against Zinoviev. They did not believe in the sincerity of Savinkov's avowals.

Savinkov understood that his hopes of deceiving those Bolsheviks who proposed working with him against Zinoviev were in vain and would never be realized . . . One must know Savinkov personally in order to understand that when he realized that all his plans had been permanently ruined, he no longer wanted to live and decided to take his own life.

Savinkov went to Russia with plans for revolutionary warfare against the Bolsheviks and, in case he was arrested, with the idea that his death would constitute a protest against the Bolsheviks.

In prison, before his trial, for a minute he assumed that it would be possible to strike a blow against some Bolsheviks by utilizing others. His adventurist nature caused him to take this bold step. But he was soon convinced that he had committed a frightful, irreparable mistake—and worse than a mistake, a crime. Having lost all hope of being able to make amends for his last mistake, he decided to end his life and at the first opportunity leaped out of the fifth-floor window.[44]

The Burtsev account of Savinkov's "confession" has been quoted at length because it is an outstanding example of a theoretical reconstruction of complex events and motives based on a "logic of the situation" approach by a sensitive observer. New evidence summarized below confirms its essentials.

During the thirteen months (July 1923–August 1924) which Sidney Reilly spent in New York seeking to win a $500,-000 lawsuit against the Baldwin Locomotive Company, he was in fairly regular communication with Savinkov in Paris. From the tone if not the explicit content of his colleague's letters, Reilly must have surmised that Savinkov, who by then was a "broken and dispirited man," was planning to return to his native land. Reilly had been assisting a former intelligence-service colleague, Sir Paul Dukes, who was lecturing in the

United States at the time, with a translation of Savinkov's novel *The Black Horse*. In greatest confidence he once turned to Dukes and said: "I am going to tell you something very, very private. I am not telling anyone else and no one must know. Savinkov is going back to Russia to give himself up. I too am going back, but I shall continue to fight." [45]

If this evidence is valid, then it follows that once Savinkov had made his decision to return (presumably months before his actual departure), the rest of his actions, and those of Reilly as well, were part of an elaborate charade meant to preserve his image and deceive the public. (This would account for Reilly's attitude during his interview with Burtsev.) But there is also a very real possibility that, as argued by Burtsev, Savinkov either before or after his return had made some sort of deal with a faction of the OGPU and believed that he could continue his struggle inside the Soviet government as he had from without. The OGPU was a very large organization, and the experience of General Kutyepov and his agents indicates that there were factions that could have been played against each other within the larger framework of the struggle for Lenin's succession, which was then going on behind the scenes. Clearly, prior arrangements had been made to provide especially humane treatment, not only for Savinkov, but also for the Dehrenthals, who in spite of their long association with Savinkov were never brought to trial. In a conversation with the American correspondent William Reswick, the OGPU chief Yagoda boasted that Savinkov had been lured back by an agent who had fallen in love with him and who had been granted "permission to stay nights in his cell," for what today would be called "compassionate purposes." The only person who conceivably fits this description is Mrs. Dehrenthal, who had for some time been Savinkov's mistress, presumably at first for the good of the cause.[46] There is a close parallel here with the intimate relationship between the British intelligence agent "Cynthia" (Elizabeth Pack) and the French press attaché Captain Charles Brousse, in Washington, D.C., during World War II.[47]

Commander Boyce's Bumble, or the Entrapment of Reilly

Savinkov's entrapment involved highly complex and mixed personal motivation, so that the closest analogy today is probably redefection. By comparison the entrapment of Reilly appears on the surface to be almost accidental, the result of escalating involvement against a background of strong ideological commitment reaching back at least as far as Reilly's wartime experience as a British agent in Russia. Reilly was far enough left in his politics that he preferred the Socialist Revolutionary terrorist Savinkov to the conservative émigré circles in Paris. In England, however, he paradoxically drew support from the British Tories—especially Churchill—to whom he turned because they were anti-Bolshevik. Reilly's own personal anticommunism was a natural, almost instinctive reaction, one shared deeply by others of his contemporaries such as Winston Churchill. It was also a visceral reaction. During the war he had written charitably that "the Germans are human beings. We can afford to be even beaten by them." The Bolsheviks were quite another matter, and here Reilly epitomizes what has been the conservative anticommunist credo ever since. Bolshevism, which was growing to maturity around him, was the "archenemy of the human race."

> If civilization does not move fast to crush this monster while there is yet time, the monster will finally overwhelm civilization . . . At any price this foul obscenity which has been born in Russia must be crushed out of existence . . . There is only one enemy. Mankind must unite in a holy alliance against this midnight terror.[48]

Although Reilly had worked for the British Secret Intelligence Service (S.I.S.) with distinction during the First World War, after hostilities ceased he was never taken on as a permanent staff member with "status." The proper Etonians in the Foreign Office regarded him as "an upstart who had no business to meddle in international politics," and the Security Service (M.I. 5) "noted his Leftist inclinations," as evidenced by his "patronage of Savinkov and the Social-Revolutionaries." [49]

Reilly's anti-Bolshevik crusade had the blessing of Churchill and the moral support of the Secret Service chiefs. But unlike the French, Polish, and Czech governments, they were unwilling to commit funds to support the various counter-revolutionary projects on which he expended a large personal fortune, finally selling most of his valuable collection of Napoleona to raise money in support of Savinkov.

Commander Ernest Boyce was the head of the British Secret Intelligence Service in Russia during the war, during which time he cooperated with Reilly on a number of covert operations. After the war Boyce had been in charge of Russian affairs in S.I.S. headquarters in London, and by January 1925 was stationed in Reval as head of the S.I.S. there. Boyce was thus responsible for the first contacts (as early as 1921) with Yakushev and with the Moscow-based resistance organization known as the Trust.[50]

The entrapment of Savinkov proved the extent of OGPU penetration into the anti-Bolshevik resistance networks formerly controlled by the Socialist Revolutionaries. The Savinkov affair should have served as a warning. Nevertheless, Boyce continued to keep up his contacts with the Trust, since S.I.S. regarded it as "a movement of considerable power within Russia," whose agents "had supplied valuable intelligence to the secret services of a number of western European countries." On the other hand, it was suspected that some reports collected through Trust channels were planted by the OGPU. British intelligence was therefore anxious to make an accurate assessment of the Trust's real strength.[51] Throughout 1924 Boyce had received a series of reports that the Trust was growing daily more powerful and even included members of the Soviet regime itself. Late in 1924 or early 1925, on one of their trips from Leningrad to Helsinki, Maria Zakharchenko and her husband, Georgi Radkovich, had visited Boyce personally. It is a tribute to Maria's powers of persuasion that she was able to convince the Commander that the Trust had prepared the way for a revolution which was to take place within the next two years. The argument was all the more persuasive because of the growing Stalin-Trotsky feud over the succession to Lenin.

Under the circumstances, what could be a more natural reaction on Boyce's part than to enlist the services of his former colleague Reilly to investigate the Trust, and to provide British intelligence with a reliable evaluation of its strength and capabilities? If it should prove to be a bona fide resistance organization, not under control of the OGPU, it would merit substantial support in the turbulent days ahead. If it was not,

British networks dependent on it could be quietly dropped. Since Reilly was not officially connected with the S.I.S., the whole operation could be conducted on an "old boy" basis between Boyce and Reilly without involving British intelligence in case anything went wrong.

The entrapment of Reilly thus began with an exchange of letters between Boyce and Reilly, who was still in New York hoping to win his $500,000 lawsuit against the Baldwin Locomotive Company. The correspondence was conducted in chatterbox code and in invisible inks, with the Trust referred to as "the Syndicate," Churchill (from whom Reilly still hoped to get support) as "Marlborough," and anticommunists as "minority interests." [52] In a long coded letter dated January 24, 1925, Boyce explained the importance he attached to the Trust and wrote that a certain "Mr. and Mrs. Krasnoshtanov" (actually Maria Zakharchenko and Georgi Radkovich) were anxious to meet him in Paris to discuss plans. In an indirect reference to the Savinkov fiasco, Boyce observed: "I am introducing this scheme to you thinking it might perhaps replace the other big scheme you were working on but which fell through in such a disastrous manner." [53] In the course of this coded correspondence, which continued through August, the Krasnoshtanovs were identified as Maria and Georgi Schultz (their most familiar alias), and General Kutyepov was named as the chief representative of the "central organization" in Paris. Reilly expressed his admiration for the General, but also his doubts about the apparent "monarchist" coloring of the organization, since he considered "any definite association with Monarchism at the present stage as fatal, as far as foreign moral and material support is concerned." [54]

During this period, at Boyce's suggestion, Reilly also communicated directly with Nikolai Nikolayevich Bunakov, "one of the Trust's more important agents in Helsinki," referred to in the correspondence as "Engineer B." Through Bunakov the Trust leaders suggested that Reilly visit Russia, meet the top officials of his organization, and judge its strength for himself. [55] Meanwhile, the lawsuit against the Baldwin Locomotive Company had been lost and with it Reilly's last chance of paying off his mounting debts. He took the news badly, literally foaming at the mouth in court and, in a typically paranoid reaction, blaming the hated Bolsheviks for his ruin. Finally, unable to put his personal finances in order, but having previously arranged for the care of his beloved Pepita in case of accident to himself,[56] he telegraphed Boyce that he and his wife would arrive for consultations in Paris on September 3, 1924.

Boyce met the Reillys on their arrival in Paris. While Pepita visited her mother in Ostend, Sidney had a number of meetings with Boyce, General Kutyepov, the journalist Burtsev, who had formerly been head of the Socialist Revolutionaries' secret service, and other émigrés.

There is no record of what went on in these discussions, but with the tragic example of Savinkov still fresh in memory it is almost certain that Burtsev and Kutyepov urged caution. According to Mrs. Reilly's narrative:

> After a few days I returned to Paris. Sidney told me that he was convinced of the sincerity and potentiality of this anti-Bolshevik organization. It had been arranged that he should meet the principals of the group on the frontier between Russia and Finland, as it was decided that a journey into Russia was very dangerous. General K. was strongly of this view. . . . General K. impressed very emphatically upon my husband the folly of crossing the border:
>
> "Let them come to you," he said. "The arrangement has been made most definitely with the people from the Moscow centre that they are to come to Helsingfors to see you there."
>
> It was arranged that I should accompany my husband as far as Hamburg and there await his return.[57]

It is significant that after months of correspondence with Reilly about the Trust, Commander Boyce, sometime after the initial meetings in Paris, left for London so that he was conveniently absent when Reilly arrived in Helsinki to meet the Trust agents. After a fortnight of conferences in Paris, the sequence of events that followed is fairly clear from Reilly's letters to his wife. He arrived in Helsinki on the twenty-first and at once got in touch with Commander Boyce's assistant, "a very intelligent youngster, keen as mustard," and Nikolai Nikolayevich Bunakov, the Trust agent with whom he had previously corresponded. Reilly described him and his position as follows:

> Although he is merely what we call a post office box, he could give me a considerable amount of useful information.

B. is a very nice fellow and I am sure you would have liked him at first sight. . . . He enjoys the full confidence of E. [Ernest Boyce] and his assistant, but, as I have said, his role is purely secondary. He took me to his flat and gave me a wonderful Russian dinner.

After dinner Maria Zakharchenko and her husband arrived and were introduced as Maria and Georgi Schultz. Reilly's letter dated September 22 describes the vivid impression Maria made on him:

> She is the head of the concern, and her very long skirt cannot disguise the trousers which she is wearing.—She is of the American school-marm type, which, strangely enough, is not uncommon in Russia, very plain and unattractive, but full of character and personality. It was most instructive to talk to her (or rather to listen to her, because she did most of the talking). She was full of information. You will understand that I cannot give you here an account of what she said, but if only 25% of what she said is based on facts (and not on self-induced delusion, as is so often the case when the wish is the father of the will) then there is really something entirely new, powerful and worth while going on in Russia.— Anyway, when I leave here—I shall be fully and definitely *"fixé là-dessus."*
>
> Now, however, comes the rub. There has been no news yet from the people we are expecting. A telegram is expected any moment and when it comes I will have to go to Wyborg [Vyborg] (a night's journey from here) to meet them. The conference will last two days at the utmost and then away.[58]

In a note apparently written an hour or two later as a postscript, Reilly states that "the telegram has come, and . . . I am leaving for Wyborg." In a letter written in Wyborg, dated September 25, Reilly continued:

> It is absolutely necessary that I should go for three days to Petrograd and Moscow. I am leaving tonight and will be back here on Tuesday morning. I want you to know that I would not have undertaken this trip unless it was absolutely essential, and if I was not convinced that there is practically no risk attached to it. I am writing this letter only for the most improbable case of mishap befalling me. Should this happen, then you must not take any steps; they will help little but may finally lead to giving the alarm to the Bolshies and

to disclosing my identity. If by any chance I should be arrested in Russia, it could be only on some minor, insignificant charge and my new friends are powerful enough to obtain my prompt liberation. . . .

My dearest darling, I am doing what I must do and I am doing it with the absolute inner assurance that, if you were with me, you would approve. You are in my thoughts always and your love will protect me. God bless you ever and ever. I love you beyond all words.[59]

Reilly's last letter was never mailed. About a month later it was simply handed to Mrs. Reilly in Paris without comment by Bunakov, who spoke nothing but Russian, and who had held onto it until then for reasons best known to himself.

There are three principal versions of what happened when Reilly left Helsinki for Vyborg, near the Finnish border, to meet Yakushev, the Trust representative. They differ in some details, but the main outline of events can be fairly accurately reconstructed.[60]

Reilly went to Vyborg on Friday, September 25, accompanied by Bunakov, Maria Zakharchenko, and Georgi Radkovich. There they met Yakushev. He obviously made a good impression on Reilly, who explained that because of the way his affairs stood, he could not go into Russia for two or three months. As a matter of fact, he planned to catch the boat the next day, Saturday, for Stettin and Hamburg. Yakushev countered with the proposition that he could arrange a fast trip which would make it possible for him to go to Moscow, meet the leaders—the Political Council—of the Trust, and still be back in Helsinki in time to catch the next boat for Stettin on Wednesday.

According to the Soviet account, Reilly's acceptance of Yakushev's proposition was so unexpected that Bunakov almost jumped up from where he was sitting. It was suggested that Reilly would need a less conspicuous suit of clothes, overcoat, cap, and shoes, in order not to attract attention across the border. Georgi Radkovich lent him his own overcoat for the journey. The other items were bought later. Yakushev promised him "a perfectly safe, if not an entirely comfortable trip." (After her husband's disappearance Mrs. Reilly later pointed out that Reilly kept his own shirt and linens, which were monogrammed with the initials S.R., so that he must have had every confidence that he would not be arrested and interrogated.)

Yakushev returned to Moscow at once to set up a staged meeting of the Political Council of the Trust for Reilly's benefit, and the latter was conducted to the border by a Captain Rosenström (an intelligence officer of the Second Finnish Division) and Georgi Radkovich. They had arrived at Kuokkala, on the Finnish side, at ten P.M. and at the border by eleven, at the regular Trust window on the Sestry River (a shallow stream marking the borderline). Reilly waded across and was met by Toyvo Vyakhy, the Soviet border guard, who had orders to use his weapon if Reilly should change his mind and decide to turn back. The seventeen-kilometer trip from the border to the Parglovo railway station on the Soviet side was made in an open Russian cart, or *telega,* and proved so uncomfortable that, in spite of the mud, Reilly preferred to get out and walk most of the way. Vyakhy put his charge safely on the train to Leningrad, where he was met by Yakushev and Shchukin, an OGPU agent who provided him with a false passport bearing the name of Steinberg.[61]

Reilly arrived in Leningrad in the morning of Saturday, September 26, and spent the day in Shchukin's apartment, where he was introduced to "Starov," allegedly a factory worker and deputy to the Moscow Soviet (then in session), before which he was scheduled to give an address on "the labor question." (Starov was in fact OGPU Commissar Pillar, a member of the special task force directing the Trust operation. He left shortly afterward for Moscow.) Mukalov, an emissary from Wrangel's forces, who had previously moved in and out of Russia through Trust channels, was also present. That evening the group took the train to Moscow, riding in the international sleeping car, and were met at the station by an alleged group of Trust operatives—Dorozhinsky, Starov again, and Shatkovsky (an ex-tsarist police colonel)—all of whom were OGPU agents.

Reilly spent the evening and the next day, Sunday, September 27, at the OGPU *dacha* in the village of Malakhovka on the outskirts of Moscow. There he was introduced to former Lieutenant General Potapov, the head of the Trust's military staff, and to the Trust's Eurasian specialist, the Red Army Commander Langovoy. When it came time to leave in order to catch the evening train to Leningrad, the party left in two cars. Reilly rode in the first, accompanied by the OGPU agents Pillar and Puzitsky (who had taken part in the earlier arrest of Savinkov). Yakushev and Potapov rode in the second car, which took them to Staunitz' quarters on Maroseika Street. It had been planned to arrest Reilly on the way to the railroad station. But he asked if he might be able to send a postcard before boarding the train, and a stop was made en route. During the interval Pillar called OGPU headquarters in the Lubyanka to explain the delay, and was ordered to make the arrest as soon as the card had been posted. (Commander Boyce later received the postcard, stamped and canceled in Moscow.) [62] According to plan, Puzitsky and other OGPU agents then boarded the train for Leningrad in order to stage an "incident"—with noise, shooting, etc.—near the village of Allekul, in which Reilly was supposed to be killed and others injured. When Reilly did not return and Maria Zakharchenko had received no news of him from Moscow, she sent a telegram which arrived on the twenty-ninth asking for an explanation.[63] In due course, the Soviet newspaper *Izvestia* announced that "In the night from the 28th to the 29th of September four smugglers attempted to cross the Finnish border into the U.S.S.R. . . . They were intercepted by our frontier troops. In the ensuing skirmish two of them were killed, a third—a Finnish soldier—was captured and the fourth mortally wounded."

Yakushev was not informed of Reilly's arrest until it had taken place, and was very much upset, for he had arranged the trip, and suspicion would inevitably fall not only on the Trust in general, but specifically on him. Meanwhile, from Helsinki Maria Zakharchenko had written him a distressing letter in which she blamed herself for Reilly's betrayal and presumed death. It was expected that she would come to Moscow to make inquiries, although she had finally been sent a chatterbox-code telegram that read: "Illness ended in death of children." To soften the blow, another scenario was staged at Staunitz' quarters, where, in addition to himself, Yakushev, General Langovoy, Zubov (an OGPU agent assigned to the Trust), and Mukalov, General Wrangel's emissary, were gathered, expecting the arrival of Maria Zakharchenko from Helsinki. Instead of Maria, her husband, Georgi Radkovich, arrived. He reported that as he and Captain Rosenström ap-

proached the border to receive Reilly, they heard cries and
shots, which they thought were probably due to a skirmish
between border guards and contrabandists. They waited until
dawn for Reilly, who, of course, failed to show up, after which
they returned empty-handed to Helsinki. Apparently Georgi
Radkovich's testimony, which was made in good faith, had its
desired effect, and the supposition that Reilly was killed or
wounded in an unfortunate accident was generally accepted.
A week later (October 8) the Warsaw representative of the
Trust wrote: "The incident was purely accidental. The Trust is
not endangered. However, it is certainly fortunate that Yakushev did not accompany Reilly." About the same time, Polish
G-2 sent gifts of gold watches and miniature monogrammed
Browning pistols to important Trust leaders—Yakushev, Potapov, Langovoy, Staunitz, and Dorozhinsky.[64] The Trust's relations with Polish intelligence were obviously not upset by the
incident.

While these scenarios centering around the entrapment of
"Britain's master spy" were being staged in Moscow, his wife
waited in vain for his arrival in Hamburg. In an exchange of
coded letters with Commander Boyce of British intelligence
she learned that the latter had received a postcard from Reilly
dated September 27, and that "before going to the hospital he
left a letter for you with instructions that it should be sent
on if he was incapable of writing himself after the operation
[that is, after his trip into Russia]. This letter is now being
sent on to Paris to you."

The letter referred to was Sidney Reilly's last communication to his wife, which was delivered to her by Bunakov in
Paris. On instructions from his superiors in British intelligence,
Boyce failed to keep an appointment with Pepita in Paris, and
when she sought him out in London he explained that it
would be dangerous for a Secret Intelligence Service official to
be seen in her company.[65] Bunakov, who spoke only Russian,
was of no assistance.

Although Bunakov was first and foremost a Trust agent,
the fact that he also took orders from Boyce and was later
executed by the OGPU as a British spy [66] indicates that he was
working both sides of the fence as a double agent. The OGPU
had won him over by bringing his brother from Moscow to
Helsinki for a visit.[67] He was probably the source of some of

the Reilly correspondence printed in *Izvestia,* June 17, 1927, for Mrs. Reilly's narrative was not published until 1931.

Before pursuing her husband's traces further, Mrs. Reilly visited one of her friends, Harold Williams of *The Times,* and arranged to have a brief announcement of Sidney's death placed in *The Times* should she wire him to do so later. She also saw another mutual friend, Captain George Hill, formerly of British intelligence, who was deeply sympathetic. When she arrived in Helsinki a few days later she found a telegram waiting for her: "Good luck to a plucky brick. Hill." Bunakov was also waiting for her, and had a room reserved in her name in a local pension (presumably an OGPU safe house), which he assured her was more secure than the best-known hotel. The next morning Maria Zakharchenko, using the name of Schultz, came to her room and, as usual, began to exert the strange influence she had over virtually everyone she met. Mrs. Reilly describes her meeting thus:

> Punctually at the hour there was a knock at the door, and in came a slender woman with pale yet attractive, capable face, steady, honest, blue eyes, obviously well bred, and answering very well to Sidney's description of her as a school ma'rm. At my first glance I decided that I could trust her. At my second I knew that I was going to like this woman.
>
> Seeing me thus, looking very mournful, very desolate, very lonely, Mme. Schultz embraced me with great emotion, telling me that she felt herself entirely responsible for my husband's death, and that she would not rest until all the circumstances had been discovered and a rescue effected if he were still alive, or a revenge secured if he were in truth dead.[68]

After a few days of fruitless inquiries Mrs. Reilly returned to Paris, and when several days later she received a coded telegram from Maria Schultz, she had the following death notice inserted in the London *Times* on December 15, 1925: "REILLY: On the 28th September, killed near the village of Allekul, Russia, by G.P.U. troops, Captain Sidney George Reilly, M.C., late R.A.F., beloved husband of Pepita N. Reilly." [69]

Nevertheless, for several years Mrs. Reilly clung passionately to the belief that her husband was still alive. She reasoned that since her husband's shirts and underwear bore the monogram S.R., and since he was wearing a watch that apparently had her inscribed photograph inside its case, surely the Soviets would have exploited his capture for propaganda purposes if he had been taken prisoner, and she refused to believe that he had been killed in the alleged border incident near Allekul.

In the weeks following Reilly's disappearance, "it was clear that something had gone seriously wrong," and British intelligence hurriedly sought to extricate itself from a politically explosive situation. Lockhart writes: "Although in the past it had been eager to use Reilly's talents, the S.I.S. was now anxious to disclaim all connection with him." [70] Pressure was exerted on Pepita to maintain silence about Reilly's presumed death, but she had his death notice published anyway. In connection with possible claims for compensation (confused by the fact that Reilly's marriage to Pepita was in fact bigamous, although sanctioned by the S.I.S.), Pepita was "blackmailed into silence with the threat that her British passport would be taken from her if she did not keep quiet about this." [71]

The realization finally dawned that for years British intelligence had been duped by the Trust, an OGPU provocation. As is customary after such fiascoes, there was a shake-up in the S.I.S. and Boyce, who had virtually delivered Reilly into OGPU custody, was relieved of his command and shifted to a minor post in Paris with the *Société Française de Tabac,* a cover organization in the French capital. To add insult to injury, "informed circles" in London "began to circulate a rumor that Reilly—of all people—might have defected to the Reds." [72]

As to what really happened to Sidney Reilly after he was taken prisoner, nothing is known for certain, and the available evidence is contradictory. Since the credibility abroad of the Trust was at stake, the Soviet authorities maintained a blanket of silence until that operation was blown with the defection to the West of Staunitz (Opperput) two years later, in the spring of 1927. After his defection Staunitz wrote that, like Savinkov, Reilly was kept in an apartment in the inner prison at the Lubyanka headquarters of the OGPU, interrogated, and later quietly shot in the back.

On June 8, 1927, the Soviet newspaper *Pravda* published an article listing the recent violations of Soviet territory by White saboteurs and terrorists which mentioned among others the case of a certain "Steinberg" who had been wounded and captured late in the summer of 1925 while attempting to cross the Finnish border with a false Soviet passport, and who, after interrogation, admitted that he was Captain Sidney George Reilly, "the notorious British spy." It was not until June 17 that *Izvestia* published a long feature article, "British Counter-intelligence at Work," which included Reilly's alleged "confessions," but said nothing of his ultimate fate.[73]

The most recent Soviet account states flatly that Reilly was executed on November 5, and reproduces extracts from the depositions he made during his prison interrogation. In one of these, a letter addressed to OGPU Chief Dzerzhinsky, dated and signed "Moscow, the Inner Prison, 30 October, 1925," Reilly allegedly stated that he was prepared to answer fully any questions regarding British intelligence, American intelligence, and Russian émigrés with whom he had had dealings.[74]

If true, since Reilly had only been arrested a week earlier, this deposition provides impressive confirmation of the speed with which the OGPU was able to break down one of their most fanatic, frustrated, and recently ineffective opponents, an agent who, during his earlier years, had certainly merited the title of "Britain's master spy." As a result of Boyce's bumble, the Commander lost his job, Reilly lost his life, and the OGPU won a cheap, ephemeral victory in the running battle of the intelligence services—a victory that cost them dearly in the end.

4
DWINDLING CREDIBILITY
AND CONTROL, 1925–27

T HE OGPU
task force running the Trust was well aware that in the long
run the Savinkov affair and the disappearance of Reilly would
seriously affect the credibility of the organization. Luckily, a
well-known Russian émigré, Vasily Vitalevich Shulgin, who was
associated with General Wrangel in Yugoslavia, provided the
OGPU with the opportunity of conducting an operation designed
to prove that Trust channels were reliable, in spite of the
"unfortunate" Reilly incident. Shulgin, a former right-wing
member of the tsarist *Duma,* or Parliament, had been active
on the White side during the civil war, and his son had disappeared without a trace in the Crimea in 1920, presumably
taken prisoner by Budenny's forces. The next year, when the
Crimea was under Soviet occupation, Shulgin had gone into
the area with a group of ten men, of whom only five returned,
without finding his missing son. When by 1924 the Trust operation was well known in émigré circles, it occurred to Shulgin
that the organization might provide a channel through which
he could continue his search. He had Klimovich, General
Wrangel's intelligence chief, approach Yakushev, the Trust
leader, on the idea. Shulgin had been convinced by a fortune-
teller that he would find his son in an insane asylum, presumably in Vinnitsa. Although he had been invited to Moscow a
year earlier, Shulgin did not leave Yugoslavia until September
1925. Neither Nikolai Chebishev, Wrangel's political consultant, who believed that the Trust was an OGPU provocation,

nor General Wrangel himself was able to persuade Shulgin to abandon the project, which for months had been an open secret in Belgrade.[1] He was met in Warsaw by the Trust representative Artamonov (Lipsky) and spent the next six weeks in Rovno, near the Polish border, growing a thick beard and otherwise preparing to disguise himself as a proletarian (as a member of the *Duma,* his former appearance was well known). Meanwhile, the unfortunate "accident" with Reilly had occurred and would certainly have caused anyone less dedicated than Shulgin to abandon the whole project.

But unknown to Shulgin, the Reilly incident in fact guaranteed the safety of his mission. Dzerzhinsky, the OGPU chief, was determined to make Shulgin's a model journey, which could be exploited for its propaganda value in general and which would prove the existence of a well-organized resistance movement with secure channels of communication in spite of occasional, if inevitable, "accidents." From Shulgin's entry through the Polish window on December 23, 1925, to his departure from Minsk on February 6, 1926, his entire trip was an elaborate scenario staged by the OGPU. He was given a false passport bearing the name Joseph Karlovich Schwartz and was accompanied to Kiev by the OGPU official Sergei Vladimirovich Dorozhinsky. In Moscow on January 4 he was handed over to the OGPU agent Shatkovsky (who had taken part in Reilly's entrapment). Shulgin met a score of Trust officials, including General Potapov, Yakushev, Staunitz, and Maria Zakharchenko. Wherever he went he found evidence of a solid, well-organized anti-Bolshevik underground. Shulgin's original purpose, the search for his son, was virtually abandoned in the staged cloak-and-dagger atmosphere that was created around him. A Trust agent went to Vinnitsa allegedly looking for Shulgin's missing son, but reported that no trace could be found and that he had presumably died and been buried under another name.[2] At Yakushev's suggestion, Shulgin was prompted to write a book about his adventures after his safe return to Yugoslavia in April 1926.

Shulgin entitled the original handwritten draft *The Smugglers,* and sent the first ten chapters to the Trust representative in Warsaw, Artamonov (Lipsky), who in turn sent it on to Moscow for typing. The manuscript was forwarded on July 11, 1926, but Shulgin did not get back a typed copy until December. There were only minor corrections, and the first part of the book was set in galleys before he received any comments from Moscow. The second half of the book, which was filled with mystic, soul-searching meditations (some of which would have displeased the Trust), was never sent to Moscow.[3] Nevertheless, the myth that it was censored for security considerations and propaganda content by high OGPU officials has persisted through the years.[4] The fact that publication was delayed until January 1927 helps lend credence to the myth. The book first appeared in Berlin under the title *Three Cities: The Story of a Trip into Red Russia (Tri stolitsy, Puteshestvie v Krassnuyu Rossiu)* and created a sensation among the Russian émigrés, who were sharply divided over it. The fact that it carried part of the Trust "message" is symbolized in the title of the French edition, *La Résurrection de la Russie* (Paris, 1927).

Months before publication of the book, news of Shulgin's trip and safe return undoubtedly helped dissipate the cloud that had hung over the Trust since the death of Reilly. P. B. Struve, who was close to General Kutyepov, made a trip to Warsaw and talked to a Trust representative there, ostensibly about finances, but actually about the growing dispute between Wrangel and Kutyepov. His real motive, so the Trust agent reported, was to emphasize that the Trust should side with Kutyepov. It was clear that Struve's mission was in part the result of rumors that Shulgin's trip had caused Wrangel to reconsider and that henceforth he would cooperate with the Trust. Nothing could have been further from the truth.[5]

So far as credibility is concerned, the Shulgin trip probably did no more than strengthen positions already held by those who either distrusted or wished to believe in the Trust. For example, Chebishev, Wrangel's political consultant, who from the outset had regarded the Trust as a fraud, wrote in his diary after Shulgin's return that Kutyepov was "playing a dangerous game with an organization working for the counterintelligence division of the OGPU." [6]

As previously indicated, no one knew better than General Kutyepov and his agents operating inside the U.S.S.R. the kind of game they were playing. According to one of them who survived, the Shulgin visit "further increased our suspicions. We began to avoid them [certain individuals] and, without appearing to do so, we continued our conspiratorial work outside Trust channels. Shulgin's visit may have resulted in 'favorable publicity,' but not so far as ourselves or our Paris Center were concerned." [7] In any case, Shulgin's book did not appear until a few months before the Trust collapsed in April 1927.

The Disappearance of Dolgorukov

The Shulgin trip, for all its elaborate staging, was at best of doubtful value as a means of restoring faith in the Trust. The strange disappearance of Prince Dolgorukov further undermined its dwindling credibility.

In prerevolutionary Russia, Prince Pavel Dimitrievich Dolgorukov had played an important role as a leader of the Kadets (Constitutional Democrats) and a member of the Governing Council of 1905. After the February Revolution he was a member of the Constituent Assembly, was arrested by the Soviet police in November 1917, and was declared an enemy of the state. He was able to escape, however, first to Constantinople and later to Paris, where he was active in émigré circles and a member of the so-called National Committee.

In the summer of 1924 Dolgorukov crossed the Soviet border from the Polish side, using a false name, was arrested by the Soviet police, and later was released.[8] According to Chebishev, General Wrangel's political consultant, this crossing was made using Trust channels,[9] in which case his release may have been arranged in order to demonstrate the influence and effectiveness of the organization, which was at the peak of its prestige and credibility at that time.

After this incident Dolgorukov published a series of articles in the émigré newspaper *Rul* under the title "A Week in the Grip of the OGPU," in which he describes his arrest and interrogation, along with a number of observations such as the following:

> The Bolsheviks have ruled now for about six years. The emigration is waiting for an explosion from within. Many people in Russia expect the push to come from outside, thus creating a vicious circle. The gulf dividing the émigrés from the Russians—even those who are anti-Bolshevik—is growing wider and wider. A link must be created between the émigrés

and the Russians so that their differences will not increase, so that there may be created between them reciprocal understanding and agreement.[10]

Two years later, in June 1926, Dolgorukov crossed into Russia from the Rumanian border a second time, again apparently through Trust channels.[11] He traveled to Kharkov, where he contacted old acquaintances from the days of his activities in the *Duma*, the Constituent Assembly, and the Kadet party. He organized resistance groups linked in cells of five members each (*piaterok*), but was betrayed to the OGPU by a former Kadet acquaintance. Rumors later circulated in the émigré press that he had been "savagely executed." On April 18, 1927, the Ukrainian OGPU chief, Balitsky, in an unusual press interview denied these rumors. He stated that Dolgorukov was still in OGPU custody, and after repeated denials had finally revealed his mission. According to Balitsky, the Prince had received written instructions, presumably in the spring of 1927, from the National Committee in Paris (meaning Kutyepov) to the effect that passive resistance was harmful to the cause, that he should organize anti-Bolshevik elements, especially among the officers, and at the proper moment—that is, at the time of an armed attack against the U.S.S.R. from the West—should strike from the rear. Dolgorukov specifically felt that it was necessary to send into Russia activist officers from the emigration. Another task of the émigrés would be to organize public opinion against the U.S.S.R. through the press. The sole active form that could be taken by the struggle against the Soviets would be a political and economic blockade.[12]

The precise date when the OGPU decided to arrest Dolgorukov rather than keep him under surveillance is unknown, but in any case as soon as his communications with Paris were cut off and premature rumors of his execution began to circulate, the credibility of the Trust operation suffered accordingly.[13]

A Last Rendezvous with Kutyepov?

The year 1926 was a bad one for the Trust. At home the first two months were taken up with the elaborate show business connected with Shulgin's trip, followed by the Dolgorukov affair in June. Then on July 26, 1926, the chief of the OGPU,

Feliks Dzerzhinsky, died and his place was taken by Vyacheslav Rudolfovich Menzhinsky. Shortly thereafter General Zayon-chovsky, the founder of the MOCR and military chief of the Trust, also died, and General Potapov, his second in command, was taken seriously ill. Yakushev used these events as an explanation or excuse for the continuing inactivity of the Trust in his arguments with Maria Zakharchenko, who kept insisting on more "direct action," i.e., *terakts*. Relations between Yakushev and Maria had deteriorated to open hostility on her part. Moreover, it is obvious from the record that during the years 1926–27 General Kutyepov was playing a double game with the Trust. This did not prevent his attending a military planning conference with Trust agents—General Potapov representing the army and a certain Zinoviev (identified only as a fleet commander) the navy. The alleged meeting took place in Helsinki from March 25 to March 28, 1927.[14]

The Soviet account of the conversations that reportedly took place at this meeting is a curious mixture of the plausible with deliberate falsehoods. For example, in response to General Potapov's question on order of battle, "What forces can we expect in case of active hostilities on Russian territory?", Kutyepov reportedly answered that five thousand troops were in training in Czechoslovakia, an absurdly high figure. As to his own terrorist squads, the first group of eight was ready to go in at any time. This last, as events were soon to prove, was certainly a statement of fact. But then, in response to General Potapov's plea that the Trust needed money, the Soviet account has Kutyepov reply:

> "There is hope of obtaining a subsidy for our organization from London. Williams, the editor of the *Times,* supports us . . . Moreover, I am happy to add that conversations are going on between the highest leaders of our organization and Hindenburg. Stresemann is also taking part in them. The conversations are being conducted personally by his Highness [the Grand Duke Nikolai] and promise to be successful." [15]

This last statement is a deliberate falsehood designed to appeal to anti-German sentiments of Nikulin's Russian readers. According to Nikolai's chief of chancellery at the time, the Grand Duke never left Paris during the period, and moreover, he thoroughly detested the Germans.[16]

Relations with Western Intelligence Agencies

The entrapment of Sidney Reilly was a blow to the prestige of British intelligence, although Soviet propaganda admitted that he entered the U.S.S.R. "on his own initiative" rather than on an official mission. After his arrest the British had to assume that any operations or agents known to Reilly were compromised, whether the Soviet boast that the OGPU had broken him was true or not. Undoubtedly most British intelligence assets in the U.S.S.R. were lost and new networks had to be painfully built up from scratch—a sweeping victory for the OGPU.

Against these gains the OGPU had to offset the loss of its at least partial surveillance of British activities related to the Trust. The OGPU also lost a valuable channel for the spread of disinformation on Soviet affairs, one they had used for years to shape a false image of Soviet reality. But the false image persisted in British "informed circles," as exemplified by the views of J. D. Gregory, the permanent Civil Service chief of the Eastern Division (Soviet desk) of the Foreign Office. In the midst of the war-scare crisis that later developed, Gregory referred to Russia as "this Asiatic menace to Locarno," but dismissed the U.S.S.R. contemptuously as lacking "the capacity to play any effective part in the affairs of Europe." [17] The British King was even more extreme in his views and held all the delusions which Trust propaganda helped to create in its target audience: "The Russians could not undertake anything, their army was rotten . . . and the whole Russian regime stood . . . on the brink of collapse." [18]

By the fall of 1925, then, the Trust had lost all credibility with British intelligence. Since the British had considerable influence, especially in the Baltic area, probably other Western intelligence agencies also began to reevaluate the situation and their relationships with the Trust.

Undoubtedly the most enthusiastic support of the Trust had come from the Polish intelligence service. One of the Polish officers directly involved, Captain V. T. Drimmer, was the Polish military attaché in Reval, Estonia. He had watched over the entire development of the Trust and was one of the first to doubt its credibility. His report on his experience is especially valuable for the light it sheds on the intelligence-evaluation process:

[The Trust] began to use diplomatic pouches to transmit its instructions abroad. When the Trust approached my liaison officer in Moscow, Lieutenant Werner, with the request to transmit its correspondence, I gave my consent. This allowed me over a period of years to control the radius of its activity and the personalities on its staff. From it I gradually began to receive information and documents which had previously been given to me by the English or Estonians. I gradually grew more and more suspicious of the Trust.

I traveled to Warsaw and explained my position and suspicions to Lieutenant Colonel Votsyansky, head of the Intelligence Division, but unfortunately met with no comprehension on his part. Consequently I decided on a risky step and went to Russia myself, explaining to my superiors that I needed to meet with my confidential agents in the Red Army. This was my second "unofficial" trip to Russia. The previous one had been a few months earlier. I used a chauffeur's passport provided for me by the Ministry of Foreign Affairs. Loaded with food supplies for our diplomats (supplies were regularly brought to our representatives in Moscow, Kharkov, and Kiev), poorly dressed, so as not to arouse the suspicions of the Chekists (security police), I arrived in Moscow.

In Moscow, in agreement with my liaison officer, I decided to visit a certain Soviet colonel, who according to our correspondence was an important Trust contact on the staff of the Red Army. My unexpected visit caught him unawares. Conversation with him strengthened my conviction that we, along with friendly Western staffs, were victims of a very large-scale provocation.

The following day, with the assistance of my liaison officer, I met with an "official" contact of the Trust. Now I was sure that we were in the hands of the Foreign Division of the OGPU.

Major Talikovsky, head of the Russian section of the Intelligence Division of the General Staff, began to contact the Trust directly. This was a major mistake, since now there was no "buffer" between the General Staff and the Trust—a function which I had performed up to this time. The only thing I could get the Intelligence Division to do was to ask the Trust to provide some serious intelligence material, such as the mobilization plans of the Red Army, which would demonstrate the reality of the Trust's (alleged) connections with the Red Army.

The Trust tried to get out of it, to procrastinate, but in

the end reported that obtaining the plans would be expensive, since they would have to be bought from someone on the Red Army staff . . . The conversations concerning the mobilization plans dragged on endlessly, and finally the Trust explained that it could not obtain the plans because a number of personnel changes had unexpectedly taken place in the Red Army staff, but that it would be possible to obtain the mobilization plans of the Soviet railroads for 10,000 American dollars. Our Intelligence [Division] agreed with the condition that it would pay $5,000 on receipt of the plans and the remaining $5,000 when they had been evaluated.

At last our General Staff received the plans. They were subsequently examined by the Research Section of the Intelligence Division and afterward by the quartermaster of the General Staff. They judged them to be genuine. General Piskor, the chief of the General Staff, took them with him to the Belvedere to Marshal Pilsudski, who requested that they be left with him for a few days.

A few days later the chief of the General Staff was again called to the Belvedere and Pilsudski told him to take back "this Soviet trash" with which the Bolsheviks were trying to deceive Poland. Then the Marshal pointed out to General Piskor a whole series of errors which had struck him after a perfunctory examination of the plans. For the most part these mistakes concerned the carrying capacities of branch railway junctions. As far as I can remember, the guiding idea of those plans was to create the impression that preparations were being made to strike the main Soviet blow against Poland in the direction of Lvov rather than in the traditional direction of the "Smolensk Gate." It was precisely this which first roused Pilsudski's suspicions, which on further examination discovered a whole series of discrepancies which had not been noticed by the staff agencies. The plans were returned, with appropriate commentaries, to the MOCR (Trust) . . . Our liaison officer with the Trust in Moscow, Major Nedinsky, reported that the rejection of the plans as forgeries came as a great surprise to the Trust.[19]

Captain Drimmer concludes his account of the so-called "mobilization plans" incident with the observation that as a result of it he informed his colleagues (Polish military agents in Reval and Riga) that the Trust was a fraud, and that the leaders of the Russian émigré organizations in both cities were likewise warned. Unfortunately Drimmer does not give dates, but since Pilsudski seized power in May 1926 and the episode took place over several months, certainly by the fall of 1926 the credibility of the Trust was nil so far as Polish intelligence was concerned, and had been seriously damaged among the émigré monarchist circles with which the Poles were in contact. This fact probably goes far to explain why the OGPU continued to cultivate the liaison with General Kutyepov so assiduously and devoted so much time and energy to the care and feeding of Maria Zakharchenko and Georgi Radkovich in Moscow.

5

INTERNAL SECURITY, CONFUSION, AND COLLAPSE

Whatever the Trust was thus rapidly losing its credibility and contacts abroad during 1926–27, the internal security problem of controlling or liquidating individual terrorists connected with the Trust became increasingly difficult. As early as 1925 one of the subgroups in Leningrad, under the leadership of Aleksandr Sergeyevich Putillov, got out of hand, in spite of the attempts of Yakushev (who had known Putillov at the academy before the Revolution) to dampen its activities. A certain naval officer with monarchist leanings, Lieutenant Zabelin, had been attracted to the group, which labeled itself "Honor and Throne," but later decided to withdraw. He had been under surveillance, and through Yakushev's intervention was posted to a station at a Black Sea port for three months to get him away from Leningrad. When he returned, following the traditional pattern of good conspiratorial discipline, he was murdered (presumably by Putillov and an accomplice). This act caused the OGPU to liquidate the entire group—although it was then too late, of course, to save Zabelin.[1]

This simple and effective method of solving management problems by liquidating troublemakers could not be applied to the Trust group in Moscow as long as Maria Zakharchenko and Georgi Radkovich were permanent guests of the organization, and were needed because of their special relationship to General Kutyepov and his Combat Corps in Paris. From the

OGPU point of view, as long as they thought they could get confidential information about the General's plans and activities through the Radkoviches, the latter had to be humored at all costs. Given Maria's fiery disposition, keeping her reasonably satisfied with "busy work" was a difficult task at best. The task was further complicated by the special relationship that gradually developed between Maria and Staunitz, who was second in command, after Yakushev, of the underground group in Moscow. Staunitz was financial manager for the MOCR and worked under commercial cover as a "Nepman." He was typical of many such operators who promoted all kinds of legitimate and black-market business deals during the period of Lenin's New Economic Policy, which successfully restored the U.S.S.R.'s war-torn economy during the years from 1921 to 1928. During the winter of 1927 Georgi Radkovich worked in an automobile repair shop in Moscow, returning late at night to the *dacha* on the outskirts of town, while Maria and Staunitz spent progressively more time alone together in the isolated cottage. They were obviously drawn together by common interests and terrorist backgrounds, and in a sense deserved each other and the ultimate fate in store for them. The triangular relationship was not without its strains. Georgi, who was not unaware of his wife's liaison and had always subordinated himself to her every whim with doglike devotion, began drinking heavily, and was picked up one night by the militia after a riotous outburst in a Moscow restaurant. When he did not show up at the *dacha* that evening, the OGPU intervened in time, and it was decided to send him off to Minsk, for the sake of the cause. Georgi submitted to the decision.[2]

The problem of the right hand not knowing what the left is doing is a perennial obstacle to the successful management of clandestine operations. It arose unexpectedly in an acute form for the OGPU in controlling the Trust in the spring of 1927, at a time when Yakushev had suffered a heart attack, and was thus incapacitated, and Pillar, the OGPU commissar directly charged with supervising the operation, had been sent out of Moscow on a special mission. His replacement, Kiakovsky, who had helped set up the Trust five years earlier, had also been out of touch with the operation for a couple of years.

According to the Soviet account, the crisis that led to the collapse of the Trust took place as follows: Sometime in late

March or early April of 1927, Pillar had sent Aleksei Zubov (the Red Army officer working as an OGPU agent inside the MOCR) and Baskakov (a Moscow policeman who belonged to the organization as a bona fide revolutionist) on a liaison mission to the Crimea. The two were to visit such southern cities as Novorossisk, Yalta, and Krasnodar in the Caucasus in an attempt to bring the underground groups in the area under the firm control of the Political Council of the parent organization, the MOCR in Moscow. Due to negligence or to the bureaucratic shuffle connected with his leaving for his new job, Pillar had apparently failed to inform other divisions of the OGPU about the Zubov-Baskakov liaison mission. In one of the cities on their itinerary, Krasnodar, the OGPU had already decided to liquidate an underground group, as it had earlier rooted out the Putillov group in Leningrad. Zubov and Baskakov were thus in imminent danger of being arrested, which would have meant the loss of one of the OGPU's most valuable agents within the Trust. Zubov was sent a warning telegram at Novorossisk to call the mission off and return at once with Baskakov, rather than to proceed to Krasnodar. Maria Zakharchenko, who by then suspected almost everyone of being an OGPU agent, knew about the mission, and had warned Baskakov in advance to keep a close watch over Zubov. For greater security the two emissaries were staying at separate hotels in Novorossisk. Baskakov, who took Maria's warning seriously, nevertheless managed to keep Zubov under close surveillance, and saw him receive a telegram at Novorossisk at the post and telegraph office. After he watched Zubov tear up the telegram and throw it in the wastebasket, Baskakov recovered the pieces and was able to make out the message: "Danger. Deadly results likely. Return." The telegram was signed "Fedorov," one of Yakushev's familiar aliases.

That evening Zubov told Baskakov that he had just received a telegram to the effect that his wife's father had died, and that they would have to cut short their inspection trip. The two MOCR representatives returned to Moscow to learn that in the meantime the OGPU had wiped out the Krasnodar underground group. This confirmed Baskakov's worst suspicions, which he related to Staunitz early the morning after his return to Moscow.

At this time, about the tenth of April, events moved rapidly to a climax. In connection with one of his many financial operations, Staunitz had allegedly swindled Roman Birk (the double agent who handled communications in Reval for the Trust) out of £2,000 (about $10,000 at the 1927 rate of exchange).[3] Staunitz had placed the money in the *dacha* for safekeeping. A meeting on Trust finances and other matters had been scheduled there for the evening after Zubov's return. Yakushev was ill, but Zubov, Staunitz, Baskakov, and Maria Zakharchenko were to be present. The date was set for two days after the sudden termination of the liaison mission to the Crimea.

In a highly excited state, after seeing Baskakov and realizing that the Trust would soon be exposed, Staunitz appeared at the *dacha* and broke the shattering news to Maria: the whole Trust operation, to which they both had devoted the last four years of their lives, was a fraud; Zubov, Yakushev, Potapov, Pillar, Artuzov, and the others connected with the entrapment of Reilly were obviously OGPU agents. The Krasnodar subgroup had just been liquidated, and they were undoubtedly next on the schedule. Their only alternative was to escape while the authorities would still obey their orders and let them through the window on the Finnish border. Maria insisted that Karinsky and Shorin, the two remaining agents of General Kutyepov, should be warned to make good their escape while there was still time. Fortunately, Georgi Radkovich had already left Minsk and was currently in Reval.

Now that their whole underground world had collapsed around them, Maria and Staunitz fled their *dacha,* taking only the barest essentials for the trip. Before they left, Staunitz could not resist the temptation of writing a brief farewell note, which he left lying open on the table.[4]

What took place at the Trust business meeting scheduled for that evening can only be surmised from circumstantial evidence. Apparently Baskakov arrived first, to find Maria and Staunitz gone, the *dacha* in disorder, and the farewell note on the table. Baskakov presumably read the note and hid in the hallway in order to ambush Zubov. When Zubov arrived, Baskakov opened fire; Zubov snatched out his own gun and fired back. Both of them were killed in the exchange of shots.

After the bodies were discovered, Zubov was given a formal burial ceremony at the Lubyanka and decorated posthumously with the Order of the Red Banner.

It was the end of the Trust.[5]

The Opperput Defection—Epilogue and Evaluation

On the evening of April 13, 1927, Maria Zakharchenko and Edward Staunitz crossed the border together at the window near the Second Finnish Division's command post. They were taken to army headquarters by Captain Rosenström, the chief intelligence officer who had so often escorted Trust agents in the past. Staunitz began writing his defector's report, in which he claimed that he had been an OGPU agent since late 1921, when he had been arrested, tortured, and brought over (at about the same time as Yakushev, with whom he claimed to have shared a cell in the inner prison of the Lubyanka). Maria reportedly wrote a series of letters to Mrs. Reilly in Paris, which indicate that she was in a state of shock. In one of them, dated May 5, 1927, she defended Staunitz in terms that indicate the depth of their ill-starred attachment to each other and hinted at a plan she had conceived to test his ultimate loyalty:

> Now I know all his [Staunitz'] past from his own lips—he has hidden nothing: he confirms many of the things that have been said of him: he states that he was forced by torture to tell all he knew when he was taken prisoner in 1921, but he states in addition that he was never a *provocateur* before his arrest. Where the truth lies I don't know. Now he is unfolding everything, he is helping the representatives of the other countries who are being fooled and surrounded by Bolshevik agents to escape from the terrible position, and he is wrecking the result of five years' work of the G.P.U.
>
> It is so easy to charge him with his past: all my soul revolts against him. But when I think that he is the only one of all those thousands and thousands, who had dared to revolt against his masters, who has had the strength to break through the hypnosis of their omnipotence, I feel that I shall behave like a coward if I turn my back on this man at this moment. You must fight against your enemy when he is strong and not when he has rendered himself of his own free will into your hands.
>
> I do not wish to justify him, I do not wish to speak of

his past which disgusts me but I have an idea which nothing can alter that we ought to give him the chance of rehabilitating himself by putting between himself and his past his blood or that of his masters. He says that is what he wants and I am going to put it to the proof. If I am right, we will acquire an ally who knows them better than we do and who will always find a means of over-reaching them.[6]

The plan that Maria had devised was to return to Russia with Staunitz on a mission of revenge. Hopefully they could bomb the OGPU headquarters, from which, in effect, their lives had been controlled and the Western intelligence agencies duped for the last four years.

General Kutyepov had already decided to send a team of terrorists into Russia as part of a stepped-up offensive, and the collapse of the Trust ended any hesitations in this regard. Accompanied by two officers, Kutyepov traveled to Helsinki, presumably to supervise the launching of the first terrorist attacks and to interview Maria Zakharchenko and Staunitz. By the end of May Kutyepov's Combat Corps went into action, and the U.S.S.R. was thrown into a major war scare which had wide repercussions both inside Russia and on the international scene.

Meanwhile, back in Moscow after exposure of the Trust, Yakushev, the organization's principal liaison agent abroad, was of no further use to the OGPU. He returned to normal civilian life, although for a time he had to leave Moscow for the sake of his own security. Yakushev died in 1936. His son, who rose to the Red Army rank of major in the Engineers during World War II, was living in Moscow in 1965.

The members of the OGPU task force that directed the operation continued in service and attained high rank within the NKVD (the successor to the OGPU). Artuzov headed the INU, the Foreign Operations Department of the NKVD, in the midthirties. He left the organization in protest against its methods in 1937 and was soon liquidated in the Great Purges. The same fate was in store for Pillar, and both have since been posthumously rehabilitated as victims of the Stalinist "cult of personality." Kiakovsky escaped a similar fate only by chance: he was accidentally murdered by a religious fanatic in Mongolia in 1932 before the purges began.

General Zayonchovsky, the military leader of the Trust, died in 1927 before the collapse. His deputy, General Potapov,

who so successfully handled military liaison with General
Wrangel and General Kutyepov, returned to regular military
duty and was reportedly teaching military history at the Frunze
Academy in Moscow in 1938, when he was retired to the
reserves. He died in 1946, having survived the purges and
World War II. General Langovoy, who continued as a leader
of the Eurasian movement after the end of the Trust, also sur-
vived. He died in Moscow in 1964, after collaborating with
Lev Nikulin in the preparation of the Soviet account of the
Trust operation.[7]

The defection of Staunitz came as a complete surprise to
the OGPU, but is portrayed in the Soviet account as if it were
almost accidental. Defectors, however, are made, not born, and
the Staunitz case was no exception. It was closely linked to
developments that took place during the first months of 1927,
when the OGPU had begun to lose its grip on the Trust. One of
Kutyepov's agents who was operating inside the U.S.S.R. at the
time has described this situation as follows:

> With respect to terrorist operations, GPU agents within
> the Trust followed a policy of trying to dissuade the emigra-
> tion from pursuing this "senseless form of struggle." How-
> ever, early in 1927 the GPU realized that among the émigrés
> the urge to begin terrorist activity was growing stronger. Then
> (according to Opperput's [Staunitz'] testimony) the GPU
> changed its line and ordered its agents to provoke acts of
> terror, provided, however, that they did not take "an anar-
> chistic form." In the opinion of the GPU agents, the only
> way this could be done would be to combine all terrorist
> operations of the émigré organizations in one center—the
> Trust. By this simple means the GPU could bring under its
> control all émigré terrorists.
>
> Our suspicions of the Trust increased, although frankly
> at that time we still didn't realize how deeply the Security
> Police Agency had penetrated the Trust. We did not fall for
> the bait of the provocations previously mentioned. On the
> contrary, we began systematically to withdraw our people
> from the Trust net. Even though we knew the entire Trust
> was infected with GPU poison, we couldn't break with it
> suddenly, as that would have resulted in our being imme-
> diately arrested . . .
>
> At that time one of the important Trust representatives
> whom we knew by the name of Staunitz, on his own initiative,

revealed that his real name was Opperput and that he was an *agent provocateur* of the GPU.

Among other things Opperput told us that the reason for his action was as follows: The GPU had begun to notice that some sort of work was going on within the Trust about which it was not informed by its agents . . . Since there were GPU agents at the very center of the Trust, the agency suspected that some of them—especially Opperput—had gone over to the side of the "counterrevolutionaries." From his acquaintants within the organization Opperput had received a warning that he would be liquidated by the GPU. This information caused him to show us his cards. He proposed that, with his aid, we should all escape across the border without delay. Actually all of us who had entered from abroad were able to escape with one exception, who was arrested and later shot. We had been warned by Opperput in time. Evidently the GPU decided to liquidate the Trust and arrests followed. Many, however, were able to hide . . . In any case, the notorious Trust ceased to exist in April 1927.

We successfully crossed the border and received instructions to break off absolutely all relations with anyone whatsoever of the remaining members of the fallen organization. The Paris center reckoned that among the survivors (even among those arrested) there might be GPU agents who were unknown to us. On the other hand, a complete break in relations with us would help save any genuine "counterrevolutionaries" among them. I can state categorically that from then on there were no relations whatsoever between the former members of the Trust remaining in Russia and our organization. . . .[8]

It must be conceded that the Trust was one of the most successful combined security police–counterintelligence operations of modern times, although both Soviet and Western claims that it achieved covert control of all the anti-Bolshevik operations of its day are highly exaggerated.

Viewed as an internal security police operation, the Trust achieved its major objectives: it facilitated police surveillance of disaffected and potentially dangerous citizens. As one contact led to another, the OGPU could build up a fairly inclusive list of individuals in the various branches of the MOCR. When they could no longer be controlled, or the net was complete, a given target group, as in Leningrad or Krasnodar, could then be quietly liquidated with a minimum of OGPU casualties. The occasional loss of one of their own agents (such as the Red Army Commander Zubov and Navy Lieutenant Zabelin) was a small price to pay for the advantages obtained by keeping the organization intact over a four-year period. Under the circumstances, a certain number of losses from individual acts of terror had to be anticipated and accepted as part of the calculated risks involved in any such security police operation.

Viewed as an intelligence provocation, the Trust operation abroad was also successful. In the early years of its existence Soviet intelligence was able to plant all kinds of disinformation in British, American, Polish, and presumably French intelligence channels. At a time when the U.S.S.R. was seeking diplomatic recognition and credits abroad, these confusing reports exaggerated the size and importance of internal resistance to the Soviet regime. Western intelligence reports, based in part on Trust handouts, undoubtedly nursed the illusion in the early 1920's that the Bolshevik regime was at best transitory. Certainly such intelligence estimates helped condition the official U.S. position toward recognition of the U.S.S.R., which remained rigidly negative until the Roosevelt administration in 1933.[9]

It is difficult to evaluate the Trust's contribution to the sowing of dissension among the White Russian émigré groups in Berlin, Paris, and Yugoslavia. Émigré movements are by definition more or less split into competing political factions, depending on the leading personalities involved, and the problem of uniting them for political-warfare purposes has historically proved very difficult of solution.[10] Undoubtedly both Yakushev and General Potapov in their liaison missions abroad were able to play one émigré faction against another, although built-in rivalries were a major factor in keeping the émigrés disunited. Ironically, the question of how to evaluate the Trust became a subject of continuing dispute between Wrangel and Kutyepov.

The Trust's influence on émigré tactics is also clearly discernible. Yakushev was highly persuasive in his arguments that terrorist tactics were counterproductive. But his line that the émigrés should conserve their assets abroad while a strong underground monarchist movement prepared the way for a counterrevolutionary seizure of power coincided with the position already taken by the VMC in Berlin before his visits. There can be little doubt that General Kutyepov's strategic-services teams, stimulated by such activists as Maria Zakharchenko, would have started their diversionary actions sooner, and probably on a larger scale, had it not been for the dampening influence of the Trust.

Both recent Soviet and earlier Western accounts of the Trust have grossly exaggerated the extent to which it was able to penetrate and influence either émigré organizations or government intelligence agencies. The Trust could secretly influence, but certainly it did not achieve covert control of anything except perhaps of the Eurasian movement. It could and did achieve surveillance of some groups or agencies with which it maintained effective liaison (such as the Polish General Staff), but it could not bend them to its control. Its most brilliant achievements were essentially theatrical: the stage-management of the Shulgin and other visits to the U.S.S.R., or the long, contrived scenario involved in the fake underground activity of Maria Zakharchenko and Georgi Radkovich.

As a covert operation designed to protect the national security of the fledgling Bolshevik regime, the Trust operation was highly successful and remains a textbook model of its kind. As in the case of many such provocations, the initial defections of Yakushev and Birk laid the foundation for its future success. However, much credit is due to skillful management on the part of the OGPU task force in charge, and to the extraordinary talents of Yakushev, the key figure in its foreign liaison activities.

Like any other covert operation, the Trust was of course expendable. It was unwittingly sacrificed for the sake of entrapping and then liquidating both Savinkov and Reilly. So far as the credibility of the Trust was concerned, these operations were major blunders, presumably motivated by a crude thirst for political revenge which characterized many later OGPU and NKVD operations. Surely Trust sources alone were adequate to demonstrate that by the time of their entrapment neither Savinkov nor Reilly was a serious threat to Soviet security.

Staunitz' defection and the collapse of the Trust caught the OGPU by surprise as events rushed to a climax in the spring of 1927, so much so that literally nothing could be salvaged from the shambles. It also seems probable that the Soviet political leadership overreacted to the next phase of the struggle —the terrorist raids of General Kutyepov's Combat Corps— with far-reaching and unforeseen consequences.

PART 2
THE SOVIET
WAR SCARE

6
OFFENSIVE AND COUNTER-OFFENSIVE: The 1927 War Scare

S_{O FAR} we have discussed only the covert or hidden side of Russian relations with the outside world, concentrating on the struggle between Soviet counterintelligence, the OGPU, and counter-revolutionary émigré groups seeking to overthrow the Bolshevik regime. We have seen how by means of the Trust, a skillfully conducted provocation, the OGPU was able not only to maintain internal security but also to keep a close watch on subversive activities directed against the U.S.S.R. from abroad. The Trust collapsed just as General Kutyepov in Paris was ready to send in his first team of terrorists, who, it was hoped, might duplicate the deeds of the Socialist Revolutionary organization *Narodnaya Volya (People's Will)*, which had helped set the stage for the Russian Revolution. This time, at least in theory, a series of spectacular assassinations and bombings might spark general unrest and lead in turn to a renewed Allied intervention and to the eventual overthrow of the Soviet regime. Ideologically such an intervention would take the form of an anticommunist crusade to restore the traditional Russian Empire to its rightful place in the community of nations, and would hopefully return the émigré leaders to positions of power and influence in the new order.

The covert operations of the period were thus an integral part of the political-warfare context and the formal international relations of the U.S.S.R. with the other great powers of Europe. Let us review the main outlines of this broader picture as it had developed by the spring of 1927.

From the Soviet point of view the period from the end of the Allied intervention and the introduction of Lenin's New Economic Policy in 1921 had been one of an extended *peredushka,* or "breathing spell." [1] During this time the U.S.S.R. had largely recovered from the excesses of War Communism, had startled the Versailles powers by its rapprochement with Germany at Rapallo, and had vigorously sought trade, credits, and diplomatic recognition abroad. Heavy-handed Comintern propaganda and abortive attempts by local Communist parties to seize power had proved major stumbling blocks to diplomatic recognition until 1924, when Great Britain took the lead and most other powers followed suit, with the notable exception of the United States, which delayed recognition until 1933.

From the outset there had always been a basic contradiction in the idea of admitting to the society of nations a revolutionary new state, the U.S.S.R., which was pledged to the violent overthrow of the social and economic system on which that society was based. The situation was rendered even more absurd by the existence of the Communist International, a worldwide organization of Communist parties directed from Moscow and openly engaged in subverting each of the governments from which the Soviet Union sought and eventually obtained recognition. In order to bridge these contradictions, the capitalist states formally accepted the Soviet fiction that the Comintern had no connections with the U.S.S.R., and most treaties of recognition included polite assurances to the effect that both of the contracting powers would refrain from hostile propaganda and subversive activities in the territory of the other. [2] In practice these pledges were routinely ignored by intelligence services and by what today would be called the "strategic services" or covert operational agencies of both the Western powers and the Soviet Union.

By means of the counterintelligence operation known as the Trust, the Soviet security police, the OGPU, had effectively penetrated most Western intelligence agencies. The Soviets were thus able to keep a close watch over British subversive activities as well as other operations directed from Poland, Finland, and the Baltic states.

The Trust had overplayed its hand by the entrapment of

"Britain's master spy," Sidney Reilly, in 1925. From this date until the sudden collapse of the Trust organization in April 1927, British intelligence operations in the U.S.S.R. were based on the new networks not connected with previous channels. After Marshal Pilsudski returned to power in May 1926, the Trust had also lost credibility with Polish intelligence.[3] On balance, however, the Soviet Union had won the first round in the battle of the intelligence services during this period.

It should be emphasized that as chief, first of the Cheka and then of the OGPU, Feliks Dzerzhinsky was very close to other top Soviet leaders, and has since become a major Soviet hero. Although Dzerzhinsky died at the end of July 1926, during the last phase of the Trust operation, his successor, V. R. Menzhinsky, also enjoyed the confidence of the Soviet leaders. The Trust was managed by the security police under a direct mandate from the Central Committee. The remarkable success of the Trust during the early years of its operation undoubtedly contributed to a Soviet feeling of security. This feeling was in turn reflected in long-range estimates of the situation formulated by party and government spokesmen. For example, although in a famous speech made on May 9, 1925, Stalin implied that a final clash between the capitalist and socialist systems (*kto-kogo* or who-whom, as Stalin put it) was the essence of the question, he spoke of a stabilization that was then taking place at both extremes of a bipolar world.[4] Then, as now, Soviet propaganda officially described Soviet foreign policy as based exclusively on the quest for peace and the peaceful coexistence of states with differing social and economic systems. War, if it came, would most probably result from competition and contradictions between rival capitalist-imperialist states. The main enemy was, of course, England, the symbol of imperialism, the moving spirit of the Allied intervention during the civil war, and later, under a Conservative government, the most likely leader (in Stalin's view) of a world crusade against communism.

In order to understand the origin of the Soviet war scare as it developed in the spring of 1927, the situation must be analyzed on at least three levels: (1) overt events (such as the Conservative party campaign to break off diplomatic relations with the U.S.S.R.); (2) Soviet military and political estimates (to the extent that these were reflected in official statements or can be surmised); and (3) Western espionage and covert operations (such as the terror raids of the Kutyepov offensive), to which the U.S.S.R. responded at first quietly and then with a maximum of publicity which sought to charge British intelligence with responsibility for almost all anti-Soviet subversive activity.

Overt Events: The Conservative Party Campaign in England

Throughout the year 1926 Soviet foreign relations with England had remained virtually stagnant. With the signing of the Locarno Treaty and Germany's entry into the League of Nations, the U.S.S.R. felt increasingly isolated. The Soviet press played up the specter of an "anti-Soviet front" under English leadership.[5] Comintern propaganda and political-warfare activities in England directly stimulated reaction. For example, Soviet propaganda and financial aid to British workers during the general strike stirred up the Conservatives to such an extent that Anglo-Soviet relations in general and the 1921 trade agreement in particular were thoroughly aired in a debate in the House of Commons on June 25, 1926. According to Arnold Toynbee, on this occasion the British Foreign Secretary, Sir Austen Chamberlain, showed that he, at least, "was sufficiently convinced of the value of Russian trade and of the dangers of an Anglo-Soviet breach to be anxious to keep the 1921 agreement in force and to maintain diplomatic relations, even though he had no intention of entering into fresh negotiations with the Soviet Government until it was prepared to observe the undertakings which it had already given" [6] (with respect to Communist propaganda and subversive activities as set forth in the treaty of recognition). Soviet initiatives during the summer of 1926 to arrange a general settlement and to improve relations were rebuffed with the reminder that first the cessation of hostile propaganda must be made an essential preliminary to more cordial relations.

The death of Krassin, the Soviet diplomatic representative in London, on November 24 provided Conservatives with a fresh opportunity to press for an open breach with Russia. In mid-December Prime Minister Stanley Baldwin received a special deputation of Conservative party members who urged that no successor to Krassin should be recognized until the U.S.S.R. agreed to cease all forms of propaganda against the

British Empire. The Conservative campaign for a complete severance of relations continued to gain impetus during January and February 1927, but not without opposition. On February 5 the Anglo-Russian Parliamentary Committee issued a protest against the efforts of "diehard reactionaries to whom the very existence of the Soviet government is a bitter grievance" to bring about a rupture, and urged instead "the establishment of full normal trade relations between the two countries." [7]

Finally yielding to Conservative pressure, the British government sent a strong note of protest to Moscow on February 23, 1927. The note included an appendix of speeches, newspaper articles, etc., illustrating the Communist propaganda to which objection was made.[8] During the debate on Anglo-Soviet relations which followed in the House of Commons on March 3, Sir Robert Horne (who helped negotiate the trade agreement of 1921) pointed out that the British note of February 23 was almost an ultimatum, and Chamberlain himself indicated that it was intended as a last solemn warning "to give the Soviet government one more opportunity to conform their conduct to the ordinary rules of international life and comity." At the same time he denied the rumor then circulating in the European press that Great Britain was attempting to form an anti-Soviet bloc. In a press conference in Geneva on March 8 at the League of Nations Council meeting, Chamberlain also denied specifically that England was inciting Poland and Rumania to take an aggressive policy toward Russia. A month later, in a speech at Birmingham on April 7, he indicated that in his opinion a diplomatic rupture with the U.S.S.R. was undesirable, since it might imperil the peace of Europe.[9]

Meanwhile, back in Moscow, the British note was heavily exploited by Soviet propaganda, including organized protests and expressions of widespread public indignation at the "interference" of the British government in Soviet internal affairs. At this stage Soviet contemporary comment blamed the Conservative diehards exclusively for the worsening of Anglo-Soviet relations. The British proletariat was virtually counted on the Soviet side. An article in *International Life,* the journal of the Soviet Foreign Commissariat, hopefully predicted that "colossal growth of mistrust in the Conservative government on the part of the working masses" would restrict its freedom to act, virtually excluding any military adventure, and thus strengthening the Kremlin position.[10]

The same April issue of *International Life* featured a review of an article entitled "A New Ring around Russia," by Louis Fischer, published in a recent (March 23) issue of the American magazine *The Nation*. According to this review, Fischer had revealed "the hidden meaning behind all recent activity of British diplomacy. His concept is quite simple and logical and in no way differs from concepts generally accepted here. A new iron ring is being forged around Russia: 'The instigator is Britain; the reason is China.' " [11]

Not only did the Foreign Commissariat journal regard Fischer's thinking as closely parallel to its own; his line of argument was repeated over and over again by Soviet leaders in the months to come. To this early line Soviet historians later added the charge that the British Conservatives were supported inside the U.S.S.R. by "Trotskyite-Zinovievite and other enemy elements." Together these forces allegedly formed "a United Front from Chamberlain to Trotsky . . . seeking to organize a Holy Crusade against the USSR." [12]

Soviet Estimates

How were these events stemming from Conservative party pressures for an Anglo-Soviet break evaluated by the Soviet leaders and reflected in their estimates of the situation as it developed in the first three months of 1927? The evidence available in open sources indicates that until mid-April they were heavily discounted, in spite of sensational propaganda exploitation at the time.

In order to reduce public anxiety, official Soviet spokesmen published a number of reassuring statements. For example, writing in *Izvestia* for January 30, Karl Radek expressed confidence that the U.S.S.R. still had ample time in which to prevent the formation of an anti-Soviet bloc and should bend every effort to that end.[13] Even after the receipt of the February 23 note, in a speech on March 1, Stalin confidently predicted that there would be no rupture of diplomatic relations with England. He also stated flatly that "There is no danger of war," because "our enemies are not yet ready for war," and because "Russia's policy of peace would make open intervention difficult." [14] In a speech in Moscow on March 29, Aleksei Rykov, the chairman of the Council of People's Commissars, estimated that although foreign military intervention in China created a threat of war in the Far East, "so far as the U.S.S.R. is concerned in the immediate future, neither war nor intervention on Soviet territory is expected. For the moment the latter is impossible. In the foreseeable future, that is in the next year and a half, it is unlikely that a war will break out, provided the present distribution of power can be preserved." [15]

On April 18, in an important report to the Congress of Soviets, Rykov summarized the recent worsening of Anglo-Soviet relations as follows:

> . . . The English conservatives are conducting a campaign in England which may, in certain circumstances, lead to a break. The rupture of diplomatic relations between two great states such as the U.S.S.R. and England is bound to have repercussions on the entire European political situation, is bound to make the maintenance of peace more difficult . . . The note [of February 23] which was received from the English government threatened a break . . .[16]

On April 6, twelve days before Rykov's report, a British-inspired raid by the Chinese on the Soviet embassy in Peking had produced a number of incriminating Comintern documents which were later given widespread publicity by the British press. On April 20 the Congress of Soviets concluded that the British note of warning and the raids against the Soviet diplomatic missions in Peking and Shanghai forced the U.S.S.R. "to be on guard" and "to do everything possible to prevent war." Since there were no Russian troops stationed in China, the danger of a "trip-wire reaction" was excluded. It would have been forestalled in any event, since Soviet policy was to avoid being provoked into military action, however limited, which could conceivably lead to reprisals and to escalating hostilities in any theater, East or West.

Nevertheless, with respect to the threat of war, Rykov completely reversed the confident line taken by both himself and Stalin at the end of March. His opening remarks sounded a note of genuine concern:

> This congress is taking place in an extremely tense and alarming international atmosphere. Our foreign policy has

developed recently in conditions where active hostility to
the Soviet Union has been growing in a number of countries
. . . There is considerable anxiety about the possibility of
preserving and securing peace. This anxiety is caused by a
number of international events of a kind which, in the history
of international affairs, have more than once occurred on
the eve of armed conflicts. Therefore, the question whether
what has been happening recently is not the prelude to or
preparation for war is the most important question of international politics . . .[17]

As might be expected, the Soviet military establishment
followed the lead of political spokesmen. On April 29 (at least
two weeks before the Arcos raid, discussed below, which is
usually regarded as having precipitated the 1927 war scare),
War Commissar Kliment E. Voroshilov summarized the Soviet
military-political situation as follows:

> *We live surrounded by governments which are taking all
> measures to incite our neighbors against us, to draw us into
> conflict by means of provocation, and to use the same provo-
> cations as justification for an armed attack against [our] prole-
> tarian government.* Such circumstances naturally account for
> the anxiety which the working masses of our Union now feel.
> Each worker and peasant is now giving serious thought to
> the condition of the armed forces, to whether we are ade-
> quately prepared to ward off the blow of the enemy if
> necessary.[18]

Even more than in Rykov's address to the Congress of
Soviets, the emphasis here is not on any external diplomatic
or military event, but on unspecified "provocations." The break
in relations occurred while Voroshilov was on a military inspection tour in the Ukraine. The following day he interpreted
the break as meaning that "war is getting closer. England still
hasn't organized enough strength to move against us today.
However, war with the imperialist powers is inevitable, and
we must be ready for it." Stressing the need for combat readiness, Voroshilov emphasized that "we do not know when the
war will begin, but we must be ready to attack at any
moment." [19]

The Covert Operational Factor: Soviet Espionage Cases, January–July 1927

Thus far we have reviewed two main factors bearing on the origin of the Soviet war scare in the spring of 1927: the anti-Bolshevik campaign of the British Conservative party and Soviet estimates of the situation. Special attention was drawn to the fact that during April the early optimism of Soviet official statements gave way to the acute anxiety expressed in Rykov's report of April 18 to the Fourth Congress of Soviets. The report itself is a strange document, a curious mixture of mistaken optimism about the worsening of relations with Russia's main enemy, England, and genuine "anxiety caused by a number of international events of the kind which . . . have more than once occurred on the eve of armed conflicts."

In surveying the visible surface of current events through April 1927, the historian and political scientist will seek in vain for elements to which Rykov referred, and which to the Soviet leaders seemed to presage a renewed Allied intervention. For this reason traditional diplomatic historians have dismissed the Soviet fear of such intervention in the spring and summer of 1927 as irrational, paranoid, or the result of "primitive thinking." [20] But a survey of Western espionage and related covert operations directed against the U.S.S.R. as the war scare developed will indicate that there were very real and substantive grounds for Soviet anxiety. Of course, neither Western nor Soviet intelligence and counterintelligence reports are available for the period. But a study of the routine press reports in *Izvestia* of espionage arrests through July 1927 will provide a striking illustration of the kind of evidence on which the Soviet picture of "hostile enemy intentions" was based.

It should be emphasized that except in three or four show-trial cases (discussed later), these reports of the arrest and trial of Western espionage agents were *not* exploited for propaganda purposes. The stories rarely made the headlines and were usually carried in the regional "News of the Republics" section on the inside pages. This being the case, there is no reason to believe that the number of incidents reported was inflated for publicity purposes to impress either domestic or foreign readers,

NUMBER OF ESPIONAGE CASES REPORTED PER MONTH,
JANUARY–JULY 1927

Month	Number
January	1
February	3
March	0
April	1
May	45
June	48
July	34*

* July figure includes 22 arrested but not sentenced until the September 13 show trial.

as was so often the case with statistics indicating industrial growth or progress.

To this already impressive statistical base should be added a large number of arrests made without any notice appearing in the press. At least a week before Staunitz' defection on April 13 and the collapse of the Trust operation, the OGPU had arrested (and presumably liquidated) subordinate monarchist groups in both Krasnodar and Ekaterinodar. Following Staunitz' defection, the remaining Trust branches in Leningrad, Nizhni Novgorod, Kiev, and Rostov-on-the-Don were also liquidated. Although for security reasons these arrests were passed over in silence by the press, they figured in the OGPU counterintelligence reports and undoubtedly contributed to the Soviet war scare in the spring of 1927.

In regard to the figures given in the table, it should be observed that for security reasons these Soviet press reports on espionage cases were deliberately vague about the time when a given agent or group of agents was apprehended. The usual indication was no more precise than the phrase "recently" or "not long ago." It may be safely assumed, however, that the average time lapse between arrest and trial was at least a month. Obviously some time was needed to extract confessions, interrogate witnesses, and prepare the case against the accused. For this reason it would probably be advisable to slide the entire table back a month in order to reconstruct the OGPU counter-intelligence picture and the Soviet leaders' perception of the security threat to their country. In other words, the OGPU probably reported a sudden increase in espionage arrests as early as mid-April 1927. This consideration alone goes far to explain the otherwise boggling note of genuine alarm which runs through Rykov's address to the Congress of Soviets on April 18, several weeks before the Arcos raid and the open break in Anglo-Soviet relations.

By mid-April 1927, then, so far as visible open events are concerned, the Soviets were expecting that at the very least the Conservative party's anti-Bolshevik campaign would lead to an eventual break in relations. At the same time, on the covert side of the picture, they had even more cause for alarm. The number of Western espionage agents sent into the U.S.S.R. was increasing dramatically by a factor of at least ten times the anticipated monthly averages. In other words, the Soviet leaders were faced with a Western intelligence offensive. This offensive provided an ominous backdrop for the open police raids against Soviet installations in Shanghai and Peking in April and the Arcos raid in London in May.

The Arcos Raid and the Break in Diplomatic Relations

After the resumption of normal trade between England and Russia under the trade agreement of 1921, the U.S.S.R. had set up a company called Arcos, Ltd., in the premises known as Soviet House at 49 Moorgate Street, London. The building also housed the official Soviet Trade Delegation, numbering roughly 350 people. At 4:30 P.M. on May 12, 1927, after the Home Secretary, Sir William Joynson-Hicks, had obtained a proper search warrant under the Official Secrets (espionage) Act, a strong force of police occupied the building and remained for the next four days, forcing open strongrooms, searching the staff, etc., ostensibly looking for what would now be called a top-secret document concerning the British armed forces. According to the search warrant, the missing document "had been conveyed to Soviet House and there reproduced by means of a photostatic apparatus." The raid was nothing if not brusque and thorough. An official by the name of Anton Miller, who was busily engaged in burning papers from a dispatch box, was forced to relinquish the box after a struggle, and the Soviet chargé d'affaires, Rosenholz, later complained that women in the building had been searched by male police officers. The allegedly stolen document was never recovered (it may have been among those burned), but on May 24 in the House of Commons, Prime Minister Baldwin stated that the evidence collected proved that "both military espionage and subversive activities throughout the British Empire and North and South America were directed and carried out from Soviet House." After two days' debate the House of Commons voted to support the government's policy by large majorities. During the debate Joynson-Hicks explained that Anton Miller, the official who was found burning secret papers when apprehended, was a Soviet cipher clerk whom Scotland Yard had kept under surveillance for six years. He had purposely *not* been arrested during this period so that he could lead the police to other espionage contacts.[21] On May 27 the Foreign Secretary, Sir Austen Chamberlain, formally severed diplomatic relations with the U.S.S.R.[22]

Naturally the Assistant Commissar for Foreign Affairs, Maksim Litvinov, protested vigorously against the raid through official diplomatic channels and demanded satisfaction "for insults suffered, and for material losses caused by the action of the police." However, a speech by Commissar Rykov to the Plenum of the Moscow Soviet on June 1, 1927, reveals far more about the Soviet concepts of the role of espionage and subversion in international relations than the formal exchange of diplomatic notes. In regard to the Arcos raid, Rykov argued that "The British Government undertook the raid solely for the purpose of creating a superficial pretext for justifying the break in relations with the Soviet Union that had already been decided upon." He claimed that "The majority of the European newspapers characterized the search [of the premises] as a Pinkerton Detective film rather than as an important justification for a break between the great powers." After a lengthy review of British espionage and subversive activities against the U.S.S.R. from 1918 to 1926, in which he quoted a number of captured documents, he concluded:

> As you see, we have here cases not only of espionage, of organizing internal uprisings against the government, but also direct atempts to restore the Romanov monarchy on the territory of our Union.

We have known all these facts for a long time. It is perfectly obvious that since we have been dealing with [Conservative party] hardheads, we could not expect anything else. But we did not see in them any reason for sending diplomatic notes or for breaking off relations . . . In our diplomatic relations we operate on a basis of fully understanding those with whom we deal. So far as we are concerned, there is not the slightest doubt that espionage is a direct function of every capitalist government, one which has been recognized by a whole series of orators in the House of Commons. For this reason Baldwin's and Chamberlain's arguments complaining about the presence of some sort of [Soviet] espionage organization will not stand up under criticism.[23]

It would be difficult to find a more frank admission from a government leader of the generally accepted role of espionage and covert operations in international relations. Even the propaganda technique of first presenting "documentary" evidence of "enemy" espionage when caught in the act oneself has since been widely practiced by all the great powers.

In August, three months after the break in relations, Soviet Foreign Commissar Chicherin wrote a highly sophisticated article, "Practical Lessons" (signed "Post-script"), to be learned from the incident:

It would be a mistake to assume that English diplomacy operates always and exclusively through the Foreign Office or its chief . . . The history of the "Zinoviev letter," the main hero of which was not [Ramsay] MacDonald, but the head of the Eastern Division, Mr. Gregory, is the clearest and most recent illustration of this situation . . . We may be sure that something like this is happening or has already taken place in the present instance. The break itself was probably not organized by Chamberlain, but by Joynson-Hicks, the Minister of Internal Affairs, apparently with the benevolent support of Churchill, the Finance Minister . . . Chamberlain may assure us and the entire world that he is not preparing anything insidious against us, but behind his back crafty designs are being plotted against us by some "Permanent Secretary" or his colleagues in the Indian Affairs Office, the Army, Navy, or Finance Ministry.[24]

Here again we have an extraordinary admission (for a Foreign Commissariat journal) that in foreign affairs the right hand of government may not be fully cognizant of what the left hand is doing by way of covert operations. Chicherin wrote from a background of bitter experiences in this regard. He frequently had reason to complain in confidence to German diplomats that both the Comintern and the OGPU had forced his hand or embarrassed Soviet diplomacy.[25]

As is always the case with such incidents, the question may be raised: How seriously did the Soviet leaders take their own propaganda? How urgently did they view the situation created by the sudden break in relations with England?

So far as the Soviet Foreign Commissariat is concerned, Litvinov, in discussing the break with a German diplomat, took the position that while the ultimate British objective could only be war, the preliminary developments would take years. At the very least war would not break out before the next elections. In the meantime, England would try to get other states to follow her anti-Soviet policy, trying first to win over "little states such as Poland and the Baltic states." [26] Since in Foreign Commissariat circles the next British election was not expected for at least a year and a half,[27] there was no sense of immediate alarm or urgency from that department.

On the other hand, there is every reason to believe that the OGPU reported the tremendous increase in espionage arrests in alarmist terms. Coinciding with the collapse of the Trust in mid-April, a sudden rush of terrorist incidents, only some of which were reported in the press, undoubtedly added to the tone of alarm in OGPU counterintelligence reports. These terrorist incidents were by no means accidental. For the most part they were planned and directed from Paris by the Russian émigré General Kutyepov and executed by members of his Combat Corps. Since these *terakts* were highly embarrassing to the OGPU, and Soviet propaganda blamed the British Conservatives and British intelligence for the crisis, the Kutyepov offensive has been neglected by Soviet and Western historians alike.[28] These covert operations added a new terrorist dimension to the wave of espionage cases which continued into the summer and form the background of the 1927 war scare as it reached its climax.

THE KUTYEPOV
OFFENSIVE

A<small>S WE</small>
have seen, for a five-year period (1922–27) the OGPU had successfully operated the Trust as a phony "monarchist" resistance organization. Two of General Kutyepov's agents, Maria Zakharchenko and her common-law husband, Georgi Radkovich, had worked within the Moscow branch of the underground organization for four years. The Trust finally collapsed with the defection of one of the OGPU's double agents, Edward Staunitz, who fled to Finland with Maria on April 13, 1927. The two delayed their flight until Georgi Radkovich and two additional agents from Paris, Karinsky and Shorin, were able to make good their escape into Poland. Later the escapees were reunited in Helsinki and joined by other members of General Kutyepov's organization.

The collapse of the Trust undoubtedly added to Soviet apprehension by cutting off the flow of intelligence obtained through Trust channels and by removing the last restraining influence over General Kutyepov and his Combat Corps. As soon as he heard the news of Staunitz' defection, the General traveled to Helsinki to interview the escapees and to plan with them a series of terrorist raids—the Kutyepov offensive.

Even before the collapse of the Trust, however, there had been an activist or terrorist side of the counterintelligence picture which was not reported in the Soviet press until June. Sometime during the winter or spring of 1927, Maria and

Georgi, in collaboration with the other agents sent from Paris, had managed to murder three OGPU agents.[1] Although for obvious security reasons these murders were not reported in *Izvestia,* they certainly did not go unnoticed in OGPU counter-intelligence reports. Moreover, as espionage arrests began to mount dramatically, the question uppermost in the OGPU interrogators' minds must have been: How many of those arrested as ordinary spies should also be counted as terrorists?

The little band of terrorists that General Kutyepov gathered together in Helsinki was divided into combat teams. The General was naturally reluctant to accept Staunitz, an ex-OGPU agent, as a bona fide member of his organization until the latter had proven himself. The only practical way he could do this would be to go back into the U.S.S.R. on a terrorist raid with Maria, as she herself suggested, adding by way of reassurance that "she would keep a gun on him [Staunitz] at all times." Staunitz was understandably reluctant to return to Russia, where, if he were apprehended by the OGPU, his death was certain, but there was no other way by which he could rehabilitate himself in the eyes of the émigrés or Maria.[2]

In any case, by the end of May 1927 General Kutyepov's Combat Corps had trained and equipped its first team of six members, each armed with two revolvers (a large Mauser or Parabellum and a small Browning), hand grenades, and large, highly explosive bombs of the Novitsky type. With the aid of guides provided by Captain Rosenström of the intelligence staff of the Second Finnish Division, they crossed the border on May 31.[3] Here they divided into two groups. One group of three, Captain Viktor Larionov and two younger lads, Sergei Solovyev and Vladimir Monomakhov, took off in the direction of Leningrad. The other, consisting of Maria Zakharchenko, Edward Staunitz, and Yuri S. Peters (alias Vosnessensky), headed for Moscow. According to Captain Larionov, "they left us and followed a footpath into the forest. We caught several glimpses of them as they moved through the fir underbrush and vanished from sight forever." [4]

What happened to the Moscow group afterward we know only from two press releases and an interview with G. G. Yagoda, deputy OGPU chief, in which he admittedly did not reveal more than the essential outlines of the story, using it as a peg for his propaganda message.[5]

By combining various Soviet accounts of the raid we can piece together what appears to be a fairly reliable picture of the basic facts.

In a discussion of suitable targets before they left, Staunitz had stated that in his opinion it would be hopeless to try to reach the offices of the OGPU chiefs in the main Lubyanka building, as they were too heavily guarded. Instead he suggested that they bomb the communal living quarters for OGPU officials, just around the corner on the Malaya Lubyanka, numbers 3–6, where there was only one guard at the door, who could be quietly done away with. The Moscow group—Maria, Staunitz, and Peters—apparently succeeded in placing a four-kilogram melinite bomb in the quarters as planned, but the fuse was defective, and at the last moment an OGPU aide was able to put it out. Otherwise there would have been several casualties, since, as Yagoda himself admitted, the bomb was powerful and had been cleverly packaged with other explosives to create maximum damage.

After placing their device, the three terrorists fled toward the western border, in the direction of Smolensk, presumably because Staunitz hoped to find shelter there with contacts he had made in the old days (1922) when he had worked with Savinkov's counterrevolutionary groups. Maria was also well known in the area. The three became separated, and Staunitz was the first to perish. At the Yanovsky liquor distillery on June 18 he was challenged by a guard to whom he appeared suspicious. Drawing his revolver, Staunitz wounded the guard and two bystanders, a laborer and a peasant, and escaped. The Byelorussian regional chief of the OGPU's Special Section (the original "OO"—*Osoboi Otdel*) was brought into the case and organized a posse with the aid of four peasants. The area was cordoned off and by a methodical screening they were able to flush Staunitz out of the bushes where he was hiding. He came out firing, however, and emptied both his Mauser and his Browning, injuring another man before dying himself in the ensuing crossfire. Having "chosen freedom" and seeking to rehabilitate himself after a lifetime of treachery and betrayal, he had found release at last.

Meanwhile, Maria Zakharchenko and Yuri Peters, who were also fleeing toward the border, had hailed a car coming down the road in the opposite direction, from Vitebsk to

Smolensk. Brandishing their weapons, they climbed into the automobile and ordered the chauffeur to turn around and drive them to the border. When he refused, they shot him and wounded his helper, who, although gravely injured, still had enough strength to wreck the automobile. At this point the two terrorists fled from the scene and hid in the surrounding woods, where the police picked up their trail in the vicinity of the Dretun railway station.

According to Yagoda at his press conference, the OGPU organized another ambush, surrounding the area with the help of local farmers. When the two terrorists tried to break through the cordon near the bakery of N Regiment they were first spotted by the wife of the regimental commander, who raised a cry of alarm and was wounded in the knee for her efforts. In the ensuing crossfire Peters was killed on the spot; Maria Zakharchenko, critically injured, died of her wounds a few hours later.[6] The fact that the ambush did take place, although perhaps not quite as Yagoda claimed, was confirmed by a former Soviet displaced person, Ivan Repin, who emigrated to the United States after the war. Repin happened to be doing his military service in a Red Army camp near the Dretun railway station and personally witnessed the shooting.[7]

The basic fact of Staunitz' death was also confirmed quite by accident in August 1942, during the German occupation of Smolensk. At that time Captain Larionov, the only surviving member of the terror squad, visited the mayor of Smolensk, Menshagin, and was invited in for a cup of tea. The assistant mayor, G. Gamziuk, was also present. Larionov writes:

> In the course of the conversation Menshagin disclosed that he had worked as a Soviet defense attorney for many years in Smolensk. In reminiscing about interesting cases in his practice he stated that in the winter of 1927 he had to defend in the local court a railroad switchman who had been guilty of sheltering a White Guardist in his cabin one night the previous June, and who was killed after an exchange of shots the following morning alongside the Smolensk sugar refinery. The man was Opperput. The switchman was sentenced to ten years in a concentration camp. The story is all the more convincing since he had no idea who I was. So far as he was concerned, I was just another émigré returning from Germany to look for his brother. Menshagin's story

has the force of documentary evidence, since it can be confirmed by Mr. Gamziuk, who also heard it and who is now living in the United States.[8]

The immediate circumstances under which Maria, Staunitz (Opperput), and Peters were liquidated are unimportant. They placed their bombs and went down fighting. Depending on one's point of view, their mission of rehabilitation and revenge was either a *beau geste* or a futile act of terror which had its just reward.

The OGPU provided a curious postscript to the epic. In spite of Yagoda's impressive press conference giving the essential facts of the story, many newspapers refused to believe that Staunitz was dead. The belief persisted that his defection was false, and that he had betrayed his comrades on their mission. Taking advantage of this situation, in September 1927 the OGPU planted a story in the London *Morning Post,* according to which Staunitz was still alive and had been decorated on July 27 with the Order of the Red Banner for his work as an *agent provocateur* with the OGPU. Under a different name he had allegedly been assigned a special mission in the Far East and had left for China.

This OGPU fable probably explains why the Soviet white book, which came out a year later, makes no mention of him whatsoever. The legend was strengthened and elaborated in the memoirs of G. A. Agabekov, who defected from his position as OGPU "resident" (station chief) in Turkey in 1929, and was assassinated in Belgium in 1938. Agabekov writes that although the first bomb placed by the team failed to go off, a later explosion shook the Lubyanka headquarters, and the following day a force of 800 OGPU agents plus a Red Army battalion organized a man hunt, combing the woods and "plunging through the deep snow," although the expedition took place in the month of June! In spite of this and similar absurdities, the Agabekov memoirs have been extensively used as a historical source, except in the most recent Soviet account of the Trust by Lev Nikulin, in which Staunitz plays a major role but is never identified as an OGPU agent.[9]

The second combat team, consisting of Captain Viktor Larionov, Vladimir Monomakhov, and Sergei Solovyev, reached Leningrad without mishap and set up a base camp in the forest of Levashovo, about twenty kilometers north of the city. The leader of the team tells what happened next in his own words in the following section.

The Larionov Story

As Captain Larionov watched Maria Zakharchenko, Staunitz, and Peters move away through the underbrush and disappear forever, his thoughts turned to his own mission, which he described in a small book entitled *A Military Foray into the U.S.S.R.* It was published in Paris four years later.[10] What does a terrorist think about himself, his companions, and his work? How does it feel to return secretly from exile on a counterrevolutionary mission to one's native land for a few hours or days, knowing that one's life is threatened by the omnipresent shadow of the local security police, in this case the dreaded OGPU? Since Larionov's expedition these questions have been asked by hundreds of other agents in similar circumstances who have never come back and have left no record of their thoughts and reactions. Hence Larionov in a sense speaks not only for himself and his two companions, Solovyev and Monomakhov, but also for many others in his narrative, here considerably abridged.

"Leningrad" . . . Formerly the Finland Station, now the *"krugovoi dorogi."* A huge crowd rumbles over the wooden planks of the platform. Dimitry and I elbow our way through—two "white Guardist bandits," "White émigrés"! [Throughout his story, Larionov calls his friend Vladimir Monomakhov by the familiar nickname "Dimitry."]

At the entrance barrier a uniformed Chekist scrutinizes the dense crowd. His face wears a stupid and confused expression. We pass by the Chekist safely in the midst of the crowd. Over there, where formerly the first- and second-class buffet stood, the sign reads: "GPU Duty Officer." Letters like any others, but these fill one with lingering misgivings.

On the steps outside the station we look eagerly at the new world opening up before our eyes. Within me a wave of spiritual exaltation at once sweeps away all the weariness of the journey and the momentary flashes of fear—fear of the conductors, of the ticket takers, of the Chekists along the way.

There could be no turning back now. Feelings of impudence, exaltation, and daring began to dominate our whole beings, mixed with derision for the whole "Soviet world" around us.

For me, an officer of the Markov brigade, a participant in General Kornilov's first campaign, it was pleasant, deliciously pleasant to feel myself here in the camp of the enemy, in this world of the Cheka:—"See, I mock your Communist sacred places, I defile them, I am walking around in front of your Chekists and militiamen who are so clever at spotting their enemies!"

And there was also the elation that comes with the realization that bridges were burned behind us . . .

Here was the first of the "holy monuments," a statue of "Ilyich" [Lenin] towering above the square in front of the station. It was in this very place that in 1917 Lenin delivered his first address to "the revolutionary proletariat" from the tower of a tank. I must say that the sculptor did not translate very accurately into cast bronze the maniacal impulsive gesture of Lenin's hand and his abnormally broad, degenerate skull.

The square was deserted. Pedestrians were walking past the bronze "Ilyich" with the same indifference they showed to familiar monuments of the past. In front of the station a loudspeaker had been placed in an empty corner. This achievement of Soviet technology must have been put there to impress distinguished foreigners arriving after a two-hour journey.

We had a moment of confusion since we didn't know which direction to take or how to get there. There were too many streetcars and they all had unfamiliar numbers. It was too far to walk and we had to move quickly and decisively. Why, we were supposed to produce the "Big Bang" right today if we could. As soon as possible we had to reconnoiter the approaches of several Soviet institutions on a list with addresses which I had been given abroad: The Plenum of the Leningrad Soviet, the Central Party Club, the School for International Minorities, the Militant Atheist School, the editorial offices of the *Leningrad Pravda,* district clubs such as the Comintern Club—there was a big selection to choose from. . . .

"Cabby!"

"Where do you want to go?"

"To the Oktober Prospekt."

"Have you got the three-ruble fare?"

"Will you take two?"

"What! With the price of oats as high as it is?"

So we finally pay the three rubles—forty francs. It's a lot of money but we haven't got time to haggle.

The Liteiny bridge . . . the beautiful Neva . . . the trellises of the green Summer Gardens, the little arched bridge over the Winter Canal, the Peter and Paul Fortress, the Champs de Mars, the Admiralty Building—my native land. How can my hand, which is unskilled in literature, portray the deep wave of feeling that swept over my starved homesick soul on seeing the beauty of my native Petersburg?

You catch this feeling best when returning to your native land like a child, eyes filled with tears of joy and happiness, not darting in like a thief in the night loaded with bombs and revolvers.

Traffic on the streets was extremely light; even the Nevsky and Oktober Prospekts were empty. Occasionally a *vanka* trotted along or an automobile of the Soviet aristocracy appeared, bumping over the potholes in the roadway which had not been repaired in years. Ordinary and even not so ordinary mortals were provided only with streetcars. Finally, the crowd on the streets was quite different than formerly, but was thinning out at that hour of the day. It was a uniform herd—government employees, workers, GPU agents, prostitutes, idling Komsomols, and various bystanders, countless provincial tour groups, Communist party representatives and delegates, and Komsomol groups of the national minorities. All this horde of many thousands of Russians, Chinese, Koreans, Bashkirs, and other such "riffraff" of the granite sidewalks offends the women, shows its teeth, eats, drinks, and occupies laughingly "living space" for the greater glory of the "God-fearing people."

Leningrad—a city of countless institutions, organizations, and schools—political, military, and such. In the crowd, along with the shaggy "Marxists" always hurrying somewhere with a shabby briefcase (a type completely foreign to the cities of Europe), there are quite a few military personnel with their erect bearing and frank open faces. You meet engineers and technicians whose intelligent faces stand out like white spots under their prerevolutionary peaked caps.

There goes a gang of prisoners led by two guards with drawn sabers on either side. The prisoners turn their frightened, deathly pale faces from one to the other guard as if seeking some sort of explanation. Who are they? Nepmen, perhaps? Private enterprisers? Or "White [Guardists]," like us?

The mute, unblinking faces of the guards. The masks, like ikons, of the OGPU. They file on and on.

Nearer the center the streets and houses become cleaner, but the Circuit Court lies in ruins—one of the real, "gigantic, bloodless Soviet achievements."

We get out of the cab at the former Armory of the General Staff. It's still used as a military warehouse. After buying a few newspapers at the gate, we go into Aleksandrovsky Park and sit down at the first bench. We look for the section with announcements of Communist meetings for the evening.

It's already three o'clock. Dimitry and I have to look over a few target institutions, buy provisions, return to the Levoshovo Woods, get a bite to eat, pick up the briefcases containing the heavy bombs, and get back to Leningrad again. Our guide who took us across the border promised to wait for us until midnight tonight at the crossroads we agreed on. We've got to force the pace of events so as not to be late to the rendezvous with our guide, especially since today is Friday. Saturday and Sunday the Bolsheviks never hold meetings because all the Soviet big shots spend the time at their *dachas*. Therefore, each hour is literally precious.

"It's got to be tonight," I said to Dimitry. "I'm not at all sure that I can make it safely across the border without the guide."

A very important person, obviously pleased with himself, enters the park through the gateway. Obviously a Chekist: leather boots, splendid riding breeches, a soft peaked cap with cavalry insignia, a new Sam Browne belt across his shoulder, and a Browning pistol in a foppish holster.

"Hm . . . mm," Dimitry mumbles. "What if . . ."

"Don't get excited, just hope that . . ."

The calfskin boots paraded on by us without stopping . . .

On the last line of the *Red Gazette,* printed in small type, we saw the following notice: "Friday at 8:30 P.M., Central Party Club. Meeting for training village propagandists. Speakers: Comrades Pelshe, Yampolsky, Rappoport, etc."

This seems to me to be what we're looking for. Well, actually I decide on my own, don't I? Dimitry is only a consulting agency for such questions.

We go along the Moika to have a look at the Central Party Club. We pass by the famous building at No. 2 on Gorokhovy Street—the Leningrad GPU. Above the building a red flag waves. As a precautionary move, instead of passing

it along the fence we cross over and go by on the other
side of the street. At the corner of Gogol and Gorokhovy
Streets we go into a delicatessen. We buy a few tins of canned
goods and two bottles of cognac to bolster our strength
and nerves. The salesmen are polite and courteous. They
bow and accompany you to the door. Our purchases cost a
lot, but we're not trying to economize.

A bootblack is sitting on his box at the next corner
and we decide to get our shoes shined. I got mine cleaned
all right but Dimitry experienced a few anxious moments. He
had just shifted one boot when he felt someone come up
behind him and stop. Dimitry glanced up sideways (during
this time I had stepped into an optical shop to buy a compass) and to his horror saw the white field shirt and red
cap band of a militiaman. Only Dimitry's calmness saved him.
Another person with different nerves would either have
started to run or would have shot it out with the militiaman,
who was merely waiting his turn to get his boots cleaned.

For two rubles I bought an inferior-grade compass, and
when I arrived at the corner where Dimitry and I had agreed
to meet he told me all about the scare he had had, now
that it was all over.

We came to the detached house on the Moika Canal
and stared at the heavy, massive front door decorated with
a small sign reading "Central Party Club and A.P.O.L.K."
(Agitation-Propaganda Division of the Leningrad Commune),
There was no one at the door. Directly in front of the house
was the bank of the Moika. A few houses to the left, if you
stood with your back to the entrance, was the Nevsky Prospekt. One or two houses to the right Kirpichny Alley seemed
to run at right angles into the banks of the Moika Canal.

I size up the situation and decide that it would be rather
convenient, after the Big Bang in the club, to dash into the
street and head for the Kirpichny Alley. On the other hand,
the Moika seriously limited the possibilities of fleeing.

We hadn't gone far from the entrance when we reached
the Nevsky Prospekt and the Comintern Club at the corner
of Fontanka Street and the Anichkova Bridge. Judging by the
papers, there was supposed to be a Komsomol meeting in the
club auditorium that evening. Leaving Dimitry on the street
and assuming a busy air, I hung around the entrance of the
club for a few minutes in order to sniff out the situation and
then returned. I didn't like what I saw: a crowd of beardless
youths still wet behind the ears. Why, we hadn't worked our

way here for that!—to settle accounts with a few youngsters who had lost their way in the Soviet dark! . . . My thoughts returned to the Central Party Club, to the meeting to prepare village propagandists, and since there wasn't enough time left for us to look at other suitable targets, I decided to honor them with my presence that evening at the Central Party Club. With this firm decision we hired a *vanka* on what was formerly Vladimir Street and rode off to the Krugovoi Station. Within half an hour the train took us to our base, where Sergei was standing guard all alone.

When we got on the train that brought us to him, our compartment was empty, but at one of the first stations a man sat down with us. He was wearing a rubberized raincoat and a service cap with high peaks and little red stars on the band. He sat opposite us and stared at us with the cold, fixed, luster-less eyes of a poisonous snake. I began to feel ill at ease and opened up the *Red Gazette* while Dimitry looked at the *Leningrad Pravda*. When I glanced furtively across at our fellow traveler from behind my paper he began to hypnotize me. At one of the stations the "man in gray" got up and left the compartment. We began a few rather unpleasant minutes of expectant waiting. But thank God we heard the engine whistle and the train moved on. The danger that threatened had passed.

Here we are at Levoshovo and here are our woods. At the ravine we turn to the right, and after following a path through the woods we whistle. There is an answering whistle, and as the thick fir branches rustle, Sergei appears:

"Well, how did it go?"

"All okay."

"I thought you'd never get back. I was feeling pretty depressed here. And then some old woman decided to collect long branches for firewood near our base. I didn't know what the hell to do, whether to 'bury' her or what!" . . .

Within the hour the train returns to Leningrad. We've got to get a quick bite to eat and get ready for the journey. We lie down in a circle. With a Finnish knife we open a can of sturgeon and a bottle of cognac. The liquor takes effect fast because we're tired and hungry. It increases our enthusiasm and readiness to bomb the hell out of all the Communists in the world. Only the time is running out. According to our watches it's 7:00 P.M. From 7:25 to 8:10 on the train to Leningrad; 8:50 at the Party Club; 9:40 back at the Krugovoi Station. . . .

Time to hit the road. We take the heavy bombs with the
fulminate-of-mercury fuses and carefully pack them in the
briefcases, each with only one safety fuse, and in brief outline I explain my plans to the young men:

We will enter the club quickly and try to get up the
stairs. If anyone tries to stop us, Dimitry will eliminate him
with a blow on the skull. If possible we must penetrate into
the hall without shooting. Sergei and Dimitry will throw
the bombs: Sergei one and Dimitry two of them. Meanwhile
I'll cover the main exit by breaking two bottles of liquid which
will instantly release an asphyxiating gas. After that we dash
to the street, swing into the Kirpichny Alley, and, depending
on the circumstances, but if possible together, we make it to
the Krugovoi Station by 9:40. If one of us doesn't make it
to the train, we will wait for him at the base until our train
comes at 10:35. After that we stop at the designated crossroads and quickly cross over the border.

That was the entire plan. It depended on speed and
boldness.

We were thoroughly armed and equipped. Slung on a
belt around my waist was a Mauser pistol with a round in
the barrel and a full cartridge clip. In the pocket of my raincoat was a Browning; in the back pocket of my pants· a
German pineapple grenade; in the side pockets of my field
jacket the flasks with the gas; in my watch pocket a dose of
cyanide. My buddies did not have any gas and only one
revolver each. But each of them had two pineapple grenades
and in their briefcases heavy bombs of the Novitsky type.
It seems that we hid all this arsenal rather nicely. We
buttoned and cinched up and looked each other over carefully. We buried our foreign currency in the moss, for who
knows, it might be unwanted evidence on our dead bodies
. . . We hide the provisions for the return trip.

We finish off the cognac down to the last drop.

"Well, let's shove off!"—We walk toward the station with
determined steps. Suddenly—I'll be damned! The train whis-
tles and clouds of white smoke rise beyond the woods. Although we know it's useless, we run after it for a few minutes
and then stop and look at each other. We hear the departing
whistle and the sound of the axles as they accelerate. "It's
gone, damn it!" We turn around dejectedly in our tracks.
How maddening that we forgot to coordinate our watches!

A complex spiritual change took place inside us. On
the one hand was the happy realization that we had a two-day

lease on life, for no Communist meetings were held on Saturday or Sunday. On the other hand, the delay created a mood like the feeling of a man sentenced to hang who has had a short reprieve. He still realizes in his thoughts that the hanging is inevitable. For us the bombing of the Party Club also meant the unavoidable finish.

And yet, how strange! There was nothing to stop us from crossing back over the border without having accomplished our mission. Of course, our honor held us back from such a retreat. It not only prevented me, an officer, from retreating, but also the two youths, who were only just becoming famous in our city for their "wild" conduct, having been expelled from one school and being generally deprived of education in their youthful years. Until our combat mission had been completed the word "retreat" simply didn't exist for us. . . .

[Saturday and Sunday were spent killing time in Leningrad, visiting theaters, and checking out possible targets of opportunity. They held to their original choice of the Central Party Club, where another meeting was scheduled for Monday night. The narrative continues as they return Sunday night.]

We returned home to our woods, about midnight. I felt uncomfortable and gloomy inside. My buddies walked along silently and I could sense that they shared my feelings. The woods were dark, lonely, and cheerless. At a point where two paths crossed in the woods we heard a low, cautious whistle:

"Quiet!"

Glancing around, we draw our revolvers, throw a round into the chamber, disperse carefully on tiptoe, and, peering into the darkness, move stealthily forward. The whistle is repeated, but is already a little farther away. And here's our hideout with everything in order: the briefcases with the bombs, and the Mausers where we left them in place. Everything was as we left it—even the moss was undisturbed. But our nerves were tense, our imaginations had pictured a scenario with Chekists in their long gray greatcoats surrounding the woods and waiting until we fell asleep so they could take us alive.

The whistle was repeated again. I felt I could never get to sleep until I found out what was making that whistle in the woods. I grabbed a Mauser and carefully, trying not to snap any twigs, crept toward the sound. After five minutes, however, I returned. The whistle was made by some sort of night bird.

We lay down on the cold, wet moss. I couldn't get to sleep. I dreamed now of a foul gray sinister city, then shadows of bygone battles rushed past; then the idea that I had been abandoned by my buddies drifted through my subconscious. My heart began to pound anxiously and repeatedly at the thought of tomorrow, and I saw clearly in front of me the image of a heavy, smooth door with a brass doorknob and a sign with the letters Ts.P.K. and A.P.O.L.K. Tomorrow, Monday, Comrades Pelshe, Yampolsky, Rappoport, etc. will appear again at the Central Party Club at a meeting "for the training of village propagandists." But we shall also drop in there without being called or invited.

The morning was especially cold. I was shivering and was surprised to see how Dimitry and Sergei crunched away at breakfast sausages and drank the cognac down to the last drop. I was too nervous to eat.

"It's time to go!" I said. "The earlier we leave, the better it will be in town. Otherwise we might be late again, and what good would that do us!"

We begin to get our equipment ready and I get pretty scared about the gases in the side pockets of my trenchcoat. I think about them all the time. Why, the glass of those phials is no thicker than in electric light bulbs!

My interlocutor in the train compartment was a Leningrad student, who had a number of interesting things to tell me. He had recently been to Moscow and had made the pilgrimage to Lenin's tomb. He described how the public filed past, one at a time under the watchful eyes of the Chekists, eyes which stripped you bare and read your thoughts. In his opinion Ilyich had long since disappeared, and in his place a wax figure was lying in the coffin. He described the last parade on the square in front of the Winter Palace, no less vividly. The tribune for the executive committee and Moscow guests had been placed directly in front of the columns with the guardian angels. Some clever Soviet type decided that the angels were undesirable, since they would be blessing the Soviet elite with the cross, and after a long discussion it was decided to throw some sort of cover over the angels with the help of a balloon. The balloon hovered over the angels all day long, to the extreme amusement of a crowd of thousands below. The covering material let down by a rope from the balloon inevitably floated past the angels. First the balloon would drift away and then the material. They never did get the job done.

I guided the conversation to the subject of antisemitism among the Komsomols. The student took up the theme.

"The other day," he said, "four Komsomol members went into a Jewish bakery shop at the same time as I did. They looked at the salesman and suddenly exclaimed in a voice loud enough to hear all over the shop: 'Ugh, Hell, this place is full of Jews! Let's get out of here, comrades!' "

He also said that here and there on walls or in latrines, scribbled by unseen hands, you find a slogan popular with the lowest classes: "Kill the Jews and save Russia!"

I turned the conversation to the Soviet leadership, to the opposition, to Trotsky. My interlocutor hadn't made much of it and wasn't interested in such high-level matters:

"Well, that's all internal affairs. It doesn't affect us." . . .

On the same day I investigated our future area of operations once more and made an important discovery. One of the houses next to the Party Club has a very irregular front yard which leads from the Moika Canal to Bolshoi Morskoi Street. This new discovery means a more favorable escape route.

We've got to act now, since we've already wasted several days to no purpose. Our money is almost gone. Our budget, which didn't anticipate an extended stay in the U.S.S.R., has been completely upset by the cost of cabs, the expensive canned goods, and the regular supply of cognac, indispensable under the rain in the woods. Today we changed half our gold reserve, three tsarist gold five-ruble pieces. We still have three left but we want to keep them as souvenirs.

We arrive at the door of the Central Party Club at exactly 8:50 P.M. A second, perhaps a minute's hesitation like before diving into the water from a great height, while I glance at my buddies. Their slightly pale faces look energetic and sternly determined.

We push open the heavy door. The half-darkness of the vestibule, luxury carpets. In front of us a staircase; on the left a cloakroom. A big table with a shaded lamp. Behind it a woman of thirty with an extremely unsympathetic, insolent, and I would say criminal-looking face. (We later learned that this was Comrade Breks.)

We hesitated . . . According to plan Dimitry was supposed to crack the skull of the first person who stood in our way in the vestibule, but before a woman he froze. I was also embarrassed. It was only after a few seconds that I felt some sort of jolt and walked briskly up to this Communist who looked at us with a questioning air.

"What do you want here, comrades?"

I answered casually, "Is this where the meeting is for training village agitators?"

"But who are you?"

"Communists."

"Second floor up—first door to the right. Sign in first in this book, comrades. Write your name and party card number. Leave your coats here in the cloakroom." I picked up the pen and wrote: "Fedorov—No. 34." As soon as I had signed in I realized how stupid it was to write down such a low party-card number. Sergei did even worse, and almost blew the whole show. He pulled his party card out of his pocket and showed it to Comrade Breks. It was a crude forgery made abroad and could easily be distinguished from the genuine article by the fact that it had the wrong kind of dust cover over it.

"What kind of card is that, comrade?" the woman asked, her interest aroused. "Do we have such cards?"

"Why, sure, in Moscow," Sergei answered foolishly.

I hurried to the cloakroom and took off my trenchcoat. Dimitry and Sergei were already removing theirs. Then we were in a new fix. We hadn't figured on taking off our raincoats and part of our military equipment was in the pockets. Almost in front of Comrade Breks's eyes we had to transfer our weapons from our coat pockets to our back pockets. Luckily Comrade Breks was too stupid to notice.

We started up the stairs. From the moment I opened the door and entered the vestibule of the Party Club, my head, my brain was working half consciously. All the surroundings —furniture, lights, the cloakroom, the staircase, the face of Comrade Breks—all were swirling in a fog. Only some internal, subconscious stimulus dictated my movements, some sort of powerful animal instinct slumbering in the depths of my ego.

There were two landings on the staircase and then the heavy, high door with an old-fashioned porcelain doorknob. I flung open the door and looked inside the room. It was a huge room with a polished parquet floor and a round table in the center. Seated at it were seven people, including two or three women. I closed the door and turned to Dimitry and Sergei: "It's no good, too few people. No use shooting at sparrows with a cannon."

We go downstairs and past Comrade Breks.

"Why so soon?" she asked in an unpleasant voice.

"We must have got the wrong address; we're from the country and don't know our way around here," I explained.

At the door of the Party Club stood a young Red Army officer who gave us a cold, piercing look. We cleared out of the entrance and walked quickly along the Moika to Nevsky Prospekt. I looked back twice but no one followed us. Apparently everything went off all right.

Immediately afterward a psychological reaction set in—a sort of massive nervous tension. Disappointment over our failure, our confusion, and this new delay overwhelmed me. Mechanically we crossed the bridge and walked along Nevsky Prospekt toward the Winter Palace. . . .

Two failures had appreciably worsened our situation. In my heart I blamed myself for not having been decisive enough. But all during the civil war I had made it a custom to listen to some sort of internal voice that was beyond logic and reason. How many times it had saved my life! Now that voice told me firmly and definitely, "Tomorrow night at the Party Club. . . ."

It was 8:45 . . . The heavy door would hardly open. I knew for sure that this was it, that everything would be all right.

It was half dark in the vestibule. Comrade Breks was talking with some short, dark-skinned Jewish man and both were bending over some sort of list. The Jew was blaming Comrade Breks for something and she was obviously very upset. The low-hung lamp highlighted their faces. Directly in front of us the staircase. To the left the cloakroom. We already knew our way around.

"Sign in, comrades, and leave your coats," she said hastily, pointing toward the cloakroom and continuing her explanations. In an uneven scrawl I wrote, "Fedorov, No. 34. Dimitry held the blotter, and this time Sergei did not take out his party card.

We go upstairs and along a corridor at the end of which is a lunchroom with a counter and beyond that the entrance to the communal living quarters. A skinny young woman comes toward us from behind the counter. With my briefcase still under my arm I bow and immediately ask, "Which way to Comrade Schirwindt's lecture?"

"The door to the right."

"Thank you very much, comrade."

The heavy oak door reached almost to the ceiling. As if it were today, I remember the carved brass doorknob . . . Everywhere the luxury of a palace. I felt no fear, no desperation, no quickening of the heartbeat. I felt exactly as if I were going about my usual work, quietly and unhurriedly.

The door opened. I stood for one or two seconds on the threshold and looked the hall over. Thirty-three heads turned in my direction at the sound of the door opening. Comrade Schirwindt, whose beard was an imitation of Trotsky's, was bent over his papers. The table occupied by the Presidium was in the center of the room. Along the walls rows of people fused together into a single monstrosity in my eyes. Pictures of Lenin and other big shots hung on the walls. Shelves with books. That's all I saw in those one or two seconds.

I step back, close the door, and whisper only one word to my buddies, "Okay," and reach for the thin phial of gas. During this second Dimitry and Sergei put down the briefcase and quietly and efficiently remove the last safety devices from the bombs. I fling open the door and step back. Sergei hurls a bomb and it bounces off in a corner. I fling a second one after it. One of the bombs sputters and then goes quiet. Another moment of silence and then suddenly a frightening unearthly roar: "Ah . . . a . . . a . . . a bomb!" Like an automaton I threw a gas bomb in the direction of the buffet and the communal living quarters and ran downstairs. On the landing a crash like the sound of a thousand panes of glass breaking all at once hit my ears and the back of my head. That was Dimitry tossing a grenade. I ran on down the staircase. Wild screams ring out all over the building. There is the sound of footsteps running and a shrieking as if thousands of rats and mice were being crushed in some gigantic press.

Wild and goggle-eyed, Comrade Breks runs up to me in the vestibule entrance.

"What happened, comrade, what happened?" She can barely pronounce the words.

"An infernal machine exploded! Run for the militia and the GPU, and be quick about it!" I shouted in a tone of command.

She ran out the door toward the Moika and let out a wild howl:

"Militia! . . . Militia!"

Sergei had already left the vestibule. My hair stood on end. For my escape into the street with the crowd of the injured Communists I had folded my cap and stuck it in my pocket while throwing off my trenchcoat in the club. I keep waiting for Dimitry, with the second phial of gas ready in one hand . . . Two seconds . . . Three seconds . . .

Dimitry comes out slowly. One hand and his forehead show a little blood. His face, however, is calm, imperturbable. Without hurrying he walks over to the cloakroom, takes his raincoat, and puts it over his arm.

"You must be out of your mind . . . Hurry . . . Make it quick!" I shout at him, tossing the gas bomb over his head up the staircase.

There's a sound of breaking glass and streams of green smoke rise higher and higher—the color of death.

At last we reach the street. On the right, toward Kirpichny Alley, a few figures. On the left, in the direction of Nevsky Prospekt, a bunch of people are running directly in front. Thirty or forty steps away are two, three, or four militiamen. I don't bother to take an accurate count. From that minute on, everything becomes foggy. But already a voice inside me speaks and cries out: "Run straight toward them!"

I ran toward the militia, waving my arms, with Dimitry running behind me. Some man darts out of the club door, all covered with stucco like flour, runs around past us, and yells: "Oooh!"

"What are you standing there staring at?" I yelled at the Soviet militiamen. "Someone threw a bomb; there are a lot of wounded. Run quickly . . . Call an ambulance . . . Quick!"

Their faces pale and frightened, the militiamen run into the Party Club.

Dimitry and I fade into the crowd. Half walking, half running, we make our way across the Nevsky Prospekt, along the Admiralty Building and under the General Staff archway . . . Under the arch, like a guardian angel, trots a cab, with fine powerful horses—a rare exception. In the front seat of the *vanka* we see the open, friendly Russian face of the driver.

"To the Krugovoi Station!"

"Is it worth two and a half rubles to you?"

"Here, take three, only drive fast!"

Dimitry waves to a young lady approaching on the side-

walk and yells something at her. Somewhat confusedly he
tells me what happened after the explosion of the bomb:

"You know, when I threw the bomb, I looked and saw
the door blow open. Well, the door blew open and hit me
on my noodle, right here on my forehead where the blood is.
When I came to and ran down the staircase, some long-haired
guy with a briefcase under his arm was dancing around in
front of me. I yelled at him: 'You there, bang, bang, what's
that hanging around your legs?' Next I pull out my revolver
and fire it point blank in his belly. The long-haired guy
clasps his waist with both hands and sinks to the floor while
I run past and see you in the vestibule." [11]

Dimitry fell silent for a moment and then said: "But
what about Sergei? He must be in a real mess. Why, he
doesn't know the city and may not make it back alone to the
station. That's a pity!"

Beyond a bend in the street we could see the familiar
building of the station with its clock. It was 9:30. Our train
for Krasno Ostrov left at 9:40, an interval of ten minutes to
wait. But those ten minutes dragged as if they were hours.
Dimitry and I walked up and down the wooden platform
alongside the almost empty evening train. We never took
our eyes off the entrance barrier, wondering whether a line
of Chekists would appear, but everything was all right. A
few passengers arrived, one by one, returning from work
with briefcases or shopping bags full of provisions. Finally
the minute hand of the clock showed 9:40 and the train,
with a jolt of its buffers, slowly pulled away from the long
platform . . .

The heavy burden of the last few days left my heart,
and I wanted to shout, "Hurrah!" Although dangers still
were ahead of us, compared to what we had just been through
they seemed like amusements. And besides, what could happen now? Well, they could take over the train and begin
to search the cars, inspect people's papers. But then, here in
the midst of the woods, field, and swamps, in the dark, Dimitry and I, with the help of our revolvers and hand grenades, we could certainly whip three or four Chekists, and
it's not likely that there would be more at a little suburban
station . . .

Well, here we are at Levoshovo. We had barely left the
rainy warm circle of light cast by the lights of the station
when we heard a familiar voice behind us: "So it's you

devils! So after the Big Bang you said to run toward Kirpichny Alley, but you . . ."

"Sergei!" Dimitry cried happily.

It seems that Sergei was already seated in the train
before it left. Since the time he ran out of the building a
whole epic had taken place. When the bomb he threw failed
to explode, he ran out on the street and was there already
when the explosion took place. He ran toward Kirpichny
Alley and turned into it. Then there was a turmoil as people
ran toward the explosion. Some doorkeeper pursued Sergei,
at the same time blowing a whistle, but he managed to fade
into the crowd on Nevsky Prospekt and took a streetcar. After
riding for forty minutes he realized that he was on the wrong
tram, changed to another, then another, and finally arrived
at the station a minute and a half before departure time. It
made no difference that he had forgotten to buy a ticket!
When the conductor came around on the train, he demanded
a penalty of two and a half times the value of the ticket,
but poor Sergei was fifty kopeks short.

"Well, sir, at the next stop, you will have to come with
me to the station GPU office."

"But comrade," Sergei pleaded, "I'm in a terrible hurry.
I'm going to visit my sick mother . . ."

The conductor was adamant. Suddenly an old Jewish
woman seated opposite took pity on him and gave him fifty
kopeks. Sergei swore by all the saints that he would pay back
the debt, and took the woman's address.

Decidedly some force up there blessed us. The fact that
Sergei, who was totally unfamiliar with the city, was saved
was really a miracle. . . .

Exchanging fragmentary impressions of our experiences
and achievements, we walked toward our base, where we
had hidden in the moss the rest of our money and a bundle
of provisions for the return trip.

At a point where another path crossed ours two peasant
girls approached us and asked: "Comrades, do you know
which path goes to Dranishky?"

"Come along with us and I'll show you where it swings
off," I replied.

We walked along the soft path through the woods together, exchanging a few phrases. At the turning point we said
a fond farewell to our traveling companions of the night, and
I felt that there was something symbolic in the way we each
went our separate paths, after shaking hands and saying,

"Until we meet again." Yes, until we meet again, perhaps not in the distant future Russia in exile from which we have just come, but in the real Russia—our unfortunate Fatherland . . .

Ten minutes later and we had reached our "home" under the fir trees. Dimitry looked at our quarters for the last time and said:

"You know, it really hasn't been so bad here. Why, I already feel a little sorry we're leaving."

[With the help of a flashlight, maps, and the compass that Larionov had bought, the three-man team was able to make its way through the night toward the point at which they had crossed the border into Russia, and within twenty-four hours they were safely back in Finland.]

Even a cursory examination of the operational details of the Larionov "military foray," as he calls it, will reveal the amateurish nature of the operation. The bombing attempt succeeded only because of the equally inept bungling of Comrade Breks. In the first place, the false Communist party cards used by Larionov's team were so badly forged that the group would have been instantly apprehended by an alert official charged with checking identification at the entrance to the Leningrad Party Club. That they were permitted to pass twice with such dubious documents was an inexcusable security break on the Soviet side. In the second place, it is clear that although disguised as Soviet citizens, the team members were not provided with adequate cover stories and identity documents in case of separation or arrest. Failure to provide elementary safeguards for brave men willing to risk their lives in such operations would be inexcusable for a modern intelligence agency. Unfortunately, such inadequate technical support probably represented the best that Kutyepov's Combat Corps could do with its pathetically limited financial means. First-class forged documents are not easy to produce, as the British SOE (Special Operations Executive) discovered at the beginning of World War II: "The first agents sent to Europe in 1941 were equipped with poorly forged documents; indeed on arrival they were warned by Resistance friends that the papers were death warrants." [12]

The incident reveals a serious flaw in Kutyepov's concepts and methods. General Kutyepov is a classic example of the spirited combat officer who regards the intelligence function with impatience and the professional counterintelligence officer as little more than a glorified policeman. He therefore tended to act as his own intelligence and counterintelligence agency, and later paid dearly for it. Although armed and equipped for combat, his special-forces teams lacked the necessary intelligence base for extended underground operations. As a result, although engaged in covert operations against a police state, his teams were no more than military raiding parties in civilian clothes.

8
COUNTERTERROR
AND CRISIS:
Stalin Crushes the Opposition

T_{HE TOP}
officials of the OGPU were not likely to forget the first week of
June 1927 and what must have seemed the longest day of the
year, June 7. In addition to the raid on the Malaya Lubyanka
in Moscow and the casualties in Leningrad, the deputy chief
of the Byelorussian OGPU, I. K. Opansky, and his aide were
killed and two of their companions injured as they were returning from the border after having arrested a Polish intelligence officer.[1]

All these casualties were a little unnerving, but except for
the sensational Leningrad bombing and the attack on Opansky
(who was in a trolley car at the time), the news of their occurrence could be hushed up by the carefully controlled Soviet
press without loss of face. But then came the bombshell that
could not be suppressed. In broad daylight on the streets of
Warsaw the Soviet ambassador to Poland, Pavel I. Voikov, was
assassinated by a mere boy, the sixteen-year-old Boris Koverda,
one of the numerous "White Guardist" émigrés then living in
the Polish capital. Since Koverda belonged to one of the
émigré monarchist organizations in Warsaw, Soviet propaganda
immediately blamed both the Polish and English governments
for "aiding and abetting White Guardist terrorists," interpreting
the murder as "a signal for other acts threatening war." [2]
Voikov himself had been one of the group of Bolsheviks who

had murdered Tsar Nikolai II and his family. This fact added
to the sensational aspects of the case, since there were many
conservatives abroad who viewed the assassination as a grim
sort of poetic justice. At the annual Ascot races a few days later
the British King confided to a German diplomat that he regarded Voikov's death as just punishment for his crimes.[3]

Against the background of the Western intelligence offensive and the Kutyepov terror raids, the murder of Voikov was
the crowning blow so far as the OGPU was concerned. William
Reswick, an American correspondent who was fairly close to
OGPU Deputy Chief G. G. Yagoda, writes: ". . . the day after
the murder of Voikov he was a changed man. He drank heavily
and seemed anxious to avoid all talk about the event . . . He
leaned close saying: 'Vladimir Isakovich, as a friend I must
advise you to avoid all such talk. The way things look to me,
we are on the verge of war.' "[4]

On June 7 Foreign Commissar Chicherin had already left
for Berlin to discuss the consequences of the Anglo-Soviet break
with German leaders, and hopefully later to thwart British
attempts to build an anti-Soviet front at the League Council
meeting which was soon to begin in Geneva.

Chicherin met the German foreign minister, Gustav Stresemann, in Baden-Baden on June 8, and if he felt any alarm at
the turn of events in Warsaw and Moscow, he did not show it.
Coolly, he told his German ally that the main danger did not
lie in a direct attack by England, in which he did not believe,
but rather in the personality of Pilsudski. The Polish dictator
was being supported in an adventurous expansionist policy by
English nationalists who wanted to widen further the breach
they had created. With regard to Chamberlain's attempt to
create an anti-Soviet front, he was also optimistic, having recently been assured by French Premier Poincaré and Foreign
Minister Briand that there would be no change in French
policy. France would not follow the English lead and break
diplomatic relations with the U.S.S.R. in spite of violently anticommunist propaganda in the press against Soviet interference
in French internal affairs. What Chicherin did fear, however,
was that in case of a Polish-Russian conflict, Pilsudski would
demand that French troops come to his aid, according to the
terms of the French-Polish alliance.[5]

Stresemann again reassured Chicherin that he would remain strictly neutral in the Anglo-Soviet dispute, and that in connection with the Locarno Treaty, France and England had not been granted troop-transit rights across Germany. Chicherin departed for Geneva apparently gratified at the outcome of his visit.[6]

The OGPU answer to General Kutyepov's terror raids was not long in coming. On June 9 *Izvestia* headlined an OGPU communiqué signed by V. R. Menzhinsky which listed the names of twenty enemy agents who had just been summarily executed. The announcement claimed that five of the victims had been working for British intelligence. The others were identified as either monarchists or terrorists in brief sketches of their counterrevolutionary careers. Three terse opening lines made up the only explanation given for the executions: "the fact that monarchist White Guardists abroad, acting on orders from and supported by foreign intelligence services, have gone over to open terroristic diversionary and wrecking operations." No mention was made of the recent assassination of Soviet Ambassador Voikov, but the European press then, and most historians since, have regarded the executions as a reprisal for this deed, overlooking the terrorism charge or dismissing it as propaganda. This is understandable, since the arrests of nearly all the victims listed had been kept secret until their execution.

Except for this one list of victims, the OGPU counterterror was also unannounced. It was applied swiftly, brutally, and silently in order to maximize fear as the news spread by word of mouth. Within a week German diplomatic posts from Odessa to Vladivostok were reporting house-to-house OGPU searches and wholesale arrests—the planned, systematic application of terror by all the resources of a police state.[7] Similar reports were undoubtedly filed by the embassies of other powers, and returning travelers told of wholesale arrests. No statistics were published, but an authoritative contemporary German source estimated that the number of arrests in Moscow alone must have been at least a thousand.[8]

In its thirst for revenge the OGPU had apparently acted hastily, without giving due thought to the psychological consequences abroad. These were immediate, and as reports of the ensuing terror multiplied, they became extremely damaging to Soviet prestige. For example, according to one of them the diplomats meeting in Geneva at the League of Nations Council "were unanimous in their judgment that the executions in Moscow represented the greatest moral defeat suffered by Soviet Russia in its existence as a state." [9]

Moscow also felt the backlash of world public opinion, which expressed itself in the form of shocked protest. The Red Cross sent the following representative telegram:

> Deeply moved, the International Committee of the Red Cross takes note of the reports coming from Moscow of mass executions . . . and . . . appeals in the name of all humanity to the feelings of moral responsibility of the Soviet authorities. The Committee urgently requests the Soviet authorities to cease and desist from measures which are an affront to justice and reason.[10]

Telegrams of protest were also sent from the British Labour party on June 20. In reply, an indignant Rykov editorial (*Izvestia,* June 29) protested against the "anti-Soviet lies and slanders in the foreign press" and argued that criminal investigation prior to the sentencing was equivalent to trial, and that, in any case, in the bitter struggle the Soviet government had no alternative to decisive action against counterrevolutionaries. Both the regime and the Comintern had counted heavily on being able to use the British trade unions in support of Soviet policy, and when they supported the Conservative government's anti-Russian line instead, it was a major blow for which the OGPU terror campaign was directly responsible.[11]

In terms of long-range public relations, the relapse back into the OGPU terror of June 1927 wiped out all the gains painfully achieved during the previous five or six years of Lenin's New Economic Policy. The belief that Russia had changed for the better in a liberal, humanitarian sense was killed with the first twenty victims, and replaced by the conviction that the U.S.S.R. remained the same ruthless police state it had always been.[12]

War Psychosis and the Diplomatic Crisis

Within the Soviet Union the terror created a psychological atmosphere of diffused anxiety in which a full-blown war psychosis developed by the end of June and continued until well into fall. The war scare at home was echoed by alarmist reports abroad, so that on June 12 the Soviet embassy in Paris had to issue an official denial of a report published two days earlier in the conservative newspaper *Le Temps* that the Soviet government intended to mobilize 800,000 men, that 350 airplanes were under construction and eight armament factories planned.[13] All kinds of alarmist rumors fed on the virtual news blockade imposed by the Soviet regime. On June 29 the German ambassador reported receiving information that the Red Army had assumed battle positions along the western frontier. This was followed by a report on July 2 indicating troop concentrations at Gomel, the westward movement of men and equipment, the construction of new military airfields, and a speedup of work in munitions plants.[14]

As part of a sustained buildup for Defense Week (July 10–17), *Izvestia* started a daily feature, "Our Reply to Chamberlain," appealing for funds for the special construction of airplanes, and listing contributions of various organizations. Combined with alarmist speeches by Soviet leaders about the imminence of war, the press campaign touched off a wave of panic buying and food hoarding which continued on into the fall. The war scare undoubtedly got out of hand very early in the summer, so much so that by the third week in June the government was reportedly sending propagandists into the country districts to allay the fears of the peasants. The agitators explained that although war was inevitable later on, there was no danger of its immediate occurrence.[15] Perhaps the most authoritative eyewitness evaluation of the situation comes from the pen of Louis Fischer, whose article "A New Ring around Russia," published in *The Nation* in March, had helped confirm Soviet fears that England was forging an anti-Soviet bloc:

> The writer arrived in Moscow toward the end of June, 1927, after a protracted stay in the West. On all sides, he was plied with the question, "When will war break out?" In vain he tried to assure Communists and non-Communists that Europe did not want war, and did not seem to be on the verge of hostile operations. Moscow knew better. Moscow was panicky. Peasants throughout the country bought large quantities of salt and hoarded their grain. A fully developed war psychosis prevailed . . . The war scare may have been calculated to arouse anti-war feeling in Europe and England. By yelling "War, War," the Soviet statesmen perhaps thought they would prevent war. But no one who lived in Russia at

the time will be shaken in his conviction that the majority of Bolsheviks were thoroughly and sincerely frightened by the prospect of immediate hostilities.[16]

An article in the April issue of *International Life,* the Soviet Foreign Commissariat journal, concluded that the British Labour movement lacked ideas and slogans, and suggested that new life might be injected into the laboring masses by the idea of a struggle against war in general, and specifically against war with the Soviet Union.[17] It may well be, as Louis Fischer suggests, that one of the complex of factors behind the Soviet war scare was an attempt to rally British Labour against both war and the Conservatives by painting the latter as embarked on a course leading inevitably to war with the U.S.S.R. Certainly as the result of the interplay of all the factors previously discussed, there were few, if any, Soviet leaders (with the possible exception of Chicherin and Litvinov) who did not believe that this was the case.

Inevitably the diplomats assembled in Geneva at the League of Nations Council meeting were drawn into the Polish-Soviet crisis that developed as a result of the Voikov murder and the exchange of notes which followed. It was felt that the Russian notes made aggressive demands on Warsaw, reminding many observers of the Austrian demands on Belgrade after the assassination of Archduke Ferdinand at Sarajevo as the guns of August were readied for World War I. Stalin himself later played up the historic analogy in an alarmist speech of his own. Because of the special relationship between Germany and Russia, the French and British foreign ministers, Briand and Chamberlain, persuaded Stresemann that he should speak for them, using his influence with Chicherin to forestall a Soviet ultimatum and to help achieve a peaceful solution of the conflict. Stresemann accepted the League of Nations mandate, and in doing so temporarily abandoned Germany's position of cautious neutrality. When the Soviets discovered that Stresemann was acting with League backing (and hence was supported by England and France), German-Soviet relations were severely strained. Although the dispute petered out before Germany was forced to choose sides, Moscow's fears were intensified that under English leadership the Western powers were preparing a war against the U.S.S.R.[18]

Thanks to the skillful diplomatic footwork of Polish Ambassador Patek in Moscow, Poland was able to give in without losing face to the Soviet demands that anti-Soviet émigré groups in Warsaw be suppressed.[19]

By the tenth of August a half-dozen White Guardist émigrés had been expelled from Poland, and a week later it was announced that more expulsions would follow.[20] By the end of the month Chicherin and Patek issued a joint statement that the Voikov murder incident was closed, and that talks about trade and nonaggression pacts would soon begin.[21] Earlier in the week Chicherin had confided to German Ambassador Brockdorff-Rantzau that Russia's threatening posture and tactics had been successful with the Poles, and had proved psychologically correct.[22] (He did not add that these same tactics had thoroughly alarmed the Western powers and had aggravated the first great international crisis of the post-Locarno period.) In contrast to these confidences, Chicherin's public statement for propaganda purposes is a classic example of the diplomatist's art: "When two states and two peoples wish to live together and work together, it would be [inexcusable] indolence on the part of their representatives if they should fail to bring about the conditions thus desired." [23] In one form or another Soviet diplomats have repeated this formula ever since whenever the occasion has called for it, most recently in connection with the peaceful-coexistence line prevailing since 1956.

Counterintelligence Indicators

While Chicherin and Patek were decompressing the Polish-Russian crisis during June, July, and August, the Soviet government executed thirteen Polish spies and sentenced six more to prison terms. Only three Polish espionage cases were tried in August as the espionage offensive petered out. This trend is obvious in the overall security picture shown in the following table, which includes espionage cases for the entire year. Whereas cases averaged over forty a month from May through July, they dropped sharply to an average of four for the next three months, August through October. (The fifty trials in November and December probably resulted from clearing out a backlog of cases rather than from a heavy increase in current espionage activity.)

In a press conference at Geneva, Foreign Secretary Chamberlain had dismissed as "paranoid" Soviet suspicions of British intentions. In the light of the hard evidence to the contrary, i.e., the OGPU espionage arrests shown in the table, it is understandable that Chamberlain suffered from what today would be called a "credibility gap" so far as Soviet leaders were concerned. The gap was widened by a naval demonstration during the last week in June, when a British squadron ostentatiously visited various Baltic ports.[24]

NUMBER OF ESPIONAGE CASES REPORTED PER MONTH, JANUARY–DECEMBER 1927

Month	Number
January	1
February	3
March	0
April	1
May	45
June	48
July	34*
August	5
September	2
October	5
November	16
December	32
Total arrests	192
Total executed	92
Total imprisoned	100

* July figures include 22 arrested but not sentenced until the September 13 show trial.

The credibility gap increased still further following press reports in mid-July that two British field-grade intelligence officers, Colonel Nesbit and Major Lloyd, had arrived in Kovno to survey the military preparedness of the Baltic states in case of a possible future war with the U.S.S.R.[25]

After the break in relations with England, Soviet propaganda tried to create the impression that almost every agent arrested was either directly or indirectly controlled by British intelligence. The intelligence agencies of the other Western

powers were rarely mentioned outright, although the nationality
of the agency with which individual agents were allegedly
affiliated was usually given in press reports of their arrest.

Although Soviet propaganda went to absurd lengths to
discover or "unmask" British direction of the Western intelligence offensive, in the trial reports only 37 of the 192 agents
arrested were in fact described as working directly under English Secret Intelligence Service (S.I.S.) supervision. In contrast,
almost twice as many (71) alleged Rumanian agents were
arrested. A striking omission is the absence of any allegedly
French agents. This may well have been due to the fact that
most agents sent from Paris were Russian émigrés, usually
provided with false Polish, Rumanian, or other non-French
passports. Although some Finnish agents were undoubtedly
apprehended, none is listed, another striking omission. They
may well be concealed among those listed as English, Latvian,
or Lithuanian. Of the arrested agents credited with foreign
intelligence-service affiliation, 71 were said to be affiliated with
Rumania, 38 with Poland, 36 with England, 18 with Latvia,
14 with Estonia.

Due to the highly charged political atmosphere created
by the intraparty struggle, or perhaps to other intangible factors, the war scare apparently reached a peak during the first
week in September, just before the first big show trial of
"English spies." On September 5 German Ambassador Brockdorff-Rantzau sent in the following summary of the situation,
in which he quotes a high Foreign Commissariat source:

> The danger of war, which up to now has been exploited
> by the political parties mainly as a means of agitation to stir
> up the masses, is now regarded as imminent by even the
> best informed members of the government. According to a
> reliable source, a leading member of the collegium of the
> Foreign Commissariat recently expressed himself literally as
> follows: "I consider war almost inevitable. We must count
> on it next year. We have reliable reports that England is
> continuing her encirclement policy with doubled zeal.
>
> "1. England will blockade Russia.
>
> "2. England will incite Poland to attack the Soviet
> Union.
>
> "The other border states are also prepared for hostili-
> ties. Finland has clearly let it be known that her readiness

can be taken for granted if England will bear the costs. Estonia apparently already has a secret treaty with Poland. Rumania's task will be to occupy Odessa. Patek's [the Polish ambassador's] assurances have no practical significance, since he has been used as a tool by Pilsudski." The Foreign Commissariat official continued: "France will probably not take part in an attack on Russia because she expects England to be weakened by it. In any case the U.S.S.R. cannot expect very much from France because the anticommunist movement in that country is surpassing all measure. War is inevitable because otherwise the anti-Soviet policy of the English government leads to an absurdity. The Conservatives can win a victory in the next elections only by a factual military attack on the Soviet Union. To be sure, no one can predict how this war will turn out. If troop transit rights are requested and Germany hesitates she will simply be run over . . ." [26]

However preposterous this scenario may seem with the advantage of forty years' historical hindsight, an excellent case can be made for it on the basis of the hard intelligence collected by the OGPU, not to mention the "reliable reports" on British intentions to which the Soviet Foreign Commissariat official referred.[27]

Showdown in Moscow

Stalin returned on July 24 from a long vacation in the Caucasus, where he had obviously been doing his homework, since he at once began to exploit the war scare to his own advantage, using it as a weapon against the opposition in his rise to dictatorial power. Within four days (June 28) under banner headlines *Izvestia* carried two full pages of Stalin's "Remarks on Current Themes," including two columns "On the Threat of War." Stalin's pedestrian prose added nothing new to the line previously taken by other Soviet leaders and expressed the general consensus that ". . . the British Tory government has definitely and concertedly undertaken to organize a war against the Soviet Union." The menace, Stalin proclaimed, was immediate: "We refer not to some vague, immaterial 'danger' of a new war, but to the real and actual *threat* of a new war in general, and of a war against the Soviet Union in particular." [28]

For the past several years Stalin had sought to communize China. Under Bukharin the Comintern had sent some of its most talented agents, such as Borodin and Roy, to the Far East for this purpose. Almost to the bitter end (April 5) Stalin had supported Chiang Kai-shek, who beginning in March 1927 had bitten the hand that fed him and by April 15 had slaughtered the Communists in Shanghai, thus bringing about the collapse of Soviet-Comintern intervention in China.[29] On May 25 a declaration signed by forty-four members of the opposition was put before the Politburo criticizing the Comintern and domestic failures of the Stalin-Bukharin bloc. The ruinous defeat in China was a blow that could not be disguised and struck a very tender nerve, since such top-level leaders as War Commissar Voroshilov, OGPU Chief Menzhinsky, and Foreign Commissar Chicherin had been members of a special Politburo committee set up early in 1926 to formulate the diplomatic line to be followed in China.[30] Under these circumstances, as one authority has put it, "the very telling nature of the opposition indictment made it all the more imperative for Stalin to destroy it if he wished to retain his authority." [31] Fortunately for Stalin, the opposition leader, Leon Trotsky, played directly into his hands in connection with the war scare. Trotsky had organized the Red Army and inspired some of its early victories in the civil war. In an open letter prepared for *Pravda,* he argued that the opposition should unseat Stalin and the other blundering Soviet leaders now that the country was once again in mortal peril. As an illustration, he pointed to the example of Clemençeau, who when the Germans were only eighty kilometers from Paris in World War I had struggled against France's incompetent leaders, had seized power, and had led his nation to victory. This unfortunate analogy gave Stalin the opening he wanted. By twisting it around, he could charge that Trotsky and the opposition were plotting civil war and treason at a time when the entire establishment should be closing ranks in the face of the common danger. OGPU agents penetrated into the opposition ranks and spread rumors that its members had been maintaining contacts with a White Guardist officer.[32] These rumors were tied in with a sensational spy story in *Izvestia* (July 10), reporting that more than twenty arrests had been made by the OGPU in connection with an English espionage ring in Leningrad. The show trial followed in September. Earlier in June, feature articles had already sought to link all current anti-Soviet covert operations with the "machinations" of the S.I.S.[33]

Rumors of a military conspiracy persisted throughout the summer and fall. Reportedly OGPU Chief Menzhinsky himself gave a long speech to the Central Committee and its Plenum in which he painted the situation in the most alarmist tones. According to Bukharin, a captured program of the conspirators proclaimed that only the Red Army could save the country from ruin, and that a military revolution was all the more desirable since it was the only means of precluding any kind of foreign intervention.[34]

In the highly charged atmosphere created by all these factors, the opposition fought a brave but hopeless battle, which its members even carried into the streets by addressing crowds of workers. On November 7, the tenth anniversary of the Bolshevik seizure of power, the last demonstrations were brutally broken up by OGPU and police agents. A week later Trotsky and Zinoviev were expelled from the party, and on December 2 an additional seventy-five members of the opposition were also expelled. By that time the war scare, which had served Stalin well, was also gone, if not forgotten. It was the end of the opposition, and within a few weeks Trotsky went into exile. Twelve years later he was murdered in Mexico by one of Stalin's security-police agents, who hacked open his head with an ice-ax.[35]

PHASE-OUT:
The End of the
Kutyepov Offensive and
the War Scare

WHILE THE fight within Soviet ranks raged throughout the summer and into the fall of 1927, General Kutyepov's Combat Corps continued its vest-pocket offensive of diversionary terrorist attacks. During July and August two more operational teams, this time composed of two men each, were trained under the supervision of Georgi Radkovich, who had escaped into Poland when the Trust collapsed in mid-April and had arrived in Helsinki in July. Radkovich also personally constructed the bombs for his teams out of dynamite and either iron or aluminum containers obtained locally. When tested, they proved to be highly destructive for their size and weight. As usual, each of the men was issued a Mauser and a smaller pistol, plus a poison kit for self-destruction in case of capture.

After several weeks of pistol practice and intensive training in handling the explosives, the group of four traveled by rail from Helsinki to the Leppyasurya station near the town of Suoyarvi. There they were met by a certain Petrov, who drove them by car a considerable distance in a northeasterly direction along the Finno-Soviet border to a rendezvous point where guides were waiting to take them across into Russia. They crossed the border without incident near Geb-Ozero (Lake Geb), where the guides left and the group split. The first team of Shorin and Sergei Solovyev (who had been on Captain

Larionov's raid in Leningrad earlier) left on August 20 for either Leningrad or Moscow. The second team of Aleksandr B. Balmassov and Aleksandr A. Solsky left a day later for Kiev, a city Balmassov knew well.

On August 21, their second day in Soviet territory, Shorin and Solovyev stumbled onto a forester by the name of Vedeshkin, who became suspicious. When he tried to arrest them near the village of Shuya they shot him down, and of course fled the area as quickly as possible. The sound of the firing drew the police to the scene. Aided by local forces, the elderly police inspector of the Karelian region organized a man hunt, using police dogs.

Meanwhile Balmassov and Solsky, who had followed along the first team's path a day later, stumbled into the police dragnet and were surrounded and arrested before they could put up any resistance. It was soon established that the prisoners were not the men who had killed the forester Vedeshkin the night before, and the man hunt continued. The first team of Shorin and Solovyev continued their flight and were able to elude the police for four more days. They were finally discovered about five o'clock in the morning on August 26 at the edge of Lake Onezhsky, a few miles from Petrozavodsk, and put up a stiff fight, wounding two Red Army soldiers, one of them seriously, before they were killed in the skirmish.[1]

Prior to the raids from Finland a Combat Corps team of three members, Nikolai Pavlovich Stroevoi, Vasily Aleksandrovich Samoilov, and A. Evon Aderkass, went into the U.S.S.R. during the last week in July from Latvia. From their show-trial testimony later in September it seems clear that the first two were betrayed to the OGPU by Aderkass, who apparently turned state's evidence.[2]

Both Stroevoi and Samoilov had fought with the White armies in the civil war and had been active in monarchist organizations abroad as émigrés in Paris and Latvia. Since 1925 they had been employed by Colonel Winter, the chief of intelligence of the Latvian General Staff. Samoilov had already crossed into Russia twice on intelligence missions and Stroevoi four times, so they were not amateurs at the business. The head of the Latvian monarchists, Prince Liven, recruited Samoilov into General Kutyepov's Combat Corps and in July got him to agree to join with Stroevoi for a special *terakt* mission.

Stroevoi, however, like many intelligence specialists, at first was skeptical about individual acts of terror. He was recruited into the Combat Corps by one of General Kutyepov's aides, Colonel Aleksandrov, in Paris, who had had a long talk with him about it in February 1927. In his trial testimony (which may have been carefully rehearsed beforehand) he gave the classical Leninist argument against terror:

> I told him [Colonel Aleksandrov] I thought assaults on private individuals do not achieve the desired goals and are even counterproductive, because each terroristic action results in reprisals on the part of the authorities, and these reprisals have a bad effect on the populace. Consequently, terroristic acts do not terrorize the powers that be, but the population; they get the opposite results from what we seek. We want to turn the populace against the powers, but instead it turns against us.[3]

Colonel Aleksandrov, of course, did not agree, and continued to sell the idea of direct action or "propaganda of the deed." At a last meeting with Stroevoi in Paris in July both Colonel Aleksandrov and General Kutyepov himself argued that with the imminence of war and the new tasks to be faced, more decisive action was imperative, and Stroevoi finally agreed to undertake the mission. Nothing came of it, as all three agents were arrested on July 26 near the town of Ostrov after crossing the border without incident. They were tried together with the surviving team, Balmassov and Solsky, in the highly publicized "case of the five monarchist terrorists," the second of two September show trials. All were sentenced to death on the twenty-fourth except for Aderkass, who got off with ten years' imprisonment in "strictest isolation." After the sentencing the presiding judge, Ulrikh, read aloud a communiqué from the Leningrad OGPU announcing that on September 21 another three-man team had crossed over from Finland and engaged the Soviet border patrol in a skirmish in which two were killed and one escaped. Solsky identified one of the dead men as the Finnish guide who had previously taken him across.[4] It was the end of a bad season for General Kutyepov's Combat Corps. Five days later, on September 29, the Finnish government expelled the remaining members of the Combat Corps, Captain Larionov, Georgi Radkovich, and Vladimir Monomakhov.[5]

As part of the price for settling the recent Polish-Russian crisis, the Poles had already begun to expell the most active émigrés from Warsaw. With the closing down of General Kutyepov's Finnish base, it was hard times everywhere in the covert-operations business. On the other hand, the Russian representative in Helsinki regarded the expulsions as only a first step, and doubted that they would be followed by action vigorous enough to enforce the agreement to stop aiding and abetting the émigrés. For their part, the Finns demanded reciprocal action on the part of the Russians, who for years had been exporting Bolshevik agents to Finland and had even organized an army battalion of Finnish Communist refugees for political-warfare purposes—forerunner of the local voluntary forces organized by Nazi Germany a decade later.[6]

For all its valor, the Kutyepov offensive thus ended not with a bang but a whimper. Casualties were high: at least 80 percent killed. The three or four brave survivors who returned to Paris could call the roll of their "golden" friends cut down fighting in the field or by OGPU firing squads later: Maria Zakharchenko, Staunitz (Opperput), Vosnessensky (Peters), Sussalin, Solovyev, Shorin, Balmassov, Solsky, Stroevoi, and Samoilov—not to mention the two unknown dead in the last foray from Finland.

On the other side of the ledger a few isolated guards, security police, or Red Army soldiers had been killed, and the one successful bombing of the Leningrad Central Party Club had caused a dozen injured. It was a high price to pay, but the direct cost of terrorist operations is seldom low, and the indirect cost in the form of police reprisals and counterterror has frequently been high.

Limitations on the Use of Terror

The Kutyepov terror raids touched off the familiar cycle of terror, counterterror, and police repression which is characteristic of revolutionary or counterrevolutionary operations. In an ironic reversal of roles the monarchist émigrés abroad sought to duplicate the feats of Savinkov and other Socialist Revolutionary terrorists on the eve of the February Revolution, which overturned the tsarist regime.

The theory behind the practice of such individual acts of terror is that they dramatize resistance to the *ancien régime,* and may produce an avalanche effect that will sweep it away. But in order to trigger an avalanche with a small explosive charge, the temperature and texture of the snow must be right. Similarly, in order for the terror raids to produce massive revolutionary effects, the political and social conditions must be such that they probably could be dispensed with anyway. Otherwise, as Lenin so aptly formulated the case against the use of terror, "the individual hero can die a beautiful death, but he is unlikely to change the political and social order." General Kutyepov's vest-pocket terror offensive is a classic example of this sound Leninist principle. On the other hand, given the political atmosphere and estimates at the time his Combat Corps went into action, a good case could be made for the offensive. Many people in high places at the time undoubtedly believed that a small spark might touch off a counter-revolutionary powder keg. This was certainly the hope and probably the conviction of the more conservative elements in the British establishment, including Churchill, Gregory (the civil service head of the Northern Division of the Foreign Office), and the King himself. In this regard, Kutyepov was traveling in the best of company.

One of the best analyses of the reasons the Kutyepov terror raids were predestined to fail comes from the Soviets themselves. A lead editorial in *Izvestia* of July 8, 1927, discusses the failure of the combat team composed of Maria Zakharchenko, Staunitz (Opperput), and Vosnessensky (Peters) to achieve its objective in terms that are generally applicable to similar covert operations. This analysis is one of the few examples of Soviet political theory in regard to covert operations and merits close attention. The article begins by noting that two days earlier (July 6) Deputy Chief Yagoda held a press conference in which he released the essential facts concerning the Zakharchenko-Staunitz mission, which the writer calls "terroristic conspiracy." The article then continues:

> However, in this case we do not really have a *conspiracy* in the proper sense of the word. By definition the most important prerequisite for a conspiracy is large-scale preparatory work inside the country against which it is directed. Although a few elements of the conspiratorial apparatus may be located abroad, the essential part, the broad base of the organization, must be within the target country which the

organization seeks to overthrow. Without such a base the
conspiracy hangs in the air, and from the very beginning
the conspirators must give careful thought to coordinating
their operations with the activity of the masses. Unless these
conditions have been met it is hopeless to dream that a
terroristic act may touch off events which will give history
a shove and serve as the opening moments of a revolution.

Nothing of the sort took place so far as the Opperput
group or other groups liquidated by the OGPU are concerned
. . . This was obviously not a conspiracy with roots in the
U.S.S.R., but rather the execution of a task directly assigned
by British intelligence and the monarchists living abroad
linked with it. These were not roots, as it were, but tentacles
stretched toward the Soviet Union from without . . .

If the terroristic acts had originated in the U.S.S.R itself, if our internal conditions were such that [individual]
terror could be converted into mass terror, then firing
squads would be powerless to stop it . . . But the twenty
agents executed [on June 9, following the murder of Soviet
Ambassador Voikov] were neither representatives of nor
spokesmen for a mass movement in our land. They were
tentacles stretched toward our land by British intelligence
and White Guardists abroad armed with English melinite
[explosive] and English grenades.

The execution of the twenty agents means that these
grenades will not explode, that these tentacles clutching our
land have been lopped off.[7]

One must sort out the anti-British propaganda chaff from
the wheat in the Yagoda interview to put it in proper perspective. Of the twenty agents summarily executed, the Soviets
themselves charged that only five were directly working for
British intelligence. Moreover, the Soviets did not claim that
more than two agents (Sussalin and Gurevich) were sent in
on terrorist missions. For the rest, no more than ordinary
espionage or routine counterrevolutionary organizational work
was involved.[8] Nevertheless, Yagoda's press interview high-
lights an important principle of covert operations designed to
overthrow a target regime: that individual or small-scale acts of
terror and violence make sense only when they are timed to
trigger a revolutionary movement that has been carefully prepared from within and which can quickly command mass
support.

Military and Diplomatic Maneuvers: The End of the War Scare

At the height of the war scare, during the first week in September, the Soviet government announced that full military maneuvers would be held in both the Leningrad and Simferol (Ukraine) districts. These were precisely the two most likely assembly areas in the event of war, and the German embassy in Moscow was concerned over the effect abroad that the military exercises might have. Chicherin, when approached on the subject, assured the German ambassador that nothing more than routine training was intended, and that there was no question of anything like a trial mobilization such as that which took place in 1914 and which contributed to the outbreak of the First World War.[9]

Chicherin was as good as his word. Although there was a partial mobilization of national resources, according to one authority:

> No large-scale mobilization of the territorial divisions seems to have taken place, not a single measure of direct mobilization put into operation. Voroshilov carried out his inspection of the Red Army in the Ukraine, but it was to maneuvers and not to military operations that Soviet troops marched out somewhat later. The situation appeared to be compounded of panic, precaution of a rudimentary kind and political calculation . . . in the struggle against the opposition.[10]

The commander of the Byelorussian military district, Marshal A. I. Yegorov, supervised the forces in his area, while General I. P. Uborevich commanded the maneuvers in the Ukraine, at which foreign military attachés were present. The exercises lasted until September 13 and were reported in *Izvestia* of that date under "News of the Republics" alongside a final feature story on "The Case of the English Spies," of whom nine were condemned to death and thirteen others to various terms of imprisonment.[11] Ten years later Uborevich, the commander of the Byelorussian maneuvers, was himself executed by an OGPU firing squad along with Marshal Tukhachevsky and five other Red Army commanders. Yegorov disappeared a year later during the purges, and presumably was also shot. Both he and Uborevich were officially rehabilitated along

with other military purge victims in 1958. They were included
by Soviet Premier Nikita Khrushchev in a list of "praiseworthy
men" who were victims of Stalinist "repression" in his closing
remarks to the 22nd Party Congress, October 27, 1961.[12]

Soviet apprehension over Poland continued on into November as a long-standing Polish-Lithuanian dispute flared up
again. The Soviet military attaché in Warsaw kept reporting
that a Polish attack on the U.S.S.R. was imminent. Chicherin
was sufficiently worried to resort to unofficial channels to com-
municate his apprehension to Washington. An American
banker, Irving T. Bush, the president of the New York Chamber of Commerce, was visiting in Russia at the time. Chicherin
confided to Bush his concern over a possible Polish attack,
and asked him to relay the message to the American ambassador in Berlin. Chicherin later explained that he used this
extraordinary means of impressing Washington with the serious-
ness of the situation, since he felt it his duty to do everything
possible "to avoid a catastrophe." [13] Returning to New York via
England, Bush repeated in a press interview his impression
that Chicherin was anxious for the United States to use its
influence with Poland to avert a conflict.[14]

The OGPU terror, as previously noted, resulted in a severe
defeat for the previously pro-Soviet wing of the British labor
movement. The British Trade Union Congress, at its annual
meeting early in September, broke all ties with Soviet trade
unions, and the Labour party resolutions a month later pointed
in the same direction.[15]

Although, with an eye to the next elections, British labor
thus severed its formal ties with the U.S.S.R., the break in
relations and the war scare had very little effect on trade and
credits between the two countries. Business as usual was the
prevailing sentiment, although Lenin's observation that the
British would trade in the ropes used to hang them applied
even more to the Soviet side of the exchange ledger. By comparison with 1926, Soviet exports to Britain increased by
£302,000 in value during the month of August.[16]

Throughout the summer and fall both British and Soviet
leaders kept the door open to negotiation in spite of the war
scare. The Soviets sent Litvinov, their deputy commissar for
foreign affairs, to Geneva in December, knowing that British
Foreign Minister Austen Chamberlain would also be there for a

League Council meeting. After some preliminary maneuvering to ensure that he would not be rebuffed, Litvinov met Chamberlain for an hour's conversation on December 5. No progress was made toward healing the breach, but a joint communiqué was issued stating that at least there had been "a frank exchange of views." The year thus ended in an atmosphere of reduced tension with the door still open for either side to begin negotiations at any time if it so desired.[17]

In this second part we have traced the origin, development, and political exploitation of the 1927 Soviet war scare on several interacting levels: (1) overt events (such as the Conservative party campaign and the Arcos raid preceding the break in Anglo-Soviet relations, and the diplomatic crisis following the murder of Voikov, the Soviet ambassador to Poland); (2) Soviet military and political estimates to the extent that these can be reconstructed from official speeches and confidential statements to German diplomats, or from other data; (3) Western espionage and covert operations (such as terror raids); (4) internal exploitation of the war scare by both sides in the Stalin-Trotsky power struggle; (5) Soviet counterintelligence and security operations as the OGPU reacted with counterterror to the Western intelligence offensive and to the Kutyepov terror raids.

Both Western and Soviet historians have traditionally regarded the Anglo-Soviet break and the Voikov incident as direct causes of the 1927 war scare. Soviet analysts have blamed the war scare on the machinations of the Conservatives and of British intelligence. Because the Soviet reaction and the degree of alarm appear to be out of all proportion to the overt incidents, Western historians have dismissed the Soviet war scare as either the result of "primitive thinking," fixed ideas, or Soviet paranoia. But there was a genuine basis for concern on the part of the Soviet leaders in the spring of 1927—a large-scale Western intelligence offensive. The Soviets were faced with a sudden expansion of Western espionage activities and terrorist diversions (which later included bombings and assassinations) directed against them. The number of espionage arrests reported increased from an average of less than two a month from January through April to forty-two during May, June, and July. This covert operational

offensive began at least a month before the Arcos raid of May
11 and the Anglo-Soviet break on the twenty-seventh, which
are generally regarded as having precipitated the 1927 war
scare. Moreover, by sheer chance this offensive coincided with
the collapse (in mid-April) of the so-called Trust, the counterintelligence operation by means of which the OGPU had kept
Western espionage under surveillance and at least partial control for five years. Taken together, these factors provide a more
rational explanation of the origin of the 1927 war scare than
theories that assume the Soviet leaders overreacted either to
specific events or to the anti-Soviet campaign of the British
Conservatives.

The assassination of Voikov in June, combined with the
terrorist raids executed by General Kutyepov's Combat Corps,
precipitated the OGPU counterterror of midsummer 1927 and
contributed to the war psychosis. The war scare was kept alive
by both sides in the Stalin-Trotsky feud and given an anti-
British twist by the spy trials. There was enough substratum
of truth to exaggerated Soviet propaganda charges of British
espionage activities to lend credibility later to the absurd claims
that characterized the purge trials of the following decade.

At the request of Britain and France, Stresemann intervened to help solve the Polish-Soviet crisis. In so doing he
temporarily abandoned Germany's position of cautious neutrality and severely strained her friendly relations with the
U.S.S.R. Although there is no documentary evidence to this
effect, the specter of a renewed Allied intervention with a
faltering Germany siding against Russia may well have strengthened Stalin's determination to force the collectivization of
agriculture and the pace of industrialization in long-range preparation for such a contingency.

As the crisis ebbed, measures taken to force White Russian émigrés to return to Paris as an operating base temporarily
ended the active use of terror by General Kutyepov's Combat
Corps. These measures compensated for the earlier collapse of
the Trust, through which the Soviet security services had kept
anti-Soviet diversions under surveillance and partial control.
In the meantime, the counterterror had wiped the slate clean of
internal resistance organizations linked with émigré groups
abroad.

The year 1927 marked the end of an epoch for the

U.S.S.R. The intelligence, counterintelligence, and covert operations that preconditioned the 1927 war scare and other external events of the day were important catalytic agents in bringing the era to a close. So far as the Soviets were concerned, the traumatic events of the year lent a new sense of urgency to their battle with Western intelligence services. The collapse of the Trust and the war scare marked the beginning of a struggle without quarter in which kidnaping and murder became the order of the day.

THE MELGUNOV OPERATIONS:
A Plan to Assassinate Stalin

D<small>URING THE</small> years 1927–28, while General Kutyepov's special forces teams were conducting their terrorist raids into the U.S.S.R., Sergei Petrovich Melgunov, the late émigré historian who at that time was the editor of the Paris newspaper *Borba za Rossiu* (*The Struggle for Russia*), was busily engaged in anti-Bolshevik propaganda and intelligence operations inside the U.S.S.R. Melgunov's activities were conducted with such tight security that they have remained virtually unknown to this day.[1] In a series of articles on the Kutyepov kidnaping written in 1955, after the passing of the Stalinist regime, Melgunov himself referred modestly to his early operations: ". . . In mid-1928, we were able (independently of Kutyepov) to infiltrate a few of our political friends into Russia for intelligence purposes. The journey of one of them was eminently successful. On his return he thoroughly enlightened us." [2]

The scope of Melgunov's operations was much broader than this passing reference indicates. Among his papers is a handwritten budget for the year 1928 which adds up to 6,820,000 francs. At the 1928 exchange rate of four francs to the dollar, this amounts to $1,705,000, of which a million francs or $250,000 was expended on terroristic acts alone!

The scope of Melgunov's activities and the size of his budget raises the question of where such large funds came from. Melgunov writes that a high-level committee had been created "for the special purpose of raising money and distributing it among the organizations actively participating in the struggle against Bolshevism." [3] Prominent among these activist groups was Kutyepov's Combat Organization, but even his special forces teams were poorly equipped and almost penniless, so it appears that the fund-raising committee was not very successful. Although the evidence is purely circumstantial, Western intelligence agencies may have provided Melgunov with considerable—and confidential—financial support.

Apparently Melgunov destroyed most of the operational records connected with his counterrevolutionary activities. Only a few agent reports remain in his archive, filed under the category "Illegal Trips into Russia." From the standpoint of his own personal security this was a wise precaution. Beginning with the kidnaping of General Kutyepov in January 1930, the OGPU systematically liquidated its opponents abroad. If Melgunov's classified papers had been compromised he would almost certainly have been liquidated. [4]

Melgunov's gain, however, is the historian's loss. For the most part, the correspondence which remains in the archive is fragmentary and, except for one or two operational reports, not very revealing. But one detailed operational report by a "master spy" appraises the resistance potential of a whole complex of controlled anti-Bolshevik groups in Moscow, Petrograd, Kiev, and elsewhere. Naturally the letters reflect the tremendous difficulties involved in carrying on conspiratorial work during the widespread terror which accompanied the 1927 war scare and continued well into 1929.

Most of the correspondence in the Melgunov archive deals with the travels, passport, and financial problems of F. D. Nazarov, a journalist who used the cover name of Ivan S. Sirotin. [5] On February 11, 1928, Nazarov arrived in Harbin, his base of operations outside the U.S.S.R. His first assignment was an illegal trip into Russia along a prearranged route from Harbin into Eastern Siberia. He was apparently sent on an intelligence or fact-finding mission with the idea that he would provide current authentic information on conditions in the U.S.S.R., which Melgunov could subsequently include in his newspaper. After completing the trip he expected to report personally to Melgunov, but presumably he returned instead to Harbin. Although Melgunov's agents provided guides for the border crossing and safe houses for contacts along the lengthy journey through Siberia to Moscow, the mission was hazardous and beset with unforeseen difficulties. Nazarov evidently entered the U.S.S.R. in August 1928 and had returned to Harbin by October 16. He describes preliminary preparations and the initial stages of his journey as follows:

There is much that is interesting. I shall begin with the operation itself. I regard it as successful. But now it must be said that the success was bought at a rather high price in terms of the patience required and the endless red tape involved. Several times I wanted to throw the whole thing over and return. There was much discussion about my identification documents. Too much importance was attached to them. I maintain that for transient work they are needed only to give the agent a sense of security. As an example I can cite my personal experience. For two weeks I didn't need them at all. But in order to obtain the documents I lost two weeks of my time and risked getting caught. You were obviously upset and did not understand what it was all about. To use a Soviet expression, I gritted my teeth and decided to see it through to the end. I succeeded. I did not spoil our relations with our contacts and they provided me with a really excellent guide.

[Having crossed the border] we had to overcome our physical weariness and cross a vast plowed zone of wet, black soil. The guide proved to be a genius at following 80 versts [a bit more than 20 miles] of impossible roads entirely at night without meeting a single living soul. Eighty versts as the crow flies, but, of course, that's not the way we were travelling. The needle of the compass swung through an arc of 180 degrees. I got tired of looking at it, and relied entirely on the irrational, animal flair of my companion. During the daylight hours we huddled together in the woods under the eaves of abandoned grain sheds. Our supply of cognac and dried sausages was quickly exhausted. The guide had friends at the other side of the 80 verst stretch. His friends, to be sure, had criminal tendencies, but were solid, commercial fellows. But when we arrived there we faced a new ordeal. His friends had been arrested. They had split among themselves and informed on each other. In short, they had all been arrested again, and once more we had to take to our heels across another zone. The operation was a brilliant success, and after another 120 versts (also as the crow flies), we came upon a neutral person living in an isolated lodge, which appeared to be entirely uninhabited. There we warmed ourselves and, as the guide expressed it, "stuffed" ourselves. The lodge was the departure point from which, after changing to city clothes, we travelled by cart to a nearby provincial city. * You are probably surprised that I have stressed the physical difficulties encountered . . . and haven't mentioned the problem of crossing the so-called fatal border. I cannot emphasize too strongly that the "fatal" border is a highly inflated myth. I convinced myself of this on my second trip. According to regulations there are two or three men per kilometer along the border, but actually I saw only heaps of stones and thick bleached grass which somehow reminded me of Peter Berngardovich [Struve's] beard. †

After leaving the provincial city I continued my raid on my own, making use of buses, taxis and first-class train compartments with reserved seats. In a word I disappeared into the masses, unnoticed by anyone and heeding no one.

After traveling two days and a night, Nazarov slipped off the train the next evening at a prearranged point. Taking the usual counter-surveillance measures, he reached a prearranged letter drop, then took the local train to the next city, where he quickly succeeded in contacting Ivan Ivanovich, the leader of a local underground resistance organization. Ivan Ivanovich had gathered around himself a large group of friends whom Nazarov met and with whom he exchanged ideas. Significantly, the group had been working together for three years and the members trusted each other. They knew Melgunov well, their program was fairly close to his, and there was a free exchange of ideas, although Nazarov seemed to them like a man "from another planet," having come from the world outside the U.S.S.R. In reporting on his trip, Nazarov attached "enormous importance to the fact that everywhere the people he met received him as one of their own. In spite of the omnipresent danger of discovery by the police the question of where to spend the night never came up." He simply stayed wherever it was most convenient at the time: "No one spoke about the

* Assuming that Nazarov entered the U.S.S.R. near the point where the railroad line from Harbin crosses the border, the city was probably Borzya, located in Eastern Siberia, approximately one hundred miles from the border at a railroad junction.

† P. B. Struve and his sister, Nadezhda, were friends of Nazarov. Struve was a leading Marxist intellectual who later became a bitter opponent of the Bolsheviks.

danger created by the fact of my presence. There was no end of kind words, handshaking, and expressions of hope that I might return safely." [6]

Probably from Rostov, Nazarov continued his journey to Moscow in order to maintain liaison with people on a list which Melgunov had given him, all of them previously active in the anti-Bolshevik underground. He was able to contact one of the leaders of the Moscow circle, Elena Aleksandrovna, and writes:

My conversation with her was like a nightmare: reproaches and complaints, fear of the GPU, and only one desire—to avoid danger. Her words: "We have suffered so much that we deserve a little pity. We are powerless. They follow every step we take, every word we speak—on the telephone, at home, in the trams, on the street." Espionage, arrests, shootings, torture—this is what she distracted me with. I interrupted, saying that I knew all this perfectly well, and asked her to talk about the cause. She answered the question and then began all over again. All this in a loud voice and with tears of anguish, while a floor-polisher was working in the next room, and a charwoman who had been recommended to her as reliable, came in. With regard to the important people which you mentioned, she said that they would not get involved in any kind of political work. After hesitating a long time she agreed to invite the people which you indicated the next day, but warned that [it was risky] and that she would not be surprised if we all fell into the hands of the GPU. She refused to give me shelter because the charwoman was under surveillance as a politically unreliable person. I left depressed, and went out on the street, where I was seized by an irrational fear that I was being followed, hounded, pursued. I took a roundabout path to cover my tracks, and it was a long time before I came to my senses. . . . The next day I did not show up at the place agreed on, and did not go to Petrograd as I said I would but in the opposite direction. It was not that I was afraid of being betrayed, but of being forced to reveal my identity in case of arrest and interrogation. Don't be surprised at this. It might not have happened, but since Moscow I have been travelling around for more than a month in Russia and have learned to recognize members of the old intelligentsia by the startled look in their eyes, which plead for mercy, by their frightened movements and guarded reticence. These are not without reason; they are ignored or held in contempt by some people, repressed or hounded by others. Sometimes they are treated with condescension but rarely with sympathy. They really do deserve to be pitied, but with rare exceptions, they are dead so far as our work is concerned. On the other hand, there are many promising prospects among the students, the young specialists, the workers and peasants who were formerly Red Army soldiers or partisans. But they are not linked together, are not organized, and for this they need our help. I was able to set up secret letter drops in Rostov and Chita [Eastern Siberia] and to organize intermediate points in the Manchurian railway stations, but cannot make further progress for lack of funds.[7]

Obviously, the problem of maintaining security in any underground operation within a police state is a major one. From the fragmentary evidence in the Melgunov archive, it appears that two basic rules were followed. First, operations were highly compartmentalized and the underground groups were kept apart. Liaison between them was handled by such agents as Nazarov who made special journeys for this purpose. Second, there was reason to believe that whenever a particular group had been penetrated by the OGPU, the individual suspected was eliminated, hopefully before the other members could be denounced to the secret police and arrested, since under torture it was assumed that they would implicate their fellow conspirators. Nazarov writes about "an extremely unpleasant incident" in which such a group "fell apart" after a new recruit was introduced into the circle by one of the members named Borya: "It was clear that he [the recruit] was brought in under control of a center which in turn was very well informed about our friends. Who knows? . . . In any case Borya's career is finished, finished forever. But let's forget him. He is now a dead body." [8]

Having returned safely to Harbin, Nazarov summed up the results of his experiences in an estimate of the situation and the resistance potential which still remained in spite of the Red Terror: [9]

The omniscience of the GPU is heavily exaggerated. It is still possible to work there. I entered Russia on the 18th of September and spent two months there. Ninety percent of the population resent the communists. Moreover, the countryside is against the city and both are against the Jews; in the new Republics the Great Russians oppose the aliens. The situation is tense. A movement could start spontaneously. Russia is entirely unlike the image formed by the emigration and by the lost souls who have left. Under the external crust there seethes a passionate life which is ready to burst forth. There are plenty of simple but skillful agitators stirring up resentment. Only the old intelligentsia and those who sided with the whites during the civil war are afraid to speak. The hatred of the countryside for the city is boundless. The influence of the Red Army is increasing. On the lower levels of the GPU there are many people who have nothing to do with communist ideology. The sentiments of the masses are against the Bolsheviks, but they are not organized. I am sending documents. Naturally, the flowers are growing among thickets of brambles and persistent work will be needed to conquer the brambles, but there is no devil so terrible that he can not be cut down to size.

. . . I shall finish a detailed report by the first of November and send it via Shanghai-Marseilles. . . . I ask you to show this report only to the people who have a need to know. If my name and location were known by the Reds, the people with whom I have contacts would suffer. . . . I am working here entirely on my own, and no one knows that I have been to Russia.[10]

The Melgunov-Nazarov correspondence affords some insight into the difficult, but by no means insurmountable, conditions under which the underground organization had to work. Nazarov's mission was principally one of liaison and intelligence collection, although he did manage to establish letter drops and support points for penetration into Russia from Manchuria through Eastern Siberia, a route which had escaped close OGPU surveillance probably because it was so infrequently used.

The more important work of organizing and controlling anti-Bolshevik resistance groups was performed by other more experienced agents. For three years one of them made regular trips into the U.S.S.R., remaining for months at a time and acting as a one-man control center. After each trip he prepared detailed operational reports on an extensive network of groups in Moscow, Kiev, Petrograd, and Smolensk, which

he personally supervised and controlled. The typescript of
one such "Organizational Report" remains in the Melgunov
archive. It is dated March 18, 1929, and signed with the
initials "N.M." and the cover name "Rudaki" (handwritten).

N.M. apparently came from a family which belonged to
the former ruling elite in Moscow, where he still had boyhood
friends. He was obviously a very competent, skillful, and
security-conscious agent. Otherwise, neither he nor the organization could have survived, since at times the OGPU investigated
his activities.

The "Organizational Report" for 1928–29 is a model
of its kind in terms of precise writing and security safeguards.
For example, the various groups or individuals which "Rudaki"
contacted are referred to only by the initials of their code
names as they appear on special lists, such as: "B.K.—See list
I-1" or "FMB—list K.-I-1." Thus, even if the report itself
were compromised or stolen, the lives of the individuals concerned would be saved.

After renewing contact in the spring of 1928 with an
underground group of twelve members in Kiev, N.M. visited
similar circles in Petrograd and Lvov, establishing liaison and
distributing literature. He then spent the next three months
in Moscow, the main base of the organization. In July 1928,
Georgi Radkovich, one of General Kutyepov's agents, exploded
a bomb in the headquarters of the OGPU. This sensational act
of terror touched off a new wave of police repression, with
intensified searches, interrogations, arrests, and so forth, so
that active underground work was suspended for the summer.
One group of eleven members drawn mainly from the intelligentsia fell apart. Its leader died and the others withdrew
from active work under pressure of the Red Terror. On the
other hand, another group of fifteen became more active, making excellent use of the Trotsky-Stalin feud and intraparty
dissension for anti-Bolshevik propaganda purposes. N.M. writes
that during this period:

> . . . I worked closely with two of my former boyhood
> friends, MMB and DAA. They were sons of a family which
> had stood at the apex of the privileged society of the past.
> Although they had not yet fallen to the very bottom of the
> oppressed classes in the present, the past continually hung
> over them like the sword of Damocles, and they were filled

with hatred of the existing system. Their political convictions, not yet fully formed, were a mixed legacy of rather right-wing tendencies and poetic, biting irreconcilability. Their slogan was "speed-up terror!" I decided to exploit this situation and we discussed the possibility of an attempt to assassinate Stalin. The Secretariat of the Ts.K.V.K.P. [The Central Committee of the Communist Party] is located on the fourth floor of the Ts.K. building situated on Staroi Square. Entrance to the building is by special permits or party cards which are not difficult to obtain. An additional permit of the managing department is demanded in the corridor of the fourth floor. Stalin visits the Secretariat once or twice a week; the remaining time he works in the Kremlin. Once a week Stalin receives especially important visitors whose names are listed in advance in the Secretariat in the order in which they are to be received. The times of the appointments are posted in the office of the permit bureau, to which there is free access. On the day before he receives visitors, a report on the list of names is made to Stalin and he arrives at the Secretariat a few minutes before the appointments begin. Under these circumstances the times of Stalin's arrival can be easily figured out in advance. He travels by automobile along Nikolskoy Street seated beside his chauffer. Of course, wherever he goes he is surrounded by a swarm of secret service agents. For this reason a direct attack on Stalin's automobile in the street is out of the question. It is much better to infiltrate into the Central Committee building before the announced time of his arrival and wait on the fifth or sixth floor by the elevator shaft. Opposite the shaft there is a big window which looks out on the street and from which every movement below can be seen. A signal that Stalin is about to enter the building should be flashed from the street to the window. The signal should be sent by someone especially placed for the purpose. This should only take a minute and, in case of a momentary or lengthy delay, the person giving the signal should not attract attention to himself. At the moment Stalin enters the building and approaches the elevator and it begins to ascend, a bomb made of a powerful explosive material which also produces a thick smoke screen should be hurled at the elevator. The explosion should be powerful enough to simultaneously destroy the canvas which screens the entrance. Taking advantage of the curtain of smoke, the person throwing the bomb can quietly leave. In the meantime, an automobile which has been especially prepared for the occasion behind the "Chinese wall" should be waiting for him. In general, the success of the project would, in the last analysis, depend on coordination and timing. I told I.V.N. the basis of the plan. He sharply rejected any such enterprise and emphatically cautioned me against it. Obviously, it would be futile to expect any help from his side for such a project. But without support, mainly financial and technical (projectiles and documents), it would be pointless to think about implementing the project. In addition M.M.B. soon left Moscow for the Caucasus. Since then our plan has been hanging in mid-air, but I hope to see it realized, and in accordance with whatever possibilities open up, I shall keep it in mind for the future.

As the first item in three pages of "'Additional Clarifications" added to his report, N.M. wrote: "With respect to an attempt to assassinate Stalin there are two opinions: I.V.N. is against and I am in favor of it. Two things are necessary: (a) the final opinion of those living abroad, and (b) support as the decisive factor." [11]

Nothing is known as to what decisions were made in Paris regarding the proposal to assassinate Stalin. If such an attempt was in fact made, it obviously failed, and any knowledge of it has been suppressed.

The plan cannot be dismissed as an idle daydream. Clearly it was based on detailed intelligence which had been painstakingly collected. The project was simple in design and required very few active participants, thus minimizing the chances of compromise in the planning stage and human failure during execution. Certainly the agent who would actually throw the bomb would be assuming almost suicidal risks. But the wave of terror and the coming excesses connected with the forced collectivization of agriculture could be expected to produce volunteers for the task. N.M. already had two such candidates with whom he had discussed the operation. In tsarist times the Socialist Revolutionary Combat organization under Boris Savinkov had carried out assassinations which in the planning stage offered far less chance for success than this project as outlined in the "Organizational Report." Had the plan been carried out either in 1929 or in 1930, the elimination of Stalin would have had a profound effect on the future of the U.S.S.R. It would certainly have "made history." In such a case it is a fascinating but purely academic exercise to speculate about what might have been. But although the stage was set and the actors ready, the project apparently never got beyond the initial planning phase. Melgunov's budget for 1928 included one million francs for terroristic acts, and presumably a comparable amount was allocated for each of the next two years. But in January 1930 General Kutyepov was kidnaped by OGPU agents in broad daylight on the streets of Paris, and this incident may well have had a decisive dampening effect on projected terrorist activities. By mid-1930 Melgunov had withdrawn from émigré affairs and retired to the country to try his hand at farming and writing history rather than making it.

PART 3
THE GOLDEN AGE
OF ORGANIZED
MAYHEM

11
NO NEED TO HOPE:
The Anisimov and
Radkovich Missions

 L IKE THE
proverbial month of March, the decade of the 1920's came in
like a lion and left like a lamb. The years 1917–20 had been
marked by abortive revolutions in Germany, Bavaria, and
Hungary. In the United States a largely imaginary Red scare
reached its climax in 1919–20, but the anti-Bolshevik legacy
was kept alive when the U.S. State Department in December
1923 published a forged Zinoviev "Letter of Instructions to
the Communist Party" which expressed the absurd hope that
"the proletarians of America" would soon "raise the Red flag
over the White House." These were the days of "dreamers,
dynamiters, and demagogues," when the last of the free-lance
anarchists occasionally exploded a homemade bomb and sent
shudders of revulsion through the bourgeois capitals of the
Western world. But the violence of the day was so unstruc-
tured, so disorganized, and so much an end in itself that it
was soon dissipated. The ideological end point of such anar-
chism had already been reached with the doctrine of "unmo-
tivated terror" of the Russian émigré philosopher Judah Gross-
man (Roshchin), who had argued in the early 1900's that the
bourgeoisie should be harassed by acts of terror committed not
for any special motive against specific individuals, but ". . .
against the bourgeoisie *as such,* for the sole crime of consti-
tuting a class hostile to the workers. Hence his term, 'unmo-
tivated terror' . . . Bombs thrown into theaters . . . swanky

restaurants and cafés—not to speak of the random stabbing or shooting of any prosperous looking person—would be the practical day to day application of this tactic." [1]

The most notable terrorist acts for the good of the anti-Bolshevik cause came not at the beginning, but at the end, of the 1920's. They were the armed raids into the U.S.S.R. of General Kutyepov's Combat Corps. This vest-pocket offensive was followed by two individual missions, one led by A. A. Anisimov and the other led by Georgi Radkovich. Both took place in 1928. Two years later, with the kidnaping of General Kutyepov in Paris, a subtle change in atmosphere began to mark the transition to the decade of the 1930's. Inside the U.S.S.R. the Soviet security police, a rapidly growing bureaucratic weed, was soon to become a pliable instrument at the disposition of Stalin in his rise to a position of absolute power. Abroad, the foreign section of the OGPU had to build new networks after the collapse of the Trust in 1927. Under the talented direction of men such as Artuzov (Abram Slutsky), head of the Foreign Department, Walter Krivitsky, and Aleksander Orlov, a highly professional corps of intelligence agents was trained and emplaced in all the capitals of Europe.

The complacent return to "normalcy" of the twenties was shattered by the Great Depression. Economic and social dislocation in turn gave rise to the intense ideological and political tension that characterized the 1930's. Following the ominous and meteoric rise of Adolf Hitler, the European world was politically and spiritually polarized after 1935 into a Communist-led antifascist left and a profascist right ready to appease Hitler at almost any price in the hope that he might be turned east against the Soviet Union. It was an age of both individual and mass subversion. National loyalties were undermined and transferred to the political cause of the right or left, and sometimes back again. Under these circumstances, treason was redefined as no more than a willingness to help the other side, and French superpatriots, alarmed to find their country with a Socialist premier, raised the slogan "Better Hitler than Léon Blum!" As we shall see in Chapter 13, Paris was transformed from a city of light into a seedbed of subversion.

By the midthirties what Hitler called the "battle of the streets" had spread from Germany to France. Violent clashes between gangs of right-wing thugs such as the *Cagoulards* and

Communist goon squads became the order of the day. The ideological "rape of the masses" (the title of a book by Serge Chakoutine) became a universal phenomenon.

The battle of the intelligence services was also intensified. A variety of competing and overlapping Nazi intelligence agencies (usually lumped together and mistakenly labeled the Gestapo) flooded western Europe with agents and created the image (largely false) of an all-powerful "fifth column" abroad.[2] Until decimated by the purges at home, the OGPU responded with a similarly intensified effort abroad. The free-floating political violence of right- and left-wing mobs in Europe was matched in the United States by the coldblooded violence of organized crime under gangster overlords. It was the heyday of the Chicago mobsters and the Dillinger-style loners. Civil crimes of violence in turn had their counterpart in political kidnaping and murder executed by the new professional "organization men" of the Nazi SD (*Sicherheitsdienst,* or Security Service) or the OGPU (renamed the NKVD after July 1934). In this muddled atmosphere, hostile propaganda could plausibly blame either the Nazi SD or its Soviet counterpart for almost any major crime. This does not mean that such charges were not based on a substratum of truth. Hugo Dewar writes:

> In March of 1938 a letter was received by the Secretary of the Juridical Section of the Secretariat of the League of Nations denouncing the existence of a "centralized Mafia of terrorists working on the territory of several states, other than their own." The writer of this letter went on to say that he could, with the help of "documents, testimony of witnesses and irrefutable political considerations," prove what was at the head of this band of assassins. No action was taken on this letter. A little over two years later its author himself was assassinated.[3]

Two outstanding case studies of the work of this "centralized Mafia," the kidnapings of General Kutyepov and General Miller, are analyzed in Chapters 12 and 14 of this book. During this decade of mass subversion and violence, General Nikolai Vladimirovich Skoblin, a prominent figure in the Paris émigré colony, won the dubious distinction of being subverted by both the Soviet and the Nazi intelligence services. Having put the finger on General Miller, he disappeared at the same time as his erstwhile chief. Before his disappearance, however, Skoblin, as a double agent, played a key role in the Nazi-Soviet frame-up known later as the Tukhachevsky affair, which makes up the last section of this book.

But this anticipates events. Let us return to the last two years of the previous decade, 1928–30, when individual remnants of General Kutyepov's Combat Corps ran their last desperate missions into the Soviet Union.

The Anisimov Mission

Although driven out of both Poland and Finland as a by-product of the 1927 Soviet war scare, small groups of General Kutyepov's Combat Corps continued their probing actions against the U.S.S.R. from bases in Paris and elsewhere. The tragic loss of Maria Zakharchenko and others who had gone before and the disillusionment that undoubtedly set in when a renewed Allied intervention failed to materialize were, of course, sobering factors. Nevertheless, at least three additional raids took place during 1928, of which the most important were the A. A. Anisimov mission and Georgi Radkovich's sensational raid on OGPU headquarters. Both these forays ended in disaster, but it seems as if Kutyepov's combat teams had adopted as their own the motto of William of Orange during his thirty years of bitter opposition to the Spanish occupation of the Netherlands: "No need to hope in order to undertake nor to succeed in order to persevere." A month after their return the two surviving members of the Anisimov group made another trip into the U.S.S.R., about which nothing is known. But during the first Anisimov mission one member of the team kept a diary, fragments of which were found in the archives of the Czechoslovak group of General Kutyepov's organization.[4] A few terse entries in this journal, dated from September 2 to October 3, 1928, tell the essential facts of the story.

The three members of the team, A. A. Anisimov, V. J. Volkov, and S. S. Voinov, met in a God-forsaken little Polish village located in a swamp near the Soviet border on September 5. Under the forceful leadership of A. A. Anisimov, the "old man" of the team, the first month was spent in physical training and conditioning, including a field "survival trip" lasting two days and nights. Anisimov also provided his men with false documents, weapons, and four hand grenades or "lemons" each.

When one of the younger men asked Anisimov what their task or goal was, he answered in terms that left no doubt that, as one who had been into the U.S.S.R. before, he had no illusions about what they could hope to accomplish:

> "I'll try to explain how it is, but I'm afraid you may not understand. All these questions will be quickly settled after you've been there awhile . . .
>
> "Stronger and more intelligent people than we have already gone in and yet have failed to carry out any great terroristic act. Why? Yes, and in Russia itself there must be some, if only a few isolated individuals [on our side] who are strong and experienced. Why have they been ineffective?
>
> ". . . You have to live there awhile yourself in order to understand how difficult Soviet conditions really are . . .
>
> ". . . Ours is a small task—a very small one. Our force is not very impressive. If you're dissatisfied you can withdraw. But right now even small tasks are necessary. You say that our firepower—our deaths, perhaps—count for little? I reply that they count for a great deal!"

By October 13 the little band had penetrated about fifty miles inside the Soviet border. An entry in Volkov's journal for that day reads in part as follows:

> I've been counting on my fingers and this must be the 13th. The days get confused. S.S. [Voinov] is lying beside me curled up like a ball with his head covered . . . But I know he's not asleep. We have hardly slept for the last three nights.
>
> I gather my thoughts together and try to find the answer to the question: "How, how did it all happen?"
>
> Having made our way around the Polish guardpost, we crossed the border on October 7 during the night. The 7th, 8th, and 9th we were en route. Everything went well, according to schedule, and we had already crossed the swamp zone. About noon on the 10th I saw A. A. [Anisimov] moving ahead through the forest. Suddenly waving his arms, he fell and did not get up again . . .
>
> For us there is no mercy, no pity!
>
> A. A. had broken his leg and lay there pale, his eyes closed. A kind of strange, cold stupor suddenly came over me from the moment I saw A. A. and realized what lay in store for us.
>
> We laid A.A. out as best we could while he never once

uttered a sound or opened his eyes. Empty-headed and stunned, we sat silently near him for maybe an hour or two or three. I don't know how long.

I got up and took a long, close look at A. A. What should we do now?

As dusk was falling, still without opening his eyes, A. A. asked us in a low voice to go find him a more comfortable place!

Unable to hold back our tears, and sobbing unashamedly, we left him. We knew that we had to. We sat down some distance away under a tree and I immediately fell asleep. [S. S.] woke me up: "Let's go back to him."

When we returned, A. A. was dead. On his chest lay a handkerchief on which he had scrawled with a pencil the words: "You must hide my body." His last instructions before dying.

We kissed our old man's hands, which were still warm, sat down, and kept watch over his body through the long night. In the gray gloom of the morning we found a shallow depression in the woods. We spent the rest of the day digging it deeper and stuffed the body into it.

What could we accomplish now?

We decided to return. Suddenly quite close by we heard gunshots; first single rounds and then bursts of firing. [S. S.] jumped up with a start and then, crouching low, ran in the direction of the shots. I followed him almost automatically while the question flashed through my mind: "What's happening?"

After we had taken a few steps the woods began to thin out. We crossed through a few low bushes and found ourselves at the edge of the forest. Bending low, we pushed aside the bushes and soon had a view of open fields. We lay down and began to take a good look around. About a half mile away a gray strip of country road was visible on which people were moving. In front and behind were cavalrymen, and in the middle of the column was a crowd of people. Who were they and how many?

"Who are they?" S.S. asked in a whisper. "Who has been taken prisoner?"

Pushing aside some branches that blocked my view, I fixed my eyes on the crowd. They were peasants—men, women, and children. Three of the men were carrying sacks on their backs, and I could make out that the sacks contained bodies. The individual feet of the corpses hung lifeless to the ground over the figures which were bent low under their burdens.

A light wind carried to us the noise of the column, the wailing and weeping of the children.

Horror-struck, [S.S.] exclaimed: "What is it? What's going on here?"

"They're taking a convoy of peasants. But look! They're taking the children too—the children!" . . . [S.S.] almost shouted: "Let's run up and shoot the bastards, the dirty s.o.b's!"

A peasant fell to his knees and immediately two horsemen from the rear ranks rode up and began to beat the fallen one. Then one of them raised his rifle and fired. The crowd fell back on either side. The wind again brought the sound of cries, of more shots, of weeping.

I closed my eyes and rested my head on the cold ground.

We took leave of A. A., making the sign of the cross over his grave.

This morning we realized the full measure of our emptiness, our stupor, our helplessness . . . As we left A. A. we took back with us his four bombs.

Thunder in the Lubyanka: The Radkovich-Monomakhov Mission

For nearly four years Maria Zakharchenko and her husband, Georgi Radkovich, were active in the Moscow underground as special guests of the OGPU-operated Trust. During this time they gave much thought to the problem of how to inflict the maximum damage on the Soviet leadership by means of a terrorist raid. N. Vinogradov, a member of Kutyepov's Combat Corps who knew them both, writes that during their stay in the U.S.S.R. the Radkoviches "had arrived at the conclusion that it would be necessary to strike at the head of the octopus, not at its tentacles." He continues:

They began long and careful preparations. Reconnaissance of the Kremlin showed that that fortress was completely out of the question. The continuous guard around it made it unassailable . . . [They] next directed all their efforts against the Lubyanka, the dread torture chambers of the Soviet inquisition. The mere names of the rulers of the Lubyanka—Dzerzhinsky, Menzhinsky, Yagoda, Trilisser—were enough to paralyze all opposition.

"Even if our attempt to blow up this torture chamber should fail," Radkovich said, "our example will serve as a summons to all those in whom the fire of freedom has not yet been extinguished."

The first try, an attempt to blow up the communal living quarters of the Chekists, fell to the lot of [Maria] Zakharchenko-Schultz and her two helpers. As is well known, this attempt, which took place on June 3, 1927, ended in failure and in the death of the participants.

[Georgi] Radkovich organized the second attempt. During his long residence in the U.S.S.R., using every precaution, he made contacts with private individuals and put them to every conceivable test. With the aid of such persons he was able to set up inside the U.S.S.R. three bases or "safe houses," one of which was in Moscow. There he was able to enlist the services of a Muscovite, a man who belonged to what was later called "the working class." D. [Vladimir] Monomakhov was chosen as his third helper—a man of exceptional self-control who had taken part in the blowing up of the Central Party Club in Leningrad.

They decided to blow up the OGPU *Kommandatura,* below which were located the offices of such important Chekists as Menzhinsky, Yagoda, and Trilisser. A date was set for the explosion, which took place on July 6, 1928. At the safe house agents who went in afterward obtained detailed information about the explosion from the Muscovite who survived the incident. He told them what he himself had seen or knew plus what he had been able to find out later from others:

"Radkovich prepared for the mission carefully and over a long period of time. The location of the *Kommandatura* was carefully studied as well as its schedule of receiving hours. An escape route was charted and means for the getaway arranged. Since strangers were not admitted after hours, special night passes were forged to gain entrance to the *Kommandatura.* Radkovich, who was a great expert in explosives, himself prepared the bombs, which combined maximum strength with portability, and finally each of the three was assigned his role.

"Although fully aware that by doing so he was signing his own death warrant, Radkovich took for himself the role of bomb-thrower. In case both of them were stopped by guards inside the *Kommandatura,* Monomakhov, using his pistol, was to clear a path for Radkovich to the stairway leading to the offices of the Chekists, then swing around immediately and rush for the entrance.

"The third man, the Muscovite, was supposed to wait outside for Monomakhov no longer than three minutes in an automobile taken from a nearby garage. In case of success he was to drive Monomakhov along a predetermined route to a railway station below Moscow where he could board a long-distance train. His ticket had been purchased in advance.

"The rescue of Monomakhov would impress the Chekists with the strength and importance of Kutyepov's organization. Under the conditions prevailing in Moscow, the use of the automobile in the operation would underline that importance. The Chekist leaders would be given to understand that there is still retribution in this world, and in the eyes of the Soviet people the all-powerful OGPU would unquestionably be undermined.

"On the night of July 6 an automobile pulled up in front of the OGPU, and Radkovich and Monomakhov stepped out. They successfully passed the document check in the vestibule. They went upstairs to the second floor and ran into two Chekists. What happened between them has not been clearly established. Perhaps the Chekists wanted to search Radkovich and Monomakhov, who immediately opened fire. Radkovich yelled at his partner: 'Run downstairs!' He rushed past him a few steps, when there was a deafening explosion of such force that Monomakhov was knocked over backward by the blow, but got up again quickly. All kinds of debris fell through clouds of smoke. Monomakhov ran downstairs, passed through the devastated vestibule and out the front door onto the street.

" 'He walked so calmly and deliberately,' the Muscovite said, 'that I lost patience and yelled, "Make it snappy!" ' "

"They drove at normal speed inside Moscow, but when they got past Serpukhovsky Street they hit the floor board. The Muscovite looked to the rear and saw that they were not being followed. He glanced in the back seat and asked in a loud voice: 'Well, how did it go? What's with Georgi?' When there was no answer he thought to himself, 'The poor guy's fallen asleep.'

"About ten miles from Moscow the motor began to misfire more and more frequently. The Muscovite turned off to one side on a country road. The automobile bounced up over a bump, came down with a bang, and the motor stopped running altogether.

"It was ten o'clock at night, and dark. To repair the damage to the car with only a pocket flashlight was out of the question. The Muscovite flashed the light around the interior of the car. Half curled up, Monomakhov was resting against the side, but the seat was covered with blood. He remained silent. The Muscovite opened the car door. With difficulty he pulled Monomakhov out and got him on his feet. The latter had lost so much blood he could hardly stand up. He had somehow been wounded in the back by the explosion. The Muscovite was able to drag Monomakhov by the shoulders into a nearby wood where he could lie down.

"The Muscovite couldn't dress the wound in the dark. What should he do? Look for help? But where and from whom? It was hopeless to tinker with the automobile in such darkness. Soon the dawn would break. No doubt an alarm had been sounded in this area. The automobile abandoned not far from the highway would certainly draw attention.

"Monomakhov came to in the cold air. With difficulty, in broken phrases, he told what had happened and was silent. A few minutes later he tried to say something again. The Muscovite leaned over him and asked: 'What did you say?' He heard Monomakhov answer: 'Save yourself! I say save yourself!' "

The explosion in the OGPU offices of the Lubyanka was so powerful that it was heard throughout the neighboring blocks. With frightened and perplexed expressions on their faces, Chekists in uniform and in civilian clothes ran out of the building. An uneasy crowd began to gather. OGPU and Red Army troops quickly put in an appearance. They immediately drove the public back off Dzerzhinsky Street and Square, detained a few suspects, and placed a guard around the entire OGPU building. Ambulances drove up and the wounded were removed. Afterward popular rumors clearly exaggerated the number of casualties, but the OGPU in its reports deliberately understated them. Apparently none of the important Chekists was injured, although rumors persistently denied that this was so.

The extent of the damage caused by the explosion to the building itself was also officially understated. But it was obvious that external balconies and railings were blown up. Workers later said that they were ordered to make all necessary repairs at once. Although they worked all night long, they were unable to finish by morning, and entrance to the *Kommandatura* was denied until the following evening. When it was then opened to the public there were no traces of the explosion left except for signs reading, "Fresh paint."

The search for any remaining participants in the explosion began at once all over the streets of Moscow and its suburbs. As might be expected, the abandoned automobile with its blood-spattered seat was quickly spotted. There was an immediate roundup in all the adjacent areas. Chekists, military units, and local inhabitants ordered out for the purpose began a careful search. Monomakhov was discovered in the heart of a small wood. They said that he shot it out with the Chekists but saved the last bullet for himself.[5]

Like other volunteers in General Kutyepov's combat teams, which for several years had penetrated into the U.S.S.R. on intelligence and terrorist missions, Georgi Radkovich was fully aware of the risks involved. His wife and friends had already lost their lives on similar raids. Viewed objectively, the cause he served was truly hopeless, but for what today would be called the true believer there is no need to hope in order to undertake. As he threw his bombs and brought a part of the hated secret police headquarters down in ruins about himself, Radkovich must have felt a moment of fulfillment and transfiguration of an intensity seldom achieved by ordinary human beings. His unknown colleagues also deserve a niche in the hall of fame of lost causes. They left no memoirs. They made no speeches before dying, and history has forgotten them. Their epitaph was unconsciously wrenched from one of them in the anguished cry: "For us there is no mercy, no pity."

12

THE KIDNAPING OF
GENERAL KUTYEPOV

A<small>FTER A</small>
long illness General Wrangel died in Brussels on April 26,
1928, and his successor, General Kutyepov, assumed command
of the ROVS, the Russian émigré military forces. Less than a
year later, in January 1929, the Grand Duke Nikolai also died
while staying on the French Riviera, leaving Kutyepov the
undisputed leader of all political as well as military operations.
Previously Kutyepov had directed émigré espionage and terrorist activities while attached to the staff of the Grand Duke.

Whether for motives of fear or revenge for the Kutyepov
offensive, or in order permanently to cripple the political-warfare potential of the ROVS, the OGPU decided that Kutyepov had
to go. Once the decision was made, given the capabilities of
the OGPU during the period, it was only a matter of time until
General Kutyepov, like Trotsky a few years later, would be
removed from the scene. His removal was one of the most
thoroughly planned and skillfully executed capers in the an-
nals of modern crime, in spite of a major blunder at the end,
so that although the operation was a brilliant success, the
patient died in the process.

Probably from the time he had been put in charge of
ROVS covert operations by the Grand Duke Nikolai in 1924,
General Kutyepov had been under OGPU surveillance. He was
well aware that he was under constant observation and used
to joke with his friends that "they" were watching him. Kutyepov lived with his wife in a modest four-room apartment on

the second floor of the building at number 26 Rue Rousselet
(in the Seventh Arrondissement), a quiet street one block off
the Boulevard Montparnasse. The Rue Rousselet itself is only
one block long and runs between the Rue Oudinot at one end
and the busy Rue de Sèvres at the other. General Kutyepov's
house was located near the middle of the block. Near the end
of the street where it runs into Rue Oudinot is a mental hospital known as the Clinic of St.-Jean de Dieu, which is fronted
by an indented parking space big enough for two cars. For
three or four Sundays before the General's disappearance a
young policeman had been observed standing on patrol at the
corner near the clinic. From time to time he would meet and
exchange a few words with a blonde woman in a beige coat.
It was afterward determined that no such policeman had been
assigned to this beat by the Paris police. The OGPU agent who
thus patiently impersonated an officer later played an important
part in the kidnaping. His presence gave the operation the
appearance of a routine arrest and was probably also designed
to remove any anxiety on General Kutyepov's part.

Three months before the event, Grigory Z. Bessedovsky,
the Soviet chargé d'affaires in Paris, had defected. He writes in
his memoirs that before his defection one of the local OGPU
agents, Yanovich, had confided to him that they had an in-
former in Kutyepov's immediate entourage, so that all of his
activities "were as clearly visible to us as if we were watching
them under a glass bell." [1] Investigation later proved that far
from being an idle boast, the statement was almost literally
true.

It was no secret to Kutyepov and his associates that his
movements to and from his apartment were under constant
observation by Soviet agents posted in two neighborhood cafés.
One, called Le Petit Beaumarchais, was located in the Rue de
Sèvres at the end of the block and gave a clear view of his
house and the entire Rue Rousselet. The other, called simply
Le Rousselet, was located near the corner at the Rue de Sèvres.
Precisely because he feared a kidnaping or assassination attempt, the General made it a rule on leaving his house always
to walk down the block into the busy Rue de Sèvres, where
his figure was well known by local shopkeepers, and of course
by the agents in the observation posts at the end of the street.

Kutyepov refused to spend official ROVS funds for a regular

bodyguard and was personally unable to afford one on his modest salary of about 1,500 francs a month. Nevertheless, knowing that he was constantly followed, he took certain precautions, which until his disappearance had seemed adequate. Already in 1926 he had been warned by the French *Sûreté* not to use the *métro*, as the police could not be responsible for his safety if he did, and an ambush was expected. For this reason the veterans of his Gallipoli forces had organized a thirty-man taxi brigade and took turns acting as his chauffeur. He made it a rule never to accept a ride from anyone whom he did not know personally and never to enter an unfamiliar building alone. The night before his disappearance, for example, the General had attended the annual celebration of the Grenadiers Regimental Association, which lasted until about one A.M.; upon leaving the meeting he declined a ride from a driver whom he failed to recognize.[2] Instead he climbed into the taxicab of Lieutenant Fortunato, who drove him back to number 26 Rue Rousselet. The next morning the General called and informed him that it would not be necessary to pick him up in the morning for church services.

Apparently two other attempts to kidnap or liquidate General Kutyepov had been planned but failed to come off. First, on October 29, 1929, a meeting of senior officers had been called in the ROVS headquarters at which Kutyepov was expected. His private secretary had already arrived and received a telephone call from an unidentified person stating that the General could not attend and had therefore called off the meeting. About this time Kutyepov himself arrived, and, of course, knew nothing about the telephone call, which may have been nothing more than the work of a *provocateur,* but may also have indicated that a kidnap attempt had been planned. If so, the plan obviously miscarried.

Second, it appears that an attempt to kidnap Kutyepov had been planned for the first week of January 1930. During that time the General had traveled to Nice to unveil a memorial plaque to the late Grand Duke Nikolai, who had died on the Riviera the previous year. According to the deposition of a Latvian émigré, a former volunteer with the White Russian forces, at 4 P.M. on January 18 the latter had boarded the Paris Express in Cannes. During a stop in Marseilles at 7 P.M., three men, all of Latvian extraction like himself, entered his compartment, and they stayed up all night talking until the train reached Paris at nine the next morning. The strangers had asked the émigré a couple of questions in French. Not wishing to reveal his nationality, he had answered in English, and then pretended to sleep during the long night's journey while eavesdropping on the conversation the strangers carried on in their native Latvian. From their conversation he discovered that they had recently been involved in an attempt against "a prominent White Russian," but that the operation had been suddenly called off. They were on their way to Paris for a similar mission and intended to stay in one of the suburbs, Fontenay-aux-Roses.[3]

Kutyepov usually attended mass in the Russian Orthodox Church of the Gallipoli Veterans Association at 81 Rue Mademoiselle, about a twenty-minute walk from his apartment. He left for church on Sunday, January 26, 1930, at about 10:30 after telling his wife that he would be back for lunch about one o'clock. He followed his normal route down the Rue Rousselet and right along the Rue de Sèvres to the corner where it crosses the Boulevard Montparnasse. At this point the boulevard angles sharply toward the Seine and becomes the Boulevard des Invalides, and the junction is marked by the *métro* station Duroc. From this point his normal route to church led him down the Rue de Sèvres (which changes to Lecourbe) toward the Rue Mademoiselle and the church. With his tall frame and black, spade-shaped beard he was a familiar figure, easily recognized by friends and neighbors, two of whom saw him that morning about 10:45 A.M. Between 10:45 and 11 A.M. he was seen at the Duroc junction of the Rue de Sèvres and the Boulevard des Invalides by an officer acquaintance. Streetcar number 89 stopped at this corner, and a White Russian taxicab driver, a veteran of the Kornilov Division, saw Kutyepov standing near the streetcar stop as if waiting for someone. Three or more witnesses stated that they saw a young woman wearing a light beige coat approach General Kutyepov [4] about this time, presumably the same woman who had previously been seen talking to the false policeman on the corner of the Rues Oudinot and Rousselet. Reportedly the taxi driver saw him a few minutes later turn down the Boulevard des Invalides toward the Rue Oudinot, instead of continuing down the Rue de Sèvres (Lecourbe) toward the church. Kutyepov was apparently taking an alternate and longer route home, one that he usually avoided for fear of an ambush. He had clearly changed his mind about going to church, where he was awaited impatiently, as a special requiem mass was to be held for a recently deceased comrade at arms. Today the trap set for him could easily be arranged with cruise cars and spotters equipped with two-way transistor radio sets. With none of this equipment available in 1930, the operation required a high level of organization and efficiency. General Kutyepov was next seen as he turned the corner of the Rue Oudinot into the Rue Rousselet, at the site of the Clinic of St.-Jean de Dieu. In the parking space in front of the clinic was a large gray Alfa-Romeo sedan, parked with its front end pointed toward the Rue Oudinot and General Kutyepov as he approached. Another car, an ordinary red Renault taxicab, was parked at the intersection of the Rues Oudinot and Rousselet, facing toward the Boulevard des Invalides, from which the General had just come, and was placed so as to observe his approach. As Kutyepov came up to the sedan, which was waiting with the door open, two powerful young men approached him, stood at attention, and invited him to enter, one on either side. He hesitated for a moment before doing so, but then got into the Alfa-Romeo between the two men. The phony policeman who had stood watch at the corner sauntered over and got into the front seat of the red taxi, and both cars, which had had their engines idling, raced off down the Rue Oudinot toward the Boulevard des Invalides. An attendant at the Clinic of St.-Jean de Dieu watched the abduction from a second-story window, and the whole operation went so smoothly that he thought the police were making a routine arrest. He called one of his friends to watch the scene, but by the time the friend reached the window it was all over.

While making their getaway, both cars were spotted twice on the Left Bank. The first observer, a police officer, saw that a struggle was going on in the back seat of the sedan. On the second occasion the cars were held up in a traffic jam at the approach to the Pont d'Alma and a certain Madame Flottes observed that a handkerchief was being pressed against the face of one of the passengers in the back seat of the Alfa-Romeo. In reply to her question as to what was going on, she was told that there had been an accident in which the unfortunate victim had had his legs crushed. They were administering ether to provide temporary relief. But the French have a proverb that nothing is so permanent as the temporary. Apparently the use of ether or chloroform was a major blunder, for although General Kutyepov had a powerful physique, he had long suffered from a heart condition. The well-known émigré surgeon Dr. Aleksinsky had advised the General against an operation requiring deep anesthesia because his heart would not be able to withstand the effects of the anesthetic that would have been necessary. It is almost certain that a generous dose of ether, combined with the physical stress of violent struggle, now proved fatal.

About four that afternoon both cars were observed parked at the edge of the moor along a deserted stretch of Normandy Beach. The occupants delivered a long package wrapped in gunnysack to a motor launch, which in turn pulled up alongside a Soviet vessel, the *Spartak*.

Naturally the kidnaping—*l'affaire Koutiépoff,* as it was called in France—created a sensation. The French government under Premier André Tardieu was strongly anticommunist, and the right-wing press welcomed an opportunity to renew its demands for a break in diplomatic relations with the U.S.S.R. From London, where he was attending a naval disarmament conference, Premier Tardieu at once ordered a full-scale investigation by two rival agencies, the Paris police under Préfet Jean Chiappe (also a staunch anticommunist) and the *Sûreté National,* corresponding to the U.S. Federal Bureau of Investigation. The *Sûreté's* top Soviet expert who bore the unfortunate name of M. Fauxpas-Bidet was put in charge of a fruitless inquiry which lasted for weeks and was sidetracked by at least eighty false clues, some of which were obviously planted as deliberate "disinformation" by Soviet agents.

Official Soviet disinformation activities were apparent early in the game. For the first five days the Soviet press entirely ignored the incident. Then on January 31, 1930, *Izvestia* published a Tass story which is a classic example of *desinformatsia:* "The French news agency Havas states that according to a communiqué published by the French police, General Kutyepov left Paris for an unknown destination." [5] This was certainly an understatement. It was also a deliberate fabrication, since neither the French police nor the Havas news agency had issued any such report. A second Tass release characterized as "idiotic" the speculations of the émigré press that General Kutyepov had been kidnaped by the OGPU, and might appear with a "confession" in Moscow. *Pravda* charged that the incident was being used as a pretext for an anti-Soviet campaign, to break off diplomatic relations and "set French imperialism on the path of an interventionist adventure." [6]

In an interview with William Owen, an English Communist named Arens, the first secretary of the Soviet embassy in Paris, made the astonishing suggestion that General Kutyepov had been kidnaped by agents of the French police.[7] Picking up the cue and making additional antiémigré propaganda, *Izvestia* charged on February 3 that Kutyepov had fled to South America, taking with him all the funds of the ROVS, the émigré military organization he commanded.[8] The charge, which was absurd on the face of it, since at that time the ROVS funds were negligible, was quickly refuted by officials of the organization and the émigré newspapers.

The predominantly anti-Soviet emigration was incensed at the kidnaping. General Goulevich, chief of the general staff of the tsarist army, addressed a formal letter of protest to the French government to which 11,726 signatures were attached.[9] Not only the Russian émigrés, but many French conservative elements were impatient with the bumbling efforts of Mr. Fauxpas-Bidet to solve the crime. Voluntary contributions to assist in the investigation poured in, and one anonymous donor deposited with the newspaper *Le Matin* a check for 500,000 francs as a reward for anyone who could produce Kutyepov dead or alive and identify the kidnapers.[10] The newspaper *La Liberté* organized two protest meetings on February 11 and 12, and after the first meeting a huge crowd, estimated at 3,000, gathered in front of the Soviet embassy on the Rue de Grenelle, shouting angrily: "Down with Dovgalevsky [the Soviet ambassador]! Give us back General Kutyepov! Death to the murderers!"

An eyewitness has described the scene from the Soviet side of the "barricade" as follows:

> Dovgalevsky declared a state of siege. Most of the Party members armed themselves and slept at the embassy. Camp beds were put up in the larger rooms, and we all took turns

at mounting guard. In case of attack we should not have hesitated to defend by force of arms this scrap of Soviet territory in the heart of Paris.

I remember sleeping on the ground floor with the secretary of the embassy, Divilkovsky, who had been wounded at Lausanne when Ambassador Vorovsky was shot. He was a nervous creature who slept badly, moaned a great deal, and had a way of starting awake, grabbing at his revolver. Ambassador Dovgalevsky, by contrast, was possessed of complete self-control. One evening there was an insolent demonstration under the embassy windows, with the French police conspicuous by their absence. I found myself behind the big entrance gate with Dovgalevsky. We expected any moment to see the great door crash down. We released the safety catches of our revolvers. The demonstration did not go that far, however.[11]

At the height of the excitement, on February 11, the rightist deputy Ybarnegaray called in the Chamber of Deputies for a break in diplomatic relations with the U.S.S.R., but before action could be taken or even a formal interpellation take place the Tardieu government fell. The ensuing crisis lasted for several weeks, and by the time Premier Tardieu formed a new government, the storm over *l'affaire Koutiépoff* had blown over.

In the interim, however, the Soviet embassy in Paris took no chances. Although the French police were never able to produce any direct evidence that the OGPU had conducted the operation, as a matter of elementary precaution Yanovich, one of the Soviet agents believed to be directly involved, and the local OGPU station chief ("resident"), Lev B. Helfand, left the country shortly after the operation.

The basic facts of the Kutyepov kidnaping were first established not by the police but by enterprising journalists with the cooperation of the Russian émigré colony, which was deeply moved by the loss of its acknowledged military leader. In spite of this cooperation, no fully satisfactory explanation was ever produced as to why General Kutyepov changed his announced intention of going to church and, returning home, walked into the trap set for him. The woman in the beige coat, who had previously been seen in the area and to whom he presumably spoke at the junction of Rue de Sèvres and the

Boulevard Montparnasse before turning back, has also never been identified.

The police investigation brought out the fact that a few days before the kidnaping General Kutyepov had traveled to Berlin for a secret meeting with two OGPU *agents provocateurs,* one of whom had visited Paris the year before. The Berlin episode in the Pension Reichhorn, January 17–18,[12] was an important preliminary stage in the kidnaping plot. According to a reliable source it took place as follows:

> General Kutyepov traveled to Berlin accompanied by Colonel A. A. Zaitsov, his deputy for covert operations against the U.S.S.R. They went to meet with two emissaries from Moscow who supposedly represented military circles. The meeting, which had been set up well in advance, had to be postponed once or twice because the people from Moscow could not make it. (Already in 1929 there were persistent rumors in circles close to General Kutyepov that contact had been made with certain high-ranking Soviet military figures.)
>
> The two people who conferred with General Kutyepov in Berlin were former colonels of the general staff of the old Russian army and later staff officers of the Soviet Army. Their names were Popov and De Roberti. Kutyepov had known the latter before the Revolution. According to Colonel A. A. Zaitsov, one of the participants, the following incident took place during the meeting, which was held in a privately owned pension in Berlin. The lengthy, cordial conversation on operational matters was interrupted when Popov had to excuse himself. As soon as Popov had left the room, De Roberti turned to General Kutyepov and requested that he be permitted to say a few words to him with no witnesses present. General Kutyepov asked his deputy (Zaitsov) to leave him alone with De Roberti. When Zaitsov stepped outside he did not go into a room apart, but stepped into a cloakroom which was separated by only a thin partition from the conference room. He could hear clearly every word spoken by De Roberti, who begged General Kutyepov not to believe anything which he and Popov had just told him. Then he warned Kutyepov that there would be an attempt to kidnap him at the beginning of May or perhaps at the end of April 1930, and that he should take extra precautions about this time. Shortly afterward Popov returned and Kutyepov

stepped into the corridor and called Zaitsov back. The conference then continued for some time. Afterward Kutyepov told Zaitsov about his conversation with De Roberti. Both agreed that the emissaries [from Moscow] were highly questionable characters, and that De Roberti's warning was made in order to win Kutyepov's confidence in at least one of them. The information about the danger which threatened in April–May, that is, in three or four months, was taken seriously. Zaitsov at once told Kutyepov that more effective security measures would have to be taken at that time.

It was not until after the kidnaping that Zaitsov told me his opinion that the [Berlin] conference had been arranged purposely in order to blunt Kutyepov's vigilance during the next few weeks. The conversation took place at the beginning of January and the kidnaping on January 26, 1930, that is, less than three weeks later.[13]

The Berlin episode provides a rational explanation for General Kutyepov's confidence with respect to his personal safety on the fateful Sunday morning during which he left his apartment never to return. He apparently believed he would be safe from ambush until April or May, and so no special security precautions, such as a personal bodyguard, were taken. The episode also makes possible a plausible explanation of how he was deflected from his normal course to church. According to this theory, when General Kutyepov met the unidentified woman in the beige coat (a person in whom he must have had considerable confidence), he was told that an important Soviet military figure (whom he may have been expecting) had arrived from Moscow and urgently wished to see him at a secret rendezvous which had been prearranged. A car was waiting for him in front of the clinic near his house and would bring him back later. The theory credits the unknown woman who spoke to him with a major role in the conspiracy.

However the trap may have been prepared for him, General Kutyepov returned to Russia to an unmarked grave rather than to the VIP suite in the Lubyanka, which had once been occupied by the terrorist Boris Savinkov and then by Sidney Reilly.

The two most obvious Soviet motives for the Kutyepov kidnaping were frequently noted by observers at the time of the incident. One was to cripple or destroy what was left of his

Combat Corps by eliminating its leader and guiding spirit. A second objective may have been the political-warfare triumph that could have resulted from a spectacular show trial. But from the Soviet point of view there was also a third compelling reason why Kutyepov's removal was necessary early in 1930 rather than later in the year. Colonel Zaitsov, Kutyepov's chief of covert operations, explained the circumstances to his assistant, Captain Galai, as follows:

> Shortly before he was kidnaped General Kutyepov was supposed to inherit a large sum of money. This inheritance would have made it possible for him to expand enormously the underground work which up to that time had been conducted with limited means and very little cash outlay. He, Zaitsov, had already been told to keep this possibility in mind. His opponents in Moscow knew exactly with what limited funds Kutyepov had had to operate up to this time. They also knew how the scale of his operations would expand when 18 million French francs would be put at his disposal. This gold had been deposited in Japan by the tsarist regime for military expenses during the First World War. Through a Japanese court, Colonel Portnyagin, the former Russian military attaché, had obtained the right personally to dispose of the 18 million francs. It had taken Colonel Portnyagin several years to obtain this right through the courts. A few years earlier Portnyagin had told General Kutyepov that as soon as he obtained these funds, the entire sum would be turned over to him for his work. At the end of 1929 Kutyepov had received a message from Portnyagin stating that the last formalities connected with the transfer would be completed in a few weeks. The OGPU was fully aware of the impending transfer of funds, and this situation alone would have made General Kutyepov's early removal imperative as a security measure from the Soviet point of view.
>
> After a short delay, the money was in fact transferred from Japan to Paris, but the soul of the undertaking, General Kutyepov, was lacking. His successors, General Miller, Dragomirov, and Globatschev, were no more than administrators and executives. Even if they had been able to surmount the security hazards involved, they were not suited to carry on the revolutionary struggle. Over the next several years the funds were dissipated for the administrative costs of maintaining cadres and in petty operations of no political or military importance.[14]

It is almost a foregone conclusion that if the OGPU had obtained its victim alive, Kutyepov would have been tortured, broken, and paraded before a show trial in Moscow. Thanks to his timely death, he was mercifully spared the indignities suffered later by most of the Old Bolsheviks and top-ranking generals who were publicly humiliated and destroyed by Stalin during the Great Purges. There is little question that if the OGPU had persuaded Kutyepov to recant and to admit the error of his ways, as they had succeeded in doing with Savinkov, the result would have been a major political-warfare victory. His death robbed them of this propaganda prize, and for all its technical precision, Operation Kutyepov ended as no more than a vulgar criminal caper.

By the end of January 1930 General Kutyepov was no more. His loss was a blow from which the ROVS never recovered. His mild-mannered successor, General Yevgeny K. Miller, was a completely different kind of personality, essentially a staff officer rather than a combat officer. Even had he been eager to conduct aggressive covert operations against the U.S.S.R. (such as the Kutyepov terrorist raids), the security hazards would have been too great. It was clear from the circumstances surrounding the kidnaping of General Kutyepov that his organization had been penetrated by OGPU agents to such an extent that further combat operations would have been suicidal. These hard lessons were also not lost on the Western intelligence agencies which might have provided the necessary backstopping for a renewed offensive. What few connections remained after the Trust episode and the Kutyepov kidnaping were sharply reduced. No intelligence agency could afford to participate actively in operations which, as the OGPU boasted, it watched "as closely as if they were under a glass bell."

The fact that the kidnaping appeared to be an "inside job" led to much speculation on the security aspects of the affair. Kutyepov was reportedly criticized by General Miller for going to a suspicious and secret appointment unguarded, without leaving a note giving details, so that a search could be made promptly if he failed to return. This is an obvious lesson, but even such precautions failed to save General Miller himself, who disappeared six years later as a result of an OGPU kidnaping plot which bore a striking resemblance to the Kutyepov incident.

Kutyepov, Melgunov, and the "Second Trust"

The key to the unsolved mystery surrounding the Kutyepov kidnaping lies in the extended battle of wits between the general and the OGPU, the Soviet security police and its network of agents abroad. For several years each of the two opponents had deceived the other in connection with the "Trust." For more than a year after the fall of the Trust, the OGPU had been unable to renew a direct contact with Kutyepov himself. It was also disturbed by the growing prestige and counterrevolutionary activities of Sergei Petrovich Melgunov, the émigré editor of *Borba za Rossiu*. Soviet authorities knew that copies of *Borba* were being smuggled into the U.S.S.R., and, according to a report of the Foreign Division of the OGPU, this situation "would bear watching." The report added that "efforts to establish direct links to the top echelon of the Melgunov group had failed." [15]

For this purpose a Soviet agent, General Alexander Nikolaevich Popov, was sent to Paris in late June 1928 and soon made contact with Melgunov. Melgunov was very favorably impressed by the Soviet general, who claimed to represent an internal Russian anti-Bolshevik organization. Melgunov not only decided to collaborate with him but also agreed to arrange a meeting between Popov and Kutyepov which took place in a Paris restaurant early in July 1928. Out of this original meeting the so-called Second Trust was born. Melgunov himself was not present, and all future contacts between the two conspirators were handled with General G. G. Korganov serving as a go-between. Melgunov insists that he had "no connections of any kind with the work of General Kutyepov's organization inside Russia." [16]

After one or two exploratory meetings during which each sounded the other out, General Popov and Melgunov agreed to collaborate in distributing copies of *Borba* in the U.S.S.R. and in the exchange of intelligence information through secret correspondence. Melgunov found much of the material provided by Popov "very important" and made use of it in his newspaper, without the slightest suspicion that he was being drawn into a provocation.[17] This may be called the propaganda aspect of the Second Trust; the operational or military side concerned General Kutyepov exclusively.

For some time, Melgunov, who was very cautious and security-conscious, had regarded one of General Kutyepov's agents, Grigory Aleksinsky, with suspicion. Earlier (in late 1927) he had failed to persuade Kutyepov to break off relations with Aleksinsky, the editor of the Paris newspaper *Rodnaya Zemlya (Native Land)* which was supported by funds from the Rumanian Military Intelligence Service, the *Siguranza.* From his own sources Melgunov had reason to believe that Aleksinsky was a double agent working for both the Soviets and the *Siguranza,* which Melgunov states "was in fact controlled by the English." His suspicions were confirmed when one of Aleksinsky's closest associates, Akasatov, was arrested as a suspected Soviet agent.[18]

In a letter from Moscow dated December 15, 1928, Melgunov learned that, working through Aleksinsky and Rumanian *Siguranza* channels, Kutyepov had sent an agent to Moscow to contact the Second Trust organization. The agent in effect claimed to represent both General Kutyepov and Melgunov, who were allegedly collaborating in their covert operations. Apparently the trip took place in November 1928. As soon as Melgunov found out about this approach, he lodged a violent protest with Kutyepov, since he objected to the security risk involved in any operation with which Aleksinsky was connected. During a stormy session the general frankly admitted his responsibility for the mission. This confrontation was the last time the two émigré leaders saw each other personally before the kidnaping which took place on January 26, 1930.

Although relations between them were strained, Melgunov was kept generally informed of Kutyepov's activities through their mutual friend, General Korganov. He and his wife also kept a detailed journal or "diary," recording important conversations and events as they occurred in the midst of "the conspiratorial bedlam" surrounding Kutyepov and himself.[19] From these "memoranda for the record" it is clear that General Kutyepov and his deputy for covert operations, Colonel Zaitsov, were playing a double-game with the OGPU and the Second Trust, represented by Popov and supposedly staffed by anti-Bolshevik Red Army officers eager to overthrow the regime. It was a dangerous game, strung along for over a year and a half, and the risks were high. But Kutyepov was anxious to recover the blow to his prestige which he suffered with the collapse of the first Trust in the spring of 1927. For its part the OGPU was eager to repair the damage done to its intelligence networks abroad, and as part of the price was willing to "cooperate" with Kutyepov and Zaitsov in keeping open certain controlled channels through which "enemy" agents were permitted to enter and leave the U.S.S.R. unharmed. Examples of this kind of *de facto* cooperation among deadly enemies, with each side attempting to reap maximum benefits at the expense of the other, are by no means unknown in the looking-glass world of covert operations. (Such arrangements have a rough counterpart in the secret Clay-Sokolovsky agreement to return defectors in the early days of the Allied occupation of Berlin after World War II.)

With regard to the Second Trust, Melgunov writes that Kutyepov sent an agent into the U.S.S.R. to contact that organization in October 1929.[20] It is extremely unlikely that the trip could have been made without the tacit connivance of the OGPU. Again, according to Melgunov, a few days before his abduction General Kutyepov had dinner with an important Russian intelligence agent, Colonel Bogdanovich, and two Soviet citizens who had entered France illegally and for whom quarters in Paris had been arranged by Colonel Zaitsov. The two visitors returned to the U.S.S.R. soon after the Kutyepov kidnaping via the Rumanian channel, and Bogdanovich, after being acquitted by a French Court, left for South America.[21] Melgunov cites as his source Captain Donchikov, who was visiting Kutyepov at the time and was asked to leave before the dinner guests arrived.

On the basis of such evidence it appears that even after returning from the Berlin meeting in mid-January with the Second Trust representatives Popov and de Roberti, General Kutyepov continued his contacts with what were presumably OGPU agents. The newspaper *Vozrozhdenie* reported that on January 24, two days before his disappearance, Kutyepov met with a triple agent who reported to the OGPU, the British Intelligence Service (S.I.S.), and the French police! Like "the woman in the beige coat" who played a role in the Kutyepov kidnaping, this agent has never been named.

The mass of circumstantial evidence gathered by Melgunov supports the theory that when General Kutyepov left for church on the fateful morning of January 26 he was deflected from his course by someone connected with the Second Trust operation and kidnaped. The last time he was seen by his deputy for covert operations, Colonel Zaitsov, was on Saturday morning the 25th. At that time Kutyepov told him to be ready for a meeting on the 27th, but said nothing about any appointment for the 26th. If Kutyepov knew in advance of such an appointment, he paid with his life for playing his cards too close to his chest. On the other hand, the OGPU had studied Kutyepov's movements very carefully for some time and may have suddenly approached him through a trusted double agent with "news" of the arrival of a high-ranking officer of the Second Trust. The general may have been caught off his guard at a time when he felt that he was relatively safe and was willing to risk another rendezvous, one which proved to be his last.

In the nightmare of suspicion which followed the kidnaping, everyone involved in the Second Trust operation naturally tried to project as favorable an image of his role as possible. Melgunov maintained a discreet silence about his correspondence with Popov,[22] and waited nearly thirty years to publish his side of the story. He was well advised to do so. If the OGPU had had any real appreciation of the extent of Melgunov's other operations inside the U.S.S.R., he would almost certainly have been next on the OGPU's list of victims to be kidnaped or killed.

Zaitsov naturally played down the extent to which both he and Kutyepov were involved with the OGPU and other intelligence agencies (such as the Rumanian *Siguranza*), but there is no reason to doubt the essential outlines of his story as told to sources close to him, such as Captain Galai.

As to the fate of General Popov and de Roberti, nothing certain is known. After the kidnaping de Roberti wrote General Korganov that all further contacts would end. Quite unexpectedly, Melgunov received a letter to the same effect from Moscow, dated February 14 and signed "Your faithful friends," thus closing the propaganda phase of the Second Trust.

Since so little certain is known about the Second Trust, it is difficult to evaluate, and in any case the two sides of the operation were distinctly separate. So far as Kutyepov is concerned, he would probably have been kidnaped in any case, with or without his involvement in the Second Trust. In this regard, Burtsev, who devoted much of his journalistic career to exposing OGPU operations, wrote a sensational article in the journal *Poslednie Novosti* for October 12, 1930, based on information from Fekhner, a secretary of the Soviet Embassy in Berlin and OGPU "resident" or chief for Europe. Fekhner, who defected after the kidnaping, later fled from Europe. He told Burtsev that the order for the kidnaping had come from the highest levels of the OGPU and that the personnel who carried it out were later called back to Moscow and liquidated. He also named both Yanovich and Helfand, two OGPU agents in Paris who fled the scene shortly after the kidnaping. Helfand later defected and escaped to Portugal. According to Fekhner it was he himself who sent a telegram to General Kutyepov inviting him to meet an important Red Army officer on the morning of the kidnaping. Since by the time of his defection this theory was already widespread in Paris, there is no reason, in the absence of concrete supporting evidence, to accept Fekhner's identification of himself as the agent who set up Kutyepov's last rendezvous. As a rule, defectors usually play up their own importance and tailor their "debriefings" to what they think their interrogators want to hear.

On balance, it must be conceded that through the Second Trust the OGPU succeeded in luring Kutyepov into an ambivalent relationship in which he eventually got beyond his depth and drowned. But, like a strong swimmer who refuses to believe that he is being swept out to sea by an undertow, Kutyepov pushed his luck beyond all reasonable limits in the last two weeks of his life and virtually closed the trap on himself.

By contrast, the OGPU failed miserably with the other side of the Second Trust, the relationship with Melgunov. As previously noted, this was mainly a disinformation operation. Melgunov found the material which was sent to him from Moscow important, and admittedly used some of it in editing his newspaper. Entirely unknown to the OGPU, however, Melgunov was also receiving intelligence reports from other agents whom he sent into the U.S.S.R. during this period. A comparison of these reports with those received from Popov shows little difference in tone and content, so far as general reporting on internal conditions is concerned. Only in one respect do the letters follow closely a key element in the OGPU line, namely a downgrading of the use of terror and its general futility. For example, after reporting on the July bombing of the OGPU headquarters by Georgi Radkovich (one of Kutyepov's agents), a letter dated September 24, 1928, from Moscow concludes: "We must assert that so far as our operations are concerned, isolated terroristic acts can never produce tangible results. They can only result in the useless sacrifice of our best people, while sowing despair and disillusionment among the weak." [23]

Melgunov played his cards very cautiously with Popov. He refused to respond to a request to send in "a representative who would be fully competent" to work on the Second Trust's military plans for "a massive popular anti-Bolshevik uprising" which was anticipated in 1929, and which was to be coordinated with "blows from abroad." Instead of falling for this ploy, Melgunov wrote Popov that it was impossible to unite the warring factions of the émigrés into an effective organization around the liberal platform of his newspaper. For this reason and "for lack of funds," he stated that he was giving up the struggle to concentrate on writing historical studies of the civil war period, such as his *Tragedy of Admiral Kolchak* and other books published the following year. This letter was written in the latter half of 1929.[24] A few months later General Kutyepov was kidnaped, and, as noted above, the OGPU itself gave up further efforts to draw Melgunov into its net. All it could show for two years of persistent effort were a few letters from Melgunov, painfully enciphered and written in secret ink under seemingly innocuous plain text. Even the formula provided for the secret ink was so crude that after a few years the chemical agents ate through the paper, so that most of the messages, if they still remain in the OGPU archives, are almost certainly illegible.[25]

A single entry in the Melgunov journal provides a fascinating postscript to the Melgunov-OGPU relationship. Written on April 29, 1928, more than a month before the arrival of General Popov and the founding of the Second Trust, the entry reads:

> S. [Melgunov] saw a military person who had just arrived
> from Moscow claiming to represent a conspiratorial organiza-
> tion. They allegedly acted on behalf of "Napoleon"—Tuk-
> hachevsky, a man without principles. S. thinks this is incor-

rect. [However,] the man inspired confidence in himself. We shall see.[26]

This is the only entry in the journal which mentions Tukhachevsky. Nor is the "military person" mentioned again.

Like General Popov and others who followed in his footsteps, this first military figure to contact Melgunov was probably an OGPU agent. He may have sensed Melgunov's negative reaction to the suggestions that Tukhachevsky was a "man without principles," for the OGPU dropped further attempts to implicate the Soviet general in its contacts with the Paris émigrés until 1935–36.

THE SKOBLIN CASE

Most observers agree that the kidnaping of General Kutyepov was at least in part an "inside job." Its success depended on an intimate knowledge of émigré affairs which could have been provided only by an agent or agents close to the General. Although never directly established, Soviet complicity was indicated by the fact that the OGPU "resident" (station chief) in Paris, Helfand, and his assistant, Yanovich, suddenly left the city shortly after the event. Mrs. Yanovich also escaped to Belgium in Soviet Ambassador Dovgalevsky's personal car a few days afterward. Sometime before the event Yanovich had boasted to another Soviet embassy official, Bessedovsky, that the OGPU observed all of Kutyepov's movements "as clearly as if he were under a glass bell." Kutyepov's bitter experience with the Trust led him to establish a special internal security organization, called the "Inner Line," in Sofia in 1927,[1] headed by Captain Klavdi A. Foss, who was officially secretary of the ROVS in Bulgaria. The purpose of this, as of any similar internal security agency, was to ferret out Soviet *agents provocateurs* among the émigrés, and to help in the selection of candidates for Kutyepov's Combat Corps, in which the presence of traitors would of course be fatal.

As the intelligence agencies of all the great powers have learned to their dismay, there are no iron-clad procedures which guarantee 100 percent security against penetration by enemy agents. Even the most trusted officials can, under certain circumstances, transfer their loyalties and defect to the "enemy." Provided he is cautious, "the defector in place" can report to an enemy agency for years without being caught. The most recent and dramatic case is that of Harold A. (Kim) Philby, the British Secret Intelligence Service official who served as a Soviet agent for thirty years before exposure. At present he is reportedly serving in Moscow in a high post with the KGB, the successor of the Cheka-GPU-OGPU-NKVD.[2]

Against the true ideological defector who stays quietly in place and serves an alien cause which he has made his own, there are no administrative or mechanical defenses except periodic "security" checks and possibly polygraph or lie-detector tests, which are at best uncertain and are often regarded as an unwanted invasion of privacy.[3] The more intelligent and capable the defector and the more responsible his position, the less likely he is to compromise himself by such obvious indicators as suddenly spending beyond his known income, riotous living, heavy gambling, and so on. Most low-level spies are apprehended because of such conspicuously aberrant behavior. But in a closed subculture such as that of the British Foreign Office, the flagrantly scandalous and socially deviant behavior of Guy Burgess and Donald Maclean, two notorious postwar defectors, was tolerated for years without drawing the proper attention of security officials. Hindsight is proverbially much better than foresight, and this is especially true with respect to detection of espionage agents. Nevertheless, it is amazing that in many instances the factor of unexplained personal income takes on significance only after an agent has been arrested and tried, or has fled to escape arrest.

In periods of great international tension, such as the classical Cold War period, 1947–53, ideological fervor may lead to an epidemic of denunciations which overburden administrative security and security-review agencies. This happened in the United States during the McCarthy period, and reached nightmare fantasy proportions during the bloody purges in the Soviet Union in 1937–38. Although legal safeguards (except in certain sensitive agencies or categories) protected most Americans from flagrant abuses, many of the disloyalty charges made during the McCarthy period also had a Kafka-like quality. For example, a brilliant Army intelligence aide was once denounced as being *simultaneously* a double agent of the Vatican

and of the Kremlin because (1) she went daily to Catholic
Lenten services in the Pentagon, and (2) no mere woman
(even an Ivy League product) could know that much about
the U.S.S.R.! Needless to say, these charges were dismissed as
coming from a sick source, which was indeed the case. But
the incident illustrates a principle that is widely applicable:
periods of high political or ideological tension produce so many
irresponsible "loyalty" denunciations that the law of diminishing returns sets in. Especially in small, closed subcultures,
charges that cannot be proved are often dismissed as irresponsible, when they may have a very real basis in fact. Thus traitors
such as Kim Philby undoubtedly benefited from the fact that
British security officials were reluctant to pursue their investiga-
tions vigorously for fear of being charged with "McCarthyism."

The high point of appeasement, the settlement at Munich
in September 1938 by which Czechoslovakia was sacrificed to
Hitler, brought in its wake a backlash of moral revulsion and
personal withdrawal or disengagement. As the French and
British politicians fumbled their way into war, the increasingly
disillusioned attitude of the man in the street was called in
French *je-m'en-foutisme,* freely translated as "To hell with it!"
After a decade of continuous application the corrosive poisons
of both Communist and Nazi propaganda (including anti-
Semitism) had eaten away at the political and social fabric of
French society until it fell apart when war finally came.

The Russian émigrés were naturally affected by the environment in which they lived. The Russian émigré colony in
Paris during the thirties numbered approximately 100,000 and
formed a political and social subculture of its own, based
largely on nostalgic and sentimental ties to the myth of a
"Holy Russia" that existed mainly in the imagination of the
later nineteenth-century Slavophiles. At first the politically
conscious members of the emigration were revolted by the
excesses of the Bolshevik Revolution and war communism.
During those years when the Soviet leadership loudly denounced
Russia's past as bourgeois and imperialist, the émigré intellectuals rightly regarded themselves as "the real custodians of
Russia's historical and cultural heritage and the standard-
bearers and spokesmen for a national Russia generally, as opposed to the world of the Third International." [4]

The introduction of Lenin's New Economic Policy in 1921

and the victory of Stalin and his policy of "Socialism in One Country" by the end of the twenties brought a significant change in the prevailing émigré attitude of hostility to the U.S.S.R. The NEP was widely misinterpreted as a return to traditional Russian patterns, and émigré intellectuals such as Nikolai Ustrialov openly declared their willingness to support the "new" Soviet regime in its defense of traditional Russian national interests. Prominent Russian-American sociologists such as Timasheff and Sorokin argued respectively that the NEP represented a "great retreat" from communism and that the U.S.S.R. was on its way to becoming a democracy under the model 1936 Soviet constitution.[5]

Stalin's doctrine of "Socialism in One Country" inevitably took on strong nationalist overtones. In 1934, following the rise of Hitler, the Stalinist regime turned to nationalistic and patriotic appeals to provide a bond of unity for the Russian masses which Marxist ideology had failed to produce. The new appeal was announced in *Pravda* on June 9, 1934, under the slogan "For the Fatherland, for its honor, glory, might, and prosperity!"[6] Nationalist historians were recalled to their posts and celebrated the tsarist military victories of such generals as Suvorov and Kutuzov. The Stalinist regime identified itself with the tsarist past and its cultural values. In a flood of historical novels and plays Peter the Great and even Ivan the Terrible were made over into Soviet heroes.[7] Based on such appeals, Soviet propaganda supported a repatriation campaign in the midthirties which had its later counterpart after World War II. A typical Soviet Communist-front organization, the Union for the Repatriation of Russians to Russia, was set up at number 12 Rue de Buci in Paris. A contemporary Soviet source states that the organization attracted six thousand to eight thousand members.[8] This is less than 10 per cent of the émigré colony, but nevertheless an impressive figure even if taken at half its face value. Staffed by the OGPU, the purpose of the organization was to screen candidates for repatriation, to weed out enemy *agents provocateurs,* and in many cases to assign applicants tasks or "good works" to prove their good faith. Needless to say, these tasks included spying on other émigrés and émigré organizations and similar OGPU-directed chores. The former Soviet intelligence chief Alexander Orlov writes that at the beginning of the Spanish Civil War in 1936, guerrilla warfare trainees (under a

Soviet commander) included "a sprinkling of German Communists from the International Brigade and about eighty former Russian tsarist officers who hoped to earn the right to return to their motherland." [9]

At the other end of the political spectrum, a significant number of Russian émigrés were attracted to Nazism as a right-wing anticommunist and anti-Semitic ideology. Like many other young men of the period, the younger generation of Russian émigrés was attracted to Nazism as "the wave of the future," one that had already restored Germany to a place in the sun. To many Young Turks in the emigration, *any* rule in Russia would be preferable to the Stalinist dictatorship. They were willing to collaborate with the Nazis in hopes that they could return to Russia as part of an anticommunist crusade, and then later seize control for themselves. Like many of their right-wing counterparts in Germany and elsewhere, they mistakenly thought that they could use Hitler instead of being used by him. During the Spanish Civil War there were Russian émigré volunteers on the Loyalist side, and pressure was put on General Miller, Kutyepov's successor as head of the ROVS, openly to proclaim support of Franco. General Miller, however, refused to commit the ROVS to the support of any foreign cause, however anticommunist or anti-Soviet it might be. He correctly foresaw that in the event of war, White Russians who joined with the Nazis could easily be branded as foreign mercenaries and would be rejected as such by Russian citizens who had no way of defending their native land against the foreign invader without at the same time supporting the hated Stalinist regime. Faced with the threat that members of his organization would be subverted by both the Nazi SD and the Soviet NKVD, General Miller decided to tighten up on security and revived the Inner Line, the internal political screening agency of the ROVS, in 1935. As a concession to the Young Turks in the military organization, he put one of their spokesmen, Major General Skoblin, in charge of the Inner Line. The appointment was also probably made in order to keep a close watch on Skoblin, who for years had been a controversial character and troublemaker within the ROVS. Skoblin's own loyalty had also long been suspected, not without reason, as events were soon to prove. Paris in the thirties was a seedbed of subversion and the Skoblin case is a classic example.

Nikolai Vladimirovich Skoblin, like Soviet Marshal Tukhachevsky, was a talented and ambitious young tsarist officer
who was determined to be either dead or a general by the age
of thirty. Both candidates made the grade, so to speak, but the
contrast between their later careers could hardly be more extreme. Tukhachevsky died a victim of Stalin's bloody purges,
but nonetheless a Soviet hero, who has since been restored to
his rightful place of honor. Skoblin simply vanished and has
never been heard from since, but his disappearance took place
under circumstances that leave no doubt that he was a traitor
to his chief, General Miller, and to the Russian émigré cause.
Skoblin even has the dubious distinction of having served both
the Soviet NKVD and the Nazi SD at the same time, an ambi-
dextrous traitor, so to speak, who was subverted by both the
left and the right extremes.

Little is known of his early career, but Geoffrey Bailey
gives the following character sketch of Skoblin:

> Small of stature, slight of build, with pale, cold, shifty
> eyes and a modest, self-effacing manner, Skoblin had emerged
> from World War I with the reputation of a reckless dare-
> devil, whose natural tactical flare made up for his lack of
> theoretical knowledge (but then these were the typical char-
> acteristics of a good Civil War commander on whichever
> side he happened to fight). Partly because of this, but also be-
> cause of the fantastic losses suffered by the White Volunteer
> Army, he had risen rapidly in its ranks until by 1920, at the
> age of twenty-seven, he was a major general, the commander
> of the crack Kornilov Division and one of the outstanding
> young hopefuls of the White military movement.
>
> And yet already in those early days there were in his
> character certain flaws—a cruelty which went beyond even
> the accepted harshness of civil wars (he made it a point of
> taking no prisoners, torturing and then hanging all captives),
> a ruthlessness bordering on opportunism, which made him a
> controversial personality and helped deny him the respect,
> rewards and recognition his personal courage and gifts of
> leadership seemed otherwise to call for.[10]

Skoblin's wife was equally colorful in her own right:

> Of peasant origin, Nadyezhda or "Nadya" Plevitzkaya
> was still a child when she ran away from home and joined
> a traveling circus. Ten years later she had become Russia's

foremost folk singer, a "Soloist of His Imperial Majesty" (the highest token of musical recognition in Tsarist Russia) and one of the most popular and best-paid artists in the country. The Revolution had interrupted her career but briefly. In 1918, she had followed her husband (who had volunteered with the Red Army) to the front, to entertain the troops with her songs. And when presently she was captured by a patrol of the already famous Kornilov Division, she was soon as popular with the Whites as she had been earlier in the opposite camp. Eventually she became the mistress of young Colonel Skoblin. In 1921 they were married, on Gallipoli, and from that moment on Plevitzkaya appeared invariably in the role of a typical "mother-commander," gay and generous in times of joy, warm and helpful in the hour of need, the "guardian angel" of the Gallipoli veterans, without whose presence and songs no White celebration, no regimental holiday could be viewed as a real success. Only a few knew her for what she was in reality: ignorant and superstitious, but at the same time sly, shrewd, ambitious, hard-boiled and soil-bound and exercising an iron grip over her handsome young husband.[11]

When one reviews what little is known of Skoblin's activities in exile, in retrospect all kinds of evidence appear to indicate that he was a security risk and perhaps an agent of a foreign power rather early in the game. As early as 1920, shortly after the Russian émigré forces under Wrangel evacuated the Crimea, there were rumors that Skoblin's wife had urged him to defect and to return to Russia. General Kutyepov, who was a good judge of character, had always mistrusted Skoblin. In 1923 Mrs. Skoblin had sung to a pro-Soviet audience at a concert in the United States, and Kutyepov had used this incident as grounds for relieving Skoblin of his command. The couple had then settled in Nice, from which they went on concert tours with General Skoblin acting as his wife's impresario and business manager. During the first few years Plevitskaya was a worldwide success. Like most people in show business, however, the Skoblins spent their money lavishly. Her age began to show (Mrs. Skoblin was four years older than her husband), her voice was not what it had been, and all this was reflected in diminishing box-office returns. By 1928 it was rumored that they were in financial difficulties.

Then suddenly, as if they had inherited a large sum of

money, the Skoblins moved from Nice to Paris in the fall of
1928 and bought a comfortable private house in the suburb
of Ozoir-la-Ferrière. Although his wife's earnings were clearly
inadequate to cover their living expenses, General Skoblin made
no attempt to supplement their income by any other job. They
even bought a car of their own—a Peugeot sedan, which was
far more of a status symbol during the Great Depression than
it has been at any time since. Later they took to spending an
average of three nights a week in town at the Hotel Pax, a
modest hotel on the Avenue Victor Hugo off the Champs-
Élysées. They kept their car on such occasions in a neighboring
garage at number 123 Rue de Longchamps, near a Russian
restaurant, the Serdechnyi, and close to the Place de Chaillot.[12]

After the fact, of course, all these indicators added up to
a classic example of the unexplained income and sudden
affluence of the low-level "defector in place" who is paid by
an intelligence agency, in this case the OGPU, for reporting on
his friends and superiors; in other words, espionage. A few
months later General Kutyepov was kidnaped, and there now
seems to be little doubt that Skoblin was one of the local agents
who kept him under constant observation. Plevitskaya even
made a virtue of necessity and, in a great display of grief and
consolation, was constantly at Mrs. Kutyepov's side in the
weeks following the General's disappearance. Captain Galai,
who knew all the principal characters involved, asserts that
there is no evidence that the Skoblins were directly involved
in the Kutyepov kidnaping. La Plevitskaya was certainly *not*
the unidentified woman in the beige coat who figured in the
case, since Mrs. Skoblin's face and figure were too striking to
have escaped positive identification. But the Skoblins dramatic
show of concern and solicitude after the event served to deflect
any possible suspicion from themselves, and was a factor in
their courting favor with General Miller, Kutyepov's successor
as head of the ROVS.

In addition to the category of income and spending habits,
security investigators also inquire into the friends and associates
a given individual keeps. "Intimate association" with known
Communists or Fascists, if proven, is *ipso facto* "derogatory
information" in United States security-clearance procedures.
The story is told of an American official who was called before
a security-review board in the 1950's and discovered, to his

amazement, that a pickup he had met in a New York bar as a young man twenty years earlier was, unknown to him, none other than the wife of a high Communist party functionary. Although admittedly this had indeed been a case of "intimate association," fortunately the U.S. government official was able to prove that the connection had been purely accidental, entirely apolitical, and indicative of nothing more than the sort of transient "moral turpitude" (also a serious charge) associated with flaming youth in the roaring twenties.

General Skoblin's association with suspect individuals and organizations was more than transient and accidental. Both he and his wife admitted having contacted a known Soviet agent in Berlin, Magdenko, a Russian émigré and former lieutenant colonel in the Kornilov Division. Skoblin also frequented the notorious Guchkov circle, with which the Soviet economist Dimitry Navashin had also been associated until his assassination, presumably by the NKVD in January 1937 in the Bois de Boulogne in Paris.

Aleksandr Ivanovich Guchkov was a former chairman of the tsarist *Duma* and for a brief period after the revolution had been a conservative Minister of War in the Provisional Government. In January 1925, while living in Berlin, Guchkov was host to meetings of the "Eurasian Movement," over which the OGPU maintained covert control even after the fall of the Trust. But according to Mikhail Spiegelglass, the deputy chief of the Foreign Division of the OGPU in 1936–37:

> The Guchkov Circle had long worked with General Bredow, Chief of Military Intelligence of the German Army. When General Bredow was executed in the Hitler purge of 1934, his department and all its foreign network came under the control of the Gestapo.[13]

Spiegelglass added that the OGPU link with the Guchkov circle was equally close, and that his agency had a man in the very center of the circle. Events later indicated that the man whom Spiegelglass had in mind was none other than General Skoblin.

By even the most charitable standards of judgment, Skoblin's associations indicated that by the early 1930's he was a doubtful security risk. Moreover, early in 1935 he was openly charged with being a Soviet agent. On February 6, a Paris

Russian-language newspaper, *The Latest News,* published a highly incriminating article in which the names of the principal figures were disguised, to avoid a libel suit, but which left no doubt that the "General xxx" referred to was Skoblin. According to this report, three years earlier, on February 22, 1932, Captain "Z" (Fedossenko) had attended in Berlin a regimental celebration during which he had a number of drinks with a former comrade of civil war days, Lieutenant Colonel Magdenko, who, like himself, had been a member of Skoblin's Kornilov Division. Under the influence of alcohol Magdenko admitted that he was now a Soviet agent working for "Ivanov," the Berlin head of Soviet military intelligence (GRU). He even tried to subvert Fedossenko, who in April 1932 returned to Berlin, joined the network, and himself became a Soviet agent known as "The Mole." Before returning to Berlin, Magdenko reportedly told Fedossenko that General Skoblin had been an agent of the OGPU since 1928.

Returning to Paris, Fedossenko claimed that he was struck by remorse and confessed everything to General Miller, who ordered him to break off all relations with "Ivanov," his GRU contact, and to report the whole matter to the French Sûreté. A few weeks later, according to Fedossenko, he was summarily dropped from the White Russian military organizations to which he belonged, not only the Kornilov Division (General Skoblin's command), but also the ROVS—the all-embracing union organization headed by General Miller. To add insult to injury, he was also scratched as an agent by the GRU.[14] Enraged at this turn of affairs, Fedossenko decided to leak the entire story to the press. Naturally, it created a sensation in émigré circles.

In addition to these scandalous public charges, General Miller had also received confidential reports through official ROVS channels indicating that Skoblin was a security risk. His representative in Finland, the émigré General Dobrovolsky, warned him on August 28 that the Finns had refused to cooperate with the ROVS, since "someone in Paris, and especially in Ozoir-la-Ferrière [Skoblin's residence], would surely betray them." Another warning followed in December that Dobrovolsky himself was breaking off all contact with Skoblin.[15]

Ironically, no official action was taken by the ROVS on these charges until the fall of 1936, when General Skoblin himself demanded that his case be reviewed by a general's court of honor. The hearing was presided over by General Erdeli.[16] The evidence was sifted and Captain Fedossenko was cross-examined, but the key witness in the case, Lieutenant Colonel Magdenko, could not be called, as he was currently imprisoned in a Munich jail. Skoblin was acquitted of the charge of being a Soviet agent by the ROVS court of honor, and later, according to one authority, "apparently enjoyed the full confidence of the Federation [ROVS], even being looked upon as Miller's right-hand man. Undoubtedly, Skoblin himself imagined that he had been completely freed from all suspicion." [17]

It was not until many years later that a Western analyst observed that General Erdeli was approvingly portrayed by Soviet propaganda as one of the "Whites who did not like to be spied upon" and as one who had succeeded in putting General Miller's security service, the Inner Line, out of action in France.[18] Although Soviet propaganda claims may be somewhat exaggerated, other sources indicate that Skoblin's position of personal *rapporteur* on security matters was abolished by General Miller in December 1936. Events later proved that Miller had been able to ease Skoblin out of his sensitive position without arousing undue suspicions on Skoblin's part. Until his disappearance Skoblin continued to believe that he had General Miller's confidence.

At the latest by 1936 Skoblin was a Soviet agent and presumably had been for several years. By then Hitler was firmly entrenched in power, and Heinrich Himmler, the chief of the RSHA, the *Reichs Sicherheits Haupt Amt,* the Nazi Central Security Organization, was busily building up his vast empire of repressive agencies. These included the Kripo, the ordinary criminal police; the Gestapo, the secret political police; and finally a combined intelligence and covert operational agency, the so-called SD *(Sicherheitsdienst)* or Security Service, under Heydrich. The SD was determined to replace German military intelligence and had stationed officers in embassies abroad who in turn recruited networks of informers or espionage agents. Skoblin was a leader of the pro-Hitler faction of the Paris émigrés, and was probably among the first to be recruited as a German agent by the SD sometime toward the end of 1936. Heydrich was not disturbed by the fact that Skoblin worked the other side of the street and also spied on the Paris emigration for the NKVD.[19] Undoubtedly his Soviet contacts also knew that Skoblin reported to Heydrich, and could thus be used to plant information in German intelligence channels. In the sequel, the Tukhachevsky affair, both powers, Nazi Germany and the Soviet Union, discovered that double agents such as Skoblin have their uses. But before Stalin's purge of the Red Army began in mid-1937, Skoblin was to play a key role in the kidnaping of General Miller and himself disappear from the scene forever.

14
THE KIDNAPING OF
GENERAL MILLER

EARLY IN
September 1937 Swiss newspapers carried the story that the bullet-ridden body of a man had been discovered on the Chamblandes road outside Lausanne. The body was that of a man in his late forties who had apparently been in robust health. There were seven machine-gun bullets in the torso and five in the head. One of the dead man's hands still clutched some strands of an unknown woman's hair. Perhaps the murder was a *crime passionel,* since the victim had not been robbed. He carried a Czechoslovakian passport bearing the name of Hans Eberhardt. The efficient Swiss police soon established the fact that the body was really that of Ignatz Reisz, a professional revolutionary of Polish origin who had served the U.S.S.R. for many years, first as an undercover agent of the Comintern and then of the Cheka, OGPU, and NKVD in turn.[1] Like many other Old Bolsheviks, he had been revolted by the first of the purge trials in August 1936, and for months had brooded about the execution of Zinoviev, Kamenev, and the fourteen additional victims. A few weeks before his death, while in Paris, he had drafted a letter of resignation from the NKVD addressed to the Central Committee of the Communist party of the U.S.S.R. in which he wrote in part:

> The letter which I am addressing to you today I should have written a long time ago, on the day the Sixteen were murdered in the cellars of the Lubianka at the command of

"The Father of the People." I kept silent then. I raised no voice of protest at the subsequent murders. . . .

Up to now I have followed you—from now on, not a step farther. Here our ways part! He who keeps silent at this hour becomes an accomplice of Stalin and a traitor to the cause of the working class and of Socialism . . . Behind me are sixteen years of underground service; that is no trifle—but I still have enough strength to begin all over again. For the salvation of Socialism requires a "New Beginning." The struggle commenced a long time ago; I shall join it . . . I am returning to freedom. Back to Lenin, to his teachings and his cause.

P.S. In 1928 I was awarded the Order of the Red Banner for services to the proletarian revolution. I am returning it herewith. To wear it simultaneously with the hangmen of the past representatives of the Russian workers is beneath my dignity.[2]

Instead of mailing the letter, Reisz made the mistake of giving it to Lydia Grosovsky, the wife of a member of the Soviet Trade Commission in Paris. She turned it over to Mikhail Spiegelglass, the deputy chief of the NKVD's Foreign Section, who had recently arrived to conduct a purge of Soviet organizations abroad. Although Reisz immediately went into hiding with his wife and child in a suburb of Lausanne, the NKVD soon tracked him down. He was murdered by two principal Soviet agents from Paris, Roland Abbiat, alias Rossi, and Etienne Martignat, assisted by an NKVD agent from Rome, Gertrude Schildbach. Gertrude had long been a close friend of the family. In her hotel room at Lausanne, which she had left suddenly, leaving her luggage behind, the police found a box of strychnine-impregnated chocolates. Apparently she had not been able to bring herself to give the chocolates to Mrs. Reisz, although she had had ample opportunity to do so before the actual assassination took place.[3] The strands of hair clutched in the dead man's hand were identified as Gertrude Schildbach's; she had obviously been used as a decoy by the murderers.

When the police investigation led to the Soviet Trade Commission in Paris, Grosovsky and a man named Beletsky suddenly left for Moscow before they could be interrogated. The Soviet embassy brought heavy pressure to bear to bury the case, but Grosovsky's wife, Lydia, was questioned by the police on December 11, and of course pleaded total ignorance of the affair. Because of the Franco-Soviet pact, the French government was clearly not interested in embarrassing the U.S.S.R. over a murder that had not even occurred on French soil. When the Swiss government demanded Mrs. Grosovsky's arrest on an extradition demand a week later, on December 17, she was soon released on the modest bail of 50,000 francs. She was supposedly kept under surveillance by the French police. Unfortunately they had only a ten-horsepower car for this purpose, while Mrs. Grosovsky had the use of a powerful American automobile provided by the Soviet Trade Commission. She went out one day in the car, easily outdistanced the French police who were trailing her, and never returned.[4] The public memory is short, but some observers recalled that six years earlier, when General Kutyepov had been kidnaped, the two OGPU agents presumably involved, Yanovich and Helfand, had also suddenly left Paris for Moscow, and that Mrs. Yanovich was whisked away to Belgium a few days later in the Soviet ambassador's personal car, which enjoyed police immunity.

It seems that the assignment to organize the assassination of Reisz had originally been given to one of his old friends and colleagues, the Soviet intelligence agent Walter Krivitsky, who simply refused the task and defected on December 5, 1937, at the height of the Great Purge in the U.S.S.R. Four years later Krivitsky himself was found in the Hotel Bellevue in Washington, D.C., shot through the head. His memoirs, *I Was Stalin's Agent,* are an important source of fairly reliable information on OGPU-NKVD operations. Clearly he knew too much, and since Stalin accepted no resignations from his team, Krivitsky had to go, just like his old friend Reisz before him. But in Stalin's book, how much was "too much"? There is no precise answer to this question. Almost the entire circle of Old Bolsheviks was exterminated before the Great Purges of 1937–38 were over. It should come as no surprise, then, that there was a series of political assassinations about the same time in Europe. These are analyzed in some detail in Hugo Dewar's authoritative *Assassins at Large.*[5]

Apparently early in December the deputy chief of the NKVD, Nikolai I. Yezhov, was ordered by Stalin to set up under his personal command a special top-secret group called the Spetsburo, or Administration of Special Tasks. This group was to carry out sensitive political operations at home and abroad, including kidnapings, murders, and provocations, some on an international scale involving the shifting of undercover agents from one theater of operations to another. Such, for example, was an operation for which Krivitsky had to supply two agents, but which was postponed, or rather which stopped at the stage of a partial dry run.

Dry Run in Paris

In his memoirs Krivitsky writes that during the first week in December 1936 he was in The Hague, where he ran a network of undercover agents in Germany, when suddenly a courier arrived from Spain with an urgent message on microfilm from A. A. Slutsky (Artuzov), then chief of the Foreign Division of the NKVD. When the microfilm was developed, it revealed the following message:

> Select from your personnel two men who can impersonate German officers. They must be impressive enough in appearance to pass for military attachés, must be accustomed to talk like army men, and must be exceptionally trustworthy and bold. Assign them to me without delay. This is of extraordinary importance. Expect to see you in Paris in a few days.[6]

Although Krivitsky was annoyed at the loss it would mean to his own operations in Germany, he ordered two suitable agents to proceed at once to Paris and arrived there himself two days later for a meeting with Slutsky. Over dinner at a Persian restaurant near the Place de l'Opéra, still resenting the loss of two of his best agents, Krivitsky asked his chief: "What the devil are you up to? Don't you people realize what you're doing?"

Slutsky answered: "Of course we do, but this is no routine affair. It involves a case of such colossal importance that I have had to drop all my other work and come here to put it through . . . If you must have it, the order is from Yezhov himself." [7]

Krivitsky heard nothing more of this "colossally important" case until several weeks later, when his two agents returned to regular duty reporting that they had been kept idle in Paris until suddenly dismissed with the explanation that "the job had been postponed." [8] He was never informed what the planned operation was, but while on a visit to Moscow in May 1937, in the corridors of the Lubyanka he ran into a colleague, Furmanov, who was responsible for counterespionage operations among White Russians abroad. Furmanov complimented him on having provided him with "a couple of first-rate men," the two who had cooled their heels in Paris on the undertaking that had been postponed six months earlier, during December 1936. Furmanov volunteered no further information, but Krivitsky knew that his colleague handled such organizations as the ROVS, General Miller's military organization, and concluded that his two men "had been commandeered for an undertaking connected with this White Russian group in France." [9]

Krivitsky returned to The Hague in May 1937, but was back in Paris again in July for a meeting with Spiegelglass, deputy chief of the Foreign Division of the OGPU. They met at Ernest Hemingway's favorite café, the Closerie des Lilas on the Boulevard Montparnasse, and Spiegelglass told him that, like Slutsky seven months earlier, he was on an "especially important mission." In the course of an animated conversation about agent networks and intelligence sources, Spiegelglass boasted that his division got its information from Germany "from inside sources. Ours doesn't come from salon conversations, but from within the Gestapo itself," and that they had been receiving such material "for the past several years." Upon further probing, Spiegelglass volunteered the information that one of his best sources of information was none other than the Guchkov circle, a group of White Russians which Krivitsky described as "having intimate links with the German Military Intelligence on the one hand, on the other close ties with the Federation of Tsarist Army Veterans [the ROVS] headed by General Eugene Miller in Paris." [10]

As previously noted, a key figure in the Guchkov circle was General Skoblin, who had previously been Miller's personal *rapporteur* on the ROVS Inner Line, with the task of screening security risks. Rarely, to borrow one of Nikita Khrushchev's expressions, has a hungrier goat been put in charge of a more inviting cabbage patch. Skoblin had been dismissed from this sensitive post in December 1936, presumably after Miller had received a warning from his agent in Finland that the Finns regarded Skoblin as a Soviet agent. But in the nine months that had since elapsed, Skoblin—at least so he thought—had regained his chief's confidence. Spiegelglass must have thought so too, since the operation for which he remained in Paris from July through late September hinged on this contingency.

The Generals Vanish

On September 22, 1937, about 10:30 A.M., General Miller arrived at his office at number 29 Rue du Colisée. As he was about to leave, at 12:10 P.M., he turned to his aide, the aging general Pavel A. Kussonsky, with the remark: "Do not think that I have gone out of my mind, but this time I am leaving a sealed message which I ask you to open only in case I do not return." [11]

Miller was due back at ROVS headquarters at 5 P.M. for an appointment with a group of émigré Russian veterans of the Northern White Army, but he failed to appear. By 8 P.M. Asmolov, the janitor who lived on the premises, called Mrs. Miller to see if he had returned directly home. He had not, and with the precedent of General Kutyepov's kidnaping six years earlier very much in mind, Mrs. Miller was alarmed when he could not be located.

Finally, after being summoned to an emergency meeting at about 11 P.M., Kussonsky remembered the sealed envelope that General Miller had left with him at noon to be opened in just such an emergency. The message read:

> I have an appointment at 12:30 today with General Skoblin at the corner of Jasmin and Raffet streets. He is to take me to a rendezvous with two German officers, one a military attaché in a neighboring country, Strohman, a colonel, the other, Herr Werner, who is attached to the local German Embassy. Both these men speak Russian well. The meeting has been arranged at the initiative of Skoblin. It is possible that this is a trap, and that is why I am leaving this notice.[12]

In spite of the hour (it was about 1 A.M. by then), General Skoblin, who with his wife was spending the night in town at their usual quarters in the Hotel Pax on the Avenue Victor Hugo, was summoned by his fellow officers to a showdown meeting at ROVS headquarters. He denied everything, in spite of the documentary evidence of the note, insisting that at 12:30

he had been lunching with his wife at the Serdechnyi restaurant on the Rue de Longchamps near the Place de Chaillot. He readily agreed with the suggestion that they should go to the police, but on the way out took advantage of a momentary lapse of vigilance on the part of the others (according to one version he asked to go to the men's room) and disappeared. This was the last that his fellow officers ever saw of him, and when they arrived at the local police station on the Place Dauphine, they had to report that both General Miller and General Skoblin had vanished.

Miller was never seen again, but about 4 A.M., when the French police began their official investigation, Mrs. Krivosheyeva, the wife of an émigré captain who owned the Kama bookstore at number 27 Avenue de Villiers in Neuilly-sûr-Seine, was awakened by persistent knocking. In response to her inquiry, General Skoblin identified himself and asked to see her husband, who had already left to sell émigré Russian newspapers at the Richelieu-Druot *métro* station. When invited in, Skoblin, who was disheveled and a little nervous, asked for a drink of water, which he gulped down, and then, with some embarrassment, borrowed 200 francs, since, as he explained, he had stupidly lost his wallet, and didn't even have carfare home. Of course, Mrs. Krivosheyeva never saw her 200 francs or General Skoblin again—nor did anyone else, except those undercover agents who presumably arranged his escape to the U.S.S.R. To this day it is not known whether he was given asylum or quietly liquidated. One thing, however, is certain: with only 200 francs in his pocket he did not travel far and conceal his identity during the man hunt that followed his disappearance without the kind of assistance that only a major covert operational agency can provide.

In sharp contrast to Skoblin's lack of funds, his wife, Plevitskaya, at the time of her arrest was carrying 7,500 francs, 50 English pounds, and 50 U.S. dollars in her purse. Her apparently foolproof alibi, accounting for all the movements of herself and Skoblin on the day of the kidnaping, broke down under police interrogation. A search of their house at Ozoir-la-Ferrière revealed that Skoblin possessed all the paraphernalia of a major espionage agent: three types of ciphers, four Yugoslav passports, and some four hundred kilograms of files and documents. The fact that none of this incriminating evidence

had been destroyed indicates that Skoblin had been caught un-
prepared for the unexpected ending to what promised to be a
flawless repetition of the kidnaping of General Kutyepov six
years earlier. Perhaps he had not been present when, in discussing the disappearance of his former chief, General Miller
remarked: "When one goes to a suspicious rendezvous, one
leaves behind a letter. That is also what Kutyepov should have
done." [13]

Most observers were convinced that General Miller had
been kidnaped by NKVD agents, but, again as in the Kutyepov
case, the evidence was indirect. When the police visited the
site of General Miller's rendezvous with Skoblin and the
"German officers," they found that in the surrounding neighborhood there was only a small milk shop (closed during the
lunch hour) from which the meeting could be observed. The
nearby buildings were either Soviet-leased or occupied by Soviet
officials, including the NKVD "resident" or chief, who used the
commercial front of the Soviet Trade Commission. Only a
block up the street, at number 41 Boulevard Montmorency, the
Soviet ambassador, Potyemkin, had leased a villa that had
been used as a school for children of Soviet officials. In spite
of the fact that the school was not in session at the time, some
activity had been noted around the villa for several days, and at
1 P.M. on the day of the kidnaping a gray Ford truck was
observed parked outside the gate.

At about the same time (shortly before one o'clock on
Wednesday the twenty-second), a White Russian veteran of
the Gallipoli Association, who knew both Miller and Skoblin
personally, happened to be standing on the balcony of a house
across the street from the villa. He recognized both generals,
who seemed to be arguing on the sidewalk outside the villa
while a third, unknown individual looked on. A few minutes
later all three had disappeared, but the gray Ford truck was
still parked outside the gate. Skoblin was also recognized
somewhat later in the day as one of two Russian-speaking
foreigners standing at the entrance to the *métro* station
Jasmin.[14]

In spite of these clues pointing toward Soviet involvement
in the affair, the French police, presumably as a result of
government pressure, delayed six weeks before searching the
villa at number 41 Boulevard Montmorency, and then only as

a result of a moving appeal from General Miller's widow addressed to President Lebrun. Naturally, at this late date, the search yielded nothing.

Sometime around 4 P.M. on the afternoon of the twenty-second the Soviet embassy truck pulled up alongside a Russian freighter, the *Maria Ulyanova,* at Le Havre, and French customs officials observed three Russian sailors while they unloaded a large, heavy trunk which was then carried on board the ship. A French maritime broker who usually handled Soviet business, and who was talking with the captain of the *Maria Ulyanova* when the incident took place, later noticed that the truck had a Paris registration number. The ship was not scheduled to leave for Leningrad until the twenty-seventh. However, in violation of harbor regulations, the captain suddenly weighed anchor five days early and, without notifying the harbor police, slipped out to sea that same evening, leaving unloaded cargo on the docks. These circumstances were so suspicious that the French government at first considered sending a destroyer to overtake the *Maria Ulyanova* and force it to return to Le Havre for a proper inspection, but the French Minister of the Interior intervened and the idea was dropped. French statesmen were naturally reluctant to create an incident that might hinder the cooperation of their ally under the Franco-Soviet pact, and which could be exploited by Hitler and Mussolini to poison the atmosphere further. M. Chovineau, the alert special police commissioner in Le Havre who had first reported the incident, was later reassigned to a menial job and resigned the service, convinced that he had been victimized. According to one analysis of the affair: "All this left a bad taste in the mouth of the public; there was a widespread suspicion . . . that a solution of the Miller case was being hampered by considerations of high politics." [15]

Technically, like the parallel case of General Kutyepov, the kidnaping of General Miller still remains unsolved, although all the circumstantial evidence points to the complicity of the OGPU-NKVD. Some analysts, such as Vladimir L. Burtsev, were convinced that Miller was first murdered by NKVD agents in the Soviet villa on the Boulevard Montmorency and that his corpse was then spirited away on the *Maria Ulyanova.*[16]

On October 25, 1937, the French police arrested Skoblin's wife, Nadezhda Plevitskaya, as an accomplice in the kidnaping

of General Miller. Her trial, which was delayed for more than
a year, began on December 5, 1938, and lasted through December 14. It was one of the *causes célèbres* of the day and
public feeling ran high. The Soviet defector Bessedovsky testified that in 1927 he had overheard an OGPU official boast that
their agent among the Russian émigrés in Paris was "a White
general, married to a singer." [17] Only Skoblin fitted this description. There was a dramatic scene in which Plevitskaya was
confronted with Mrs. Miller, whose friendship she had cultivated for six years, and who begged her to tell all she knew.
Mrs. Skoblin stubbornly denied any inside knowledge of
General Miller's abduction, but she did volunteer the strange
remark that by that time she imagined that both the vanished
generals were safely in the U.S.S.R. She even suggested that
she be allowed to go there herself, as she was sure she would
be able to find the missing men.

But the court had other plans for her, and on December
14, 1938, Mrs. Skoblin was convicted and sentenced to twenty
years' hard labor, one of the harshest peacetime sentences ever
handed down against a woman by French justice. La Plevitskaya served only six years of her sentence. She died in Rennes
prison for women in October 1944, still faithful to the cause in
which she had reportedly enlisted her husband, and carrying
whatever secrets she guarded with her to the grave.[18]

General Miller was a harmless, elderly man of sixty-seven
when he vanished. During the six years of his stewardship as
head of the ROVS, aggressive covert operations against the
U.S.S.R. had been abandoned. The few survivors of General
Kutyepov's Combat Corps had scattered and returned to normal peaceful pursuits. Georgi Radkovich's bomb hurled in the
headquarters of the Lubyanka was the last of such gestures.
With networks of NKVD-controlled agents, including General
Skoblin, at the very center of their military organizations, the
Kremlin knew that it had nothing to fear from the Russian
émigrés abroad. Under these circumstances the questions arose
then and still puzzle analysts: Why was General Miller kidnaped? What compelling motive led to the liquidation of *both*
Miller and Skoblin?

In the earlier Kutyepov case it was presumed that a major
show trial was planned, an objective thwarted by his death.
France at the time was ruled by a hostile anti-Soviet govern-

ment, the U.S.S.R. had just emerged from a genuine war scare, and a show trial could have been used to propagandize the bugaboo of a renewed Allied intervention. But by the time of General Miller's disappearance in September 1937 the international situation had changed almost beyond recognition with the rise to power of Adolf Hitler and the prospect of a second world war looming on the horizon. The U.S.S.R., after denouncing the League of Nations for years as a "league of brigands," joined it in September 1934 in the hope that it might be possible to create some kind of "collective security" against the menace of a Germany that had been secretly rearming (with Soviet help) for several years. In May 1935 the U.S.S.R. forged the first links in what it hoped might develop into an effective alliance against Hitler. A mutual-assistance treaty was signed with France on May 2, 1935, followed by a similar treaty with Czechoslovakia on May 16. However, not to be caught short by any possible French defection, the Soviet Union made her pledge to come to Czechoslovakia's aid dependent on France's doing likewise. Finally, in 1935, the Comintern switched its propaganda from the isolationism of the 1928 "hard line" and began to beat the drums for the formation of a so-called popular front against war and fascism. Although the Franco-Soviet pact was drawn up in May 1935, it was a full year before it was ratified by the French Assembly on May 27, 1936, and the following week Hitler occupied the Rhineland, his first and boldest bid to overturn the status quo, and one to which France and England responded with no more than talk. Ironically, Hitler used the ratification of the Franco-Soviet pact as the pretext for this move. Coming as it did in September 1937, the Miller kidnaping might have seriously disturbed French-Soviet relations, although, as we have seen, the Soviet government was spared the embarrassment of having the *Maria Ulyanova* forcibly seized and searched by the French Navy. Since Skoblin's wife, Plevitskaya, was no longer a Russian citizen, the U.S.S.R. was indifferent to her fate, and Soviet propaganda blamed the Miller affair, not implausibly, on Hitler's SD.[19]

Since under these political circumstances the U.S.S.R. might better have left Generals Miller and Skoblin alone, why, in the last analysis, was the powerful organizational apparatus of the NKVD set in motion to eliminate an apparently inoffensive old man in Paris? Perhaps the only kind of answer that makes sense can be suggested by analogy. When a gangland figure is suddenly liquidated, the two most logical motives that suggest themselves to the police are (1) revenge and (2) the probability that the victim knew too much. Revenge can be excluded in General Miller's case, but the presumption that Miller and Skoblin knew too much remains. But this line of reasoning apparently raises as many questions as it answers. For example, they knew too much about what? And why should such knowledge require that they be liquidated? Plausible answers to these questions are extremely complex and are related to the whole tangled skein of developments which led to the breakdown of the Franco-Soviet alliance against Hitler, and to the bloody purge of the Soviet military establishment. These developments are taken up in the next part of the book. The Tukhachevsky affair marked the beginning of the military purge. Paradoxically, the purges in turn paved the way for Stalin's deal with Hitler, which touched off World War II.

PART 4
THE TUKHACHEVSKY
AFFAIR

SECRET SOVIET-GERMAN MILITARY COLLABORATION

T HE TUKHACHEVSKY
affair was far more than a minor intelligence or disinformation
operation. The credibility of the conspiracy story (that Tukhachevsky and his colleagues were plotting the overthrow of
Stalin in cahoots with German generals) derived from the
tangled and often contradictory course of Soviet foreign policy
over the preceding two decades. It began with the story of
secret German-Soviet military collaboration up to the advent
of Hitler, for falsified documents of this period provided evidence on which the case against the Soviet generals was based.

Having at last decided that National Socialist Germany
was a threat to the peace in the spring of 1935, Stalin sought
the open support of France and England in an alliance system
which, if given military teeth, might conceivably have frustrated
Hitler's expansionist aims. But even before Hitler occupied the
Rhineland in 1936 and the French generals proved themselves
to be somewhat reluctant tigers, Stalin secretly began private
approaches to Hitler, using NKVD channels. These early feelers
were fruitless, but when taken up again later they led eventually
to the Nazi-Soviet pact of August 1939 and to the outbreak
of war. Meanwhile, in order to wipe the slate clean of any
possible opposition, either political or military, Stalin instigated
the Great Purges of 1936–38. In order to build up a credible
case against his military leaders, he spread false rumors of

their collaboration with German generals in the so-called Tukhachevsky conspiracy.

An examination of the evidence leads to the conclusion that Stalin conceived the operation at the latest by 1935–36, when the original disinformation was planted in Paris with General Skoblin, who, as we have seen, had become a double agent of both the Soviet and German intelligence services. The tragic drama unfolded slowly and in deepest secrecy over the next two years until it finally broke in the military purge of June 1937. Two years later, when Hitler turned against Stalin (to the latter's astonishment) and Nazi armies stormed into the U.S.S.R., the enormous Russian casualties and prisoner-of-war losses were part of the ultimate cost of Stalin's successful but disastrous intelligence caper. Before turning to these later developments, let us first look at a brief sketch of the central figure in the Tukhachevsky affair.

A Red Star Is Born

Mikhail N. Tukhachevsky was born in Penza in 1893. His family was poor but aristocratic and boasted of two grand pianos at which Anton Rubinstein, the composer, used to play. The young Misha, like another young aristocrat of an earlier generation, Peter Alekseyevich Kropotkin, was first introduced to military and court life as a page in the Imperial Cadet Corps. But unlike Kropotkin, who was revolted by the repressive court atmosphere and became an "anarchist prince," the young Tukhachevsky went on to the Aleksandrovsky Military Academy and was commissioned as a junior lieutenant in 1914 as World War I began. He was then twenty-one and eager to win fame on the battlefield. But his dreams of military prowess were cut short a year later when he was taken prisoner by the Germans on the eastern front. Five times he tried to escape, only to be recaptured each time. On the last occasion he was lodged in the maximum-security fortress of Ingolstadt in Camp IX, along with a young French captain by the name of Charles de Gaulle.

Tukhachevsky impressed his fellow prisoners with his brooding ambition, his Russophilism, and his determination to find an outlet for his restless energies in war. He once said to a fellow prisoner, "To me war is everything. At thirty I shall be either a general or dead." [1] He was unable to escape from Ingolstadt until 1917 and did not reach Moscow until late that autumn, after the Bolshevik seizure of power and the beginning of the civil war. Casting his lot with the Bolsheviks rather than the White armies, he was first assigned to training troops in the Moscow area, where he drew the attention of War Commissar Trotsky. Tukhachevsky joined the Communist party in April 1918 and by early summer was sent to the eastern front to take over as a Red Army division commander. The revolt of the Czech legion had created a confused critical situation in this, the upper Volga area.

Thanks to Trotsky's patronage, Tukhachevsky was given command of the First Red Army, which took Simbirsk in September 1918. The following March he commanded the Fifth Red Army and, crossing the Urals, played an outstanding role in the Soviet counteroffensive against the armies of the White admiral Kolchak. Described as "brilliant, quick of mind, with a streak of cruelty allied to an impetuousness which bordered on the rash, Tukhachevsky displayed strategic talents and tactical abilities of a conspicuously high order," which made him "on more than one occasion the saviour of the Eastern front." [2] In January 1920 he was transferred to the northern Caucasus, but by April the Poles were menacing in the west, and to meet this challenge Tukhachevsky was put in command of all Soviet forces on the western front, at the age of twenty-seven. A Red star was born, and the scrappy prisoner had made good his boast of achieving fame or death before he was thirty.

The Polish campaign began disastrously for the Soviets as General Jozef Pilsudski's forces moved into the western Ukraine and took Kiev. The Soviets launched a smashing counteroffensive which by August brought the Red Army almost to Warsaw. The city might have fallen if Yegorov, in command of the southern flank with the First Cavalry Army, had given Tukhachevsky the support he requested instead of driving west to Lvov. Significantly, Stalin was Yegorov's political commissar at the time. Both Lenin and Trotsky had to intervene personally to redirect the First Cavalry Army toward Warsaw, but by then Tukhachevsky's left flank was overextended, and soon the Red forces were compelled to retreat into home territory. A dispute over the strategic blunders of the Polish campaign continued in the highest Soviet military circles for years, although Tukhachevsky's reputation emerged unscathed. If anything, it was enhanced, and the young commander was called upon to crush the Kronstadt mutiny in March 1921 and a peasant uprising in Tambov later that spring.

Throughout the 1920's Tukhachevsky served in alternate staff and command positions and in 1931 was appointed to the Commissariat of Defense as deputy to its chief, Kliment E. Voroshilov. As chief of ordnance, Tukhachevsky was responsible for weapons development and modernization of the Red Army. Like his former fellow prisoner de Gaulle, he favored a professional army and pioneered in the development of both armor and parachute troops. Unlike de Gaulle, Tukhachevsky had gathered around him a group of young professionals and other admirers who were devoted to his teachings. His star continued to rise, and it reached its zenith in 1935, when, at the age of forty-two, he became one of the first five marshals of the Soviet Union, along with Voroshilov, Budenny, Blyukher, and Yegorov. Of this shining constellation only two remain alive today, Voroshilov and Budenny. The others had all been shot or had disappeared within three years as Stalin decimated the Soviet high command in the 1937–38 purges.

Special Division R: German-Soviet Military Collaboration

Both Germany and the U.S.S.R. were excluded from the negotiations that led to the Versailles Treaty and thus in the immediate postwar period were known as "the outcasts of Versailles." Nothing could have been more natural, since misery loves company, than their subsequent getting together, a rapprochement formalized in the famous Treaty of Rapallo of April 1922, which alarmed and astonished the rest of Europe. Long before this dramatic event, representatives of both powers had laid the groundwork for a mutually profitable military collaboration which lasted until the rise to power of Hitler, and which was one of the best-guarded secrets of the interwar period. Thanks to this cooperation, Germany was able to bypass some of the disarmament provisions of the Versailles Treaty and to achieve a substantial degree of military training and preparation so that Hitler could fling his military challenge to the Western world less than five years after seizing power.

It all began in the Berlin Moabit prison in February

1919. Karl Radek, one of the Bolshevik leaders who had taken part in the abortive Berlin uprising known as the Spartacus Rebellion, had been thrown in jail and, according to his account, treated rather roughly at first. Gradually, however, he was given better treatment and even permitted to obtain German and foreign newspapers. From the London *Times* he found out that the Soviet government of the Ukraine had appointed him its ambassador in an attempt to spring him from prison. His jailers were unimpressed with his newly acquired rank, but soon afterward he was presented with a fancy chamber pot, which he describes as "a present of prime necessity," observing: "I immediately came to the conclusion that the affair was a strange reflection of some kind of change in world politics . . . 'Small causes frequently have great consequences,' said some ancient . . . Here great causes led to tiny consequences." [3]

Radek was soon transferred to a comfortable room in the prison, and his quarters "turned into a political salon, where young Communist leaders came for advice, statesmen to air their views—and officers to talk about possible military collaboration, particularly against Poland." [4] Among Radek's distinguished visitors were Walther Rathenau (German Foreign Minister at the time of the Rapallo Treaty), General Baron Eugen von Reibnitz, and Admiral Hintze. Although Radek was not an officially accredited representative of the U.S.S.R., these friendly exploratory talks went on for months until his repatriation in January 1920. Meanwhile, Walther Rathenau had set up a high-level industrial "study commission" to investigate the Soviet scene, and sometime late in 1920 General Hans von Seeckt, head of the German War Ministry, organized the top-secret "Special Group R" (which was soon expanded to a division) to conduct whatever military collaboration might be arranged with the Red Army. The latter had already proved itself to be an effective fighting force when Tukhachevsky drove to the gates of Warsaw, as we have seen. Special Division R established offices in both Berlin and Moscow. Colonel von der Lieth-Thomsen, one of Germany's leading flying officers, was put in charge of the Moscow office, known as *Zentrale Moskau*.[5] His deputy was "Herr Neuman," the cover name used by Oskar von Niedermayer, a colorful major who had acquired fame during World War I as leader of a German military expedition to Afghanistan, and thought of himself as a sort of German Lawrence of Arabia. To handle military-industrial arrangements the War Ministry organized a sort of holding company with the deceptively innocent name of Trade Enterprises Development Company, known as GEFU (from the initials of its name in German, *Gesellschaft zur Förderung gewerblicher Unternehmungen*). By 1923 a capital fund of 75 million gold reichsmarks (about $18 million) had been provided. Contracts signed in 1922 and 1923 granted the Junkers Corporation concessions for the manufacture of airplane motors at Fili, a suburb of Moscow. A joint stock company, Bersol, was founded for manufacturing poison gases at Trotsk in Samara province. German technicians assisted the Russians in manufacturing ammunition at plants in Zlatoust, Tula, and Petrograd.[6] In return, the German War Ministry received a share of the production. For example, in September 1926 three Russian boats delivered 300,000 shells plus gunpowder and fuses disguised as pig iron or aluminum.[7] It was in connection with this shipment that the first major leak occurred. The agreement with Junkers aircraft provided for an annual production of 300 machines, of which the Russians took 60 in return for supplying raw materials and labor to assist the German technicians.[8]

Even more important than these joint research and development projects were the agreements providing schools for training personnel and testing weapons. The Germans needed and obtained a flying school near Lipetsk in Tambov province, about 250 miles southeast of Moscow. A regular staff of sixty German military and civilian instructors, aided by an additional hundred technicians, provided the training, and by 1925, disguised as Squadron 4 of the Red Air Force, the German *Luftwaffe* was born. At the Lipetsk "private flying school" about 120 fighter pilots were trained by 1933, plus an additional 100 aerial observers. Many of these trainees later became leading officers of the *Luftwaffe*.[9]

A comparable tank-training school, called a "heavy vehicle experimental and test station," was set up on the river Kama, near the town of Kazan.[10] Although the Soviets signed an agreement establishing the school in December 1926, they at first refused to lend any tanks, and the opening was delayed until the spring of 1929. By then the German firms of Krupp, Daimler, and Rheinmetall had built their first "light tractors," as they were called, the prototypes of the later German *Panzerwagen*.[11] The first shipment of six tanks, which were transported in sections and then reassembled at the Kazan school, arrived in August 1929. In addition to the German source of supply, the Soviet government placed an order for some sixty tanks with the British Board of Trade in March 1930. Since the U.S.S.R. had no automotive or tractor industry of any importance before 1932, the first Soviet experiments with tanks and their use in war took place in close collaboration with the German technicians assigned to the Kazan school.[12]

For their part, the Soviet armed forces benefited greatly from the exchange of officers and observers. In this phase of collaboration an estimated "minimum of 120 Soviet senior officers passed through German training courses or were attached for training to German units." [13] After a 7,000-mile inspection tour of Red Army units in the summer of 1931, the German military attaché Colonel (later General) Ernst Köstring observed that German military influence was visible in all aspects of the Soviet Army: "Our views and methods go through theirs like a red thread." [14]

German-Soviet military collaboration lasted for almost twelve years. One authority has summarized the mutually advantageous results as follows:

> . . . There seems little doubt that both armies had considerably profited from it, and that the rapid German rearmament, especially in the air, would have been impossible without this preliminary work. It should be borne in mind, however, that the Red Army too, with its lack of technical experience, had learnt a great deal from its German instructors and from the German plans and designs handed over to it—on balance it was perhaps the chief gainer. It is one of the ironies of history that the two armies were to show on the battlefield how much they had gained from the secret understanding that came to an end a mere eight years before Hitler decided upon the invasion of Soviet Russia.[15]

The fact that German-Soviet military collaboration was taking place was kept secret from the rest of the world for at least four years. This is a remarkable security achievement for an operation of such scope and magnitude. The War Ministry played its cards very close to the chest. The military exchange of personnel was handled exclusively by the Berlin office and the *Zentrale Moskau* of Special Division R, rather than through either the German embassy in Moscow or the military attaché's office. As a result, according to Gustav Hilger, a key figure in collaboration on the diplomatic level, "the government appears to have lost not only control over German-Soviet military collaboration, but seems to have had only the sketchiest knowledge of the activities and deals of [General] von Seeckt and his officers . . . German officers in Russia made wholly irresponsible statements and proposed fantastic deals . . . [which later] were nothing but a source of embarrassment" to the German ambassador.[16] The story broke and the whole operation was blown when the *Manchester Guardian* published an article full of revelations on the subject in December 1926. Following this exposure in the press, an attack by the Social Democratic deputy Scheidemann brought about the fall of the German cabinet. The Social Democratic newspaper *Vorwärts* speculated gleefully that the German Army troops that had bloodily suppressed the 1923 Communist uprisings had probably used Russian-made ammunition to do the job.[17]

The furor in the press led to nothing more than a token investigation by the Foreign Affairs Committee of the Reichstag. The entire matter was quickly hushed up, and the military collaboration not only continued but was intensified. The Socialist deputy Scheidemann, who had raised the scandal in the Reichstag, was even branded a traitor by conservatives. In spite of Socialist propaganda put forth as a matter of longstanding principle against armaments and war, evasion of the Versailles Treaty provisions and the rearmament program were broadly supported by the German public. A program of such scope and magnitude could be kept secret only because it rested on a genuine consensus. According to Gustav Hilger: "In the opinion of the solid, respectable citizen, the military affairs of the Reich were beyond public discussion." He adds:

> The German judiciary also cooperated to keep the critics and tattlers quiet. When the *Münchener Post,* on January 19, 1927, published the names of Reichswehr officers on temporary duty in Russia, its editor was indicted for treason. In the summer of 1930 a Captain Amlinger crashed while testing a fighter plane in Russia, and his widow published the customary death notice with the

remark that her husband had died "for his German fatherland in far-away Russia while practicing his flying profession." Here too the authorities quickly moved in to suppress the story.[18]

In the perennial battle of intelligence and counterintelligence services, the German-Soviet military collaboration repre-
sents a major triumph comparable to the security achieved by
the United States with its Manhattan Project, the general cover
name for its secret atomic weapons development program. In
the various German-Soviet military exchanges the strictest
security precautions were taken. German officers training in
Russia were officially "retired" from active lists. Personal and
place names were changed and the true nature of various
contracts disguised. (Later these security measures made it
relatively easy to forge incriminating documents by changing
key words in such a way that the sense of the whole could be
misconstrued.) Likewise the names of Russian officers attached
to the German War Ministry and attending General Staff
courses were disguised. For example, Army Commander I. P.
Uborevich became "Herr Ulrich." [19] Even after the 1926 revelations the German War Ministry was able to conceal the scope
and importance of its continuing military collaboration with
the Soviets. As late as 1931 the following report of Colonel
James Marshall Cornwall, the British military attaché in Berlin,
indicates how poorly informed British intelligence could be on
this vital subject:

> The relations between the German and Soviet Russian
> military authorities remain somewhat of a mystery. Such co-
> operation as exists is purely on the basis of reciprocal bene-
> fit, but it appears that relations have been less cordial of
> late, and there have certainly been fewer exchanges of visits
> between senior staff officers of the two countries. The prac-
> tice of seconding German officers in order to practice flying
> in Russia, prevalent from 1927 to 1930, seems to have
> recently ceased. There are certainly no German officer in-
> structors attached to the Soviet army. A new German un-
> official military representative, Colonel Koestring, has been
> sent to Moscow. The cooling off of German-Soviet relations
> may be in part attributed to the violent propaganda campaign
> directed against the Reichswehr by the Communist party.[20]

The Interallied Control Commission had been set up after

the war as a watchdog committee to report on German violations of the disarmament provisions of the Versailles Treaty.
It depended for its information mainly on the intelligence
services of Great Britain, France, and Belgium, and in its
report number 45 of December 1924 noted a number of violations. But it met with such strong passive resistance on the
part of the local authorities that it phased out of operation
shortly thereafter and German internal military preparation
henceforth was monitored only by the separate intelligence
agencies of the Entente powers.[21] Moreover, Germany was
brought back into the European community and relations with
France and Great Britain were normalized, symbolized by the
"Spirit of Locarno" in 1926. Under these conditions, German
rearmament in violation of the Versailles Treaty, while reported by the intelligence agencies, was in effect condoned by
their foreign offices and governments, since nothing was done
about it. The same observation applies to the information collected by British and French intelligence about German-Soviet
military collaboration, information that was, of course, much
more limited than their knowledge of local developments in
Germany itself. For example, in 1930 a German counterintelligence officer, Lieutenant Colonel von Bredow, was informed
by a senior official of the agency that the British War Office
was not worried about the increasing strength of the German
army and navy, but did follow (along with the French and
Belgians) developments in German air strength.[22] Under these
circumstances, aided by the knowledge and experience gained
in the U.S.S.R., German clandestine or semiclandestine rearmament was well under way before Hitler later openly announced
his preparations for war. On the Soviet side of the picture, from
the outset the policy of collaboration with Germany had the
approval of Stalin. Marshal Voroshilov, the Commissar of War
(or Defense) from 1925 to 1930, sought wherever possible to
expand and multiply contacts. It was Voroshilov who received
the senior German officers when they arrived in Moscow,
providing unbroken contact with such important General Staff
figures as Blomberg (1928), Hammerstein-Equord and Kühl-
ental (1929), Halm and Heye (1930), and General Adams
(1931–32).[23] Ironically, Voroshilov was one of the few Soviet
staff officers who later escaped being purged on charges of
conspiring with the Germans during the exchanges. Of the

other four marshals promoted to that exalted rank in November 1935 (Budenny, Blyukher [Galin], Yegorov, and Tukhachevsky), only the last two were involved in collaboration with the German Army, and then relatively late in the game. Tukhachevsky, who had originally been a protégé of Trotsky, was in something of a temporary eclipse after Stalin's victory over the opposition in the fall of 1927. He had been virtually excluded from the brisk interchange of Soviet and German senior officers taking place at that time (1927–28), and his name does not appear on the record as a participant in joint military or war-industry ventures until 1931–32.[24] In the fall of 1932 Tukhachevsky was a deputy commissar of defense under Voroshilov, and Yegorov was chief of the Red Army staff when both were invited to attend the German fall maneuvers. Tukhachevsky remained a few days after the maneuvers to inspect arms plants in the west of Germany. There is no indication that Tukhachevsky's friendly visit had any appreciable affect on German-Soviet political or military relations. On the contrary, ever since the 1927 war scare Stalin had probably had some second thoughts about the ultimate reliability of Germany. The formal basis of Soviet-German relations during this period was the Berlin Treaty of April 1926, by which both powers reaffirmed Rapallo, promised to remain neutral if either were attacked, and also promised not to join any hostile political or economic coalitions against each other. The treaty came up for renewal after five years in 1931. It is significant that German Chancellor Brüning tried to keep the renewal secret in order not to alarm the French, and that the Reichstag did not ratify the new treaty for nearly two years (May 1933).[25] By then Hitler had seized power, but had not yet embarked on an anti-Soviet policy. Ratification by the Reichstag was purely routine and signified nothing more than the fact that Hitler as yet had no intention of making a sudden break in relations with Moscow.[26] As a form of reinsurance, nonaggression pacts were signed with Poland (July 25) and France (November 29, 1932). At the end of 1932 Schleicher, not Hitler, was appointed chancellor. The Nazi vote fell in the elections, the Communist party (KPD) registered gains, and Molotov's report on the foreign situation on January 23, 1933, was exceedingly complacent.[27] Seven days later, on January 30, to the astonishment of all the experts, Hitler came to power.

It was four years before Stalin and the other Soviet leaders grasped the full significance of the fact, but they were already living in an age dominated by Hitler.

The End of a Profitable Friendship

The Soviet leaders were in excellent company in their failure to take note of Hitler or to evaluate his potential importance on the German scene. In 1929 the former British ambassador in Berlin, Lord D'Abernon, published his memoirs, *An Ambassador of Peace,* and mentioned Hitler only once, in a footnote on pages 51–52. After noting Hitler's arrest and condemnation for having taken part in the 1923 Bavarian uprising, the former ambassador adds: "He was finally released after six months and bound over for the rest of his sentence, thereafter fading into oblivion." [28] Even such astute and well-informed political analysts as Dr. Arnold Wolfers (then director of studies at the Berlin Hochschule für Politik) and the historian Arnold Toynbee confidently predicted the failure of the Nazis to capture the electorate and regarded the threat of dictatorship as minimal.[29]

However honestly mistaken Western analysts may have been in their early judgments of Hitler and the Nazi movement, they were quickly able to reevaluate the situation once Hitler had replaced the Weimar Republic with a repressive police-state regime. Soviet leaders and analysts, on the other hand, were blinded for years by ideological preconceptions that distorted their view of the world. Communist theory held that sooner or later revolution in Germany was inevitable because of the built-in contradictions—the class struggle, etc.—of the capitalist system. Paradoxically, Hitler's seizure of power was actually welcomed by some Soviet spokesmen. It was believed that Hitler's repressive measures would inevitably speed up the revolution, which so far had failed to materialize (notably in the abortive 1923 uprisings) but was now believed to be just around the corner. The very day after Hitler's seizure of power, *Izvestia* confidently predicted that the moment was near when the struggle for power among the competing factions inside Germany would be transformed into open class warfare. Because the Socialist parties were the Communists' main rivals for working-class support, ever since 1928 the general line had called for a struggle without quarter against what Soviet propaganda called the "social fascists" or "Socialist traitors." For this reason the Communists cooperated with the Nazis in a campaign against the Social Democratic party and its leaders, thus removing the one vital center of opposition inside Germany that could conceivably have stopped Hitler before it was too late. Led astray by this kind of ideological blindness, the Communists persisted in this folly for four long years until the realization finally dawned in the Kremlin that stopping Hitler was more important than beating local Social Democratic rivals. Then the general line abruptly changed, calling for cooperation with the Socialists in a popular front against war and fascism. By that time most of the Social Democratic leaders were rotting away in concentration camps and there were few left to cooperate with.

Meanwhile, on the diplomatic and government level, in spite of Hitler's anticommunist tirades and his liquidation of the German Communist party, Soviet leaders continued to express a desire to maintain good relations with Nazi Germany. According to Gustav Hilger, German counselor of embassy in Moscow, Soviet diplomats "never tired of pointing out how well Moscow got along with Italy and Turkey, even though the Communist parties there were completely outlawed. The official Soviet line on that subject was summed up when Litvinov [the foreign minister] said: 'We don't care if you shoot your German Communists.' " [30]

Hilger added that long after Hitler had cut off friendly exchanges and embarked on an openly anti-Soviet policy

> we found among many Soviet leaders a deep and lasting nostalgia for the old days of German-Soviet collaboration, and some of them were frank enough to voice this nostalgia before their German friends. . . . In spite of Germany's aggressive designs, Radek insisted upon his friendly feelings toward the German people . . . He allegedly voiced great admiration for the organizing talent of the National Socialists, the power of their movement, and the devoted enthusiasm of its youth. "In the faces of brown-shirted German students," he exclaimed, "we see the same dedication and inspiration that once brightened the faces of Red Army officer candidates and the volunteers of 1813. [A reference to the Prussian volunteers in the war of liberation against Napoleon.] There are

magnificent lads in the SA and SS. You'll see, the day will come when they'll be throwing hand grenades for us." [31]

The day came in January 1937 when this conversation was used against Radek at his own treason trial.

In return for his extended tour of German installations in the summer of 1932, Tukhachevsky invited his opposite number, General von Bockelberg (the head of German ordnance, the *Heereswaffenamt*), to visit Soviet installations. The trip took place from May 8 to 28, 1933, in the friendliest atmosphere, and at a dinner party Voroshilov loudly stressed his intention to maintain ties between the two armies. No sooner had the German mission left, however, than orders went out from the Soviet side to cut off all further exchanges and to close down such cooperative enterprises as the flying school at Lipetsk. Within five months it was all over. The installations had been closed down and the final toasts drunk by starry-eyed Soviet and German officers. In a frank talk with the German embassy counselor von Twardovski on October 31, Tukhachevsky admitted that the exchanges had been broken off as "a political consequence" of the conviction that German policy was taking an anti-Soviet direction. Obviously disturbed by the termination of such a mutually profitable relationship, officials on both sides expressed the hope that the cooperation might be renewed again "in another form" in the future. In a long conversation the next day with von Twardovski, Tukhachevsky stressed that in spite of the recent political developments, the Red Army command would always remember the German Army's valuable aid in building up Russia's forces. As he took leave he said in French, a language in which he was also fluent, "Don't forget, my friend, that it is politics, your politics alone that separates us and not our feelings, our most friendly feelings towards the *Reichswehr*." [32] That Tukhachevsky's farewell to the German Army was spoken in French was more than an example of the irony of history. It also symbolized developments that had taken place at a rapid pace since April 8, when the first French military attaché to the Soviet Union had arrived in Moscow, apparently ready to step into the place being vacated by the Germans.

When von Twardovski was transferred to Berlin two years

later, in October 1935, a farewell reception was given in his honor at the German embassy. Even at that late date Tukhachevsky expressed his regrets over the break in military collaboration. "If Germany and Soviet Russia were to march together," he said, "they could dictate peace to all the world; but if they were to clash, the Germans would find out that the Red Army had learned a lot in the meantime." [33]

By one of the ironies of history, Tukhachevsky's words were echoed a decade and a world war later by one of his former fellow prisoners of war, Charles de Gaulle: "For France and Russia to be united is to be strong; to be separated means danger. This is truly a categorical imperative of geography, experience and common sense." [34]

This was the rationale behind the Franco-Soviet rapprochement that followed the breakup with Nazi Germany, and to which we now turn our attention.

16
FRANCE AND
THE U.S.S.R.:
The Alliance That Never Was

T HE GERMANS
were in the midst of closing down their clandestine military installations in the U.S.S.R. when Soviet Foreign Minister Maksim Litvinov arrived in Paris during the first week in July 1933 and broadly hinted that since French and Russian national interests were not in conflict, "there is no obstacle to further political and economic rapprochement." By August the first "cultural exchanges" began, and by the first of September, the leader of the French Radical-Socialist party, former Premier Édouard Herriot, spent ten days on a gala visit during which he was received by Litvinov and Molotov, and banquets in his honor were attended by such important military figures as Voroshilov, Tukhachevsky, and Budenny. Three days after the Russian and German officers who closed down the Lipetsk aviation school had drunk their farewell toasts and exchanged regrets, the young French air minister, Pierre Cot, and his entourage arrived for an official visit. The German military attaché wrote with ill-disguised envy:

> The reception of the Minister [Pierre Cot] had the character of an international military tribute, new for Russia: tricolor decorations at the airport and at the hotel; guard of honor reviewed by the Minister as they marched by; honorary escort by a Russian fighter wing of the 20th Air Brigade on the flight from Kharkov to Moscow . . .[1]

Pierre Cot returned to Paris with a Soviet proposition for a tight security pact with teeth in it, that is, an "unconditional alliance" by which each party would pledge to come to the assistance of the other wherever attacked. But this was not what the French government or Foreign Ministry had in mind. The rapprochement with the U.S.S.R. was meant merely to break up the collaboration between the German Wehrmacht and the Red Army, thus protecting France's ally Poland. Another partition expressed in the phrase "to push Poland back to her ethnographic frontiers" had been the unspoken maximal aim behind the many years of Soviet-German collaboration.[2]

Since the new French relationship with the U.S.S.R. was conceived in negative terms, as a means of keeping Germany and Russia apart, there was no sense of urgency on the French side in pursuing the idea of an alliance. Moreover, the project fell into the hands of Pierre Laval, who became foreign minister after the assassination of the King of Yugoslavia and Louis Barthou in Marseilles in October 1934. At a cabinet meeting the previous June (according to the notes of a fellow cabinet officer), Laval had declared himself "categorically in favor of an accord with *Germany* and hostile to a rapprochement with Russia, which would bring us the Internationale and the Red Flag." [3] History could hardly have picked a more unlikely choice to negotiate the Franco-Soviet pact than the devious Laval, a veritable prince of appeasers—so much so that Churchill regarded him as an outright German agent.[4] Laval fought a delaying action by pushing a grandiose scheme for a general mutual-assistance pact, a so-called Eastern Locarno, to which France, the U.S.S.R., Poland, the Baltic states, Czechoslovakia, and even Finland would be signatories—a proposal that, as Laval no doubt expected, was stillborn. Nevertheless, pressure for a bilateral Franco-Soviet agreement mounted in the spring of 1935, and limited military exchanges took place. An estimated forty French officers were attached to Soviet aviation and armored and infantry units, and an equal number of Russian officers were sent to France.[5] Laval's hand was finally forced, however, by Hitler's declaration of open rearmament of March 16, 1935, in which he raked over the arms restrictions of the Versailles Treaty and announced to a stunned world that Germany was restoring universal military training and would soon have an army of thirty-six divisions—about 600,000 men, compared to the 405,000-man French army stationed in metropolitan France.[6]

The Soviets had secretly aided German rearmament for twelve years and knew the advances being made in aviation and tanks, so the Russian reaction to Hitler's bold announcement was both angry and immediate. An *Izvestia* editorial declared:

> Everything depends on whether or not the powers against whom this policy is directed will be able to work out quickly a system of mutual assistance against the event of German aggression. . . . Time demands a speedy consultation of the powers interested in the preservation of peace. Time demands rapid decision.[7]

Laval was invited to Moscow forthwith to negotiate a treaty of mutual assistance, which was signed in Paris on May 2, 1935. It was made contingent on a complementary Soviet-Czechoslovak mutual-assistance pact, signed on May 16. Under the terms of the agreement the U.S.S.R. promised to come to Czechoslovakia's assistance only after France honored its obligations to that country. Thus the U.S.S.R. hedged against finding itself in a possible war with Germany while France held back. The Soviets were fully aware that Laval would have preferred to do business with Hitler, and this "escape clause" was, as events proved later, a wise precaution against a last-minute defection on the part of their new-found and reluctant ally.

The U.S.S.R. lacked a common Soviet-Czech frontier, but planned to come to Czechoslovakia's aid by airlifting forces in the event of a German attack. The head of the Frunze Military Academy, Shaposhnikov, attended the late-summer maneuvers of the Czech Army in western Slovakia. In return, French, Italian, and Czech observers were present at the autumn maneuvers of the Red Army.[8] When, under Foreign Minister Paul-Boncour, preliminary negotiations first began in December 1933, the French General Staff, and especially General Maxime Weygand, were warm partisans of the pact.[9] However, two years later, after the pact was signed, a negative reaction set in, and French military leaders gave it only grudging support at best. In briefing General Maurice Gamelin on November 16 on the Franco-Soviet pact, Laval expressed his mistrust of the Russians and the treaty, from which, he said, he had eliminated "the most dangerous parts." [10] Gamelin, the chief of staff, himself was convinced of the political value of the pact, since the U.S.S.R. "represented the only great counterweight vis-à-vis Germany." [11] However, as Laval left for Moscow, General Louis Maurin, who was war minister when the pact was signed, told the cabinet: "From the military point of view the Russian alliance is devoid of interest." [12] The Maginot Line was nearing completion in 1935 and the strategic thinking of the French High Command was purely defensive. General Maurin in public debate raised the crucial question:

> How can anyone believe that we are still dreaming of the offensive when we have spent billions to establish a fortified barrier? Would we be foolish enough to go out beyond that barrier into I know not what sort of adventure? [13]

For their part, the Soviets might well have asked: If the French high command has no intention of moving its forces beyond the Maginot Line, of what value is a pledge to come to our assistance in case we're attacked? Under these circumstances, after the pact was signed, the Soviet ambassador in Paris, Potemkin, pressed Colonel Fabry, minister of war in Laval's cabinet, in July 1935 for a military convention which would put some teeth in the agreement. According to Paul Reynaud, "Fabry refused . . . without consulting either the Council of National Defense or the Supreme Military Committee." [14]

Without joint military planning and arrangements to meet a possible German attack in either direction, east toward Czechoslovakia and the U.S.S.R. or west toward France, the Franco-Soviet pact was nothing more than a Platonic gesture. We have mentioned the "Maginot Line mentality" of the French high command. But even if this were suddenly to change for the better, what were the capabilities of the French for taking the offensive? On March 31, 1935, Marshal Tukhachevsky had published a sensational article in *Pravda* in which he compared the offensive capabilities of the German armed forces with those of the French, of which he was extremely critical: "The French Army, with its twenty divisions, hastily assembled units, and slow rate of expansion by stages under mobilization, is already incapable of active opposition to Germany." [15]

However, from the Soviet point of view even a reluctant ally would be better than none in the event that Hitler should drive east toward the U.S.S.R. Neither Germany nor the U.S.S.R. could afford to fight a two-front war, as both powers had learned from bitter experience. Therefore, even if the Soviet military leaders rated the French Army as weak on the offensive, the very fact of its existence on Hitler's western flank would hopefully act as a deterrent against any adventurous moves in the east. Besides, in spite of much noisy propaganda to the contrary, in 1934–35 the U.S.S.R. did not believe that war was imminent and that its ally in the west would be called upon to make good its pledges. Let us take a brief look at Soviet war-scare propaganda during this period.

Communist Propaganda and the Fake 1935 War Scare

During the long-drawn-out negotiations leading to the Franco-Soviet pact, Communist propaganda, which began on a complacent note in 1934, ended with a full-fledged but phony war scare in the spring of 1935, designed to create a political atmosphere favorable to signing the pact and to consolidating a popular front against war and fascism.

For intelligence purposes it is important to distinguish between the Soviet attitude toward "imperialist war" in general —that is, wars in which other powers, preferably capitalist, may slug each other into a state of exhaustion—and any possible war in which the brunt of the attack will be borne by the U.S.S.R. Preparations for an "imperialist war" in the West were becoming increasingly apparent in the early 1930's. Far from disturbing Soviet policy-makers, the prospects of such a war were viewed complacently, if not actually welcomed (provided the blows were not directed against the U.S.S.R.). As late as January 26, 1934 (after the rise of Hitler's star, it should be noted), Stalin had arrived at the following estimate:

> Things are orienting themselves toward a new imperialist war as the outcome of the present situation. There is evidently no reason to suppose that the war will really settle anything. On the contrary, it should foul up the situation even more. So much the better: it will certainly unleash the revolu-

tion and will jeopardize the very existence of capitalism in a number of countries, as was the case during the first imperialist war.[16]

On January 29, 1935, almost exactly a year after Stalin's complacent estimate, Molotov, addressing the Seventh Soviet Congress of the U.S.S.R., struck a genuine note of alarm:

> We have to take into consideration that the immediate danger of war has increased for the U.S.S.R. Certain influential circles in Japan have already long since openly been speaking about war against the Soviet Union. It must not be forgotten that there is now in Europe a ruling party openly declaring its historical task to be the seizure of territory in the Soviet Union.
>
> Not to see a new war approaching means to close one's eyes to the chief danger.[17]

The Molotov speech was reported verbatim in the February 9, 1935, issue of *International Press Correspondence,* the Kremlin-published weekly publicity organ of the Comintern, but the "war danger" theme was not given front-page treatment until the February 23 issue, which ran the banner headline: THE DANGER OF WAR IS EXCEEDINGLY ACUTE, THE FIGHT AGAINST THE WARMONGERS MUST BE INCREASED AT ALL COSTS. This heavy emphasis on the war danger continued throughout the month of March.

Should this heavy publicity campaign have been taken as an authentic indication that the U.S.S.R. really *believed* that at the time (1) war was either imminent or inevitable, or (2) that the Soviet Union was in imminent danger of being attacked by Nazi Germany, already labeled as the principal and most dangerous enemy of the U.S.S.R. among the "imperialist powers" of the West?

These questions are the sort that perennially crop up in intelligence estimates, and without reasonably full historical documentation (as in the case of similar Nazi estimates contained in captured documents) they cannot be finally answered one way or another. However, a study of Soviet propaganda of the period can shed some light on the matter. So far as France is concerned, an examination of the data sheets indicates that the war scare was used (1) to build up public opinion in favor of the Franco-Soviet mutual-assistance pact (actually signed on May 2) and (2) to win wide popular support for the developing antifascist (and therefore antiwar) people's front. There is additional evidence that the imminence of "the coming war" (so highly touted by Soviet propaganda as "dangerously near" in March) was not taken too seriously in the Kremlin. In the April 20 issue of *International Press Correspondence*, Tukhachevsky, writing on the "War Plans of Present-Day Germany," gives a complete summary of the German order of battle: troop strengths, forces available for an "army of invasion," etc. In the final section, entitled "Hitler's Anti-Soviet and Revenge Plans," after quoting *Mein Kampf* to prove "the anti-Soviet attitude of Hitler," he goes on to state, however: "It is clear that Hitler's imperialist schemes have not only an anti-Soviet direction." [18] Hitler, Tukhachevsky averred, was aiming primarily not at the U.S.S.R., but at a war of revenge and aggrandizement in the west and south—against France, Belgium, Czechoslovakia, and Austria. Although there is no evidence that Tukhachevsky seriously believed that Germany then represented an imminent threat to the U.S.S.R., it is astonishing how accurately he put his finger on the areas into which Hitler would move (as soon as he dared), but in the wrong sequence.

Propaganda analysis might also have turned up other indications that the Soviet-inspired war scare of March 1935 was not taken seriously at its point of origin, the Kremlin. One such indication is the question of the arming of the Soviet Union's allies. The French Communist party continued its antipreparedness, antimilitarist slogans and policy, even after the signing of the mutual-assistance pact in May. The main target was the extension of military service to two years. At the beginning of March 1935, the month of the "acute war danger" campaign, the policy of the "united antifascist front" did *not* in any way alter the basic local Communist attitude of treason to one's country and loyalty only to the U.S.S.R., the only "fatherland" of all honest workers, democrats, etc. (Signalized by the now famous October 1948 speech of Maurice Thorez, a return to this basic platform of treason later "shocked" the Western world.) By the same token, the French Communists bitterly opposed French rearmament and extension of military service to two years to meet the growing Nazi threat. It was not until June 15, 1935, more than a month after the mutual-assistance

pact of May 2, that the Kremlin, realizing the treasonable in-
consistency of "revolutionary defeatism," i.e., the revolutionary
slogan of the defeat of one's own country, grudgingly decided
that, in the event of a Nazi attack on France, the Communists
might defend their own country.

It is most improbable that if in March 1935 the Soviet
leaders had really believed war imminent they would have
continued to oppose the rearming of their main ally abroad
and to insist as late as June 1935 that their followers in France
must refuse to oppose a Nazi attack.[19]

Tukhachevsky's European Junket

During the last week in January 1936 it was announced
that Marshal Tukhachevsky would accompany Soviet Foreign
Minister Litvinov to London to attend the state funeral of
King George V. Whereas Litvinov flew directly to London, arriving on January 26, Tukhachevsky broke his journey for a
few hours in Berlin. This first stop on what later became a
highly publicized European junket led to persistent reports
that the Soviet marshal used the occasion to renew contact with
General Blomberg, and presumably with other German officers
who had previously been active in the Red Army–*Reichswehr*
collaboration which had been broken off by the Soviets in
May 1933. To be sure, a reservoir of personal goodwill toward
the German generals still existed among their Russian counterparts in spite of the break and Hitler's violent anticommunist
tirades. However plausible rumors of renewed contacts during
Tukhachevsky's stopover may be, they are almost certainly
false. After Tukhachevsky's execution, U.S. Chargé d'Affaires
Loy Henderson queried German Ambassador von Schulenburg
in this regard and the Ambassador replied:

> Prior to going to France last year Marshal Tukhachevsky
> had asked the German Military Attaché in Moscow if it would
> be possible for him to have a chat with General Blomberg
> while passing through Berlin . . . this request was made with
> the full knowledge and approval of the Kremlin . . . my Gov-
> ernment [Berlin] felt that in view of the tense political rela-
> tions between the two countries it would not be proper . . .
> Marshal Tukhachevsky thereafter passed through Berlin with-
> out meeting any German officials.[20]

None of this was unknown to Stalin, since Tukhachevsky's entire junket was undoubtedly planned and cleared in advance. Tukhachevsky arrived in London on January 27, took part in the funeral ceremonies, and remained for almost two weeks, during which time he made the acquaintance of the French chief of staff, General Maurice Gamelin, also present for the solemn occasion. Gamelin invited him to visit France on his return journey and, accompanied by Vitvot Putna, the Soviet military attaché in London, Tukhachevsky spent a week as a guest of the French General Staff. The Soviet representatives visited various military installations, such as aircraft plants, airfields, and tank parks, in which they showed a keen interest. At a small dinner party Tukhachevsky made no attempt to conceal the fact that for intelligence purposes he kept up certain German contacts, but indicated that he wanted to see an intensification of relations between the French and Red armies. Significantly, the Soviet marshal told General Gamelin that he expected Hitler's next move would be the reoccupation of the Rhineland!

The presence of a Soviet marshal naturally aroused a great deal of speculative interest in the French press, and Tukhachevsky's highly ambivalent but "typically Russian" behavior at a celebrated banquet in the Soviet embassy created a furor. Whether by accident or by design, Tukhachevsky used the occasion to advise Rumanian Foreign Minister Titulescu to look to Germany (rather than his French ally) for rescue, and, waxing eloquent on the phenomenal growth of the German Air Force, exclaimed to the fellow-traveling French journalist Madame Tabouis: *"Ils sont déjà invincibles!"* ("They are already invincible!") Such remarks, coming from the man designated to command the Soviet forces in the event of war, created considerable misgiving in French military circles.[21] If Tukhachevsky had been determined to prove that the Russians at times behave like "baptized bears," he could hardly have put on a more convincing performance.

Since Tukhachevsky was executed the following year (June 12, 1937) for an alleged anti-Stalinist plot, and this was his last trip abroad, the legend has developed that he used the occasion for conspiratorial meetings with representatives of General Miller's ROVS, the organization of Russian émigré officers in London, Paris, and Berlin. Without exception the legend rests on unconfirmed reports or dark hints from highly dubious sources. For example, Abshagen, the biographer of Admiral Canaris, chief of the German intelligence service, writes that Canaris knew Tukhachevsky was "by no means guiltless," [22] a statement that could be applied to a saint. The British journalist Ian Colvin writes that Tukhachevsky not only "met emissaries of General Miller and the White Russian *émigrés* of Paris," but also that in Berlin "a German communist agent, named Blimiel, had managed to slip into a small private meeting between the Marshal and some of the *émigrés* of Germany." [23] The source of this story is Ernst Niekisch, presumably an NKVD agent arrested by Heydrich, who allegedly shared a prison cell with Blimiel. Beyond this "the whole incident is without any other circumstantial confirmation whatsoever." [24]

No one knew better than Tukhachevsky that he would be under constant NKVD surveillance during his trip abroad. He must also have known that the émigré organizations were thoroughly penetrated by Soviet agents and that any contact with them would be literally the kiss of death. Such illicit contacts are not easily arranged under the most favorable circumstances. For this reason alone, it is extremely unlikely that they took place during Tukhachevsky's busy spring trip. Moreover, in January 1930 General Kutyepov had been kidnaped on the streets of Paris, and his anti-Soviet Combat Corps had been disbanded and dispersed. General Miller, his mild-mannered successor, had long since given up covert political operations as far too risky. Even had it been possible to arrange illicit contacts with his émigré organization, it is difficult to imagine what a tough combat officer like Tukhachevsky would hope to accomplish by them. It is significant that most of these tales of Tukhachevsky's so-called illicit contacts can be traced to presumably NKVD sources, and that they arose after his execution, and were designed to lend a sort of retroactive support to the conspiracy charges made against him later by his Soviet executioners.

The Rhineland Crisis

A defensive alliance against a revisionist or aggressive power is held together by a shared fear of aggression. Remove that fear and the cement that holds it together dissolves. Something like this happened to the NATO alliance as the fear of Soviet aggression on the European continent dissolved in an unprecedented flood of visiting Soviet firemen and affability after the death of Stalin and the end of the classic Cold War period in 1953. Terrified by the prospect of a thermonuclear holocaust, the post-Stalin Soviet leaders opted for a policy of coexistence in preference to one of no existence. By withdrawing from Austria in 1955 and reducing their huge standing armies from 175 to about 85 divisions, they gradually removed the fear of Soviet aggression which in Stalin's day had given rise to the NATO alliance and held it together. By contrast, in the mid-1930's the fear of Nazi aggression mounted but, paradoxically, the nascent alliance system that might have blocked Hitler's bid for control of Europe never materialized. Why?

There are no simple answers to this kind of question. In general terms, however, two principles apply. First, a defensive alliance is no better than the joint military planning and arrangements that put teeth into it. In case a threatening enemy strikes, arms and men have to be allocated to stop him. This kind of planning can be done only by a genuinely cooperative effort of the allied military staffs. Vigorous, wholehearted staff work, widely publicized, may frequently deter an aggressor and avert war. But in an age of mass armies the ultimate strength of an alliance derives from the popular consensus on which it is based. In other words, a commitment to go to war to defend an ally is meaningful only to the extent that it is supported by the people who may be called upon to fight. In the case of France (and England) in the mid-1930's, the popular consensus that might have given strength to an alliance to stop Hitler was lacking. In spite of the massive Communist propaganda campaign to drum up support for the Franco-Soviet pact, the French Parliament delayed ratification for nearly a year (February 27, 1936) after it was signed. By then the delay itself had greatly reduced the political impact of the treaty, and Stalin could hardly fail to draw the proper conclusion from this reluctance to ratify a commitment. If there were any remaining doubts as to what his French ally would do in a showdown, they were soon to be dispelled by the French and British reaction to Hitler's occupation of the Rhineland in March 1936.

On January 24, 1936, about the same time that Marshal
Tukhachevsky was leaving Moscow for his spring visit to London and Paris, Pierre-Étienne Flandin became French foreign
minister in the Sarraut cabinet. Like Tukhachevsky, Flandin
expected Hitler to make his next move into the demilitarized
zone of the Rhineland. He writes that from the moment he assumed office, "I had but one preoccupation: the Rhineland." [25]
At the funeral of King George V, Flandin had asked British
Prime Minister Stanley Baldwin and Foreign Secretary Anthony
Eden what England would do if Germany broke the Locarno
Treaty by moving into the Rhineland. Instead of answering,
Baldwin asked Flandin what decision the French government
had reached. A few days later, back in Paris, Flandin in turn
asked the Supreme Military Committee what military measures
could be taken immediately, and was told by his war minister
"that the French Army had been given an entirely defensive
character and had nothing prepared." Nevertheless, he was
authorized by the cabinet to tell Mr. Eden that "the French
Government would place all its forces . . . at the disposal of
the League of Nations to oppose by force a violation of
treaties," and he was to invoke British aid under the Locarno
Treaty. Six weeks later, when Hitler's troops moved into the
Rhineland, Flandin discovered that behind those brave words
"all that was envisaged was to man the Maginot Line and to
move two divisions from the Rhône Valley to the eastern
frontier." He added that for action in the Rhineland the General Staff demanded a general mobilization. This provoked
turmoil in the cabinet: " 'A general mobilization six weeks
before a general election, what folly!' declared some of my
colleagues." [26]

On the very day of Hitler's reoccupation of the Rhineland,
Poland offered to mobilize immediately in support of any
military moves her French ally might make. But, although
Flandin later admitted that he "could have forced Britain's
hand" and "believed that Britain would have stood by her en-
gagements," he called for consultations. These took place first
in Paris on March 10 and later in London. And thus instead of
an immediate and forceful reply to Hitler's incredible gamble,
both the French and British governments took "a middle line
between action and inaction—they talked." [27] During the
Rhineland negotiations in London, Flandin lunched with some

members of the House of Commons, and reportedly, "speaking with a cold passion which impressed us all," said that if he had obtained the approval of the British government he would have acted, and had every reason to believe that "the Germans would have withdrawn without firing a shot." [28]

Flandin's conclusion at the time of the crisis has been widely accepted by historians since. Top military circles in Germany recognized the tremendous odds against the Rhineland gamble and anticipated prompt Franco-British resistance to which the invading German forces would have no alternative but to submit.[29] As Namier puts it: "Had France taken immediate military action, Hitler would have suffered a fatal check, which might have brought down his regime, and would, in any case, have put an end to his treaty infringements." [30]

As might be expected in view of the backdrop of war-scare propaganda emanating from Moscow, Soviet reaction to the Rhineland reoccupation was immediate and alarmist. At the League of Nations Council meeting on March 17 Litvinov asked whether by a policy of inaction the League would condone the extension of German hegemony over all of Europe.[31] Two days later the Soviet ambassador in London, I. Maisky, in a speech on the war danger stressed the desire to see created "in a short space of time" a peace front that would be capable of talking to an aggressor "in a language of tanks and machine-guns." [32] The popular front of the Socialist and Communist parties won the election in May, and the Socialist premier, Léon Blum, was faced with the problem of adding to the Franco-Soviet pact effective military arrangements capable of talking such a language. Thanks to the paralysis shown during the Rhineland crisis, this task was now much more difficult than it might have been before. For the Rhineland crisis revealed for the first time a mutually interreacting Anglo-French paralysis of will which later characterized each of the crises produced by Hitler's political and territorial expansion. It also revealed the fatal tendency to seek relief from tension in endless consultation, "negotiation," and wishful thinking. In this sense the Rhineland crisis was a sort of dry run for Munich. As one authority summed up the situation: "Even *The Times* hailed the impact of this charge of explosive on the fabric of international confidence with a leader entitled 'A Chance to Rebuild'—a comment which no doubt applies in a sense to any devastated area, provided the foundations have not been irremediably shaken." [33]

On October 14 Belgium renounced her military agreement with France and reverted to a position of "neutrality." This seriously undermined French Maginot Line strategy, which depended on an initial concentration of combined forces behind the Antwerp-Liège-Arlon line. Since Great Britain and France would honor Belgian neutrality and Hitler almost certainly would not, this gave the German forces a great advantage on the offensive. Under the circumstances the tempo of cooperation with France's Russian ally should have increased markedly. It did not. The new French ambassador to the U.S.S.R., Robert Coulondre, arrived in Moscow in October armed with instructions that could be reduced to "No preventive war, no Soviet interference in French internal affairs, and possible military aid should war be inescapable." Admiral Darlan had shown little or no cooperation in arranging the exchange of naval attachés.[34] In a frank exchange of views, U.S.S.R. President Kalinin complained about French failure to provide promised equipment, pointing out, significantly, that German industry had offered to deliver unlimited supplies on credit. "Including arms," Litvinov added.

The Ambassador was forced to recognize that the French technical departments had acted irresponsibly. The Admiralty had revoked its offer of naval guns and the War Ministry supplied only obsolete artillery.[35] Only firm and decisive action on the part of Premier Léon Blum could have corrected this situation. But whatever action Blum may have contemplated was choked off by a complex net of intrigue which began to unfold in late 1936 and early 1937. The plot, which is the heart of what later was called the Tukhachevsky affair, was first spun in Moscow, and apparently sprang from the paranoid depths of Stalin's mind as he plunged into the unprecedented bloodletting of the 1937–38 purges.

The Morning After: Soviet Military Preparations

As an aftermath of the Rhineland crisis, the U.S.S.R. took measures designed to put teeth into its mutual-assistance pact with Czechoslovakia. Since the Soviet Union had no border with Czechoslovakia, Russian ground forces could not come to her defense without prior consent from Poland or Rumania. It was assumed that such passage had been blocked since January 1934, when Colonel Joseph Beck, Polish minister of foreign affairs, signed a pact with Hitler by which both parties renounced the use of force in the settlement of disputes for a ten-year period. Aware of Hitler's appetite for expansion, Beck thus hoped to secure for Poland the temporary immunity of being the last to be eaten. By the spring and summer of 1936 public opinion in Poland had become increasingly pro-German and anti-French, "a tendency encouraged by local anti-Semitism and the character of the Polish Government." [36] However, at this stage Polish reluctance to permit passage of Russian ground forces did not exclude plans to come to the aid of Czechoslovakia based on the use of Soviet air power.

In the March 1936 debate on the Rhineland crisis, the statement was made in the House of Commons that at that time no agreement yet existed for the Soviet use of Czech airfields and installations. Apparently this situation was quickly remedied when the chief of the Red Air Force, Ya. I. Alksnis, and a group of senior Soviet officers arrived in Prague on July 15. In return Czech General Krejvi attended the Red Army autumn maneuvers and was favorably impressed. The British and French military missions also attended these maneuvers.[37]

Czechoslovakia had a well-developed airfield system, adequately screened by an efficient army. In the event of German attack, these fields could be used as advanced bases by Soviet bombers while Red Army mechanized forces drove rapidly west, with passage either assured beforehand or simply taken by force later. Powerful striking forces for such an operation could be assembled from Yakir's group in the southwest or Uborevich's command to the northwest. Given the size and efficiency of the Czech forces, contingency planning for joint offensive operations with the Red Army looked attractive enough in principle.[38] That nothing concrete ever developed was due in part to the reluctance of the French General Staff to follow through with joint plans after the Rhineland crisis. But an equally important factor was Stalin's long-range objective of eliminating all possible political and military opposition to himself and his policy of appeasing Hitler, which culminated in the Nazi-Soviet pact of August 1939 and World War II. In the controversy that has raged over Munich and appeasement, Western historians have concentrated on French and English shortcomings, since these have been obvious and the record open. Soviet appeasement has been seriously neglected by both Western and Soviet historians because of the secrecy clamped over the record, and because Stalin himself deliberately excluded his responsible military and political advisers from his secret, personal diplomacy and covert operations, such as the disinformation behind the purging of Marshal Tukhachevsky and the Soviet High Command. In the following sections an attempt is made to trace Stalin's appeasement policy, which runs like a hidden red thread beneath the savage holocaust of the political and military purges.

Soviet Appeasement and the Purges

Up to the time of the Great Purge, Soviet leadership was divided on the line of policy that should be followed with reference to Hitler. Bukharin has summarized the initial Soviet reaction to Hitler as follows:

> In the first few months after Hitler's seizure of power, it seemed to us in Russia that the Third Reich would be merely *a passing phase in Germany's history,* that Hitler would be able to remain in the saddle only a few months, to be followed quickly by a severe crash and revolution. That the "imperialists" of England and France would permit Germany, their "hereditary foe," to carry out her rearmament plans was generally regarded as impossible; neither were Hitler's mouthings about a campaign against Russia taken seriously. Gradually, however, we began to realize that the situation was far more serious than we had thought, that no preventive measures against Hitler by the Western powers could be expected, and that preparations for a campaign against Russia were in full swing.[39]

As a result the revolutionary intellectuals of the Bolshevik Old Guard, many of them of Jewish origin, formed a group that was opposed to fascism on moral grounds and sincerely supported "the politics of the anti-fascist Popular Front and the diplomacy of collective security which Foreign Commissar Litvinov pursued vigorously in the middle 1930's." [40] The intellectual leader of this group was Bukharin, who in an impassioned speech at the 17th Party Congress in January 1934 had warned against Hitlerism's cult of blood and violence and forecast an inevitable clash with it. Later, as editor of *Izvestia,* he continued to hammer away on this theme until his arrest and liquidation in the last of the three purge show trials.

Opposing the Old Bolsheviks, who favored moderation in the use of repressive measures at home and support of the antifascist struggle abroad, stood Stalin. Stalin could not have cared less about the moral or ideological aspects of fascism. He made this clear in his address to the 17th Party Congress in early 1934, when he denied that the U.S.S.R. had "taken an orientation toward France and Poland," and held the door open for an agreement with Hitler, pointing out that while he was "not enthusiastic about the fascist regime in Germany," ideology was no problem, "if only for the reason that fascism in Italy, for example, has not prevented the U.S.S.R. from establishing the best relations with that country." [41]

Two months after this speech, which might be called Exhibit A in the Soviet record of appeasement, Hitler carried out his bloody purge of the Roehm wing of his followers on "the night of the long knives," June 20, 1934. As Kennan observes: "This exhibition of ruthless brutality against party comrades made a profound impression upon Stalin. . . . He was, I am sure, filled with admiration. From now on, there was no stopping him." [42] According to Krivitsky, the blood purge convinced Stalin that Hitler had consolidated his power and strengthened his inclination to make a deal with him. It probably also provided Stalin with both a model and, if one were needed, a stimulus for eliminating his own internal opposition. Certainly almost all those who opposed Hitler on moral or antifascist grounds and strove to create a united front with Western liberals against him were later purged.[43] In fact, Nicolaevsky claims that "as a rule, the fate of any one person in the years of the Great Purge is a true indication of his sincerity as regards this policy: with few exceptions all of its *sincere* supporters were liquidated." [44]

Hitler's denunciation of the Franco-Soviet pact and simultaneous occupation of the Rhineland on March 7, 1936, was a contemptuous gesture that might well have led to a break in Soviet relations with Germany. Instead, although in his speech in London on March 19 Soviet Ambassador Maisky called for an effective peace front backed by tanks and machine guns, he also kept the door open for a deal with Hitler, emphasizing that Germany had not taken "the hand stretched out

to her." On the same day in Moscow, Molotov, in an interview
with a French reporter, M. Chastenet of *Le Temps,* noted that
while the Soviet *public* was aroused by Hitler's anti-Soviet
tirades, by contrast the government "thinks an improvement in
Soviet-German relations possible." [45] Under the circumstances,
this was tantamount to saying that Stalin considered such an
agreement *desirable,* and these two speeches taken together may
be regarded as Exhibit B in the record of Soviet appeasement.
The fact that Hitler did not respond to these overtures, did not
grasp the hand publicly extended toward him, in no way discouraged Stalin. On the contrary, rejection probably acted as
an additional stimulus to Stalin to clear the slate for ultimate
agreement by destroying every element of opposition which
could conceivably stand in his way. Within a few days after
German occupation of the Rhineland, Stalin secretly ordered
the preparation of the trial of Kamenev and Zinoviev and
fourteen others accused of forming a so-called Trotskyite-
Zinovievite terrorist center, the first of the three great show
trials that marked the main phases of the purge process.[46]

It is important to understand why in Stalin's thinking
half-measures would not do and why party members who were
antifascist had to be eliminated as a class. Perhaps the best
explanation is by Professor Robert C. Tucker in a recent essay
on the purge trials:

> . . . It was not simply that these people, including the
> great majority of Old Bolshevik leaders, would have found it
> very hard to stomach a treaty with the Nazis. To understand
> Stalin's special motive for getting rid of them, we must re-
> member that he visualized the coming pact with Hitler as
> more than merely a way of securing temporary safety from
> invasion and buying time for further defense preparation.
> What he contemplated, as his alliance with Hitler in 1939–
> 1941 showed in retrospect, was a kind of Moscow-Berlin
> axis, an active collaboration of the two dictatorships for ter-
> ritorial expansion, the division of spheres of influence in
> Eastern Europe, the Balkans, and even the Middle East. Now
> the Old Bolsheviks and other party members who shared their
> outlook were revolutionaries, not old-fashioned Russian im-
> perialists. They could have gone along, if reluctantly, with a
> simple nonaggression arrangement with Berlin. But a policy
> of outright imperialistic aggression in collaboration with Nazi
> Germany would have been extremely repugnant to very many

of them, as Stalin knew. Nor could the Polish Communist party (which was simply dissolved in the Great Purge) be expected to acquiesce supinely in a new partition of Poland between Russia and Germany. Consequently, to get a fully free hand for the diplomacy of the Soviet-Nazi alliance, Stalin needed to eliminate or expel thousands of foreign as well as Soviet Communists and to achieve in external as well as internal policy the absolute autocracy that, as we have seen, only the Great Purge brought him.[47]

The first show trial took place in August 1936. The second trial of seventeen, including Piatakov and Karl Radek, former head of the Comintern, all of whom were accused of forming an "Anti-Soviet Trotskyite Center," took place in January 1937. Bukharin and Rykov, former chairman of the Council of People's Commissars (from April 1922 to December 1930), led the list of twenty-one defendants in the last trial of the "Anti-Soviet Bloc of Rights and Trotskyites" in March 1938. In each of the trials, names of victims slated for arrest or execution were mentioned, or previous charges were renewed and amplified. For example, Marshal Tukhachevsky and one of his colleagues, V. K. Putna, were mentioned by Radek in the second trial. They had been summarily executed in June 1937 and their names were blackened again in the last trial by the charge that they headed a "military conspiratorial organization" linked with the larger conspiracy of which Bukharin and others were the alleged ringleaders.[48]

Since Stalin's death the Soviet regime has admitted that all the alleged counterrevolutionary conspiracies publicized in the trials were nonexistent. In his secret speech to the 1956 20th Congress, Khrushchev reported that a special investigating committee appointed by the Central Committee found "nothing tangible" on which the treason charges of the purge period were based. The post-Stalin revelations confirm the earlier testimony of such high-ranking secret-police officials as Krivitsky, that Stalin personally conceived, planned, and directed the entire process,[49] although he was absent in the Caucasus when the first trial began. As usual, Stalin managed to stay in the background, but he presided over the spectacle, in Kennan's apt description, "with diabolical, cynical composure, with his customary self-deprecating manner of having nothing to do with it at all—but presumably enjoying every minute of it, relishing every new exhibition of the misery and degradation and helplessness of his former aides and associates." [50]

Stalin the Father Figure

For years Stalin had built up a public image of himself as a sort of benevolent father figure, the close associate and successor of Lenin, watching over the interests of his flock from the empyrean heights of the Kremlin. Many of the purge victims themselves believed that the senseless violence of the NKVD had been concealed from Stalin, and from their prison cells addressed anguished appeals to the leader in whom they never lost faith. For example, Khrushchev told the 22nd Party Congress in 1961 that General I. E. Yakir, who was arrested along with Marshal Tukhachevsky in 1937, shouted at the moment of his execution: "Long live the party, long live Stalin!" [51]

In his rare contacts with foreign diplomats Stalin studiously projected the image of a warm, outgoing personality. A junior American diplomat's wife (who had certainly never met him) once described him as "dreamy." During Ambassador Joseph E. Davies' farewell call at the Soviet Foreign Commissariat on June 5, 1938, Stalin suddenly showed up and remained for a long talk. Afterward Davies wrote:

> He greeted me cordially with a smile and with great simplicity, but also with a real dignity. He gives the impression of a strong mind which is composed and wise. His brown eye is exceedingly kindly and gentle. A child would like to sit in his lap and a dog would sidle up to him. [52]

Only a few of those who thus came in privileged and fleeting contact with Stalin suspected that the outward mask concealed a cold, calculating, and (in Khrushchev's words) "a sickly, suspicious man." Stalin's close associates, of course, knew that he had a vengeful nature. One summer night in 1923 Stalin had said to Kamenev and Dzerzhinsky, who was then head of the OGPU: "To choose one's victim, to prepare one's plans minutely, to slake an implacable vengeance, and then to go to bed . . . There is nothing sweeter in the world." In a conversation with Kamenev in July 1928 Bukharin compared Stalin to Genghis Khan and warned that he "knows only vengeance . . . We must remember his theory of sweet revenge." [53]

We now know from the memoirs of Stalin's daughter, Svetlana Alliluyeva, that after Stalin drove his wife to suicide in the fall of 1932, "The first few days he was in a state of shock." [54] Externally life remained much the same, "But inwardly things had changed catastrophically. Something had snapped inside my father." [55] Svetlana writes that Stalin underwent "a psychological metamorphosis," after which "he was in the grip of an iron logic whereby once you've said A, then B and C have to follow. Once he accepted the premise that X was his enemy, the premise became axiomatic, and no matter what the facts might be, they had to be made to fit." [56]

No one was more familiar with NKVD methods of torture than Stalin, and yet Svetlana writes:

> What my father didn't want to realize was that in the cellars of the secret police X, Y and Z could be made to testify to anything. That was the domain of Beria, Yezhov and the other executioners, whom nature had endowed with a special talent for that sort of thing. . . .
>
> At this point—and this was where his cruel, implacable nature showed itself—the past ceased to exist for him. Years of friendship and fighting side by side in a common cause might as well never have been. Difficult as it is to understand, he could wipe it all out at a stroke—and X would be doomed. "So you've betrayed me," some inner demon would whisper. "I don't even know you anymore." Remembering his old attitude toward them, men and women he'd worked with for years, colleagues and friends of long standing, might plead with him, but it was all in vain. He was deaf to them already. He couldn't go back. He couldn't even remember.[57]

Svetlana's analysis of the timing of Stalin's metamorphosis was strikingly confirmed by a succession of dramatic events in September 1936. During the first show trial in August, the prosecutor, Andrei Vyshinsky, announced that evidence had turned up implicating Bukharin, Rykov, Tomsky, and others, which was being investigated. Tomsky committed suicide under the strain, but on September 14 a brief announcement appeared in *Pravda* stating that the investigation of Bukharin and Rykov was being called off due to lack of incriminating evidence.[58]

Bukharin was apparently supported by G. G. Yagoda, the chief of the secret police. Stalin's reaction came quickly. In a dramatic telegram sent from Sochi on September 25, Stalin demanded the replacement of Yagoda by N. I. Yezhov and called for the merciless purging of traitors and unreliable elements from party ranks. The police should now do the things they had failed to do four years earlier. This was the time of his wife's suicide, when "something snapped" inside, and apparently for the first time he demanded the death penalty against his opponents.[59]

From the time Yezhov took over as head of the NKVD until his execution and replacement in December 1938 by Lavrenty P. Beria, the Great Purge took on fantastic proportions. An estimated eight to nine million perished, including the cream of the party, military, and government elite. "In a vast conflagration of mock justice, torture, and brutality, at least two-thirds of the governing class of Russia literally devoured and destroyed itself."[60] Khrushchev himself has admitted that the Soviet order was hard put to survive the holocaust and "the tremendous loss of cadres suffered as a result of the baseless and false mass repressions in 1937–1938."[61]

DISINFORMATION, PLOT, AND COUNTERPLOT

B Y THE
fall of 1936 Stalin had decided to make a deal with Hitler and
began to speed up the purge of all internal *political* opposition.
By December the *Yezhovshchina* (the "time of Yezhov," the
Grand Inquisitor of the Great Purge) was well under way. The
next step was to set in motion a covert operation which would
justify the killing of his top *military* leadership, which in
Stalin's sick delusional world might also conceivably stand in
the way of his contemplated settlement with Hitler. This would
be a most delicate piece of surgery requiring instruments that
could cut both ways and injure the hands of the surgeon.

Beginning with the first Five-Year Plan in 1928, the forced
collectivization of agriculture had resulted in terrible hardships
for the Russian people. In a famous article in March 1930,
Stalin had called a halt to early excesses and had placed the
blame on his subordinates. But in the famine of 1932 millions
of peasants had starved in the Ukraine and the north Caucasus.
The collectivization program was resumed, and at least five
million alleged kulaks ("rich peasants") had been deported by
1932. About a million others perished in forced labor camps
under the harsh administration of the NKVD.[1] Thus when the
Great Purge began, the liquidation of a political elite that had
inflicted such hardships evoked little sympathy on the part of
the disaffected population.

There is no solid evidence to support rumors that such

army leaders as Blyukher opposed collectivization, although they were certainly aware that it gravely injured morale.[2] Nevertheless, at the time of the purges the Red Army was probably the one institution that still commanded widespread popular support. According to Weissberg, the army "was as well loved among the masses of the people as the G.P.U. was hated." He adds a personal reminiscence by way of illustration:

> I well remember my own feelings. In February, 1937, after I had already been summoned to the G.P.U. three times, I was walking in a very depressed mood along the Ulitsa Pushkina in Khartov when I met a column of the Red Army. The men were singing, and the sight of them brought tears to my eyes. Inwardly I had already finished with the Communist Party, but the Red Army still remained the symbol of the great revolution for me.[3]

Given the popular support of the Red Army, Stalin must have realized that a sudden brutal killing of his top military leaders would entail too much of a calculated risk. The case against them would have to be carefully prepared, and would require incriminating evidence that would be credible not only to the public, but also to those military leaders who survived. Obviously, something more would be required than the kind of manufactured evidence being produced by the NKVD for the political show trials, the first of which was already under way. The incriminating material would be all the more convincing if part of it came from abroad and from unimpeachable high-level sources. Although the evidence to support it is circumstantial, this line of reasoning best accounts for the origin of the "Tukhachevsky conspiracy," which Khrushchev himself declared nonexistent in a speech to the 22nd Party Congress in 1961.

According to Nicolaevsky, I. A. Serov, an old-line Chekist who made his career while working under A. N. Poskrebyshev in Stalin's personal secretariat, "was chiefly responsible for the execution of Tukhachevsky and his co-defendants." Serov also headed "the 'Special Sector' of the NKVD, which, working on direct instructions from Stalin's personal secretariat, was given the most responsible assignments connected with the liquidation of Stalin's major adversaries."[4] It appears that Stalin worked through such special channels to plant disinformation about Tukhachevsky abroad. Such reports would then be picked up not only by NKVD agents, but also by Western intelligence agents, thus gaining in credibility. For example, in Bella Fromm's *Blood and Banquets, A Berlin Social Diary,* the entry for October 24, 1936, refers to a report by an agent, "Henry," of the French ambassador's staff:

> The Nazis snub the Russians in public, but I know that privately they have been in close contact with an extensive clique of Russian Army officers. Quite a plot, too. Involves some of Marshal Tukhachevsky's highest staff officers. The clique entered into an agreement to effect the removal of Stalin. Afterward a pact with Germany against the world . . .[5]

But an obscure agent in the French embassy in Berlin and his informant were probably no more than secondary sources of the Tukhachevsky conspiracy rumors. Krivitsky writes that the émigré general Skoblin was used by Stalin as the original channel "in his frame-up of the most loyal generals of the Red Army." [6] This version of the source of the original disinformation has recently been confirmed by a member of the Soviet General Staff, Dashichev, as follows:

> Now for a word about the trial of our military leaders (the Tukhachevsky-Yakir group). The false evidence which was designed to permit their condemnation was prepared by the Gestapo; but the idea was Stalin's. He suggested it to the fascist leaders through the intermediary of General Skoblin. Unfortunately, the documents concerning this affair are inaccessible.[7]

For this reason—that is, because he knew too much—the émigré general Miller was kidnaped through the intermediary of General Skoblin in Paris on September 22, 1937 (see Chapter 14 above). Both generals were presumably killed at the time or shortly thereafter; they have never been heard from since. Krivitsky writes that "this bold crime was perpetrated in order to destroy the one uncontrolled source of information, apart from the Gestapo [SD] itself, as to the source of Stalin's 'evidence' against the Red Army Chiefs and the channels through which it travelled." [8]

Evaluation

How was Skoblin's report of an alleged Tukhachevsky conspiracy received and evaluated by Heydrich and his associates in the *Sicherheitsdienst?* What are the relevant facts bearing on the situation by which a plausible model of their evaluation can be reconstructed? First, it should be noted that Skoblin had been reporting on émigré affairs for almost a year; that is, since the end of 1935, when Heydrich set up a "section of the SD dealing with political intelligence on the U.S.S.R. (later known as Referat VI C)." [9] There is every reason to believe that during this period of several months Skoblin regularly turned in complete and well-informed reports on émigré affairs. He was undoubtedly rated by the SD as a "usually reliable" or "B" source on the U.S. rating scale. Second, as noted above, reports had already been circulated in intelligence circles (at least in the *Abwehr*) that on his European trip to London, Paris, and Berlin, Tukhachevsky had contacted the ROVS, the émigré officers' association in which Skoblin was a prominent figure. These earlier reports thus pointed to Tukhachevsky himself as the original source of Skoblin's information. Reports from a third source, "Henry" of the French embassy, may also have been collated with the others to provide further confirmation.[10] The amateurs in Heydrich's intelligence agency (they had been in business only about a year) would almost certainly collate Skoblin's report with such background information. If Heydrich and his aides had worked out an evaluation rating scale (which they probably had not), Skoblin's report would have been described as "coming from a reliable source" and "probably true"—a B2 rating on the U.S. scale. But one of Germany's most experienced intelligence specialists, SS Colonel *(Hauptsturmführer)* Erich Jahnke, warned that the report might well be a trick of Stalin's, because it came through Skoblin, who was a well-known NKVD agent. Jahnke at that time was an intelligence consultant to Rudolf Hess.[11] He had served with distinction in German military intelligence from 1914 to 1933 and had been responsible for such exploits as blowing up the New York docks (the "Long Tom explosions") during World War I. SS General Hermann Behrens (who was later hanged for his war crimes by the Yugoslavs in Belgrade in 1946) also supported Jahnke's warning [12] that Stalin's purpose in passing the report was to have incriminating evidence against his own military leaders fed back into NKVD channels from an external source and at the same time to sow distrust between Hitler and his top military leaders.

Whether it was suggested by Skoblin or was his own inspiration, Heydrich hit upon the idea of adding additional forged material to the evidence provided by Skoblin in order to incriminate high-ranking German generals as well as their Soviet counterparts. There is little doubt that Heydrich was motivated by a fierce hatred of the military establishment and had for years nursed a grudge because he had been dishonorably discharged as a junior officer from the navy. The fact that Skoblin was an NKVD agent and that the report might be false in no way bothered Heydrich if he could use it to strike a low blow against both the Soviet and the German military leaders. Fearing that Jahnke's negative evaluation might interfere with his scheme, Heydrich had him placed under house arrest.[13]

Dissemination

That NKVD agents had also penetrated Heydrich's *Sicherheitsdienst* is a matter of record: the famous Soviet spy R. Sorge, who at that time was stationed in Japan, also reported through special channels to the SD in Berlin.[14] Stalin may have received reports on the progress of his provocation from several intelligence agents in Berlin.[15] But he made sure the knowledge of the alleged conspiracy also reached Czech President Dr. Eduard Benes, who promptly relayed the report back to him through NKVD channels.[16] This maneuver served a double purpose. It tested Benes's loyalty to Stalin, a test the Czech leader passed with flying colors. Second, it provided additional high-level confirmation from another external and "usually reliable source" of the original disinformation. This fact in itself became one more damning bit of evidence to be used against the Soviet generals.

In his memoirs Benes writes that Hitler had tried to get him to sign a secret nonaggression pact in the fall of 1936, without the knowledge of either the German or Czech foreign ministers. For this purpose Benes had been approached twice, on November 13 and again on December 19, in the greatest secrecy by two special envoys, Count von Trauttmansdorff and

Professor Karl Haushofer, the Nazi "geopolitical" expert. In the second half of January 1937 Benes received a report (apparently from his ambassador Dr. Vojtech Mastny) from Berlin of a conversation with Trauttmansdorff in which the latter, "as a slip of the tongue," had unwittingly revealed that Hitler was negotiating "with the anti-Stalin clique in the U.S.S.R., Marshal Tukhachevsky, Rykov, and others. Hitler expected these negotiations to be successful and he was therefore not interested in bringing the discussions [about a secret nonaggression pact with Czechoslovakia] to a speedy conclusion . . . I at once informed the Soviet Minister at Prague, Alexandrovsky, of what I had learned from Berlin." [17]

What Benes calls "a slip of the tongue" by a high-level Nazi official selected by Hitler to negotiate behind the back of his own Foreign Office has all the marks of a calculated leak. Apparently Hitler correctly assumed that the report would be promptly relayed by Benes to Stalin, and the way would be paved for forwarding the dossier of forged evidence as soon as it was ready. What is most amazing in retrospect is that the report was apparently accepted at face value by Benes. Benes was well aware that both the German generals and the Red Army commanders were under constant surveillance by the secret police of their respective countries. Since the secret military collaboration had long since been broken off, how were the alleged conspirators able to evade the watchful eye of the secret police and "negotiate" an agreement? None of these obvious questions casting doubt on the credibility of the Tukhachevsky conspiracy story seems to have occurred to either Benes or Churchill.[18]

Although he does not mention it in his memoirs, Benes not only informed Stalin of the alleged conspiracy, but also the French Premier Léon Blum. To paraphrase an old story, it would seem that the three fastest means of disseminating a secret message at that time were "telephone, telegraph, and tele-Benes." This had important consequences, which were apparently unforeseen. Benes writes that on June 4, 1936, when Blum became premier, he "had sent me a message that France would never again behave with such weakness" as when Hitler occupied the Rhineland "and assured me that his government would be strong and firm toward Germany, and that we might count on this. This was really France's last stand. The Foreign

Minister, J. Paul-Boncour, sent me a number of messages in the same strain." [19]

For two years Léon Blum tried to put some teeth in the Franco-Soviet pact in spite of the "reticence" of his general staff. He testified to a postwar investigating committee that a secret report from Benes on the alleged Tukhachevsky conspiracy finally discouraged these efforts:

> At the end of 1936, I gave up bringing pressure to bear on the Minister of National Defence and on the General Staff in order to give the alliance its character of military solidarity. . . . [I had just received], in a private and friendly way from my friend M. Eduard Benes, a piece of advice transmitted by my son who was making a short stay in Prague, which counselled me urgently to take the greatest precaution in our relations with the Soviet General Staff. According to his own intelligence service—the Czech intelligence enjoyed a well-deserved reputation in Europe—those behind the Soviet General Staff were maintaining relations with Germany which gave ground for suspicion . . . It was this warning, given at the end of 1936, which crippled in some fashion the tenacious effort that I had been making for several months to invest the Franco-Soviet alliance with all its significance, and profit in the military sphere.[20]

It is ironic that in his bumbling way, Benes, who later complained bitterly about the Munich settlement, contributed directly to undermining effective Franco-Soviet military collaboration, which might have saved his country.[21]

Forging and Transmitting the Documents

Thus far we have traced the origin of the idea of the Tukhachevsky conspiracy from Stalin, its originator, through the émigré general Skoblin in Paris to Heydrich, chief of the Nazi *Sicherheitsdienst*. As soon as Jahnke, the old intelligence hand who warned that it was a provocation, had been put under house arrest, Heydrich took the material he had received from Skoblin to Hitler and obtained permission to add forged evidence that would fully implicate the German General Staff in a fake plot to liquidate both Stalin and Hitler. The original material was given a new dimension by including a forged correspondence including signatures of General von Seeckt, Trotsky, Tukhachevsky, and others who had been active in the years of secret German-Soviet military collaboration. As previously noted, Tukhachevsky himself was not actively involved in these exchanges (as a matter of open record) until 1931 to 1932, when he attended the fall maneuvers in Germany. Many of the original documents were deliberately deceptive, with personal and place names disguised. By means of astute alterations, plus added notes and "buck slips" (forwarding memos), some of the documents could easily be made to appear incriminating. Although he was aware of the suspicious background of the original Tukhachevsky conspiracy report, SS General Hermann Behrens, one of Heydrich's loyal deputies in the SD, played a major role in "filling out" the documentation with the assistance of another officer attached to the organization.[22] Behrens probably obtained adequate materials, including specimen signatures of the principal figures, by the simple expedient of requesting them through channels.[23] Obtaining a competent forger to duplicate the signatures, and one who could be sworn to absolute secrecy, was more difficult. However, according to one account, a skilled engraver was found who reproduced some fifteen pages of selected "documents" in a matter of hours while an SS major, Alfred Naujocks, stood guard. Information that these documents were available was then leaked to NKVD agents in Prague. Naujocks was soon contacted by "Hans," an NKVD agent in Berlin, who bought a photocopy of the collection for 50,000 marks,[24] and the documents presumably were sent on to Moscow via the Prague NKVD channel.

The problem of timing in the preparation and delivery of the forged dossier is an important one which has so far defied investigation due to the difficulty of distinguishing between "preparation" and "action" in a covert operation of this kind.[25] The accounts by former SD personnel date the systematic forging in April (Hoettl) and delivery in the middle of May 1937 (Schellenberg). Since the announcement of Tukhachevsky's transfer from Moscow to the command of the Volga Military District had already been made on May 11, it has been argued that the forged SD file had little bearing on his fate.[26] The only documentary evidence from the German side (the SD request for Tukhachevsky's prisoner-of-war file with his signature) is dated February 1937, and if the actual forging took only a few days (the figure "four days" is mentioned in at least two accounts), it seems reasonable to assume that the SD file reached Moscow by the beginning of March at the latest. This supposition is supported by the fact that in a speech to the Central Committee on March 3 on "Shortcomings in Party Work and on the Methods Used for Liquidation of Trotskyite and Other Double-Crossers," Stalin hinted darkly at the untold harm that "a few spies within the ranks of the Red Army could do to the country." [27] Having received the SD file, Stalin could proceed to prepare the public for the coming killings. It is important to note that according to Naujocks, the NKVD was content to buy no more than a photo copy of the incriminating SD evidence. This means that they *wanted* to accept it as authentic without any serious evaluation. Erasures, alterations, chemical analyses of inks, papers, etc., would almost certainly have revealed the forged nature of the originals if such had been delivered.[28] But Stalin and his executioners in the NKVD were not about to challenge the pedigree of the gift horse delivered to them by Heydrich's SD. In Erickson's apt formulation: ". . . at last the NKVD had within its possession material which could be used against the army . . . the poisoned bread cast upon the waters was bringing its final return." [29]

18

THE MILITARY PURGE,
JUNE 1937

I NCREDIBLE AS
it may seem, sometime in May 1935 (the month during which
the U.S.S.R. signed interlocking defense pacts with France
and Czechoslovakia), Stalin posted an envoy to Berlin whose
mission was to work for an improvement in Soviet-German
relations. His name was Yevgeny Gnedin, and he was an NKVD
agent who served as press attaché with the rank of secretary of
the Soviet embassy. (He later became head of the press department of the Soviet Foreign Commissariat and, although arrested, survived the purges, returning to Moscow after Stalin's
death.) [1] Apparently it was not until December 13, 1935, that
Gnedin had an opportunity for an extended conversation with
a representative of Rosenberg's foreign political office, responsible for Nazi party policy toward the U.S.S.R. His name was
Duercksen (not to be confused with von Dirksen, the former
German ambassador to Moscow). Duercksen reported that
Gnedin was a former journalist who had worked for some
years in the German Department of the NKVD and who made
"an intelligent impression." Gnedin stated "frankly" that

> he had been sent to Berlin with direct instructions to work
> energetically for an improvement of German-Soviet relations.
> But . . . [he] had gradually come to the conclusion that there
> was no desire on the German side to improve them. . . . He re-
> peatedly expressed his regret that the two countries which de-
> pended so much on each other were not able to arrive at a
> better relationship.[2]

Almost a year later (October 12, 1936), after German-Soviet relations had continued to deteriorate, Gnedin returned to the same theme. Duercksen reports:

> G. tried to convince me that he had come to Berlin eighteen months ago with specific instructions to study the possibility of an improvement in our relations. . . . Today, as a result of the Nuremburg speeches and of other things, the Soviet Union took a very negative view of such a possibility. But he only wanted to say there was no reason why the former attitude should not return.[3]

These overtures (which Duercksen found "astonishing"), and the Kandelaki mission which soon followed, may be regarded as the first tentative steps leading ultimately to the Nazi-Soviet pact of August 1939 and the unleashing of World War II. Apparently these maneuvers were kept secret from the Soviet government agencies that would normally have been involved or informed: from Litvinov and the Commissariat of Foreign Affairs, from the Council of People's Commissars (the Soviet equivalent of the cabinet), and from the Central Executive Committee. They were kept secret for very good reasons. As Krivitsky observes: "Since Stalin was executing his Old Bolshevik comrades as Nazi spies at the same time that he was himself conducting these secret negotiations with Hitler, they obviously could not be made widely known."[4]

The resources of Soviet intelligence were brought to bear in a number of indirect ways to impress Hitler favorably. For example, during the Spanish Civil War the latest Soviet fighter planes were permitted to fall by "mistake" into German hands. According to Orlov, a former NKVD chief, the German experts who examined them "were amazed at the quality and performance of the planes, which in some respects surpassed German fighters . . . Evidently, Stalin wanted to impress on Hitler that the Soviet Union was much stronger and better armed than he thought and that it would be wiser for Germany to have Russia as a partner than an opponent."[5] Orlov later observed that during the Hitler period "the NKVD intelligence in Germany acted very cautiously, not only because it was afraid of the Gestapo, but also because it feared Stalin, who in case of a spy scandal in Germany would berate the NKVD for jeopardizing his relations with Hitler."[6]

After Gnedin had obviously failed in his goodwill mission, Stalin switched to another channel, the Soviet trade delegation in Berlin, headed by David Kandelaki, a fellow Georgian and reportedly a former schoolmate of Stalin. In December 1936 Kandelaki approached Dr. Hjalmar Schacht, Hitler's finance and economics minister, and inquired about the prospects of enlarging Soviet-German trade. He was told that before this could take place, Communist-inspired agitation in Germany would first have to cease. Having made his initial exploratory pitch, Kandelaki then left for Moscow, accompanied by Friedrichson of the NKVD, to report to Stalin.[7] Presumably Kandelaki used the interview with Schacht to renew on December 24 a short-term trade and foreign-exchange treaty that had been signed the previous April.[8]

After reporting these meager results, Kandelaki and Friedrichson returned to Berlin in January 1937, and on January 29 once again appeared before Schacht on instructions from Stalin and Molotov with a written proposal that the two governments should open direct negotiations, either through regular embassy channels or in secret.[9] Apparently the Soviet proposal aimed at broader agreements than the short-term trade treaty already signed, and in an oblique reference to the Gnedin mission it observed that this was not the first time the Soviets had suggested such agreements. When pressed on whether the Russian proposals might be taken up, Schacht was noncommittal, and replied that certain guarantees (a reference to clamping down on Comintern agitation) would have to be forthcoming. He passed the proposals on to Neurath in the German Foreign Ministry, who briefed Hitler on them on February 10. Hitler reportedly felt that no practical result could be obtained from taking them up at that time.[10]

Krivitsky had been informed by NKVD sources in December that it would be "only a matter of three or four months before we come to terms with Hitler." His informant, A. A. Slutsky, head of the NKVD's Foreign Section (INU), told him: "Matters have gone so far that I can give you Stalin's own view in his own words. He recently said to Yezhov: 'In the immediate future we shall consummate an agreement with Germany.' "[11] Apparently this was overoptimistic, since there is nothing in the files to support such a rosy forecast.[12] As a matter of routine the trade treaties continued to be renewed

every so often, but it was not until the summer and fall of
1938 that both sides expressed a desire to relax tensions somewhat. Their respective propaganda agencies were directed "to
restrain themselves and cease attacking the other country . . .
the first visible indication that a change in the relations between
the Soviet Union and Germany was in the offing." [13] What in
retrospect is so remarkable about the secret Gnedin-Kandelaki
contacts in 1935–37 is that they were precisely the sort of
thing for which the top Soviet and military leaders were being
tried and executed at the time and on into December 1938,
when Yezhov himself was liquidated and the worst of the
terror abated.

Propaganda Preparation: The Second Show Trial

Although largely forgotten outside the U.S.S.R. today,
each of the three Moscow show trials was front-page news in
its day. The first two trials were used as propaganda preparation, naming future victims and creating an atmosphere of
terror for the military purge which took place in June 1937.
The kind of slow, methodic preparation that characterized
most of Stalin's moves began early in the year with the January
trial of the "Trotskyite Center" allegedly led by Karl Radek
and others. One by one, under merciless hammering by the
prosecutor, Andrei Vyshinsky, a galaxy of former Soviet
leaders confessed to a huge conspiracy involving espionage on
behalf of Germany. Walter Krivitsky, who was then head of the
NKVD's western European intelligence network, read about the
trial daily in the press from his station at The Hague. He writes:

> I was sitting at home with my wife and child, reading the
> testimony given on the evening of January 24, when my eye
> was startled by a line quoted in court from Radek's secret
> confession. Radek had stated that General Putna, lately Soviet
> military attaché in Great Britain and a prisoner of the OGPU
> for several months, had come to him "with a request from
> Tukhachevsky." [After quoting this line from Radek's confes-
> sion, the Prosecutor Vyshinsky then mentioned Tukhachev-
> sky's name no less than five times in his next three questions.]
>
> When I read this I was so profoundly shocked that my
> wife asked me what had happened. I handed her the paper,
> saying: "Tukhachevsky is doomed!"
>
> She read the report, but remained calm.

"But Radek again and again absolved Tukhachevsky from any connection with the conspiracy," she said.

"Exactly," I said. "Does Tukhachevsky need absolution from Radek? Do you think for a moment that Radek would dare of his own accord to drag Tukhachevsky's name into that trial? No, Vyshinsky put Tukhachevsky's name in Radek's mouth. And Stalin prompted Vyshinsky. Don't you understand that Radek speaks for Vyshinsky, and Vyshinsky for Stalin? I tell you Tukhachevsky is doomed."

. . . Stalin and Yezhov had forged a ring around Tukhachevsky and perhaps other ranking generals of the high command. It was certain to me that all secret preparations had been made, and that the process of closing in upon them in the open had begun.[14]

The Net Closes—From the Ides of March to May Day

The last full-dress appearance of the Soviet military leaders in Moscow was at a gala dinner party given by the American ambassador, Joseph E. Davies, on March 23, 1937, in honor of the Red Army. In his diary Davies wrote:

About 60 sat down at the Embassy table. They included the "High Command of the Army and Navy" and various notables . . . One was impressed by the fine appearance of these men—strong, healthy, and with fine faces. Their uniforms were resplendent with the various insignia of rank and various decorations, including "The Order of Lenin," etc.

This was the first and last occasion of its kind, for the Ambassador later noted: "Within nine weeks eleven of the principal officers of the army and navy were tried by court-martial and shot, among them Marshal Tukhachevsky and four other generals of the high command who were among our dinner guests." [15] The unconscious parallel with the last supper and the possibility that these men with their "fine faces" might have been betrayed or "framed" never occurred to Davies, a former lawyer. He had already accepted as valid the Soviet verdict against Radek and other "Trotskyites" condemned at the second show trial in January.[16]

Ironically, it was presumably in March that Stalin received the faked evidence from Germany of an alleged conspiracy between German and Red Army leaders. It was also on March 18, a few days before U.S. Ambassador Davies' dinner for the

Red Army high command, that Yezhov denounced NKVD chief Yagoda, replaced him, and shortly thereafter brought into the organization a staff of two hundred loyal henchmen to intensify the purge.[17]

Krivitsky had arrived in Moscow to report to Yezhov on the unfortunate effect of the two treason trials abroad, which "had been to shake the faith of pro-Soviet elements . . . The sweep of Stalin's purge was increasing daily, and it was working havoc in Western Europe." He describes the local scene and the thickening police-state atmosphere surrounding the military leaders as follows:

> When I reached Moscow I found an atmosphere of terror even in the highest offices of the government. The extent of the purge was greater, not less, than had been reported abroad. One by one, men who had been my friends and associates since the civil war, hardened and trusted and loyal officers of the general staff and other departments of the Red Army, were disappearing. No one knew whether he would be at his desk the next day. There was not a shadow of doubt that Stalin was drawing his nets around the entire high command of the Red Army. . . .
>
> By the end of April it became an open secret that Marshal Tukhachevsky, Vice-Commissar of War Gamarnik, and a number of other high-ranking generals were caught in the rapidly tightening net woven by Stalin's special agents. These leaders were still at liberty, but they were marked men. They were shunned at social affairs. It was considered dangerous to be seen speaking to them. They walked alone. Silence surrounded them.
>
> The last time I saw my old chief, Marshal Tukhachevsky, was on May 1, 1937, at the celebration on Red Square. . . .
>
> The marshal was walking across the square. He was alone. His hands were in his pockets. Who could guess the thoughts of this man who took care almost to saunter in the May Day sunshine, knowing he was doomed? He paused for a moment, glanced round the Red Square massed with humanity and adorned with banners, and then proceeded to the space in front of the Tomb, where the Red Army generals were accustomed to review parades.
>
> Tukhachevsky was the first to arrive there. He took his place and stood motionless, his hands still in his pockets. Some minutes later Marshal Yegorov came up. He did not

salute Tukhachevsky nor glance at him, but took the place beside him as if he were alone. A moment passed, and Vice-Commissar Gamarnik walked up. He again did not salute either of his comrades, but took the next place as though he did not see them.

Presently the line was complete. I gazed at these men, whom I knew to be loyal and devoted servants of the revolution and of the Soviet government. It was quite apparent that they knew their fate. That was why they refrained from greeting one another. . . . The military parade flowed by. It is customary for the Army generals to remain in their places for the civilian parade which follows. But this time Tukhachevsky did not stay. During the intermission between the two parades, he stepped out of line and walked away. His hands still in his pockets, he passed through the cleared lanes, out of the Red Square, out of sight.[18]

The showdown between the NKVD and the Red Army had begun in Spain before it reached Moscow. Already on February 4 General Kleber (whose real name was Stern) was relieved of the command of the International Brigade, was transferred to Málaga, and then vanished after arrest by the NKVD. The small Soviet military force of about two thousand in Spain was commanded by Berzin, the chief of army intelligence, who successfully directed the defense of Madrid in 1936. He was assisted by Stashevsky, a Red Army commander. But the NKVD moved in everywhere virtually to seize control of the republic with a policy of kidnaping, killing, and terror.[19] The Soviet security police had control of everything except tactical military operations while the Army watched with dismay. Berzin and Stashevsky complained through channels and the latter traveled to Moscow to brief Stalin and Tukhachevsky in April 1937, but by then the Marshal was powerless to help. (The situation was a preview of the relationship between the German Army and the Nazi security police during the German occupation of Russia, when SS and SD atrocities totally alienated an originally friendly population.) [20] George Kennan has observed that the Soviet intervention in Spain was the last manifestation of liberal antifascism in the U.S.S.R., and that almost without exception Stalin later exterminated all who had participated in what initially was an idealistically motivated crusade.[21]

While this struggle was going on in Spain, back in Moscow

lesser military leaders began to disappear into the Lubyanka cellars with increasing frequency—men like General Putna, who had been named in the January show trial by Radek, or Army Commander A. I. Kork, head of the Frunze Military Academy, who had been attacked in April in *Krasnaya zvezda* (Red Star), the Army newspaper.[22] An article in *Pravda* for April 28 on the need for the Soviet military to master politics as well as technique clearly suggested changes that were not long in coming. On May 10–11 the hated system of "dual command" and political commissars was reintroduced. At the same time a series of personnel changes in the high command was announced. Marshal A. I. Yegorov was relieved as chief of the General Staff and replaced by B. M. Shaposhnikov. I. E. Yakir was transferred from Kiev to command of the Leningrad Military District. Marshal Tukhachevsky was posted to a provincial outpost, the Volga Military District, comprising three territorial divisions and a couple of tank battalions. By the end of the month changes had been announced in the command of most of the military districts, but many of the reassigned men were arrested by the NKVD before arriving at their new posts.[23]

On the day he left Moscow (May 22) to return to The Hague, Krivitsky went to Mikhail Frinovsky, a deputy chief of the NKVD, while "hourly reports came in of fresh arrests," and asked him directly:

> "Tell me, what's going on? What's going on in the country?" I demanded of Frinovsky. "How can I leave in these circumstances? How can I do my work without knowing what it's all about? What shall I say to my comrades abroad?"
> "It's a conspiracy!" replied Frinovsky. "We've just uncovered a gigantic conspiracy in the Army, such a conspiracy as history has never known. And we've just now learned of a plot to kill Nikolai Ivanovich [Yezhov] himself! But we've got them all. We've got everything under control." [24]

It is significant that from his vantage point near the apex of the NKVD, Frinovsky spoke only of "a gigantic conspiracy" suddenly discovered within the Army, but made no mention whatever of the "Tukhachevsky plot," fabricated by Heydrich's SD. This means that an entirely separate NKVD dossier was already in existence proving the case against the Red Army leaders based on *internal* evidence alone. It wasn't until much later, sometime early in July, that Krivitsky learned from Spiegelglass, deputy chief of the Foreign Division of the NKVD, that evidence had been obtained "from Germany too—from inside sources . . . [not] from salon conversation but from within the Gestapo itself." [25]

The NKVD case for an internal counterrevolutionary organization was extremely weak, to put it mildly. It is difficult to build up convincing evidence from scraps of disgruntled conversation remembered from chance meetings, etc. Bukharin and other witnesses who appeared at the third show trial in March 1938 had been worked over by the secret police for months. Their roles had been carefully rehearsed and they were supposed to present conclusive evidence that the Soviet military leaders (who by then had been shot and could not defend themselves) had planned a military coup d'état or "palace revolution" the year before. The prosecutor's case was full of the most glaring contradictions. For example, Tukhachevsky was supposed "simultaneously to attend a ceremony in London and raise rebellion in Moscow . . . The whole thing was preposterous and inane." [26] Since this was the case almost a year *after* the military purge, it is obvious that in June 1937 the NKVD dossier needed strengthening badly if it was to be convincing. That strengthening came from the German side, from the dossier forged by Heydrich's SD and kept secret from all but Stalin, Yezhov, and the few agents involved in transmission and delivery of the forged documents.

Before killing his top military leaders, Stalin not only needed evidence against them which would be convincing, but also needed to present that evidence, in closed session of course, to a large number of their colleagues. Otherwise he would run the risk that a genuine military coup d'état might develop. Stalin also knew that without retaining a hard core of officers who would remain loyal to him it would be impossible to reform the Red Army into an effective fighting force after the killings. To achieve both these objectives, an extraordinary session of the Military Soviet attached to the Commissariat of Defense was held from June 1 to 4.[27] It appears that military district commanders from various regions of the U.S.S.R. also attended. (A rough American equivalent would be an expanded conference of the Joint Chiefs of Staff and the National Security

Council to which U.S. military district commanders would also be invited.) [28]

The immediate occasion for the conference was the determined opposition of Marshal Tukhachevsky and other top-level commanders to the reimposition of political-commissar control over military commanders, which had been announced on May 10–11, along with certain changes in the High Command. According to Colonel Phillip R. Faymonville, the U.S. military attaché, it was

> inconceivable that trained military men like Marshal Tukhachevsky and Komandarms [Generals] Yakir, Uborevich, and Kork could have approved of a system under which the single authority of the military commander, only recently achieved after great tribulation, should be once more divided with political officers. This innovation, coming after twenty years of loyal service by the Red Army . . . could only have enraged Marshal Tukhachevsky and the military commanders who agreed with him. . . . The general military conference which took place from June 1st to 4th appears to have been called to deal with this crisis: whether or not the measures . . . were to be enforced in the face of the determined opposition of Marshal Tukhachevsky.[29]

Apparently it was also at this general conference that the combined evidence from the two sources, the internally prepared NKVD dossier plus the forged German documents, was presented to a stunned audience. A senior émigré Russian officer claims to have had a conversation with a member of the supposed tribunal which reportedly passed judgment on the condemned officers. According to this source, "the accused did not confess, but the *documentary* evidence produced against them was overwhelming and convincing." [30]

Stalin's original bit of disinformation, the false report of a Tukhachevsky conspiracy to overthrow the regime and set up a military dictatorship, had been transmitted through the renegade émigré general Skoblin to Heydrich's *Sicherheitsdienst* in Berlin. From there, amplified and strengthened by skillfully forged documents, it had returned to the Kremlin along NKVD channels in ample time to be used by Stalin as a decisive weapon against the last potential source of leadership which could rival his own. In retrospect it may seem incredible that a small sheaf of forged documents—and photostat copies, at that—could have convinced the other Red Army commanders that their most talented and respected leaders were guilty of treason in their contacts with their German counterparts. But in an atmosphere charged with fear, suspicion, and denunciation, the threshold of disbelief lowers remarkably, as German officers who survived the Hitler period and American officials who lived through the much milder hysteria of the McCarthy period can testify. The subconscious drive to go along with denunciations can be a powerful motivating factor when one's life and the lives of one's family can be jeopardized by the slightest show of opposition. Moreover, in Stalin's sick world, denunciation was not only the ultimate test of loyalty to himself, but a positive virtue in itself. Somewhat later, about the middle of the year 1937, according to recent testimony of a General Staff officer, Anfilov:

> Stalin declared to another meeting: "Voroshilov and I arrived in Tsaritsyn [later renamed Stalingrad, now Volgograd] in 1918, and within a week we had unmasked all the enemies of the people, whereas you, you're not even capable of unmasking your neighbors." Voroshilov at once interrupted to declare himself entirely in agreement with Stalin and to invite us to denounce our own friends and colleagues. It makes me sick to the stomach to see Voroshilov on the tribune when a parade passes in review.[31]

Part of the "sons against fathers" cleavage that haunts both post-Stalin Russia and post-Hitler Germany stems from the inability of the postwar generation to project itself into the purge-ridden atmosphere of a police state. In today's relatively free environment there are few Soviet fathers who can give wholly convincing and satisfactory answers to the embarrassing question: "Where were you when your friends and colleagues were being herded off to forced labor camps?" Even Ilya Ehrenburg's plea, "We thought (perhaps we wanted to think) that Stalin knew nothing about the senseless acts of violence committed against the Communists, against the intelligentsia," leaves much to be desired.[32]

By the first week in June, then, with the meeting of the general military conference in Moscow the stage had been set. Stalin had achieved, if not complete credibility, at least a numbed suspension of disbelief in the hollowness of the charges made against the accused. A basis had been laid for the "justice" soon to be meted out. The air was thick with rumors of arrests and of the suicide of Ya. B. Gamarnik, the head of the Political Administration of the Red Army (who was almost certainly murdered in prison).[33] In a report dated June 8, Loy Henderson, the chargé d'affaires at the U.S. embassy, wrote:

> The Embassy agrees with the view of a number of competent foreign observers in Moscow that the arrests and shifting of army personnel and the changes which are being made in the army structure are prompted by lack of confidence on the part of Stalin and the little Party group around him in the absolute loyalty to themselves of certain sections of the Red Army. Whether the Kremlin will go so far as to charge that there has been a gigantic Red Army plot remains to be seen . . . The press is already commencing to charge Gamarnik with Fascist espionage and treachery, the usual synonyms for lack of enthusiasm over Stalin's leadership.[34]

The answer to the question of what would happen next vas not long in coming. Four days later, on June 11, *Pravda* :arried an announcement that

> . . . the case of Tukhachevsky, Yakir, Uborevich, Kork, Eideman, Feldman, Primakov, and Putna, who had been arrested by the Commissariat for Internal Affairs at various dates, has been completed and the case has been turned over to the court. The above-mentioned prisoners are charged with violation of their military obligations (oath of allegiance), treason to the Fatherland, treason to the peoples of the U.S.S.R., and treason to the workers' and peasants' Red Army.
>
> The investigation has established that the accused, and also Gamarnik, who committed suicide, participated in anti-State connections with leading military circles of a certain foreign nation [Germany] which follows an unfriendly policy in regard to the U.S.S.R. Being in the military secret service of this nation, the accused systematically supplied the military circles of this nation with espionage information concerning the condition of the Red Army, conducted wrecking work designed to weaken the Red Army, and endeavored to prepare the defeat of the Red Army in case of an armed attack

upon the [U.S.S.R.], and it was their purpose to facilitate the restoration of the power of the landowners and capitalists in the U.S.S.R.

All of the accused have pleaded guilty in the fullest measure to the charges brought against them.

The hearing of the case will take place today June 11 at a closed special judicial session of the Supreme Court of the U.S.S.R., consisting of the Chairman V. Ulrich, Chief of the Military Collegium of the Supreme Court, and the following members of the court.[35]

There followed the names and titles of Alksnis, Budenny, Blyukher, Shaposhnikov, Corniv [sic] (read Belov), Dybenko, Kashirin, and Goryachev.

In reporting on this announcement, Colonel Faymonville, the U.S. military attaché, reasoned if the NKVD had in fact had any hard evidence of treasonable activity on the part of the accused, it was "inconceivable" that they "could have retained their high places and their freedom until June 1st" (the opening of the general military conference in Moscow). As to the charge that the accused sold out to the Germans, he observed that there "was not enough money in Germany to purchase the entire group alleged to have been corrupted. Men with the characters of the accused do not become traitors." Noting that the preparations for Soviet espionage trials took months, he reported that "In time of peace, or even the half-peace which exists in Europe today, and particularly with commanders as eminent as the accused, it is inconceivable that a treason trial could be completed in a single day." [36]

The controversy over whether the accused were brought to trial is largely semantic, since it hinges on what the various sources have meant by the word "trial." [37] Certainly, nothing like the previous show trials, which took months to stage, ever took place. On the other hand, some sort of drumhead court-martial, presumably "a closed special hearing of the Supreme Court," [38] gave its rubber-stamp approval to Stalin's accusations and orders. In the fear-ridden atmosphere of the day, any other alternative would have been unthinkable. It is unlikely that the official records of this travesty of Soviet justice will ever be made public (if they have not long since been destroyed). These records have not been made available to even the most reliable party propagandists, such as the late Lev Nikulin, who have published biographies rehabilitating Tukhachevsky. Hence, accounts of "the trial" by Soviet journalists or novelists are largely apocryphal or at best based on hearsay evidence.

Count von Schulenberg, the German ambassador, who made his own investigation of the affair, told U.S. Chargé d'Affaires Loy Henderson that

> when in Berlin on leave, he told the appropriate German authorities that it was necessary for him as German Ambassador to the Soviet Union to know whether there was any truth in the conspiracy charges. He was assured that "there had been absolutely no illicit direct or indirect connections between any of the generals in question and German officials." . . .[39]

Tukhachevsky and the other executed officers have long since been officially rehabilitated and the treason charges against them dismissed. The question of their alleged guilt is thus academic. Nevertheless, from an intelligence point of view, the reaction to the executions by the western European embassies in Moscow is still of interest. Loy Henderson, the U.S. chargé d'affaires, reported on June 23: "Insofar as the Embassy can ascertain not one diplomatic mission here, nor a single foreign observer in Moscow whose opinion bears weight, believed that the executed Red Army officers were guilty of the crimes attributed to them." Returning to this point in a subsequent dispatch on September 30, Henderson wrote:

> Neither I, nor any of the Secretaries on duty in the Mission [including George F. Kennan and Charles E. Bohlen] have as yet been convinced that the eight generals were guilty of the crimes attributed to them . . . In the meantime, [the Embassy] continues to adhere to the view that the downfall of the generals was due to the fact that Stalin did not feel sure of their unconditional loyalty to himself.[40]

In striking contrast to this evaluation of the situation by the professional Foreign Service officers of the embassy, the ambassador, Joseph E. Davies, wrote a long estimate on July 28, in which he absolved Stalin of responsibility for the executions as follows:

> . . . generally speaking, in diplomatic circles here responsibility for these executions, in a strictly personal sense,

is not attributed to Stalin. He commands a great deal of respect, outside of these terrible happenings. He is considered to be a clean-living, modest, retiring, single-purposed man, with a one-track mind, devoted to communism and the elevation of the proletariat. The responsibility is generally attributed to the "action of the party" through its party leaders.[41]

Davies had had nothing but the highest praise for Tukhachevsky and his fellow officers when they had attended a gala dinner party at the embassy in April. In July, however, after Tukhachevsky had been executed, Davies retroactively changed his evaluation of the Marshal: "Tukhachevsky had the reputation of being a very able man. He did not impress me very much. He had a rather fresh and boyish appearance, was rather overweight for his size, and looked like a man who enjoys good living." [42] In direct contradiction to the reports of his embassy staff (which included Henderson, Kennan, and Bohlen), Davies writes: "It is generally accepted by members of the Diplomatic Corps that the accused must have been guilty of an offense which in the Soviet Union would merit the death penalty." [43]

Twice in his reports Davies implies that the French ambassador, Robert Coulondre, also believed in the reality of the alleged Tukhachevsky conspiracy.[44] By contrast, the chargé d'affaires, Loy Henderson, in his report dated June 23 writes:

> The French Ambassador has told me in confidence . . . he was convinced that no formal conspiracy had evolved and that he did not believe that the executed officers had formed treasonous contacts with Germany or any other foreign power.[45]

It would be difficult to find more striking examples of a wider divergence between amateur and professional intelligence reporting than that illustrated in these dispatches concerning the Tukhachevsky affair from the U.S. embassy in Moscow.

Finally, Coulondre's ultimate evaluation of the "Tukhachevsky conspiracy" provides a striking illustration of what in intelligence circles is called "feedback," in this case the re-echo in Moscow of Stalin's original disinformation played through Paris, Berlin, and Prague. The original French embassy reaction to the executions was reported as follows in Henderson's telegram of June 13, 1937:

There is a rumor among the Soviet population that the intelligence service of the French Army first discovered that the Red Army officers were involved in a conspiracy with agents of the German Government to overthrow Stalin and communicated their findings to the Soviet Government. The Embassy is not in a position to state whether there is any foundation for this rumor, which is ridiculed by the French Embassy here. Even though the French military intelligence service may have found cause to be concerned at friendly relations existing between certain Soviet and German officers and the prevalence of friendly feelings for Germany among the higher officers of the Red Army, the Embassy nevertheless is not convinced that the condemned men were guilty of the crimes attributed to them.[46]

Coulondre was at a loss to explain the origin of this rumor until after an interview with V. P. Potemkin, deputy chief of the Commissariat of Foreign Affairs, during which he pressed the diplomat for an explanation. Potemkin had been stationed in Paris as Soviet ambassador to France as recently as February 1937, before returning to Moscow to assume his new position. According to Potemkin:

Last February during a reception Daladier [the French premier] took me aside and told me confidentially that he had learned from a good source that contacts had been made between representatives of the Reich and members of the Soviet High Command and that a deal had been made to organize a military plot, the overthrow of the Bolshevik Government and the conclusion of an agreement with Berlin.

Potemkin then added: "In suppressing the traitors we have shown our fidelity to the Franco-Soviet entente and have affirmed the continuity of our political orientation." [47]

When writing his memoirs many years after the executions (they were published in 1950), Coulondre observed that "This [conversation] could explain the rumor in Moscow according to which my embassy had denounced Tukhachevsky." He then hedged on his original evaluation of the guilt question based on the information in Churchill's memoirs which came through Benes, concluding: "It would thus seem probable [*peu douteux*] that there was a military plot." Coulondre then qualified this conclusion as follows: "However, the fact that the Czechoslovak police was informed of the plot by the GPU makes the whole affair somewhat suspect." [48] This is a classic example of diplomatic understatement.

Military-Diplomatic Consequences

So far as the Western powers are concerned, the most important and far-reaching result of the military purge was its effect on estimates of Soviet military capabilities. U.S. Chargé d'Affaires Loy Henderson's estimate was probably shared by the military attachés of the Western powers: "It is the consensus of opinion of competent observers here that the morale and self-confidence of the armed forces from top to bottom has received a severe shock from which they cannot recover for some time." [49] The British embassy estimate was even more emphatic. Noting that about 65 percent of all general officers had been killed, British observers believed that the purges "had thrown the General Staff and Higher Command into such appalling chaos and disorganization for the time being that one could not possibly tell what might or might not happen in the event of a major operation." [50]

Ambassador Schulenburg, who had been one of the architects of German-Soviet collaboration, observed that "the removal of most of the higher command, their replacement by insufficiently trained younger men, and the reintroduction of political commissars have brought about a not inconsiderable weakening of the striking power of the Red Army." [51]

Curiously, U.S. Ambassador Davies was the only contemporary observer to hold an opposite view. He writes:

> The elimination of higher commanders by the purge . . . had resulted in the promotion of many of the younger officers who, while lacking the experience of their predecessors, probably made up for it in greater energy and devotion and loyalty to the government . . . [The purge also] resulted in a feeling of greater security on the part of the average soldier, and the belief that his fate was now in the hands of more trustworthy and loyal officers than "the Trotskyite traitors who met the fate they deserved." [52]

After the German invasion of the U.S.S.R. in June 1941, Davies reinterpreted the Moscow trials as proving the existence of a Nazi fifth column in Russia, spearheaded by Tukhachevsky and his military colleagues. His article "How Russia

Blasted Hitler's Spy Machine," written for *American Magazine* and included in *Mission to Moscow,* concluded with the reassuring statement: "There were no Fifth Columnists in Russia in 1941—they had shot them. The purge had cleansed the country and rid it of treason." [53] However mistaken this example of historical hindsight may be, Davies was instinctively right when he wrote at the time of the military purge:

> . . . these shootings have probably been more serious in their adverse effects on conditions in Europe, outside of Russia, than on conditions within the Soviet Union. There is no doubt that the confidence of France and England in the stability of a potential eastern European ally must have been severely shaken by these events.[54]

While France was in the midst of a cabinet crisis, Hitler moved into Austria March 11–13, 1938, and it was universally expected that his next move would be against Czechoslovakia. This would invoke the interlocking Franco-Soviet and Czech-Soviet pacts, under which the U.S.S.R. had pledged to come to Czechoslovakia's assistance, but only if France would honor her commitment to do so first. Léon Blum had hastily formed a cabinet with Paul-Boncour as Foreign Minister on March 13, and on March 14 Blum reaffirmed France's intention to support Czechoslovakia.[55] Meanwhile, on March 15 a Soviet spokesman stated that the U.S.S.R. would go to the aid of Czechoslovakia if the latter were attacked, provided France did likewise. As if returning a ping-pong ball, on March 23 French Foreign Minister Paul-Boncour again reaffirmed France's intention to support Czechoslovakia. But all was certainly not well beneath this visible exchange of reassurances. Even in the heyday of the Blum Popular Front government, France had been a reluctant ally of the Soviets. After receiving the Stalin-inspired disinformation about an alleged Tukhachevsky plot from Benes in December 1936, Blum had given up trying to put some steel into the Franco-Soviet pact. On the very day of Paul-Boncour's reassuring statement, Soviet Foreign Minister Litvinov conferred with U.S. Ambassador Davies on the Czechoslovakian situation. Davies writes:

> He [Litvinov] made the rather startling statement that there was danger that Czechoslovakia might voluntarily yield to Germany because she had no confidence in France and

was completely surrounded. For that matter, Litvinov stated frankly, "France has no confidence in the Soviet Union and the Soviet Union has no confidence in France." [56]

Within a matter of days another cabinet crisis reinforced Soviet lack of confidence in her reluctant French ally.

The new Daladier cabinet was formed without Socialist participation and with Georges Bonnet as foreign minister on April 10. Two days later the quasi-official newspaper *Le Temps* featured an article by the jurist Joseph Barthélemy which argued that France was not obliged to go to war to save Czechoslovakia. In case of war the Soviet regime would collapse and another Brest-Litovsk would follow. How could the U.S.S.R. come to Czechoslovakia's aid when the Czech airfields would be overrun in three weeks? [57] M. Coulondre reported that the Soviets made a dry-run test of the feasibility of such aid by flying sixty Soviet bombers to the airfield at Uzhorod in eastern Slovakia,[58] but the crux of the matter was that there were no military agreements between the U.S.S.R. and Czechoslovakia under which aid could have been supplied. Benes himself had never pressed for a military agreement, since—although he was more than eager to provide Stalin with secret intelligence— he prided himself on a "Western orientation." [59] Having been the first to undermine Blum's confidence in the U.S.S.R. with the story of the Tukhachevsky conspiracy, Benes was not likely to press for firm military agreements, although he obviously did not interfere with Soviet preliminary military preparations.

Soviet policy toward Czechoslovakia at this time was typically ambiguous. For publicity purposes President Kalinin told a delegation of Czech workers on May 11: "The Soviet Union has invariably fulfilled all its treaties concluded with other States in all their consequences and will do so in this case also. It will if called upon fulfil to the last letter all its obligations to Czechoslovakia and France." [60]

On the other hand, in a speech in Leningrad on June 23, Litvinov went out of his way to emphasize that the U.S.S.R. would reserve complete freedom of choice in any contingency that might arise over Czechoslovakia. Soviet intelligence was probably aware that at a private luncheon on May 10 with American and Canadian journalists, British Prime Minister

Neville Chamberlain had reportedly expressed the view that Russia neither could nor would fight for Czechoslovakia, and that France was incapable of doing so.[61] Taking his cue from rumors current in London in May that Chamberlain had indicated that cession of the Sudetenland to Germany would be the best solution of the crisis, Litvinov ominously hinted that the Czech government would "find reasonable limits for concessions." This key passage, which might be called "Exhibit C" in the Soviet record of appeasement, reads as follows:

> Our peace policy compels us, naturally, to wish that conflicts arising between Czechoslovakia and its neighbours be settled peacefully, but we strictly refrain from giving any unsolicited advice to the Czechoslovak Government, for we believe in its peaceful intentions, and consider that it is its own judge in internal political affairs; that it will itself find reasonable limits for concessions compatible with its prestige, sovereignty, and independence as a State.[62]

In this remarkable speech, given three months before the Munich crisis in September, Litvinov deliberately isolated the U.S.S.R. in advance from whatever arrangements would be made by "the states responsible for the postwar international order," and relieved his government "of responsibility for the further development of events." The relevant passage follows:

> As you see, comrades, the Soviet Government is by no means indifferent to present international events; on the contrary, it is ready to fulfil and does fulfil completely its duty of international solidarity as a consistent and ardent fighter for peace. . . . Quite recently it reminded the peaceful Powers of the need for urgent collective measures to save mankind from the new sanguinary war that is approaching. This appeal was not heard, but the Soviet Government, at least, has relieved itself of responsibility for the further development of events. I should point out that the Soviet Union asks nothing for itself, does not wish to impose itself on anybody as partner or ally, but merely agrees to collective cooperation, for the situation that has arisen is especially dangerous not for the Soviet Union, but primarily for the small countries, and secondly for the States responsible for the postwar international order.[63]

The implication that the U.S.S.R. did not regard itself as "responsible for the postwar international order" and that the fate of Czechoslovakia would be left to France, England, and Germany is clear, and was not lost on the German embassy in Moscow, which interpreted Litvinov's speech as a very "objective" statement of opinion about German policy.[64] By thus writing off Czechoslovakia in advance, Stalin in effect gave his future ally Hitler *carte blanche* to press for maximum German demands at Munich. Since Churchill has described the British and French cabinets at this time as presenting to Hitler "a front of two overripe melons crushed together; whereas what was needed was a gleam of steel," the result was a foregone conclusion.

On September 12, just three days before Chamberlain flew to Berchtesgaden for his famous confrontation with Hitler, Ambassador Coulondre learned from his Czech colleague, Fierlinger, that the Kremlin did not believe that France and England were prepared to go to war for Czechoslovakia.[65] Since the machinery of the interlocking Franco-Soviet and Soviet-Czech pacts put the onus on France, which in turn deferred to the British position, the U.S.S.R. could and did promise aid without seriously risking that its bluff would be called. In a speech at the League of Nations on September 21, Litvinov revealed that in reply to a Czech question, asked two days earlier, whether the U.S.S.R. would stand by its obligations if France did, his government's gallant reply was "a clear answer in the affirmative." [66]

Winston Churchill was out of the British government during the Munich crisis, but his considered judgment in his memoirs is based on the principle that "there is no merit in putting off a war for a year if, when it comes, it is a far worse war, or a harder one to win." He had been approached by the Soviet ambassador, Ivan Maisky (who feared a rebuff from the Foreign Office), on September 2. Maisky told him that the U.S.S.R. was resolved to fulfill its obligations to Czechoslovakia and had suggested immediate staff conversations between Russia, France, and Czechoslovakia, and consultation between Russia and the Western powers. Churchill immediately transmitted the communication to Lord Halifax but received a "guarded reply." Churchill did not doubt Russia's willingness at that time "to join the Western Powers and go to all lengths to save Czechoslovakia." [67]

Churchill had no way of knowing that Maisky was referring to conversations between Litvinov, French Foreign Minister Bonnet, and Ambassador Coulondre, who was on leave in France during August. Litvinov had rejected the idea of forcing Poland to permit passage of Soviet troops—the only really effective way of aiding Czechoslovakia in case of war—since this "would make the U.S.S.R. look like an aggressor, and this we cannot do." Bonnet regarded the Soviet position as "dilatory." When Coulondre returned to Moscow in mid-September, he could get no satisfaction out of Potemkin at the Soviet Foreign Commissariat, who remained "completely dumb," and referred him back to Litvinov, who was still in Geneva! [68]

This was the cold substratum of reality behind the Soviet façade of promises as the Munich crisis matured. Thus the legend has developed that only the U.S.S.R. stood firmly by her commitments to Czechoslovakia and that during the mid-thirties there was a real possibility of an effective coalition of the U.S.S.R., France, and Great Britain which might have frustrated Hitler's ambitions and prevented the catastrophe of World War II. The legend is false on two counts. First, as George Kennan points out, because of the Great Purge

> . . . Stalin's Russia was never a fit partner for the West in the cause of resistance to fascism. Russia herself was, throughout these years, the scene of the most nightmarish, Orwellian orgies of modern totalitarianism. . . . To the moral cause of an antifascist coalition, the Soviet government of 1934 to 1937 could have added little but hesitant, halfway measures, and a nauseating hypocrisy.[69]

Second, the bungling Anglo-French appeasement of Hitler was perfectly open and publicly supported after Munich. By contrast, Stalin's appeasement of Hitler was carefully concealed from the public and even from Western intelligence agencies until the news of the Nazi-Soviet pact burst like a bombshell in August 1939. The pact was meant to unleash World War II, which was clearly envisaged by both Stalin and Hitler when they signed it. Western appeasement of Hitler necessitated the temporary loss of independence for Czechoslovakia. Stalin's appeasement involved the murderous liquidation of tens of thousands of both the party and the military elite, and seriously threatened the ability of the nation to survive the Nazi onslaught when it came two years later. Thus, in Erickson's apt formulation, Soviet policy at the time of the Czechoslovak crisis was "a policy as cynical and self-interested as the western powers' was dubious . . . The inevitable exclusion of the Soviet Union from the Munich settlement completed a self-imposed isolation, and made it imperative for Stalin to proceed with his private policy of negotiating an agreement with Hitler." [70]

Postlude: The German Attack on Russia

The military purge had far-reaching effects on military estimates before and after the Nazi onslaught against Russia, which was unleashed in the early-morning hours of June 21, 1941. So far as political leadership around Hitler was concerned, General Goering stated in November 1937 that the Red Army had "ceased to exist as a fighting force." [71] Late in October 1938 an important article in *Deutsche Wehr* took the line that the "Tukhachevsky conspiracy" was widely supported throughout the Red Army, which was held to be seething with dissidence and unrest. The Red Army was merely waiting for the right moment and the right "Bonaparte" (since Tukhachevsky had failed) to revolt against the regime. The fact that the U.S.S.R. did not intervene in the Czech crisis was interpreted as due only in part to the fact that its leadership had been decimated by the purges. "An even greater factor was probably the fear in the Kremlin of a Red Bonaparte." [72]

This kind of wishful thinking later undoubtedly influenced German military estimates in the planning period for the Russian campaign. The invasion plans and estimates were strongly influenced by the political assumption that resistance would collapse after the first few weeks of fighting along the Russian border.

This assumption, which became the inarticulate major premise underlying all German military planning for the Russian campaign, was never seriously examined by the German high command. It was simply accepted as axiomatic that the U.S.S.R. was "a colossus with feet of clay and no head," that the Russian people hated the regime so intensely that, after the first heavy blow, "the whole Bolshevik system would burst like a soap bubble." [73]

According to a recent Soviet source, Dashichev of the General Staff, the military purge was also a major factor in the decision to strike before the Red Army could be rebuilt. He states that:

> Hitler strongly influenced the decision of the German military leaders at a summit meeting during which he declared: "The Red Army has been decapitated. Eighty per cent of its commanders have been liquidated. The Red Army is weaker than it has ever been." This is the fundamental factor which caused him to make the decision: he had to wage war before new cadres could be re-formed. Every historian should have the courage to state this truth.[74]

That Hitler's estimate of the damage done to the Red Army by the purges may have been a little high is unimportant. Not only the wealth of material in captured German documents, but also recent Soviet memoirs bear witness to the repeated blunders by the Russian high command and admittedly inferior leadership on lower command levels in the initial stages of the campaign. Only the heroic efforts of those like General A. V. Gorbatov, who survived the purge, many of whom were recalled from forced labor camps, averted disaster. It should also be borne in mind that in spite of staggering initial losses and chaotic command conditions, the mass of the Red Army fought a stubborn patriotic defense against the foreign invader.[75]

In the days following the German invasion of the U.S.S.R. in June 1941, almost all Western experts also predicted a Russian collapse within a matter of months. The crucial question in Washington was whether vital supplies, desperately needed in Great Britain, should be diverted to Russia, since they would be lost and wasted in the event of a speedy Russian collapse. Ironically, however wrong he may have been on his evaluation of the military purge, it was former Ambassador Davies who "virtually alone among the President's advisers in those doubtful June days . . . counseled a policy of all-out aid to the retreating Soviets." Davies' optimistic counsel carried the day with President Roosevelt, who distrusted the career Foreign Service professionals, "who were better able to discern the disabilities in the Soviet system which the regime sought to conceal . . . while Davies merely overlooked them. Thus Davies was right for the wrong reasons, whereas his fellow diplomats were wrong but for the right reasons." [76]

The U.S.S.R. sustained, by conservative estimate, a minimum of twenty million casualties in World War II. How many of these were the needless result of Stalin's policy of appeasing Hitler, a policy he continued blindly until German planes were already dive-bombing and strafing the Soviet troops, will remain a matter of disputed value judgments. To those losses must be added the hundreds of thousands who were directly slaughtered in the purges and the several millions who later perished in forced labor camps. The revolution may have devoured some of its children in any case, but Stalin's appeasement crucified the best.

19
INTELLIGENCE
OPERATIONS
AND THE ROAD
TO WAR

IN THE
fall of 1946 the late Boris Nicolaevsky, one of the earliest
Soviet émigrés and experts, observed that in order to understand the real motives behind foreign policy one must study
the battle of the secret intelligence services which goes on con-
tinuously beneath the surface of historical events.[1] In the preceding chapters we have examined some of the major episodes
in the clash between Soviet and selected Western intelligence
agencies in the European theater during the 1920's and 1930's
as the Great Powers blundered their way into World War II.
We have concentrated on reconstructing the story of what
happened in this struggle in an attempt to lift the veil of
secrecy and often deliberate deception which has covered it.
The task remains of assessing the significance of these covert
operations.

How should the success or failure of these covert operations be judged? How did they affect the attitudes and the
decisions of Soviet leaders and their Western rivals? How did
they help set the scene for World War II? Keeping in mind
such questions, let us review briefly the major episodes and
operations with which we have been concerned. It should be
emphasized that our observations are tentative value judgments
drawn from incomplete data—from which other quite different
conclusions may be drawn.

In the first part of the book the historical setting, development, and collapse of the legendary Trust operation was examined. It will be recalled that after their seizure of power in November 1917, the Bolshevik leaders soon resorted to terror to consolidate their regime. The instrument used for this purpose was "the All-Russian Extraordinary Commission" (Cheka for short) "for combatting counterrevolution and sabotage," set up in December 1917. Thousands of internal enemies were ruthlessly liquidated during the confused period of War Communism, Allied intervention, and civil war. The Cheka (renamed the OGPU in 1923) next turned its attention to the suppression of counterrevolutionary activities directed from abroad. In addition to acting as an internal security service, the OGPU, through its Foreign Department, began active counter-espionage and covert operations outside the U.S.S.R. (Most governments divide internal security functions and foreign espionage, including covert operations, between two separate agencies—such as the FBI and the CIA respectively.)

One of the OGPU's first and most successful foreign ventures was the Trust operation. Thanks to a lucky break the OGPU was able to win over A. A. Yakushev, a leader in a Moscow-based resistance organization with links to like-minded émigré groups in the Baltic States and in Berlin. The organization was given commercial cover by the OGPU and renamed the Trust. As most of the émigré groups abroad were used by Western intelligence organizations, through the Trust the OGPU was able to some extent to penetrate these organizations (at least in the field) and to keep their activities under surveillance for roughly five years (1922–27). Through the Trust, Western intelligence agencies (mainly those of Great Britain, Poland, France, and even the United States) were fed a steady diet of disinformation mixed with some reliable reports. Moreover, during his travels as foreign liaison officer to Berlin, Paris, and Yugoslavia, Yakushev was very effective in presenting the Trust's ideological and tactical line to émigré resistance groups (and indirectly to Western intelligence agencies). The line, which was carefully tailored to what those target groups wanted to hear, was anti-interventionist: because the hated Bolshevik regime would inevitably collapse anyway, outside intervention was unnecessary. Aggressive covert operations against the U.S.S.R., such as guerrilla warfare, sabotage, and similar *terakts* (acts of terror), would be counterproductive. They would result in crushing counterterror by the OGPU and would prematurely destroy the Trust, the powerful resistance organization which would supply political leadership when the proper moment to strike came. Meanwhile, the Trust needed only moral and financial support in return for intelligence (read disinformation) which it alone could provide.

During the 1920's disinformation provided by the Trust undoubtedly reinforced the strongly anti-Bolshevik attitudes of such Conservative *eminences grises* within the British Establishment as Sir Eyre Crowe, the permanent civil service head of the Foreign Office, and J. D. Gregory, head of the Northern (Russian) Section. Also affected were such figures as Admiral (later Sir Hugh) Sinclair, the head of the S.I.S. until his death in November 1939, when his deputy, Stewart Menzies, took over the service.[2]

Operationally, however, even if the small Conservative in-group which ran the S.I.S. had been inclined to do so, it is unlikely that the agency was capable of mounting terrorist operations against the U.S.S.R. during the Trust period. The best evidence in this regard is the bumbling way in which the S.I.S. handled the western European operations of Savinkov, Elvengren, and Reilly, ending in the latter's entrapment by the OGPU.

The restraining influence of the Trust on the anti-Soviet operations of General Kutyepov's strategic services teams directed from Paris is clearly discernible. They would undoubtedly have started their terrorist raids sooner and probably on a larger scale had it not been for the Trust. But, here again; capabilities were limited by lack of funds, which were not available until 1930. Indeed, it seems likely that one of the major motives behind the kidnaping of General Kutyepov was the Soviet fear of what his organization might achieve once it had adequate funds.

So far as internal security is concerned, the Trust was a major success: the OGPU was able to keep under surveillance a potentially dangerous resistance organization, to liquidate individuals and groups which got out of control, and to suppress acts of terror against the regime. In this regard the operation was a textbook model of its kind.

The Trust also provided Soviet leadership with a sense of

security during a critical period (the early years of the NEP) when all energies were badly needed to rebuild the Soviet economy, which had been reduced to a shambles by War Communism and civil war.

Both in regard to maintaining internal security and in terms of deceiving and penetrating rival agencies abroad, the OGPU, through the Trust, clearly won the first round of the struggle between Soviet and Western intelligence agencies, at least so far as the Poles and the British were concerned. The Trust leaders, including Yakushev, however, were themselves deceived by General Kutyepov who, contrary to legend, realized at the outset that the Trust was a provocation but took a calculated risk to use its channels to collect intelligence. Two of his best-known agents, Maria Zakharchenko and her husband Georgi Radkovich, actually worked within the Trust in Moscow for more than three years, knowing all the while that the organization was controlled by the OGPU.

The Trust was needlessly compromised in 1924–25 for the sake of the entrapment and liquidation of the terrorist Boris Savinkov and the legendary British agent Sidney Reilly, although neither represented a serious threat to Soviet security at the time. It appears that as a result of the astonishingly favorable response to early Trust contacts abroad, the OGPU mistakenly believed that Western intelligence agencies could be deceived indefinitely. The attempt to counterbalance the damage done by the Reilly affair with the elaborately staged Shulgin visit to the U.S.S.R. failed. Only those who wanted to be deceived by Shulgin's escapade were impressed by it. Moreover, in spite of numerous signs of compromise, the Staunitz defection and the collapse of the Trust in the spring of 1927 obviously caught the OGPU by surprise, so that nothing could be saved from the wreckage. It is also clear from Soviet reaction to events at this time that the OGPU had not developed reliable replacement networks to fall back on—always a serious blunder in such operations.

The loss of Savinkov and especially Reilly was a severe blow to the prestige of the British S.I.S. It closed an epoch which began with the legendary wartime and postwar exploits of such agents as Bruce Lockhart, Reilly, Somerset Maugham, Sir Paul Dukes, and Captain George Hill, and ended with the misadventures of Georgi Elvengren. The Reilly affair was a sobering incident for the S.I.S. Incompetent agents such as Commander Boyce (who was mainly responsible for Reilly's loss) were transferred to obscure and less responsible posts. Old networks were scrapped and within two years' time had been replaced, so that by the spring of 1927 the British intelligence community was back in business again, busily collecting information from the Baltic windows, Leningrad and Moscow. (The term "community" is used to include both the S.I.S. and British Military Intelligence.) Although circumstantial, evidence indicates that, contrary to Soviet propaganda at the time, most of these new networks were controlled not by S.I.S. but by the British military establishment.

This leads to certain observations about the role of intelligence agencies in the 1927 war scare. It is clear from the evidence that the combined Western intelligence agencies conducted a major offensive against the U.S.S.R. in the spring of 1927. The Soviet press reported a dramatic increase of espionage cases from an average of two a month for the period January–April to forty-two a month during May, June, and July. Surviving émigré sources affirm that a collection effort of this magnitude was far beyond the capabilities of General Kutyepov's Combat Corps, which launched its own vest-pocket offensive of terrorist raids after the collapse of the Trust in mid-April. A sudden sharp increase in "enemy" espionage is usually taken as an indication of impending hostilities. This is standard intelligence doctrine based on military experience. The OGPU thus had every reason to be alarmed by the Western intelligence offensive. Moreover, Anglo-Soviet relations had been deteriorating under Conservative party pressure since February. After the Arcos raid on Soviet installations in London in mid-May, the British severed relations on the twenty-seventh. By the first week in June, General Kutyepov's Strategic Services teams had launched their terror raids, and bombs were exploding in Leningrad. On June 7 the Soviet ambassador to Poland was assassinated in broad daylight in Warsaw by a young émigré terrorist, precipitating a Polish-Soviet crisis. Cut off from its previous Trust intelligence sources, the OGPU was apparently floundering in the dark. It responded with a wave of arrests and executions. The execution of the first twenty victims was highly publicized and produced a backlash of moral revulsion abroad, destroying the favorable Soviet image which

had slowly been building during the NEP period. For the
most part, however, the OGPU counterterror was applied swiftly
and silently to maximize its effects internally, with arrests running into the thousands.

The OGPU undoubtedly overreacted to the dramatic events
outlined above. There is evidence that Georgi Chicherin, the
head of the Soviet Foreign Commissariat, and his deputy,
Maksim Litvinov, downgraded the threat of renewed Allied
intervention. But most of the Soviet leadership and certainly
the general public, informed by deliberately alarmist propaganda, took the war scare seriously. In connection with the
fierce internal power struggle in the Soviet Union which
reached a climax in November 1927, Stalin skillfully exploited the war scare to expel Trotsky and seventy-five members of the opposition from Moscow. The internal crisis coincided with the disastrous failure of Comintern intervention in
China, for which scapegoats had also to be found. By the end
of the year the war scare had played out, Stalin had crushed
the opposition, and the OGPU had wiped the slate clean of
internal resistance organizations linked with General Kutyepov
abroad.

By intervening at British and French requests to help
solve the Polish-Soviet crisis, German Chancellor Stresemann
severely strained German-Soviet relations, which had been
friendly and cooperative for several years. The spectre of a
renewed Allied intervention, with a faltering Germany siding
against Russia, may well have strengthened Stalin's determination to force the collectivization of agriculture and the pace
of industrialization in long-range preparation for such a
contingency.

The Western intelligence offensive and the Kutyepov terror
raids which lay behind the 1927 war scare were thus important factors in bringing the NEP period to a close. British
Prime Minister Austen Chamberlain dismissed Soviet fears
of a renewed Allied intervention as paranoid. It may well be
that he was never briefed by his own advisers on these operations, which, as evaluated by the OGPU, were a serious threat
to Soviet security.

After the collapse of the Trust, the Foreign Department
of the OGPU was faced with the problem of creating new net-

works abroad, and the war scare lent a new sense of urgency to its battle with Western intelligence services.

Top priority was given to establishing new links with General Kutyepov and with S. P. Melgunov, whose émigré newspaper in Paris stood for a policy of "revolutionary activism." For this purpose the OGPU sent General A. N. Popov to Paris in late June to set up the so-called "Second Trust," a provocation in which both Melgunov and Kutyepov were implicated, although the operations of these two leaders were entirely separate. Melgunov arranged for exchange of information with Popov and for distribution of his newspaper inside the U.S.S.R. Unknown to the OGPU, however, Melgunov had already established two separate underground networks which were engaged in subversive anti-Bolshevik operations. The scale of these operations is indicated by a budget for the year 1928 of over $1,705,000, of which $250,000 alone was earmarked for "terroristic acts." In view of the wave of OGPU terror which began with the 1927 war scare and continued well into 1929, the conduct of such operations must be regarded as a major achievement which has remained virtually unknown until the present.

In 1928–29 one of Melgunov's agents conceived a well-laid plan to assassinate Stalin, which was quite within the capabilities of the organization. But the project apparently never got beyond the planning stage. After the kidnaping of General Kutyepov in January 1930, Melgunov withdrew from émigré affairs, retired to the country, and devoted most of his energies to writing history. He was probably well advised to leave the hazardous business of covert operations: if the OGPU had realized the scope of his activities, he too would almost certainly have been liquidated.

Whereas Soviet intelligence failed to draw Melgunov into its net by means of the Second Trust, it was more successful with General Kutyepov, who sent agents into the U.S.S.R. through Rumania using new OGPU-controlled channels. Besides this deadly and highly ambivalent game, General Kutyepov's special forces teams continued their sporadic terror raids into the Soviet Union well into 1928. They were soon decimated, although in an amazing penetration Georgi Radkovich exploded a bomb in the Lubyanka headquarters of the OGPU, a dramatic gesture of suicidal desperation. In retaliation, and in order permanently to cripple what was left of his combat corps, the OGPU kidnaped General Kutyepov. New evidence in the Melgunov archive indicates that the OGPU exploited Kutyepov's contacts with General Popov and other agents of the Second Trust for this purpose. Apparently the OGPU succeeded in luring Kutyepov into an ambivalent relationship in which, in spite of warnings, he got beyond his depth and virtually closed the trap on himself. Presumably the purpose of the kidnaping was to capture the general alive. The operation was thoroughly planned and executed, but Kutyepov himself died in the process. The Soviet regime was thus deprived of the opportunity of staging a sensational show trial—a characteristic feature of its political operations during the 1930's.

The OGPU quickly recovered its balance after the 1927 war scare. Renamed the NKVD in 1934, it was effectively used to suppress resistance to collectivization and the forced industrialization of the Five-Year Plans by familiar police-state methods—extermination or deportation to forced labor camps. These repressive functions of the NKVD have been widely publicized in the West, and today even in the U.S.S.R., through the novels of Alexander Solzhenitsyn, especially his *One Day in the Life of Ivan Denisovich,* a moving story of life in one of the Stalinist labor camps.

In contrast to the voluminous literature on Soviet terror and the purges, the foreign operations of the OGPU-NKVD have been neglected. The kidnaping of General Kutyepov indicates that by 1930 the Foreign Department of the OGPU had successfully built new, smoothly functioning operational networks within three years after the collapse of the Trust—a remarkable achievement by any standard of performance.

Operations such as the kidnaping of General Kutyepov (and later of General Miller) attracted unfavorable attention to the Soviet embassy in Paris, from which they had presumably been directed. To avoid future embarrassment from such incidents, the NKVD developed a system of underground or "illegal" station chiefs and agents who remained under deep cover, frequently posing as nationals of the country in which they operated. Such "illegal" agents are not protected by diplomatic status and risk the usual severe penalties for espionage if apprehended by local police or security agencies. To survive for long, the undercover agent must have extensive training, considerable language skills, and nerves of steel. He must also be motivated by patriotic or ideological dedication to the cause he serves, since no amount of pay will really compensate for the mental strain and risks involved. To Americans, a notorious example of such undercover agents is Colonel Rudolf I. Abel, the extraordinarily talented Soviet "illegal" who operated in the New York City area in the 1950's and was exchanged for the American U-2 pilot Francis Gary Powers in February 1962.

Alexander Orlov, the Soviet defector who wrote the intelligence training manual used in the NKVD during this period, writes: "By 1934–35 the Soviet underground intelligence had achieved maturity and grown into a force which no country could ignore." [3] Under the talented direction of Artuzov (Abram Slutsky), the Foreign Department of the NKVD had trained a highly professional corps of intelligence officers and had emplaced them on two levels, legal and illegal, in all the major European capitals. The covert operational capabilities of the NKVD were amply demonstrated in a whole series of kidnapings and assassinations during this decade of organized mayhem. Defectors such as Grigory Agabekov, Ignatz Reisz, and others were tracked down and murdered, and NKVD agents terrorized even Red Army commanders taking part in the Spanish Civil War.

The decade was also one of individual and mass subversion, especially after the rise of Hitler and the civil war in Spain which polarized political attitudes and passions. Against the background of the Great Depression these events shook man's political and social loyalties to a degree unparalleled since (except perhaps by American intervention in Vietnam in the 1960's). The NKVD profited immensely from these conditions. After the kidnaping of Kutyepov, General Skoblin, who had previously been recruited as a Soviet agent (probably in 1927–28), worked his way up in Paris émigré circles and in 1936 played a major role in the disappearance of General Miller. The same pattern repeated itself in the careers of other Soviet agents recruited during the 1930's. Harold (Kim) Philby was recruited in Vienna in 1933. The subversion of Guy Burgess and Donald Maclean followed later, and the agent careers of all three were inextricably mixed for almost thirty years. Kim Philby not only rose to key positions in British intelligence but also worked closely with the CIA and the FBI after World War II and did not seek asylum in the U.S.S.R., his "spiritual home," until February 1963.[4] During this same period the NKVD recruited Harry Gold who later played a key role in industrial espionage against the U.S., including ferreting out atomic secrets during the Manhattan project.[5]

Sensational publicity, including publication of Philby's memoirs both in Moscow and abroad, has created the impression that the KGB, the current successor to the NKVD, deserves the credit for his subversion and subsequent career. This is deliberately misleading. The remarkable group of Soviet agents recruited in the 1930's (Philby, Maclean, Burgess, Sorge, and others) were won over and trained by men such as Artuzov, the head of the NKVD's Foreign Department, who with Trilisser, Pillar, and others supervised the earlier Trust operation. This brilliant corps of professionals has probably not been equaled before or since in the intelligence agencies of the major powers. Certainly their bumbling British counterparts in the 1930's were not in the same league.[6] The upper ranks of the NKVD were decimated in the purges and never lived to see the remarkable payoff from their work two or three decades later. To add insult to injury, in the pompous ceremonial speeches celebrating the fiftieth anniversary of the Soviet state security organs, their names were not even mentioned,[7] perhaps because some of them, such as Walter Krivitsky and Alexander Orlov, had defected. Others, such as Artuzov, who in 1937 resigned from the service in protest against its police-state methods, were soon liquidated in the purges.

After the rise of Hitler, from 1934–35 on Soviet intelligence had to compete with new rivals such as the *Abwehr* (German Military Intelligence) and the *Sicherheitsdienst* (SD), the Foreign Intelligence Division of Heinrich Himmler's sprawling secret police empire. Again, as in the competition with the British S.I.S., the superior capabilities of the NKVD and its staff of trained professionals soon became apparent in its encounter with SD Chief Reinhard Heydrich's amateurs. The SD was quickly penetrated at several levels,[8] and the NKVD made effective use of a number of double agents who reported to both Western and Soviet intelligence agencies. For its part, the SD also knew that some of its agents, such as the émigré general Skoblin, were double agents working for the NKVD and perhaps other intelligence services as well. The SD thus could deliberately feed intelligence information and misinformation into NKVD channels, knowing that such reports would reach the Lubyanka in Moscow. As it turned out, such channels were indispensable in the development of the Tukhachevsky affair which Stalin used as justification for the purge of the Red Army, a major turning point on the road to World War II.

The Tukhachevsky affair was far more than a minor intelligence or disinformation operation. The NKVD claimed to have discovered that Tukhachevsky and seven high-ranking Soviet generals had plotted the overthrow of Stalin in secret collaboration with German generals, who were likewise unhappy with Hitler. The so-called trial and execution of the accused in June 1937 touched off a bloody purge which decimated the Soviet high command. The credibility of this story derived from the fact that at the time both the German and Soviet General Staffs were indeed unhappy with their respective dictators, and from the tangled and often contradictory course of Soviet foreign policy over the preceding two decades. It began with thirteen years of secret German-Soviet military collaboration up to the advent of Hitler.

The groundwork for this military collaboration by which Germany bypassed disarmament provisions of the Versailles Treaty was laid as early as 1920, two years before the open rapprochement between Germany and the U.S.S.R. formalized in the Treaty of Rapallo. The Germans were able to set up ammunition, aircraft, tank, and poison gas factories in the U.S.S.R. under the direction of a "Special Division R" created by General Hans von Seeckt. A flying school was set up at Lipetsk, southeast of Moscow, where in 1925 the German *Luftwaffe* was born, disguised as Squadron No. 4 of the Red Air Force. Even more important was the annual exchange of officers during which a minimum of 120 senior Soviet officers passed through German training courses or were attached for training to German units. This highly profitable cooperation continued for roughly twelve years and not only had the approval of Stalin but was also personally monitored by Marshal Voroshilov, the Soviet Commissar for Defense. His deputy, Marshal Tukhachevsky, who modernized the Red Army and made it into an effective fighting force, was an enthusiastic supporter of this mutually profitable collaboration, which was regretfully broken off sometime in 1933 after the rise of Hitler. As late as 1935, at a nostalgic farewell party for the German military attaché in Moscow, Tukhachevsky predicted: "If Germany and Soviet Russia were to march together, they could dictate peace to all the world; but if they were to clash, the Germans would find out that the Red Army had learned a lot in the meantime."

A few days after the Germans closed down the Lipetsk Aviation School, high-ranking French officials, including the young Air Minister Pierre Cot (who later won a Lenin Peace Prize), visited Moscow amid much fanfare, and French officers began to take the place of the departing Germans. By March 1935 an estimated forty French officers were attached to Soviet aviation, tank, and infantry units. In exchange, an equal number of Russian officers were posted to France. Tukhachevsky had been present at all important negotiations from the outset, so that he was now regarded as decidedly pro-French by German embassy sources in Moscow.[9] Stalin had personally urged Voroshilov to "join the French!" At this time he was clearly interested in exploring the possibility of building some sort of coalition of Western powers to offset the Nazi threat to European stability. This course became known as the policy of collective security proclaimed by Soviet Foreign Commissar Maksim Litvinov in impassioned speeches delivered to the League of Nations, which the U.S.S.R. had joined in 1934 after having denounced it for years as a league of "capitalist-imperialist brigands." Litvinov, who in 1930 had replaced Chicherin as Commissar of Foreign Affairs, had never paid more than lip service to the Rapallo policy of friendship with Germany,[10] and its corollary, the long years of secret German-Soviet military collaboration. Like Bukharin and a number of other Old Bolsheviks in the Politburo, Litvinov took the Nazi menace seriously and thought it required the cooperative resistance of the peaceful powers.[11] It has been persuasively argued by Henry L. Roberts that "there were at least two contending lines of foreign policy within the Politburo, and perhaps in Stalin's own mind, in the 1930's: one the 'Litvinov policy,' . . . the other the policy which emerged with the [Nazi-Soviet] pact of August 23, 1939.'[12] Stalin skillfully held on to both options simultaneously, but the weight of the evidence, including the Tukhachevsky affair, supports George F. Kennan's view that Stalin was "playing desperately" for the Rapallo line,[13] and that during this period Soviet entry into the League of Nations, collective security, and the Franco-Soviet and Soviet-Czech pacts were regarded by Stalin not as ends in themselves but as means of making Hitler realize the advantages of a friendly Soviet Russia.[14]

Certainly in 1934, in a speech to the 17th Party Congress, Stalin denied that the U.S.S.R. had "taken an orientation toward France and Poland," and held the door open for an agreement with Hitler. When the Nazi dictator marched contemptuously into the Rhineland in March 1936, Stalin's ambassador in London, Maisky, called for an effective "peace front," but at the same time emphasized that, unfortunately, Germany had not taken "the hand stretched out to her" by the Soviets. On the same day in Moscow, Molotov, in a published interview with a French reporter, said his government still thought "an improvement in Soviet-German relations possible." Clearly the wish was father to the thought. Similar statements by British or French statesmen have since been branded "appeasement." These early Soviet manifestations of the same syndrome have gone virtually unnoticed.

So far as the French leaders were concerned, the purpose of their military exchanges with the Soviet Union was to drive a wedge between the U.S.S.R. and Germany in order to protect France's ally, Poland. The French military establishment balked at providing any significant military aid to the Russians. At a cabinet meeting in June 1933, Pierre Laval (who became Foreign Minister in October 1934) declared himself categorically in favor of an accord with *Germany,* not with the U.S.S.R. Although circumstances forced Laval to negotiate the Franco-Soviet pact, which was signed in May 1935, Laval did his utmost to delay it, and afterwards at a briefing for General Gamelin, the French Chief of Staff, boasted that he had eliminated "the most dangerous parts."

As for the French generals, after spending billions of francs on the Maginot Line, which was nearing completion in 1935, they had no intention of moving beyond it to come to the aid of Czechoslovakia. There was no joint French-Soviet military planning to meet a possible German attack to the

east against the Czechs or to the west against France, so that
in fact the mutual assistance treaty was a dead letter from the
outset. These military facts of life were hammered home during
the Rhineland crisis, when neither France nor Great Britain
moved to crush Hitler at a time when they had overwhelming
military superiority and could easily have called his bluff. After
this major turning point on the road to World War II, it was
doubtful whether either country would move decisively against
Hitler as long as influential groups in both countries nourished
the secret hope that the Nazi military machine could somehow
be turned against the U.S.S.R. and the Red Menace in the East.
This assumption was coupled with the illusion that "peace in
our time" could be bought by giving in to each of Hitler's "last"
territorial demands. Thus, when war finally came, France and
England had nothing but a heap of broken promises "to point
to as a reminder that hope, divorced from power, is not a
policy"—the aphorism applied by Philip Mosely to American
policy toward eastern Europe after the war.

There is every reason to believe that Soviet intelligence
was able correctly to assess both French and British aims and
intentions during this period. The best evidence to support this
contention is that even before the Rhineland crisis, Stalin, keeping his options open, began to use secret NKVD channels to bid
for a renewal of friendly relations with Nazi Germany. For this
purpose a special NKVD emissary repeatedly contacted members
of Rosenberg's Foreign Political Office, which was responsible
for Nazi party policy toward the U.S.S.R., from December 1935
through October 1936. David Kandelaki, head of the Soviet
Trade Delegation in Berlin, assisted by the NKVD agent Friedrichson, tried again in December 1936 and January 1937, with
instructions signed by Stalin and Molotov, proposing negotiations aimed at broader agreements than short-term trade treaties.
According to new evidence recently brought to light, some
of these secret overtures were brought to the attention of the
American chargé d'affaires in Berlin by friendly sources who
reported that negotiations aimed at improving German-Russian
relations were going on in the summer of 1936. The American
consul in Geneva even filed a report in August that the anticipated German-Soviet rapprochement would have as its corollary a "rupture of German-Polish friendship." [15]

The fact that Hitler did not respond to these persistent

overtures and grasp the hand extended to him did not discourage Stalin. Quite the contrary, and the Rhineland crisis merely added a new sense of urgency to his efforts to make a deal with Hitler which would turn the *Wehrmacht* west.

What Stalin had in mind was something much more than a simple nonaggression pact to protect his vulnerable western frontier. He envisaged a long-range partnership in which the two dictators would divide Europe, the Balkans, and even the Middle East into spheres of interest and imperialist expansion. This view is supported by the secret protocols attached to the Nazi-Soviet pact when it was finally signed on August 23, 1939. That this option meant the unleashing of a second world war was an additional argument in its favor so far as Stalin was concerned. According to Gustav Hilger:

> For years Stalin had both prophesied and desired a war among the "capitalistic imperialist" powers in the West which it was hoped would (a) remove the danger of capitalist encirclement of the U.S.S.R.; (b) would weaken the capitalistic powers; and (c) pave the way for communist aspirations in the west. Stalin's greatest fear, after the rise to power of National Socialist Germany, was that the Western Powers would come to an understanding with Germany at the expense of the U.S.S.R. . . . Stalin's speculations as a statesman were prompted by his hopes as a Communist, that, once Germany had reached an understanding with Russia in the East, she would turn against Poland and the West. In such an event, Stalin hoped that, with time on the side of the U.S.S.R., the ensuing war would eventually bring about a situation in Western Europe in which he could intervene to shape European relations in a direction favorable to the U.S.S.R. and to the ideals of world revolution.[16]

Stalin's long-range ambition, a working partnership with Hitler under which each dictator could pursue his expansionist aims in the spheres of interest later agreed upon, was probably a major factor (but to be sure not the only factor) in precipitating the political purges of 1936–38. Stalin knew that most of the Old Bolshevik leaders would go along with a simple nonaggression pact with Berlin, either with or without a return to the close German-Soviet military collaboration of the good old days before the advent of Hitler. But "a policy of outright imperialistic aggression in collaboration with Nazi Germany would have been extremely repugnant to them." [17] After all, it was a cardinal tenet of the communist faith that imperialism was a besetting sin of capitalism, so much so that for years the powers outside the socialist camp were inevitably branded as "capitalist-imperialist." Therefore, in Stalin's reasoning, the Old Bolsheviks had to go. They were charged with treason and paraded before the public in three elaborate show trials from August 1936 through March 1938. In the purges which accompanied the trials, Stalin wiped the slate clean of any possible political opposition to his long-range plans. In an atmosphere of unprecedented terror and denunciations, all those who may have doubted the charges or opposed the purge itself were swept away.

The liquidation of the political elite responsible for the hardships and brutalities connected with the collectivization of agriculture and the Five-Year Plans evoked little sympathy from the Soviet public. The political leadership may have been respected or feared, but it was certainly not beloved. The military elite was in a different category. Among the disaffected population, the Red Army was probably the one institution that still commmanded widespread popular support. Why Stalin felt it necessary to wipe out the Soviet military elite as well as the Old Bolsheviks remains a major unsolved mystery in spite of John Erickson's monumental study, *The Soviet High Command,* which sets forth in great detail the relationship between Stalin and his military leaders.[18] Certainly as late as 1935 many high-ranking officers, including Marshal Tukhachevsky, looked back with nostalgia to the years of secret military collaboration with Germany which had proved so profitable in building up the Soviet military establishment.

Knowing the popular support of the Red Army, Stalin probably realized that a sudden, brutal killing of his top military leaders would involve too much of a calculated risk. The case against them would have to be long and carefully prepared. The evidence against whatever group he planned to charge with conspiracy and treason would have to be good enough to convince their fellow officers. Otherwise he would risk a genuine revolt by the only sector of the Soviet elite outside the NKVD which had control of the physical instruments of power in the Soviet state. Malicious gossip and denunciations extracted by manipulative persuasion and torture—the kind of evidence being produced by the NKVD for the political show trials—would not suffice. The incriminating material would be greatly strengthened if evidence could be introduced which came from abroad and from unimpeachable high-level sources.

Marshal Tukhachevsky had been an observer at the autumn maneuvers of the German Army in 1932. Accompanied by Litvinov he had attended the state funeral of King George V in London in January 1936, returning by way of Paris (where he spent a turbulent week as a guest of the French General Staff) and Berlin, where it was rumored that he had made "secret" contacts with German officers and even with Russian émigrés. Thus Tukhachevsky was a natural target for the charge of heading a conspiracy among disaffected Soviet generals to overthrow Stalin.[19] There is convincing evidence that this charge of an alleged "Tukhachevsky plot" originated with Stalin himself, and that he planted it with the émigré general Skoblin in Paris sometime in December 1936. Skoblin had long been an NKVD agent, and it was also well known by his superiors that he had turned double-agent and also reported on émigré affairs to the SD, the Nazi security service responsible for foreign political intelligence and covert operations. Skoblin promptly relayed the report of a Tukhachevsky plot to Reinhard Heydrich, the SD chief, who took it to Hitler with the idea of forging documents which would prove treasonable contacts between certain high-ranking *German* generals and their alleged Russian counterparts. An old intelligence hand (Jahnke), who warned that the report was disinformation deliberately planted by Stalin for his own purposes, was placed under house arrest by Heydrich while the incriminating documents were being forged. Rumors of the alleged conspiracy were leaked probably by both the NKVD and the SD in Berlin, where they were picked up by Czech intelligence and reached President Benes. In late December 1936, Benes wrote an urgent letter relaying the disinformation to French Premier Leon Blum. This confidential letter was transmitted personally by the French Premier's son, Paul, who was visiting Prague at the time. After receiving Benes' "friendly warning," Blum relaxed the pressure which for several months he had been putting on the French military establishment to put some teeth into the Franco-Soviet pact.

In the last half of January 1937, Benes received another
report, apparently from his Ambassador in Berlin, that Hitler
was secretly negotiating with an "anti-Stalin clique in the
U.S.S.R., Marshal Tukhachevsky, Rykov, and others." Although the report was clearly a deliberate leak from a high
Nazi official, Benes promptly and dutifully relayed it to Stalin.[20]
By playing his role of "honest intelligence broker," Benes thus
contributed directly to undermining any effective Franco-Soviet
military collaboration.

After the incriminating documents had been forged by
the SD, a photocopy of the collection was sold to an agent in
Berlin and transmitted through NKVD channels, probably by
way of Prague, to Moscow. Meanwhile, for some months the
NKVD had been busily preparing a case against the Soviet military leaders based on evidence collected from local sources.
In a tense, fear-ridden atmosphere filled with rumors of denunciations, suicides, and impending arrests, a conference of top
military leaders, including commanding generals from regional
military districts, was held in Moscow from June 1 to 4,
1937. Apparently it was at this conference that Marshal
Tukhachevsky and certain other leaders were charged with
treasonable contacts with their German counterparts. The
charges were supported by evidence from two sources, the
internally prepared NKVD dossiers and the forged German documents. Reportedly the audience was stunned. The accused
angrily denied the charges, but the documentary evidence was
so convincing that Stalin never lost the confidence of those
officers who survived the military purge which followed. On
June 11 *Pravda* announced that Tukhachevsky, Yakir, Uborevich, Kork, Eideman, Feldman, Primakov, and Putna had
pleaded guilty to charges of treason and were to be tried by a
special tribunal. Certainly the accused plus an estimated 35,000
other general officers, the cream of the Soviet high command,
were liquidated in the military purge which followed. On June
23, Loy Henderson, the U.S. chargé d'affaires in Moscow, reported that: "Insofar as the Embassy can ascertain, not one
diplomatic mission here, nor a single foreign observer in Moscow whose opinion bears weight, believed that the executed
Red Army officers were guilty of the crimes attributed to
them." [21] With the survivors of both the political and military
purges cowed into submission or herded into forced labor

camps, Stalin had achieved a position of total dictatorship. Any conceivable source of opposition to his long-range plan to establish a working partnership with Hitler had been wiped out.

Viewed as a disinformation operation or provocation, the Tukhachevsky affair was certainly one of the most successful in modern history. It represented a major NKVD achievement, far exceeding reasonable results in comparable covert operations. Nevertheless, Artuzov, the brilliant head of the Foreign Department, and his aides soon perished in the purge themselves.

To guard against compromise and retain textbook model secrecy after the event, one further operation was necessary. According to Walter Krivitsky, General Skoblin, the double-agent used as the original Western source of the story, and his superior, General Miller, in Paris had to be removed from the scene. Accordingly, Skoblin was assigned his last mission, to lure General Miller into an NKVD trap to facilitate his kidnaping, which took place on September 22, 1937. The operation would have gone according to plan except that Miller left a note stating that he had a rendezvous with Skoblin and suspected a trap. Although apprehended by his associates, Skoblin managed to escape and vanished forever. His wife was later sentenced by a French court to twenty years' hard labor for her part as an accomplice in the kidnaping. Skoblin himself, who was of no further use to the NKVD, was presumably quietly liquidated, thus assuring security, since from the Soviet point of view it was unlikely that the Nazi SD would reveal its cooperation in the operation. But in a gross breach of security, Heydrich could not refrain from boasting to his associates of his role in the affair before he himself was assassinated in May 1942 by Czech paratroopers working for the British. Walter Krivitsky, the NKVD agent in The Hague who was also involved, defected in the fall of 1937 and was liquidated in a Washington hotel room in February 1941, two years after the publication of his memoirs which have since been a major source of information on the Tukhachevsky affair. (Krivitsky had refused to organize the assassination of his friend and fellow agent, Ignatz Reisz.)

The Tukhachevsky plot was thus a catalytic agent in producing the military purge. During the two-year interval before the outbreak of World War II, the purge of the

Soviet high command had important effects on the military plans and estimates of all the Western powers. In November 1937 General Goering stated that the Red Army "had ceased to exist as a fighting force." [22] Hitler moved into Austria in March 1938, and it was universally expected that his next move would be against Czechoslovakia, invoking the inter-locking Soviet-Czech and Franco-Soviet pacts under which the U.S.S.R. had pledged to come to the aid of Czechoslovakia, but only if France would honor her commitment to do so first. On March 23, French Foreign Minister Paul-Boncour reaffirmed France's intention to support Czechoslovakia, but for the last year and a half, after receiving from Benes the Stalin-inspired disinformation about the "Tukhachevsky plot," Premier Blum had given up his efforts to put some steel into the Franco-Soviet pact. On the very day of Paul-Boncour's bravely reassuring speech, Litvinov told U.S. Ambassador Davies in Moscow that "France has no confidence in the Soviet Union and the Soviet Union no confidence in France." [23] At the end of May the British Embassy observed that the purge had produced "appalling chaos and disorganization" in the Red Army General Staff and high command. Under these circumstances, ". . . there was no good hoping vainly that the Russians might be of some value as a counterpoise to the Germans . . . even a partial military adventure of demonstration on their part was improbable." [24] At this time (May 1938) reports were already circulating in London that in the view of British Prime Minister Neville Chamberlain, Russia neither could nor would fight for Czechoslovakia, and that France was also incapable of doing so. Therefore the best solution to the mounting crisis was for the Czechs to cede the Sudetenland to Germany.

Soviet intelligence, of course, promptly picked up these reports. Three months before the showdown at Munich in September, in an important speech on the international situation Litvinov suggested that the Czechoslovak government would "find reasonable limits for concessions." This is the very essence of appeasement, which both Western and Soviet historians have since represented as an exclusively Anglo-French disgrace. The Soviet Foreign Minister went even further. He deliberately isolated the U.S.S.R. from whatever arrangements would be made and relieved his government "of responsibility for the further development of events." [25] By writing off Czechoslovakia in advance, Stalin in effect gave his future ally Hitler a free hand to press for maximum demands. This self-imposed isolation was the cold substratum of reality behind the Soviet façade of promises as the Munich crisis matured.

Soviet propaganda has made much of the myth that only the U.S.S.R. stood firmly by her commitments to Czechoslovakia during the mid-thirties. Churchill and other Western historians have added the illusion that there was a real possibility of an effective coalition of the U.S.S.R., France, and Great Britain which might have frustrated Hitler's ambitions and prevented catastrophe. Anglo-French appeasement is an open record. By contrast, Stalin's persistent efforts to make a deal with Hitler, beginning even before the Rhineland crisis of 1936, much less Munich, were carefully concealed from Western intelligence agencies and apparently from his own Foreign Commissariat as well. An NKVD intelligence operation, the Tukhachevsky affair, played a significant role in precipitating the military purge and in laying the groundwork for the Nazi-Soviet pact, which in turn was the signal for World War II. Ironically, the working partnership with Hitler which Stalin finally achieved at such tremendous human cost fell apart after two years, in spite of his frantic efforts to keep it going. Hitler's decision to attack the U.S.S.R. was undoubtedly influenced by the purges and by the argument that the odds of winning would be greatly increased if the attack took place before the Red Army could rebuild its cadres, decimated by the purges.

The Russians suffered a minimum of twenty million casualties in World War II. Nearly four million prisoners were taken in the first few months of battle. How many of these losses were the needless result of Stalin's delusions will long remain a matter of dispute. Since the Red Army later proved its mettle and turned the tide of the war at Stalingrad, Tukhachevsky's 1935 prophecy ultimately proved true: that if Germany and Russia were to clash, the Germans would find out that the Red Army had learned a lot from the many years of secret military collaboration. In the meantime, however, Stalin's policy of appeasement had devoured the best of the Revolution's children.

NOTES

Chapter 1 / Yakushev: The Recruitment, Care, and Feeding of a Double Agent

1. E. H. Carr, *The Bolshevik Revolution, 1917–1923* (London, 1950), I, 168, citing *Izvestia* for September 3 and 7, 1928, and the *Weekly Cheka Report* no. 6 (1918), p. 19.
2. *Ibid.*, p. 167.
3. V. I. Lenin, *Sochineniya,* XXIV, 612–13, cited in *ibid.*, p. 174.
4. Lev Nikulin, *Mertvaya Zyb* (Moscow, 1966), pp. 22–25.
5. See Leonard Schapiro, *The Communist Party of the Soviet Union* (New York, 1960), pp. 328–29.
6. Stalin-Shaposhnikov telegram (no. 001919, dated September 15, 1941). From an order of Lieutenant General Lukin of the 19th (Soviet) Army found among documents captured near Vyasma by the German *Abwehr* Command III and forwarded by Army Group Middle on December 12, 1941 (OKW/688). (Citation according to the original nomenclature on the records formerly held in the GSA archives in Alexandria, Virginia).
7. Biographical sketches on Artuzov, Pillar, and Kiakovsky were compiled from data in Nikulin, *Mertvaya Zyb*, pp. 367–68, and Geoffrey Bailey, *The Conspirators* (New York, 1960), *passim*.
8. For a vivid firsthand account of Soviet methods of interrogation and extraction of confessions, see Alexander Weissberg, *The Accused* (New York, 1951). For the best fictional account of the purge-trial period, see Victor Serge, *The Case of Comrade Tulayev* (New York, 1950).
9. Bailey, *Conspirators*, p. 65.
10. Nikulin, *Mertvaya Zyb*, pp. 13–14, 32–33.
11. For examples of U.S.-British intelligence collaboration at the Baltic stations, see U.S. National Archives, State Department Decimal File no. 811.OOB, *passim*.
12. For full text of the letter, see S. Melgunov, "Legenda i deistvitelnost," in the bi-monthly magazine, *Vozrozhdenie*, XIV (March–April 1951), 145–46. (Not to be confused with the daily newspaper of the same name.)
13. According to Nikulin, *Mertvaya Zyb*, p. 161, "Vasily" was the cover name later used by Rtishchev, head of the Political Council of the MOCR in 1923.
14. Melgunov "Legenda," pp. 148–52.

Chapter 2 / Operations at Home and Liaison Abroad

1. This account of the Kiakovsky-Kolesnikov mission is drawn from Lev Nikulin, *Mertvaya Zyb* (Moscow, 1966), pp. 89–95, previously published in *Moskva,* no. 6, pp. 45–49. It corresponds closely to Western accounts, and there is no reason to doubt its essential accuracy.
2. Nikulin, *Mertvaya Zyb,* p. 96.
3. For details see Nikolai Chebishev, "Trest, istoria odnoi legendy," in the Paris émigré newspaper *Vozrozhdenie,* nos. 3748 and 3754 (September 7 and 13, 1935).
4. E. H. Carr, *The Bolshevik Revolution, 1917–1923* (London, 1950), III, 156.
5. This account of Birk's defection is based on Nikulin, *Mertvaya Zyb,* pp. 100–11. While it is unconfirmed by Western sources, there is no reason seriously to doubt its essential outlines. It goes far to explain the remarkable speed and effectiveness with which the Trust was able to place its reports (containing a mixture of some reliable information and a great deal of "disinformation") into Western intelligence channels. Roman Birk later fled to Berlin in the spring of 1927 as the Trust operation ended.
6. V. T. Drimmer, "Trest," *Chasovoi* (*La Sentinelle,* Brussels), no. 480 (June 1966), p. 21 (an abridged version by the editor V. V. Orekhov of Drimmer's original article in Polish published in the Paris journal *Kultura*). Captain V. T. Drimmer of Polish intelligence (Army G-2) served for six years as military attaché in Reval and was in close official contact with the Trust.
7. For examples of the correspondence, see Melgunov, "Legenda," *Vozrozhdenie,* XIV (March–April 1951), 145–50.
8. See the correspondence quoted by Nikulin, *Mertvaya Zyb,* p. 118.
9. Nikulin is ambiguous in his handling of Zayonchovsky. In the first draft of his chronicle, published in the magazine *Moskva,* Zayonchovsky is mentioned at most only three or four times, and then as a mere figurehead. Moreover, Nikulin has General Potapov, the new chief of staff under the Trust, explain to Yakushev: "I recently came in contact with your 'Supreme Emissary.' What limitations, what a pitiful mental horizon, what poverty of ideas!" (*Moskva,* June 1965, p. 72.) This is the kind of treatment given to so-called negative heroes in Soviet fiction. However, in a new chapter added to the 1966 version (chap. 41, pp. 192–95), Nikulin depicts Zayonchovsky as a major Trust figure receiving instructions from the top echelon of the OGPU (Artuzov) on how to deceive a young visiting officer (Arapov) from Berlin.
10. The fact that the MOCR had its own ideology and tactics is completely ignored in the Soviet chronicle of the Trust operation. It is also minimized in most Western accounts, some of which assume that in real life there never was an MOCR or other resistance group in Moscow, and that the Trust itself was a complete fabrication or hoax built from scratch. (See Richard Wraga, "Trest," *Vozrozhdenie,* no. 7 [January–February 1950]; Geoffrey Bailey, *The Conspirators* [New York, 1960].)

   As a sort of press agent for the security police, Nikulin creates the impression that the OGPU successfully imposed its own ideology and tactics on both the MOCR and the VMC in Berlin. According to the Soviet version, Dzerzhinsky and other OGPU officials worked out a Trust ideology and tactical line which Yakushev then successfully sold to monarchist leaders in Berlin and Paris. Reduced to its simplest terms, the Trust line was "anti-interventionist": The future of Russia would depend on internal developments. A collapse was inevitable anyway, so intervention from outside was unnecessary to begin with, and the use of terror would be counterproductive. It would result in crushing counterterror by the OGPU and would destroy everything built up secretly by the MOCR, which needed only financial help from abroad. Future political leadership should come from *inside* Russia, from those who daily risked their lives in the struggle against the regime.

11. Quoted by Melgunov, "Legendy [sic] i deistvitelnost," *Vozrozhdenie*, XV (May–June 1951), 118 (not to be confused with the earlier article, "Legenda" in Vol. XIV).

12. Shirinsky-Shikhmatov was the principal contributor to the two VMC publications, *Dvuglavyi Orel* (*Double-headed Eagle*) and *Ezhenedelny* (*Weekly*). He was also head of the Russian monarchist youth group known as the Assembly of Youth Abroad and author of a number of its programs and resolutions.

13. Melgunov, "Legenda," *Vozrozhdenie*, XIV (March–April 1951), 150–51.

14. *Ibid.*, p. 151.

15. On the Vorovsky assassination see Carr, *Bolshevik Revolution*, III, 489, and Nikulin, *Mertvaya Zyb*, p. 99.

16. *Ibid.*, pp. 222–23.

17. *Ibid.*, pp. 127–28.

18. *Ibid.*, pp. 127–28. Nikulin implies that Yakushev overheard the discussion after the door closed behind him. This is most unlikely. Experienced intelligence officers do not carry on confidential conversations at that high a noise level. Nikulin's report of the discussion is probably false, although it is based on the work of Chebishev, the only one present who has written about it. For Chebishev's account of the meeting, see *Vozrozhdenie*, no. 3702 (July 23, 1935).

19. Personal confirmation by Von Lampe to a Paris source, by telephone, February 15, 1967. (Von Lampe died later in the spring of 1967.)

20. Personal confirmation by Von Lampe to a Paris source, by telephone, February 15, 1967.

21. Nikulin, *Mertvaya Zyb*, p. 140.

22. Melgunov, "Legendy" [sic], *Vozrozhdenie*, XV (May–June, 1951), 129.

23. N. Vinogradov to the author, July 26, 1967; see also his article, "Pravda o svidanii bolshevitskago agenta yakusheva-fedorova s velikim kniazem nikolaem nikolaevichem," *Vozrozhdenie*, XLVIII (December 1955), 114 (hereafter cited as "Pravda").

24. Nikulin, *Mertvaya Zyb*, p. 143.

25. *Ibid.*, pp. 170–72. In a letter to the author dated July 26, 1967, Vinogradov ridicules Nikulin's statement that arrangements were made to quarter some of General Wrangel's forces in groups of fifteen in "green *dachas*"—houses hidden in the forest along the border.

26. Nikulin, *Mertvaya Zyb*, pp. 178–79.

27. *Ibid.*, pp. 162–63, 225–26, 245–46 (no dates are given).

28. *Ibid.*, p. 339.

29. *Ibid.*, p. 158.

30. Quoted by Donald W. Treadgold, "The Ideology of the White Movements: Wrangel's 'Leftist Policy from Rightist Hands,'" in *Russian Thought and Politics*, Harvard Slavic Studies, IV, 494.

31. Peter Ryss, "Revolutionnoe delo A. P. Kutyepova," in *General Kutyepov, Sbornik Statei* (Paris, 1934), p. 363.

32. *Ibid.*, pp. 359–60.

33. Quoted by Chebishev, "Trest," *Vozrozhdenie*, no. 3769 (September 28, 1935).

34. *Ibid.*

35. Vinograd, "Pravda," *Vozrozhdenie*, XLVIII (December 1955), 112–13.

36. *Ibid.*, p. 114.

37. As quoted by Vinogradov, *loc. cit.*

38. *Ibid.*, pp. 115–17. A copy of Maria Zakharchenko's report on their border crossing under Trust auspices—the only written testimony she left—was given by General Kutyepov to N. Vinogradov and incorporated by the latter in his *Vozrozhdenie* article.

39. Chebishev, "Trest," *Vozrozhdenie*, no. 3723 (August 13, 1935), pt. 5.

40. Sidney George Reilly, *The Adventures of Sidney Reilly: Britain's Master Spy* (London, 1931), p. 126.
41. Nikulin, *Mertvaya Zyb*, pp. 62–63.
42. *Ibid.*, pp. 332–40; Chebishev, "Trest," *Vozrozhdenie*, no. 3718 (August 8, 1935).
43. Nikulin, *Mertvaya Zyb*, p. 340.
44. *Ibid.*, p. 174.
45. Viktor A. Larionov, personal interview. Larionov discussed the case with Maria Zakharchenko in the spring of 1927. See also Vinogradov, "K istorii Boevoi Organizatsii Gen. A. P. Kutyepova," *Chasovoi* (Brussels), no. 320 (June 1952), p. 7.
46. Nikulin, *Mertvaya Zyb*, p. 315.
47. Melgunov, "Legendy," *Vozrozhdenie*, XV (May–June 1951), 127.
48. *Ibid.* Only five of Kutyepov's agents have been positively identified as having entered the U.S.S.R. through Trest channels: the two Radkoviches, Korinsky, Shorin, and Sussalin. During the three years that General Kutyepov maintained operational liaison with the Trust, 1924–27, this connection was far more sophisticated than the simple "deceiver-deceived" relationship portrayed in Nikulin's Soviet account or in the superficial Western version of either Geoffrey Bailey or Richard Wraga. The latter gave the impression that General Kutyepov was completely duped by the OGPU.
49. Agent "X," *"Trest i GPU,"* *Segodnya* (Riga), October 27, 1927.
50. Vinogradov, "Iz proshlogo: o tak nazyvaemom 'treste,' " in the New York émigré journal *Pereklichka*, V, nos. 136–37 (March–April 1963), 10. See also "Pravda," *Vozrozhdenie*, XLVIII (December 1955), 117–18.
51. Nikulin, *Mertvaya Zyb*, pp. 199–202.
52. Vinogradov, "Pravda," *Vozrozhdenie*, XLVIII (December 1955), 118. Vinogradov insists that this was the only meeting that took place (letter to the author, July 26, 1967). The Soviet account claims that there were two additional meetings with the Grand Duke, one on August 27, 1923, the second in July 1925 (Nikulin, *Mertvaya Zyb*, pp. 137–38, 244–47).
53. Nikulin, *Mertvaya Zyb*, pp. 199–202.
54. *Ibid.*, pp. 237–38.
55. *Ibid.*, p. 248.
56. See Vinogradov, "Iz proshlogo," *Pereklichka*, nos. 126–27 (May–June 1962), p. 19.
57. Melgunov, "Legendy," *Vozrozhdenie*, XV (May–June 1951), 127 n.
58. If Monkewitz had been subverted by the OGPU (another coup equivalent to the case of Yakushev), one would expect that a *roman chronique* designed to propagandize OGPU triumphs would have exploited his subversion, but he is mentioned only once in Nikulin's account, in a paragraph added to the text of the book (p. 248), and is missing altogether in the first draft published in *Moskva*.
59. Nikulin, *Mertvaya Zyb*, p. 261.

Chapter 3 / Savinkov, Elvengren, and Reilly

1. Sidney George Reilly, *The Adventures of Sidney Reilly: Britain's Master Spy* (London, 1931), p. 122 (Mrs. Reilly's narrative).
2. For a biography of Reilly, which includes considerable material on Savinkov, see Robin Bruce Lockhart, *Ace of Spies* (London, 1967).
3. For complete texts, see *Izvestia*, June 16 and 17, 1927.
4. Reilly testimony, *Izvestia*, June 17, 1927.
5. In this regard see especially the article "Konets savinkova" by Vl. Lebedev, in *Volya Rossii* (Prague), XIV–XV (September 1924), 184–89.
6. Lockhart, *Ace of Spies*, p. 100.
7. George A. Hill, *Go Spy the Land, Being the Adventures of I.K. 8 of the British Secret Service* (London, 1932), pp. 194–96.

8. Winston Churchill, *Great Contemporaries* (London, 1937) pp. 126–32.
9. Somerset Maugham, "The Terrorist," *Redbook,* October 1943.
10. *Izvestia,* May 13, 1925.
11. Churchill, *Great Contemporaries,* p. 110.
12. As reported by Walter Duranty in *The Curious Lottery* (New York, 1929), p. 122. For the Russian text, less florid but equally moving, see Boris V. Savinkov, *Protsess Borisa Savinkova,* 2nd ed. (Berlin, 1924), p. 107.
13. Lockhart, *Ace of Spies,* p. 73, n. 1.
14. *Izvestia,* June 16, 1927.
15. George A. Hill, *Go Spy the Land,* pp. 195–96.
16. Vl. Lebedev, "Konets savinkova," *Volya Rossii,* XIV–XV (September 1924), 184.
17. For an analysis of the campaign, which touched off a long dispute among the Soviet High Command, see John Erickson, *The Soviet High Command* (London, 1962), pp. 91–110.
18. Alexander Orlov, *Handbook of Intelligence and Guerrilla Warfare* (Ann Arbor, Mich., 1963), p. 172.
19. Geoffrey Bailey, *The Conspirators* (New York, 1960), p. 34.
20. *Izvestia,* June 16, 1927.
21. General Gayda was later falsely accused of being a Bolshevik agent (Bailey, *Conspirators,* p. 34). In this regard see the article by the former Soviet intelligence officer G. Dumbadze, "Pravda o Gen. Gayda," in *Pereklichka* (New York), no. 129 (August 1962), pp. 11–12.
22. Lockhart, *Ace of Spies,* pp. 88, 103.
23. *Izvestia,* June 16, 1927.
24. Lockhart, *Ace of Spies,* p. 112.
25. The *Torgprom* (a Russian abbreviation of *Torgovo-promyshlennyi-komitet*) is described as "a counterrevolutionary organization founded in 1920 which united powerful Russian capitalists living abroad" (Nikulin, *Mertvaya Zyb,* p. 245 n.).
26. *Izvestia,* June 16, 1927.
27. *Ibid.,* June 16, 1927.
28. *Ibid.,* June 17, 1927.
29. Lockhart, *Ace of Spies,* pp. 126–27. On Orlov's forgeries, including a document suggesting that Senator Borah accepted Soviet bribes, see Paul W. Blackstock, *Agents of Deceit* (Chicago, 1966), pp. 78–80.
30. *Izvestia,* June 17, 1927.
31. *Ibid.* This is apparently the action mistakenly attributed by Bailey (*Conspirators,* pp. 34–35) to Savinkov and Reilly. Bailey's summary is borrowed (without attribution) by Lev Nikulin, *Mertvaya Zyb* (Moscow, 1966), p. 255. Both Bailey and Nikulin erroneously state that Chicherin was returning from the Hague Conference. According to a former British intelligence agent, Captain George A. Hill, who was present at the conference, ". . . it was only a secondary affair, attended for the most part by sober economists, and shepherded by politicians of the second rank" (*Dreaded Hour* [London, 1936], p. 246).
32. *Izvestia,* June 17, 1927.
33. *Izvestia,* June 16, 1927.
34. Churchill, *Great Contemporaries,* pp. 126–32.
35. See Nikulin, *Mertvaya Zyb,* p. 256.
36. Reilly testimony, *Izvestia,* June 17, 1927.
37. Reilly, *Adventures,* pp. 113–14.
38. Nikulin, *Mertvaya Zyb,* pp. 257–58. See also Grigori Z. Bessedovsky, *Na putyakh k termidoru: Iz vospominanii byshogo sovetskogo diplomata* (Paris, 1930), II, 69 ff. Although Bessedovsky, a Soviet chargé d'affaires in Paris who defected in 1929, later produced a score of fraudulent Soviet memoirs, there is no reason to doubt the general reliability of this early work. (On his later falsifications, see Blackstock, *Agents of Deceit,* pp. 171–85.)
39. Robert H. Bruce Lockhart, *Memoirs of a British Agent* (London, 1932), pp. 178–79.

40. Nikulin, *Mertvaya Zyb*, p. 62.
41. William Reswick, *I Dreamt Revolution* (Chicago, 1952), p. 9. (The author has known at least one Soviet defector who returned for similar motives to certain death during the Stalinist regime.)
42. Churchill, *Great Contemporaries*, p. 110. Since by this time Trotsky was already pitted in a deadly struggle against the Stalin-Zinoviev-Kamenev triumvirate for Lenin's succession, he should probably be excluded as a source. It is much more likely that the invitation was another OGPU provocation, and an integral part of the entrapment operation.
43. Reilly, *Adventures*, pp. 146–47. Although Pepita (Mrs. Reilly) knew no Russian at this time, her husband undoubtedly briefed her on the substance of what happened, and there is no reason to doubt the essential facts as they are related by her. Certainly Reilly considered Savinkov's plan to return as "utter madness" (Robin B. Lockhart, *Ace of Spies*, p. 117).
44. *Segodnya*, October 18, 1927.
45. Quoted by Robin B. Lockhart, *Ace of Spies*, pp. 115–16, without documentation, but presumably from either Dukes himself or his private papers.
46. Reswick, *I Dreamt Revolution*, p. 11.
47. See *Time*, December 20, 1963, p. 17.
48. Reilly, *Adventures*, pp. 28–29.
49. Lockhart, *Ace of Spies*, p. 96. (The S.I.S., which is responsible for foreign espionage and covert operations, is designated M.I.6, formerly M.I.1.C. The Security Service, which is responsible for internal security and counterespionage at home, is known as M.I.5. The "M.I.," which stands for Military Intelligence, is a misleading anachronism, as this function is performed by a Directorate of Intelligence of the Ministry of Defense in Whitehall.)
50. *Ibid.*, pp. 132–35.
51. *Ibid.*, p. 117.
52. For reproductions of several of the letters, see Reilly, *Adventures*, *passim*; see also Lockhart, *Ace of Spies*, pp. 132–35.
53. Reilly, *Adventures*, p. 174; Lockhart, *Ace of Spies*, p. 132.
54. Reilly, *Adventures*, pp. 178–81.
55. Lockhart, *Ace of Spies*, p. 135.
56. *Ibid.*, p. 129, 137.
57. Reilly, *Adventures*, pp. 184–85. According to Vinogradov, Mrs. Reilly's statement (deleted above) that she and her husband dined with General Kutyepov the night before they left Paris is hardly credible, but the rest of the paragraph rings true.
58. *Ibid.*, p. 190.
59. *Ibid.*, pp. 199–203.
60. Maria Zakharchenko, who escaped from Moscow in April 1927 with Staunitz (Opperput), gave a detailed account to Mrs. Reilly, which the latter includes in her narrative; Staunitz gave an account to the press and to intelligence agencies in Helsinki. Most Western versions, such as that of Bailey (*Conspirators*, pp. 67–71), are based on Staunitz' testimony. Lev Nikulin (*Mertvaya Zyb*, pp. 270–75) has a lengthy recital apparently based in part on documentary materials such as Yakushev's reports to the OGPU, Reilly's interrogation reports, and a letter from Toyvo Vyakhy, a Soviet guard who met Reilly at the border. Although written for obvious propaganda purposes, Nikulin's version of the affair is probably more accurate in some details and at least as reliable in general as the Zakharchenko and Staunitz accounts. Finally, Reilly's biographer Robin Bruce Lockhart (*Ace of Spies*, pp. 166–86) has taken his account verbatim from Nikulin, adding a page of comment on the "many glaring and unnecessary inaccuracies" in the Russian original (although his translation has a number of deletions or abridgements which are nowhere indicated). A comparative content analysis will demonstrate that Nikulin "adapted" much of his material from Bailey, who in turn frequently borrows without attribu-

tion from unreliable secondary sources. Although indirect, the evidence is convincing that Nikulin was permitted access to few if any original NKVD materials on either Savinkov or Reilly, indicating that both cases are still "sensitive" so far as the Soviet authorities are concerned.

61. Nikulin, *Mertvaya Zyb,* p. 270. Nikulin claims that Vyakhy is still living and provided him with a letter describing his role in the operation and clarifying several details.

62. The above version of Reilly's arrest, based mainly on Nikulin, explains the postcard incident, which is missing from the Staunitz account—but then Staunitz had no way of knowing about it.

63. Nikulin, *Mertvaya Zyb,* p. 275.

64. *Ibid.,* p. 282.

65. Lockhart, *Ace of Spies,* pp. 145–46.

66. *Izvestia,* June 9 and July 10, 1927.

67. Nikulin, *Mertvaya Zyb,* pp. 264–65.

68. Reilly, *Adventures,* pp. 215–16.

69. Quoted in Lockhart, *Ace of Spies,* p. 146.

70. *Ibid.,* p. 145.

71. *Ibid.,* p. 146 n.

72. *Ibid.,* p. 147.

73. *Izvestia,* June 17, 1927.

74. Nikulin, *Mertvaya Zyb,* p. 280. Since no U.S. agencies were involved in the Reilly case, Nikulin's reference to American intelligence is a crude attempt to make a propaganda point in the current campaign to glamorize the Soviet security agencies.

Chapter 4 / Dwindling Credibility and Control, 1925–27

1. Nikolai Chebishev, "Trest, istoria odnoi legendy," *Vozrozhdenie,* no. 3715, August 5, 1935.

2. Lev Nikulin, *Mertvaya Zyb* (Moscow, 1966), pp. 283–93.

3. For details based on documents from intelligence files (including Shulgin-Lipsky correspondence), see S. L. Voitsekhovsky, "P. B. Struve v Varshave," in the magazine *Vozrozhdenie,* IX (May–June 1950), 141–44.

4. See, for example, Nikulin, *Mertvaya Zyb,* p. 294. At the end of World War II Shulgin was reportedly turned over to the Soviet authorities, sent to a concentration camp, later released, and is currently (1966) living in Moscow. The forthcoming publication of his memoirs has been announced. Nikulin quotes him as reminiscing on his trip, but nevertheless reports the fable of Trest censorship which he apparently took from Chebishev, Wraga, Bailey, or some other Western source.

5. Voitsekhovsky, "P. B. Struve," pp. 144–48.

6. Chebishev, "Trest," *Vozrozhdenie,* no. 3178 (August 18, 1935), pt. 4.

7. Agent "X," "Trest i GPU," *Segodnya* (Riga), October 27, 1927.

8. *Izvestia,* April 19, 1927, p. 4.

9. Chebishev, "Trest," *Vozrozhdenie,* no. 3723 (August 13, 1935).

10. Quoted by the Ukrainian OGPU chief, Balitsky, in a press interview published in *Izvestia,* April 19, 1927.

11. Chebishev, "Trest," *loc. cit.*

12. *Izvestia,* April 19, 1927.

13. Three weeks after official Soviet assurances that Dolgorukov was safely in OGPU custody, he was summarily executed along with nineteen other accused spies following the assassination of Voikov, the Soviet ambassador in Warsaw, by a young émigré terrorist, and his name had the dubious honor of heading the list (*Izvestia,* June 9, 1927). It is interesting to note that when diplomatic relations with England were broken off on May 27, and a full-scale war scare began, the political line and operational plans attributed to Dolgorukov and the National

Committee in Paris were ascribed by Soviet propaganda to the British Conservative Party diehards and British intelligence.

14. Nikulin, *Mertvaya Zyb*, pp. 345–49. Bailey mentions the visit twice, claiming that it took place "some time in March, 1927 . . . in the Finnish border town of Terijoki" (*The Conspirators* [New York, 1960], pp. 59, 83). However, there is absolutely no documentary evidence known to this author that such a meeting ever in fact took place.

15. Nikulin, *Mertvaya Zyb*, p. 348.

16. Personal interview with Vladimir Popott, Paris, March 1967. The alleged statement also supports the Soviet propaganda line that a broad anti-Soviet coalition was secretly taking shape in the spring of 1927 in preparation for a renewed Allied intervention.

17. J. D. Gregory, memorandum for the record of conversation with the German Counsellor of Embassy, Herr Dickhoff, May 25, 1927. See former German Foreign Ministry files, British Foreign Office collection, 6698/H 105676-680.

18. Sthamer to Foreign Office, June 16, 1927 (British Foreign Office collection, 2860/D 558893).

19. V. T. Drimmer, "Trest," *Chasovoi* (*La Sentinelle,* Brussels), no. 480 (June 1966), pp. 21–23. (Based on secondary sources, the Wraga and Bailey accounts of this incident are rather sketchy by comparison with Drimmer's, and the entire episode is ridiculed as preposterous by N. Vinogradov in *Pereklichka,* no. 129 (August 1962), p. 10. Naturally the Soviet account says nothing of this major blow to the status of the Trust.)

Chapter 5   /   Internal Security, Confusion, and Collapse

1. Lev Nikulin, *Mertvaya Zyb* (Moscow, 1966), pp. 202–16, 218–21.

2. *Ibid.,* pp. 324–30, 340–42. While Nikulin's account of this alleged triangular relationship is by no means implausible, there is no reliable evidence in Western sources to support it.

3. Since there is no evidence that Staunitz took out any large sum of money at the time of his defection, the story of the alleged swindle may have been invented by Nikulin to further discredit a "negative hero," as required by the tenets of "socialist realism."

4. Nikulin, *Mertvaya Zyb,* pp. 349–51, 353–57.

5. *Ibid.,* pp. 357–60.

6. George Sidney Reilly, *The Adventures of George Sidney Reilly: Britain's Master Spy* (London, 1931), pp. 260–64. Since the Reilly memoirs were in fact written by a ghostwriter-journalist, this letter may be apocryphal, although it is certainly *ben trovato* (Robin Bruce Lockhart, *Ace of Spies* [London, 1967], pp. 7–8). In his biography of Reilly, Lockhart himself cites several such letters (*ibid., passim*).

7. Nikulin, *Mertvaya Zyb,* pp. 366–70.

8. Agent "X," "Trest i GPU," *Segodnya* (Riga), October 27, 1927.

9. For recent evidence in this regard, see Paul W. Blackstock, *Agents of Deceit* (Chicago, 1966), chap. 5, "American Recognition of Russia and the Zinoviev Instructions," pp. 81–102.

10. On the use of émigrés for political warfare purposes, see Blackstock, *The Strategy of Subversion* (Chicago, 1964), chap. 7, "The Problem of Counter-Elites and Operational Control," pp. 158–66. Nikolai Chebishev gives ample evidence that Yakushev was able to sharpen the differences between Wrangel and Kutyepov and thus to reduce cooperation in the common cause ("Trest, istoria odnoi legendy," *Vozrozhdenie,* nos. 3702–3780 [July 23–October 9, 1935], *passim*).

Chapter 6 / Offensive and Counteroffensive: The 1927 War Scare

1. In the midst of the war-scare crisis, Mikhail Tomsky began an important speech "On War and Peace": "Today the Soviet Union is entering a new period which can be characterized as marking the end of the *peredushka*" (*Izvestia,* June 12, 1927, p. 4).
2. *Cf.* E. H. Carr, *Socialism in One Country* (London, 1963), III, pt. 1, 15–19.
3. The principal Western accounts of the Trust are: (1) a series of five articles in the Riga (Latvia) Russian newspaper *Segodnya* dated October 27–28 and November 1, 1927 (Opperput's testimony; his official army interrogation reports were destroyed by Finnish intelligence in 1946 to avoid possible Soviet capture); (2) a series of eighteen articles titled "Trest, istoria odnoi legendy" by Nikolai Chebishev, in the Paris Russian-language newspaper *Vozrozhdenie,* appearing at irregular intervals beginning with no. 3702 of July 23 and ending with no. 3780 of October 9, 1935; (3) an article by Richard Wraga, "Trest," in the magazine *Vozrozhdenie,* no. 7 (January–February 1950); (4) two articles by S. Melgunov, the editor of *Vozrozhdenie,* in issues no. 14 and 15 (March–June 1951); (5) Geoffrey Bailey, *The Conspirators* (New York, 1960), pt. 1, "The Trust"; (6) a series of thirteen critical review articles by N. Vinogradov in the New York émigré journal *Pereklichka,* appearing at irregular intervals during 1962–63; (7) the recent *roman chronique* by Lev Nikulin, *Mertvaya Zyb* (Moscow, 1966), a Soviet account of the operation which is based in part on official documents but is intended primarily to improve the OGPU image and should be used with caution.
4. Josef Stalin, "Report to the Fourteenth Conference of the Russian Communist Party," in *Leninism* (Moscow, 1934), I, 152–53.
5. *Cf.* Otto Hoetzsch, "Russlands Aussenpolitische Lage und Aussenpolitik," *Osteuropa,* II (February 1927), 396–97.
6. Arnold Toynbee, *Survey of International Affairs, 1927* (London, 1929), p. 264.
7. *Times* (London), February 7, 1927, cited in Toynbee, *Survey of International Affairs,* p. 265.
8. For the text of this note and the Soviet reply of February 26, see the British Parliamentary paper *Command,* 2822, 1927.
9. Arnold Toynbee, *Survey of International Affairs,* p. 266.
10. F. Novinsky, "Tendenzii vnutrennevo razvitia Anglii," in *Mezhdunarodnaya zhizn,* April 1924, p. 24.
11. For the complete text of Fischer's article, see *The Nation,* March 23, 1927.
12. F. D. Volkov, *Anglo-sovetskie otnosheniia (1917–1929)* (Moscow, 1958), p. 282. The Volkov account of the Conservative campaign and the break in relations (*op. cit.,* pp. 257–344) is highly colored in the worst Stalinist tradition. For a more objective treatment see V. I. Popov, *Anglo-sovetskie otnosheniia (1927–1929)* (Moscow, 1958). For a recent, post-Stalinist version, edited in part by Soviet Foreign Minister Andrei Gromyko, see B. N. Ponomareva, A. A. Gromyko, and B. M. Khostova, eds., *Istoria vneshnei politiki SSSR (1917–1945)* (Moscow, 1966), I, 229–43.
13. *Izvestia,* January 30, 1927.
14. *Pravda,* March 1, 1927, p. 3, col. 7.
15. *Izvestia,* March 30, 1927.
16. *Izvestia,* April 20, 1927, p. 2. Rykov's allusion to "declarations of certain English ministers" may refer to Chamberlain's Geneva press conference of March 8 and to his Birmingham speech of April 7, noted above.

17. *Izvestia,* June 12, 1927.
18. *Izvestia,* April 30, 1927; italics by Voroshilov.
19. May 31, 1927 (dateline May 28, Tass, from Artemovsk, Ukraine).
20. See Louis Fischer, *The Soviets in World Affairs* (Princeton, N.J., 1951), p. 72: "In retrospect, the danger of war was certainly overestimated by Moscow partly because of the primitive thinking in which the Bolsheviks indulged in these matters." See also Gustav Hilger and A. G. Meyers, *The Incompatible Allies* (New York, 1953), p. 215.
21. *Izvestia,* June 4, 1927.
22. For a semiofficial account of the Arcos incident, see Toynbee, *Survey of International Affairs,* pp. 266–71.
23. *Izvestia,* June 2, 1927.
24. Grigory V. Chicherin, "Uroki praktiki," *Mezhdunarodnaya zhizn,* no. 8 (August 1927), p. 59. For Chicherin's use of the pen name "Post-script," see T. H. Von Laue, "Soviet Diplomacy: G. V. Chicherin," in G. A. Craig and F. Gilbert, *The Diplomats, 1919–1939* (Princeton, N.J., 1953), p. 263, n. 72.
25. For illustrative cases see Hilger and Meyers, *Incompatible Allies, passim.* For a specific case in which Chicherin promised to take up the problem of Comintern and press interference when he returned to Moscow, see the circular telegram Wallroth to Moscow Embassy, June 14, 1927 (British Foreign Office collection, 2860/D 558859).
26. Hey to German Foreign Office, May 27, 1927 (British Foreign Office collection, 2860/D 558737–39).
27. See the article by I. Taigin, "Anglo-Sovetskii razryv," in *Mezhdunarodnaya zhizn,* no. 7 (July 1927), p. 11.
28. The official Soviet white book on the subject is N. N. Kichkassov, *Byelogvardeiski terror protiv SSSR (White Guardist Terror against the U.S.S.R.)* (Moscow, 1928). Although substantially correct in the account of some incidents, the book completely ignores the role of Staunitz, the OGPU agent who defected from the Trust and later was a leading figure in the Kutyepov offensive.

Chapter 7 / The Kutyepov Offensive

1. Naimsky in Leningrad, Turov-Ginsburg and Orlov in or near Moscow. For details see N. Vinogradov, "Iz proshlogo: o tak nazyvaemom 'Treste,' " in *Pereklichka,* nos. 136–37 (March–April 1963), p. 10.
2. *Ibid.,* p. 14; Nikolai Chebishev, "Trest, istoria odnoi legendy," *Vozrozhdenie,* no. 3769 (September 28, 1935).
3. N. N. Kichkassov, *Byelogvardeiski terror protiv SSSR* (Moscow, 1928), p. 40. This is the official Soviet white book on the subject. However, it makes no mention whatever of Staunitz, indicating reluctance to admit that an OGPU agent could defect, a fiction which continues into the present.
4. Vinogradov in *Pereklichka,* nos. 136–37 (March–April 1963), p. 15. According to Kichkassov, two additional members of the team, A. B. Balmassov and A. A. Solsky, were turned back because the guides were afraid to risk crossing the border with such a large group (*Byelogvardeiski terror,* p. 40).
5. *Izvestia,* July 5, 6, and 7 (Yagoda interview). Yagoda later became OGPU chief but perished himself during the 1937–38 purges. The official Soviet white-book version of the story (Kichkassov, *Byelogvardeiski terror*) is essentially the same as the original OGPU account except that no mention is made of Staunitz, who reappears thirty-eight years later in Lev Nikulin's chronicle of the Trust.
6. G. G. Yagoda, *Izvestia,* July 6, 1927.
7. Vinogradov in *Pereklichka,* nos. 136–37 (March–April 1963), p. 16.
8. Cited in *ibid.,* p. 16, and confirmed in a personal interview with Larionov in Munich, 1967.
9. For an exposé of the absurdities in Agabekov's memoirs, see Vinogradov

in *Pereklichka,* nos. 132–33 (November–December 1962), pp. 21–22. Vinogradov is also highly critical of errors in the early literature on the Trust: Chebishev, "Trest"; Richard Wraga, "Trest," *Vozrozhdenie,* no. 7 (January–February 1950); and more recently Geoffrey Bailey, *The Conspirators* (New York, 1960).

10. V. A. Larionov, *Boevaya vylazka v SSSR* (Paris, 1931).
11. The Soviet account (Kichkassov, *Byelogvardeiski terror*) reads: "Comrade Yampolsky was able to escape from the room and selflessly seized the bandit with both arms. The latter drew a pistol and shot Comrade Yampolsky in the trunk."
12. E. H. Cookridge, *Set Europe Ablaze* (New York, 1967), p. 38.

Chapter 8 / Counterterror and Crisis: Stalin Crushes the Opposition

1. *Izvestia,* June 9, 1927. The OGPU later claimed (in the London *Morning Post,* September 1927) that the Opansky murder had been executed by Staunitz, acting on orders from Moscow! See N. Vinogradov in *Pereklichka,* nos. 136–37 (March–April 1963), p. 15.
2. See the *Izvestia* editorials "On Provocation and Murder," June 8 and 9, 1927. The June 9 editorial also referred to "the senseless bombing in Leningrad" (by Captain Larionov's team) and "acts of banditry in Minsk" (the murder of OGPU Deputy Chief Opansky).
3. Sthamer to German Foreign Ministry, June 16, 1927 (British Foreign Office collection, 2860/D558893).
4. William Reswick, *I Dreamt Revolution* (Chicago, 1952), p. 182.
5. Wellroth to Moscow Embassy, June 14, 1927 (British Foreign Office collection, 2860/D558857–58).
6. Harvey L. Dyck, "German-Soviet Relations and the Anglo-Soviet Break, 1927," *Slavic Review,* XXV, no. 1 (March 1966), 76, which cites an extract from minutes of a Cabinet meeting, June 9, 1927 (British Foreign Office collection).
7. Moscow to German Foreign Ministry, June 16, 1927 (British Foreign Office collection, 2860/D558894–95).
8. Otto Hoetzsch, "Russlands Aussenpolitische Lage und Aussenpolitik," *Osteuropa,* II (February 1927), 603.
9. Stresemann to German Foreign Ministry, June 15, 1927 (British Foreign Office collection, 2860/D558862–63).
10. Hoetzsch, "Russlands Aussenpolitische Lage," pp. 604–5.
11. *Ibid.,* p. 609; *Izvestia,* June 29, 1927.
12. Hoetzsch, "Russlands Aussenpolitische Lage," p. 605.
13. Arnold Toynbee, *Survey of International Affairs, 1927* (London, 1929), p. 274, n. 2.
14. Rantzau to Foreign Ministry, June 29, 1927 (British Foreign Office collection, 9524/E671669–70); Dirksen to Reichswehr Ministry, July 2, 1927 (9480/H276430–31).
15. Toynbee, *Survey of International Affairs,* p. 275.
16. Louis Fischer, *The Soviets in World Affairs* (Princeton, N.J., 1951), II, 741.
17. F. Novinsky, "Tendentzii vnutrennevo razvitia Anglii," *Mezhdunarodnaya zhizn,* no. 4 (April 1927), p. 25.
18. For an excellent discussion of Germany's position in the crisis, see Dyck, "German-Soviet Relations." See also K. Rosenbaum, *Community of Fate* (Syracuse, 1965), pp. 246–50.
19. *Izvestia,* August 7, 1927.
20. *Izvestia,* August 10 and 17, 1927.
21. *Izvestia,* August 31, 1927.
22. Rantzau to German Foreign Ministry, August 28, 1927 (British Foreign Office collection, 2860/D5588947–48).
23. Quoted in Otto Hoetzsch, "Russlands Aussenpolitische Lage," p. 610.

24. *Izvestia,* June 26 and 28, 1927.
25. *Izvestia,* July 12, 1927.
26. Rantzau to German Foreign Ministry, September 5, 1927 (British Foreign Office collection, 2860/D558955–56).
27. The table below provides a detailed breakdown of espionage cases reported for the year.
28. Josef Stalin, "On the Threat of War," *Izvestia,* July 28, 1927. (For an English translation, see J. Degras, *Soviet Documents on Foreign Policy* [London, 1951].)

SOVIET ESPIONAGE CASES,
January–December 1927

Intelligence-Service Affiliation	Location[a]	Total	Executed	Imprisoned	Date Reported
Polish	Minsk	1	0	1	January 16, 1927[b]
Estonian	Leningrad	3	1	2	February 17, 1927[b]
Polish	Kharkhov	1	0	1	April 19, 1927[b]
Latvian	Leningrad	18	0	18	May 9 and 27, 1927[b]
Polish	Kiev	3	3	0	May 28, 1927[b]
Polish	Kiev	3	1	2	May 29, 1927[b]
Polish	Kiev	10	0	10	May 31, 1927[b]
Rumanian	Odessa	11	8	3	May 31, 1927[b]
English and monarchist	Moscow	20	20[c]	0	June 9, 1927[b]
Rumanian	Odessa	12	10	2	June 11–12, 1927[b]
Rumanian	Odessa	8	5	3	June 15, 1927[b]
English	Leningrad	2	2	0	June 17, 1927[b]
Polish	Kharkhov	3	2	1	June 18, 1927[b]
Polish	Kharkhov, Zhitomir	2	2	0	June 29, 1927[b]
Polish	Kharkhov	1	1	0	June 30, 1927[h]
Polish	Minsk	9	5	4	July 3, 1927[b]
English	Leningrad	1	1	0	July 6, 1927[b]
English	Leningrad	22	9	13	July 11, 1927[b]
Rumanian	Odessa	1	0	1	July 17, 1927[b]
Polish	Minsk	1	1	0	July 20, 1927[b]
Rumanian	Tiraspol	1	1	0	August 19, 1927[b]
English	Leningrad	1	1	0	August 24, 1927[b]
Polish	Vitebsk	3	2	1	August 30, 1927[b]
Rumanian	Balta (Odessa), Ukraine	1	0	1	September 9, 1927[b]
Polish	Minsk	1	0	1	September 10, 1927[b]
English	Leningrad	......	......	......	September 13 show trial previously announced July 11[b]
English	Leningrad	5	3	2	October 25, 1927[b]
Rumanian	Tiraspol	5	3	2	November 5, 1927[d]
Estonian	Leningrad	11	3[e]	8[e]	November 23, 1927[d]
Rumanian	Kharkhov	29	7	22	December 2, 1927[d]
Rumanian	Odessa	2	1	1	December 11, 1927[d]
Rumanian	Kiev	1	0	1	December 16, 1927[b]

[a] Russian city from which the news story was filed, indicating the approximate area involved.
[b] *Izvestia.*
[c] Summary execution of 5 English and 15 monarchist terrorists.
[d] *Pravda.*
[e] Estimated.

29. H. Seton-Watson, *From Lenin to Khrushchev* (New York, 1960), pp. 142–43.
30. John Erickson, *The Soviet High Command* (London, 1962), p. 287 n.
31. See Leonard Schapiro, *The Communist Party of the Soviet Union* (New York, 1959), p. 303.
32. *Ibid.*, p. 305.
33. *Izvestia*, June 16 and 17, July 10, September 6, 7, 8, and 13. See also the lead editorial, "Otkuda oni," in *Izvestia*, July 8.
34. *Segodnya* (Riga), November 8, 1927.
35. Schapiro, *Communist Party*, p. 306. For excellent accounts of the Trotsky murder, see Hugo Dewar, *Assassins at Large* (Boston, 1952), *passim;* and Isaac Don Levine, *The Mind of an Assassin* (New York, 1959).

Chapter 9   /   Phase-Out: The End of the Kutyepov Offensive and the War Scare

1. The above account is based mainly on N. N. Kichkassov, *Byelogvardeiski terror protiv SSSR* (Moscow, 1928), pp. 44–46. See also the comprehensive report, "Delo pyati monarkhistov-terroristov," *Pravda*, September 17, 1927.
2. See Aderkass testimony in the section "Dopros von-Aderkass," *Izvestia*, September 23, 1927.
3. Stenogram of September 21, 1927, quoted in Kichkassov, *Byelogvardeiski terror*, p. 47.
4. *Pravda*, September 24, 1927. See also the full-page feature articles in *Izvestia*, September 22–25, 1927.
5. *Segodnya* (Riga), September 30, 1927.
6. Grundherr to German Foreign Office, October 4, 1927 (British Foreign Office collection, 2860/D559058–59). The dispatch mentions specifically that with the help of the French ambassador, Georgi Radkovich had left for Paris.
7. "Otkuda oni," *Izvestia*, July 8, 1927.
8. To the extent that any of the charges against the accused were made public, they are included in the brief paragraph that identifies each of the victims in the OGPU announcement in *Izvestia*, June 9, 1927.
9. Rantzau to the German Foreign Ministry, September 1, 1927 (British Foreign Office collection, 2860/D558949–50).
10. John Erickson, *The Soviet High Command* (London, 1962), p. 285.
11. *Izvestia*, September 13, 1927.
12. Erickson, *Soviet High Command*, p. 447. Other military purge victims mentioned were Tukhachevsky, Yakir, Kork, and Eideman. Most of these Red Army commanders were rehabilitated in a special supplementary volume, no. 51, of the 1958 edition of the *Great Soviet Encyclopedia*.
13. Stresemann to Rantzau, November 3, 1927 (British Foreign Office collection, 2860/D559098–99), and Rantzau's reply, November 11, 1927 (2860/D559106–07).
14. *Manchester Guardian*, November 4, 1927, as cited by Arnold Toynbee, *Survey of International Affairs, 1927* (London, 1929), p. 275, n. 5. Toynbee also notes that Mr. B. Sullivan, a British trade-union delegate at the tenth anniversary of the October Revolution, found the Soviet public obsessed with the fear of war and convinced that Chamberlain was deeply engaged in anti-Soviet plots.
15. Otto Hoetzsch, "Russlands Aussenpolitik und Aussenpolitische Lage," *Osteuropa* III (1927–28), 2.
16. *Ibid.*
17. Toynbee, *Survey of International Affairs*, pp. 277–78.

Chapter 10 / The Melgunov Operations: A Plan to Assassinate Stalin

1. The recent opening of the Melgunov archive (deposited by his wife with the London School of Economics after his death in 1956) makes it possible for historians to study some of these operations as indicated by agent reports and correspondence, some of which is still enciphered. The present account is based on a study of these and other documents in the Melgunov archive.
2. C. P. Melgunov, "Zagadki v dele generala Kutepova," in *Russkaya Mysl'*, no. 812, October 25, 1955. The original manuscript and the typescript are in the Melgunov archive, Box 18 (e), papka 11.
3. Melgunov, "Zagadki," *Russkaya Mysl'*, no. 806, October 11, 1955. As leading members of the committee he names the industrialist O. Gukasov, the generals A. I. Denikin and A. P. Kutyepov, A. P. Markov (a collaborator of the historian P. N. Miliukov), M. M. Fedorov, and himself.
4. Melgunov was in fact drawn into a Soviet provocation, the so-called "Second Trust," but collaborated with the OGPU solely for purposes of distributing propaganda and exchanging information.
5. Many of the letters are in cipher text or mixed plain text and cipher. Others are handwritten in clear text but are in part unreadable. Typescripts for most of the letters are included, but in many cases do not include the entire handwritten text. The book used for the cipher is not indicated, and the volume of cipher text is not large enough to break by ordinary cryptanalysis. There is no reason to assume, however, that the unbroken texts contain material which differs substantially from the portions which have been recovered.
6. Excerpts from a handwritten, clear-text letter dated November 25 (?), 1928, and obviously posted outside the U.S.S.R. Melgunov archive, Box 18 (d), papka 9, "Nelegalnye poezdki v SSSR."
7. Excerpts from an enciphered letter written in Harbin and dated November 1, 1928. Melgunov archive, Box 18 (d), papka 9.
8. Handwritten, plain-text letter dated November 27 (?), 1928, and presumably posted from Harbin. Melgunov archive, Box 18 (d), papka 9, "Nelegalnye poezdki v Rossiu."
9. An authoritative contemporary German source estimates the OGPU had made at least a thousand arrests in Moscow alone during the summer of 1927.
10. Enciphered letter dated November 16, 1928, marked "Harbin." The identical text was enciphered a second time and presumably sent by a different channel. The work sheets used in decipherment are in Melgunov's handwriting—a clearly recognizable scrawl. Melgunov archive, Box 18 (d), papka 9.
11. Melgunov archive, Box 18 (e), papka 9, "Organizatsionnyi doklad v 1928–1929 g."

Chapter 11 / No Need to Hope: The Anisimov and Radkovich Missions

1. Max Nomad, *Dreamers, Dynamiters, and Demagogues* (New York, 1964), p. 31.
2. In this regard see Louis de Jong, *The German Fifth Column in World War II* (Chicago, 1956).
3. Hugo Dewar, *Assassins at Large* (Boston, 1952), p. ix.
4. Reproduced in *Chasovoi* (*La Sentinelle*, Brussels), no. 313 (November 1951), pp. 11–15.

5. N. Vinogradov and M. Kritsky, "Vzryv v OGPU 6-go iulia 1928 g," *Vozrozhdenie*, no. 71 (November 1957), pp. 103–7.

Chapter 12 / The Kidnaping of General Kutyepov

1. Grigory Z. Bessedovsky, *Na putyakh k termidoru* (Paris, 1930), p. 245.
2. B. Bajanov and N. Alexeiev, *L'Enlèvement du Général Kutyepov* (Paris, 1950), p. 38, on which the present account is largely based. See also the account in Geoffrey Bailey, *The Conspirators* (New York, 1960), pp. 99–117.
3. Bajanov and Alexeiev, *L'Enlèvement*, pp. 25–26.
4. See the *Literary Digest* account, CIV, no. 9 (March 1, 1930), 13.
5. *Izvestia*, January 31, 1930.
6. *Pravda*, February 3, 1930.
7. Bajanov and Alexeiev, *L'Enlèvement*, p. 76.
8. *Izvestia*, February 3, 1930.
9. *Literary Digest, loc. cit.*
10. Bajanov and Alexeiev, *L'Enlèvement*, p. 81.
11. Alexander Barmine, *One Who Survived* (New York, 1945), p. 186.
12. Bajanov and Alexeiev, *L'Enlèvement*, pp. 78–79.
13. N. Galai to Paul W. Blackstock, May 12, 1967. At the time of the incident Captain Galai, a former White Army officer, was Zaitsov's assistant for military-technical affairs.
14. Galai to Blackstock, May 19, 1967.
15. S. P. Melgunov, "Zagadki v dele generala Kutepova," a series of ten articles published in *Russkaya Mysl'* (Paris, beginning with no. 806, October 11, 1955, through no. 819, November 10, 1955, hereafter cited as "Zagadki"). Melgunov's source for the OGPU report cited is given as I. V. Gessen. See *Russkaya Mysl'*, no. 806, October 11, 1955. The present summary account of the Second Trust operation is based on these articles plus additional material from the recently opened Melgunov archive in the library of the London School of Economics.
16. Melgunov, "Zagadki," *Russkaya Mysl'*, no. 806, October 11, 1955.
17. *Ibid.* Five of these letters are published in *Russkaya Mysl'*, no. 810, October 20, 1955, and No. 812, October 25, 1955.
18. For a detailed account of the checkered careers of both Aleksinsky and Akasatov, see Melgunov, "Zagadki," *Russkaya Mysl'*, no. 810, October 20, 1955, and no. 812, October 25, 1955.
19. Melgunov archive, Box 18 (b), papka 5, Vypiski iz dnevnika P.E.M., 1926–32, and Box 18 (b), papka 2, Pisma i dokumenty, 1925–30, Konspir. rabota provokatora. See also the "Zagadki" series of articles cited above, which draws heavily on these sources.
20. Melgunov, "Zagadki," *Russkaya Mysl'*, no. 815, November 1, 1955. Melgunov implies that the agent was General Steifon, and cites as a source the journalist Burtsev, who claimed that while serving as counter-intelligence officers in Bulgaria and Serbia, Kutyepov's deputy Zaitsov and Steifon "systematically played a double-game with the bolshevists among whom they maintained an extensive network of provocateurs" (no. 813, October 27, 1955).
21. Melgunov, "Zagadki," *Russkaya Mysl'*, no. 815, November 1, 1955.
22. Actually, as indicated in his "Zagadki" articles and by a few additional partially enciphered letters in the Melgunov archive, most of the Melgunov-Popov correspondence originated in Moscow.
23. Published by Melgunov, "Zagadki," *Russkaya Mysl'*, no. 807, October 13, 1955.
24. Disillusioned with the émigré movement, Melgunov and his wife retired to the country in 1930 and became "farmers." They did not return to Paris until after World War II, when Melgunov took over the editorship of the magazine *Vozrozhdenie* in 1946.

25. The OGPU cryptographers were also clumsy. One of the letters dated September 6, 1928, contained a number of enciphering errors as evidenced by Melgunov's work sheets, which he used in trying to decipher it. In five lines of cipher text Melgunov obviously had great difficulty in trying to decipher five groups (83/14, 74/11, 80/7, 83/8, and 83/5), for each of which he jotted down several possible plain-text equivalents. Five additional groups were totally illegible. (Melgunov archive, Box 18 (d), papka 9, "Nelegalnye poezdki v Rossiu.")
26. Melgunov archive, Box 18 (b), papka 5, "Vypiski iz dnevnika P.E.M., 1926–1932."

Chapter 13 / The Skoblin Case

1. Hugo Dewar, *Assassins at Large* (Boston, 1952), p. 10.
2. See the authoritative article by Geoffrey McDermott, "James Bond Could Have Learned from Philby," in the *New York Times Magazine,* November 12, 1967.
3. In this regard see Vance Packard, *The Naked Society* (New York, 1964).
4. Geoffrey Bailey, *The Conspirators* (New York, 1960), p. 130.
5. Nicholas V. Riasanovsky, *A History of Russia* (New York, 1963), pp. 638–39. See also N. S. Timasheff, *The Great Retreat* (New York, 1944), and P. A. Sorokin, *Russia and the United States* (New York, 1946).
6. Quoted in Merle Fainsod, *How Russia Is Ruled* (Cambridge, Mass., 1954), p. 113.
7. *Ibid.*
8. L. Gedar, *Antisovetskaya politika frantsuskogo imperializma* (Moscow and Leningrad, 1931), p. 67.
9. Alexander Orlov, *Handbook of Intelligence and Guerrilla Warfare* (Ann Arbor, Mich., 1963), p. 172.
10. Bailey, *Conspirators,* p. 121.
11. *Ibid.,* pp. 121–22.
12. *Ibid.,* p. 231.
13. Quoted by Walter Krivitsky, *I Was Stalin's Agent* (London, 1939), p. 260.
14. *Posledniye novosti,* February 1, 2, 6, and 20, 1935.
15. Bailey, *Conspirators,* p. 125.
16. Dewar, *Assassins at Large,* p. 17.
17. *Ibid.,* p. 4. According to Dewar, the hearing took place in 1935.
18. *Ibid.,* p. 17. See also *International Press Correspondence,* no. 48 (November 6, 1937).
19. Gert Buchheit, *Der Deutsche Geheimdienst* (Munich, 1966), p. 163.

Chapter 14 / The Kidnaping of General Miller

1. For a full account of the Reisz murder in English, see Hugo Dewar, *Assassins at Large* (Boston, 1952), which is based largely on Victor Serge, Maurice Wullens, and Alfred Rosmer, *L'Assassinat politique et l'URSS* (Paris, 1938).
2. Quoted in *ibid.,* pp. 34–35.
3. *Ibid.,* p. 36.
4. *Ibid.,* p. 41.
5. In addition to the Reisz case, Dewar analyzes the assassinations of Dimitry Navashin (January 1936), Leon Sedov (Trotsky's son, 1938), Rudolf Klement (Trotsky's translator, 1938), Lieutenant Colonel Evhen Konovalec (Ukrainian nationalist leader, 1938), Willi Muenzenberg

(Comintern propagandist, 1940), and Leon Trotsky (1940), plus a large number of NKVD-instigated assassinations during the civil war in Spain.

6. Walter Krivitsky, *I Was Stalin's Agent* (London, 1939), p. 235.
7. *Ibid.*, pp. 237–38.
8. Geoffrey Bailey, *The Conspirators* (New York, 1960), p. 228.
9. Krivitsky, *I Was Stalin's Agent*, pp. 253–54.
10. *Ibid.*, pp. 257–59.
11. Quoted in *ibid.*, p. 260.
12. As quoted in *ibid.*, pp. 260–61. Slightly variant versions are given in Bailey, *Conspirators*, p. 234; Dewar, *Assassins at Large*, p. 3; and Joseph Bornstein, *The Politics of Murder* (New York, 1950), p. 78. The other principal source, one that makes a strong case for NKVD responsibility for the murder of Miller, is Vladimir L. Burtsev, *Bolshevitskie gangstery v Parizhe* (Paris, 1939).
13. Quoted by Bailey, *Conspirators*, p. 234.
14. *Ibid.*, pp. 256–57.
15. Dewar, *Assassins at Large*, p. 9.
16. See Burtsev, *Bolshevitskie gangstery*, especially chap. 13, pp. 92–99.
17. Quoted in Ig. Opishnya, "Tukhachevsky i Skoblin," *Vozrozhdenie*, March 1955, p. 109.
18. Dewar, *Assassins at Large*, pp. 11–12.
19. See the article "Hitler and the Russian White Guards in France" in the Comintern organ *International Press Correspondence*, no. 48 (November 6, 1937).

Chapter 15 / Secret Soviet-German Military Collaboration

1. R. Gul, *Tukhachevsky, krassnyi marshal* (Berlin, n.d.), p. 42.
2. John Erickson, *The Soviet High Command* (London, 1962), p. 58.
3. Quoted by Gustav Hilger and A. G. Meyers, *The Incompatible Allies* (New York, 1953), p. 190.
4. *Ibid.*, p. 191.
5. F. L. Carsten, *The Reichswehr and Politics, 1918 to 1933* (Oxford, 1966), p. 232.
6. Hilger and Meyers, *Incompatible Allies*, pp. 193–94.
7. Carsten, *Reichswehr and Politics*, p. 234.
8. Erickson, *Soviet High Command*, p. 157.
9. Carsten, *Reichswehr and Politics*, p. 359.
10. Hence the cover name Operation Kama, sometimes mistakenly applied to German-Soviet military collaboration as a whole. For example, see Geoffrey Bailey, *The Conspirators* (New York, 1960), pp. 196, 199.
11. Carsten, *Reichswehr and Politics*, pp. 236, 273.
12. Erickson, *Soviet High Command*, pp. 269–70.
13. *Ibid.*, p. 280.
14. Quoted in Hilger and Meyers, *Incompatible Allies*, p. 207.
15. Carsten, "The Reichswehr and the Red Army, 1920–1933," *Survey* (London), October 1962, p. 132.
16. Hilger and Meyers, *Incompatible Allies*, pp. 199–200. In spite of Hilger's complaint, the captured German Foreign Office files contain some 1,500 pages of documents. See especially 4564H/E162514-164069: Mil. Angelegenheiten mit Russland, Büro d. Staatssekretär 17 March 1923– 18 May 1930 (Erickson, *Soviet High Command*, p. 696, n. 39).
17. Hilger and Meyers, *Incompatible Allies*, p. 204.
18. *Ibid.*, p. 203, n. 15.
19. Erickson, *Soviet High Command*, p. 273.
20. Ernest L. Woodward and Rohan Butler, eds., *Documents on British Foreign Policy 1919–1939*, 2nd ser., II (London, 1947), 520–21, quoted in Hilger and Meyers, *Incompatible Allies*, p. 207 n.
21. Carsten, *Reichswehr and Politics*, pp. 148, 210, 359.
22. *Ibid.*, p. 359.

23. Erickson, *Soviet High Command,* p. 272.
24. *Ibid.,* p. 279.
25. Hilger and Meyers, *Incompatible Allies,* pp. 146–47.
26. *Ibid.,* p. 253.
27. Erickson, *Soviet High Command,* pp. 342–43.
28. Quoted by G. M. Gathorne-Hardy in *A Short History of International Affairs* (London, 1950), p. 357.
29. *Ibid.,* pp. 357–58.
30. Hilger and Meyers, *Incompatible Allies,* p. 252.
31. *Ibid.,* pp. 267–68.
32. Erickson, *Soviet High Command,* pp. 346–48.
33. Hilger and Meyers, *Incompatible Allies,* p. 271.
34. Quoted in William Evans Scott, *Alliance Against Hitler* (Durham, N.C., 1962), p. 2.

Chapter 16 / France and the U.S.S.R.: The Alliance That Never Was

1. Quoted in William Evans Scott, *Alliance Against Hitler* (Durham, N.C., 1962), p. 120.
2. Gustav Hilger and A. G. Meyers, *The Incompatible Allies* (New York, 1935), p. 154.
3. Edouard Herriot, *Jadis,* II, 437, quoted in Scott, *Alliance Against Hitler,* p. 209.
4. Lewis B. Namier, *Europe in Decay* (London, 1950), pp. 14, 35, 92–105.
5. John Erickson, *The Soviet High Command* (London, 1962), pp. 385–86.
6. Scott, *Alliance Against Hitler,* p. 231.
7. *Ibid.,* p. 232. (The quotation is taken from a dispatch of the American chargé d'affaires in Moscow, Mr. Wiley.)
8. Erickson, *Soviet High Command,* p. 344.
9. J. Paul-Boncour, *Entre deux guerres* (New York, 1947), II, 371.
10. *Ibid.,* p. 400.
11. Scott, *Alliance Against Hitler,* p. 196.
12. Quoted in Namier, *Europe in Decay,* p. 36.
13. Quoted in Scott, *Alliance Against Hitler,* p. 229.
14. Quoted in Namier, *Europe in Decay,* p. 36.
15. Jane Degras, ed., *Soviet Documents on Foreign Policy* (London, 1953), III, 125.
16. Josef Stalin, "Report to the XVIth Congress of the Communist Party," in *Les Questions du Leninisme* (Paris, 1947), II, 139 (my translation).
17. *International Press Correspondence,* English ed., XV, no. 6 (February 9, 1935), 175.
18. *Ibid.,* XV, no. 17 (April 20, 1935), 452.
19. For a content analysis of Communist propaganda in the period of transition to the popular front, see Department of the Army, Office of the Assistant Chief of Staff, G-2, *Analysis of Soviet and French Communist Propaganda,* Intelligence Research Project no. 6317 (Washington), August 10, 1951 [sic].
20. Quoted by Loy Henderson, dispatch no. 598 (unpublished), September 30, 1937 (National Archives file no. 861. 20/429).
21. Erickson, *Soviet High Command,* p. 413. See also the account in Geneviève Tabouis, *Ils m'ont appelée Cassandre* (New York, 1942), pp. 248–49.
22. K. H. Abshagen, *Canaris* (Stuttgart, 1949), p. 168. Geoffrey Bailey accepts as true rumors that "during his spring trip to Western Europe, he [Tukhachevsky] had not shunned contacts with certain White emigres" (*The Conspirators* [New York, 1960], p. 217).
23. Ian Colvin, *Master Spy* (New York, 1951), p. 41.
24. Erickson, *Soviet High Command,* p. 729, n. 27; see also pp. 413–14.
25. Quoted in Namier, *Europe in Decay,* p. 17.

26. *Ibid.*, p. 20.
27. The phrase is Paul Reynaud's, quoted in *ibid.*, p. 25.
28. *Ibid.*, p. 11.
29. G. M. Gathorne-Hardy, *A Short History of International Affairs* (London, 1950), p. 421.
30. Namier, *Europe in Decay*, p. 6.
31. Degras, ed., *Soviet Documents*, III, 173–74.
32. *Ibid.*, p. 179.
33. Gathorne-Hardy, *Short History*, p. 422.
34. Erickson, *Soviet High Command*, p. 431.
35. Robert Coulondre, *De Staline à Hitler, Souvenirs de deux ambassades, 1936–1939* (Paris, 1950), pp. 33–34.
36. Gathorne-Hardy, *Short History*, p. 369.
37. Erickson, *Soviet High Command*, p. 427.
38. *Ibid.*, p. 419.
39. Quoted in "The Letter of an Old Bolshevik and Other Essays by Boris I. Nicolaevsky," in *Power and the Soviet Elite*, edited by Janet D. Zagoria (New York, 1965), pp. 30–31.
40. Robert C. Tucker and Stephen F. Cohen, *The Great Purge Trial* (New York, 1965), p. xxxv. For a detailed analysis of the split between Stalin and Bukharin on domestic and foreign policy issues at this time, see Robert M. Slusser, "The Role of the Foreign Ministry," in *Russian Foreign Policy: Essays in Historical Perspective*, edited by Ivo J. Lederer (New Haven, 1962), pp. 217–28.
41. Degras, ed., *Soviet Documents*, III, 70.
42. George F. Kennan, *Russia and the West under Lenin and Stalin* (Boston, 1961), p. 302.
43. Tucker and Cohen, *Great Purge Trial*, p. xxxvi.
44. In *Power and the Soviet Elite*, p. 89.
45. Quoted in Erickson, *Soviet High Command*, p. 416.
46. Kennan, *Russia and the West*, pp. 305–6.
47. Tucker and Cohen, *Great Purge Trial*, p. xxxvi.
48. *Ibid.*, p. xi. For a detailed analysis of these charges and an exposé of their absurdity, see Erickson, *Soviet High Command*, pp. 481–88.
49. Tucker and Cohen, *Great Purge Trial*, p. xxiv.
50. Kennan, *Russia and the West*, p. 308.
51. *Documents of the Twenty-second Congress of the CPSU* (New York, 1961), I, 228.
52. Joseph E. Davies, *Mission to Moscow* (New York, 1941), pp. 356–57.
53. Boris Souvarine, *Stalin: A Critical Survey of Bolshevism* (New York, 1939), p. 485.
54. Svetlana Alliluyeva, *Twenty Letters to a Friend* (New York, 1967), p. 112.
55. *Ibid.*, p. 123.
56. *Ibid.*, p. 78.
57. *Ibid.*, pp. 78–79.
58. Robert Slusser cites Nicolaevsky's *Letter of an Old Bolshevik* (in *Power and the Soviet Elite*, ed. Zagoria, p. 60) as evidence that pressure to end the investigation was brought to bear by "several members of the Politburo" ("The Role of the Foreign Ministry," in *Russian Foreign Policy*, ed. Lederer, pp. 220–21).
59. Kennan first pointed this out in 1960, seven years before its confirmation by Stalin's daughter (*Russia and the West*, p. 307)!
60. *Ibid.* For the estimate of nine million victims and an explanation of the computations on which it is based, see Alexander Weissberg, *The Accused* (New York, 1951), pp. 318–25.
61. Quoted in Tucker and Cohen, *Great Purge Trial*, p. xxvii.

Chapter 17 / Disinformation, Plot, and Counterplot

1. Hugh Seton-Watson, *From Lenin to Khrushchev* (New York, 1960) pp. 158–59. For an eyewitness account of a typical incident, see "The Anisimov Mission" in Chapter 10 above.
2. See John Erickson, *The Soviet High Command* (London, 1962), p. 356 and p. 722, n. 105, on E. Wollenberg's claim in *The Red Army* that Blyukher presented an ultimatum to Stalin demanding a relaxation of collectivization in eastern Siberia in order to assure defense of the area. Wollenberg's source is apparently Walter Krivitsky, who goes so far as to claim that "Stalin's power at that time [1933] hung so delicately in the balance that he was forced to capitulate. Sweeping concessions were granted to the peasants in Marshal Bluecher's district" (*I Was Stalin's Agent* [London, 1939], p. 245).
3. Alexander Weissberg, *The Accused* (New York, 1951), p. 371.
4. Janet D. Zagoria, ed., *Power and the Soviet Elite* (New York, 1965), p. 195.
5. Bella Fromm, *Blood and Banquets, A Berlin Social Diary* (New York, 1942), p. 231.
6. Walter Krivitsky, *I Was Stalin's Agent*, pp. 234–35.
7. *Le Nouvel Observateur*, no. 109 (December 14–20, 1966), p. 17. The quotation is from an apparently authentic document, a stenographic report or "protocol" of a closed discussion of Stalin's war guilt which took place at the Institute of Marxism-Leninism with both historians and General Staff officers present. (Although this document is generally accepted as authentic, for an extended argument against its validity see Christian Duevel, *First-Rate Documents or Forgeries? A Comparative Analysis of Protocols of Closed Meetings at the Institute of Marxism-Leninism in Moscow*," Radio Liberty research report CRD 529/67 [Munich, 1967].)
8. Krivitsky, *I Was Stalin's Agent*, p. 235.
9. Joachim Pindter, "Heydrich und die Affaire Tuchatschewski," in the *Frankfurter Allgemeine Zeitung*, November 28, 1961. An obviously well-informed source in his own right, Pindter is critical of both the Schellenberg and Bailey versions of the affair (Walter Schellenberg, *The Schellenberg Memoirs* [London, 1956]; Geoffrey Bailey, *The Conspirators* [New York, 1960]).
10. See Fromm, *Blood and Banquets*, p. 231.
11. Erickson, *Soviet High Command*, p. 434.
12. Pindter, "Heydrich und die Affaire Tuchatschewski."
13. Erickson, *Soviet High Command*, p. 414.
14. Chalmers Johnson, *An Instance of Treason, Ozaki Hotsumi and the Sorge Spy Ring* (Stanford, Calif., 1964), pp. 170–73.
15. According to Horst Falkenhagen (presumably an alias of Walter Hoettl or Hagen), Canaris, the chief of the *Abwehr*, knew that there were four OGPU agents in the Berlin headquarters of the Gestapo. See his article "Verhängnisvolles Zusammenspiel: Rote Armee und Reichswehr," in *Die Neue Zeitung*, October 2, 1948. See also Alexander Orlov, *Handbook of Intelligence and Guerrilla Warfare* (Ann Arbor, Mich., 1963), *passim*.
16. Winston Churchill (*The Second World War* [London, 1948], I, 224), in a footnote states there is reason to believe that Benes first received a report of the alleged Tukhachevsky plot from the Czech police through the OGPU, "who wished it to reach Stalin from a friendly foreign source." This information was apparently supplied to Churchill by British intelligence as an editorial afterthought or correction. In the text Churchill indicates (1) that Benes was informed in "a message from a high military source in Germany" in the autumn of 1936, and (2) that Benes was made aware of "communications passing through

the Soviet Embassy in Prague between important personages in Russia and the German Government."

17. Eduard Benes, *Memoirs of Dr. Eduard Benes* (London, 1954), pp. 14–20 and 47, n. 8. Actually Hitler was not seriously interested in a nonaggression pact which might later tie his hands, and "Haushofer was instructed to drag out the negotiations, which meant that they were to be dropped" (Gerhard L. Weinberg, "Secret Hitler-Benes Negotiations in 1936–1937," *Journal of Central European Affairs,* January 1960, p. 373).

18. For a biting analysis of the absurdities in what both Benes and Churchill have written on the subject, see the article by Boris Souvarine, "L'Affaire Toukhatchevski," in *Le Contrat Social,* III, no. 4 (July 1959), 206–8.

19. Benes, *Memoirs,* p. 34.

20. Quoted by Paul Reynaud, *In the Thick of the Fight, 1930–1945* (London, 1955), pp. 58–59.

21. Apparently Benes died still believing in the Tukhachevsky conspiracy story, according to a letter from his nephew, Vaclav Benes.

22. Pindter, "Heydrich und die Affaire Tuchatschewski." Erickson writes that "it has been possible to confirm this from a private source who was also implicated" (*Soviet High Command,* p. 735, n. 26). SS Major Alfred Naujocks claims to have been the other officer involved. See his lurid account (as told to a German journalist) in Günter Peis, *The Man Who Started the War* (New York, 1962), chap. 5.

23. Erickson writes that "on the question of signatures, *Zweigstelle Dresden* records a loan to the *Wehramt* Ausl. VI from February–November, 1937, of 11th Infantry Brigade files which contained a specimen of Tukhachevsky's signature as a prisoner-of-war in Germany. See OKH Records (Part I), The National Archives, Washington, D.C." (*Soviet High Command,* p. 435 n.). Various accounts that Heydrich approached Canaris directly for correspondence (K. H. Abshagen, *Canaris* [Stuttgart, 1949], p. 116; Peter Kleist, *Zwischen Hitler und Stalin* [Bonn, 1950], p. 213) or that the *Abwehr* offices were burglarized for this purpose (Schellenberg, *Memoirs,* p. 48; Peis, *Man Who Started the War,* p. 73) are hardly credible. According to General Dr. Karl Spalcke (at that time a first lieutenant and the Russian expert in the *Abwehr's* Foreign Armies [T-3] Division), Canaris was not informed of the operation until it was all over (*Der Spiegel,* no. 49 [November 28, 1966], p. 96; part 7 of the series *Der Orden unter dem Todtenkopf,* by Heinz Höhne).

24. Peis, *Man Who Started the War,* pp. 72–82. Stripped of its sensational journalistic wrappings, the outline of events in Naujocks' story is credible and corresponds closely to the reconstruction by Erickson, who concludes that "Although many details concerning its preparation remain obscure, the existence of the forged material cannot be held seriously in doubt" (*Soviet High Command,* p. 457).

25. Erickson, *Soviet High Command,* pp. 731–32, n. 87.

26. *Der Spiegel,* no. 49 (November 28, 1966), p. 94.

27. For the texts of Stalin's March speeches, see W. P. and Z. K. Coates, *The Moscow Trial (January 1937) and Two Speeches by Joseph Stalin* (London, Anglo-Russian Parliamentary Committee, 1937).

28. The standard handbook on detecting such forgeries is *Suspect Documents* (New York, 1958), by Wilson R. Harrison of the British Home Office. However, most of the technical methods employed today in detecting criminal forgeries were known in the mid-1930's.

29. Erickson, *Soviet High Command,* p. 457.

Chapter 18 / The Military Purge, June 1937

1. *Survey* (London), no. 44 (October 1963), p. 128 (a translation of hitherto unpublished captured German documents under the title "Moscow and the Nazis").
2. *Ibid.,* pp. 129–30 (from EAP 250-d-18-15, AA/Amt Osten, microfilm T 81/14, National Archives, Washington, D.C.).
3. *Ibid.,* p. 132.
4. Walter Krivitsky, *I Was Stalin's Agent* (London, 1939), p. 249.
5. Alexander Orlov, *Handbook of Intelligence and Guerrilla Warfare* (Ann Arbor, Mich., 1963), pp. 22–23.
6. *Ibid.,* pp. 106–7.
7. John Erickson, *The Soviet High Command* (London, 1962), p. 432.
8. Gustav Hilger and A. G. Meyers, *The Incompatible Allies* (New York, 1953), p. 284.
9. Erickson, *Soviet High Command,* pp. 432, 453.
10. *Ibid.,* p. 453.
11. Krivitsky, *I Was Stalin's Agent,* p. 237.
12. Erickson, *Soviet High Command,* p. 458. (Erickson was apparently unaware of the recently discovered Duercksen memoranda.)
13. Hilger and Meyers, *The Incompatible Allies,* pp. 288–89. A German embassy official (Hilger?) told the U.S. chargé (Kirk) in Moscow on June 22, 1938, that discussions had been held with the Soviet trade delegation in Berlin "about two months ago," indicating that this channel, which was eventually used for political rapprochement, was kept open (*Foreign Relations of the United States, Diplomatic Papers, The Soviet Union 1933–1939* [Washington, 1952], pp. 584–85).
14. Krivitsky, *I Was Stalin's Agent,* pp. 238–40.
15. Joseph E. Davies, *Mission to Moscow* (New York, 1941), pp. 132–33.
16. *Ibid.,* p. 43.
17. Erickson, *Soviet High Command,* p. 455, based on Krivitsky, *I Was Stalin's Agent,* p. 167.
18. Krivitsky, *I Was Stalin's Agent,* pp. 248–51.
19. Erickson, *Soviet High Command,* pp. 429–31.
20. For a definitive study of the German occupation of the U.S.S.R., see Alexander Dallin, *German Rule in Russia, 1941–1945* (New York, 1957).
21. George F. Kennan, *Russia and the West under Lenin and Stalin* (Boston, 1961), p. 311. During the postwar period of "de-Stalinization," the Soviet author Alexander Solzhenitsyn in his short novel "An Incident at Krechetovka Station" gives a sympathetic portrayal of a young idealist who tried to volunteer for duty in Spain and was rebuffed. See Alexander Solzhenitsyn, *We Never Make Mistakes,* two short novels translated from the Russian with an Introduction by Paul W. Blackstock (Columbia, S.C., 1963), pp. 50–51. For an incisive portrayal of the NKVD role in Spain, see Victor Serge, *The Case of Comrade Tulayev* (New York, 1950), pp. 108–42.
22. Kork had been instrumental in recruiting Roman Birk to work as a double agent for the GPU in the early Dzerzhinsky days, when the Trust operation was first launched (see Chapter 2 above).
23. Erickson, *Soviet High Command,* pp. 460–61.
24. Krivitsky, *I Was Stalin's Agent,* p. 253.
25. *Ibid.,* p. 257.
26. Erickson, *Soviet High Command,* p. 488. For the complete trial testimony, see Robert C. Tucker and Stephen F. Cohen, *The Great Purge Trial* (New York, 1965).
27. Erickson, *Soviet High Command,* p. 462.
28. According to Ambassador Davies: "That such a conference was in fact held and that a very large number of officers were present here in Moscow at that time seem to be confirmed by foreign military observers

who saw many of these Red Army officers whom they met in different
parts of the Soviet Union" (*Mission to Moscow*, p. 200).

29. Military Attaché, Moscow, U.S.S.R., report no. 875, June 17, 1937
    (Record Group 165/MID, File 2037–1833, National Archives, Wash-
    ington, D.C.). I am indebted to Mr. Richard Bauer, GSA, for de-
    classification of this report.

30. As quoted by Leonard Schapiro, "The Great Purge," in B. H. Liddell
    Hart, *The Soviet Army* (London, 1956), p. 70. See also Erickson, *Soviet
    High Command*, p. 736, n. 46. (This report was confirmed by Leonard
    Schapiro in an interview in February 1967. Further investigation has
    indicated that the officer in question was Major M. F. Vasiliev, who
    was connected with the Vlassov movement and lived in Ireland after
    the war, but later redefected to the U.S.S.R.) Robert Conquest, in his
    exhaustive study *The Great Terror: Stalin's Purge of the Thirties* (New
    York, 1968), cites a recent Soviet source indicating that the agenda of
    the extraordinary meeting of the military Soviet attached to the Com-
    missariat of Defense "consisted of a single item—the exposure of the
    counter-revolutionary military-fascist organization, reported on by Stalin
    personally" (p. 222). The same source (Yu P. Petrov, *Partiynoe Stroi-
    tel'stvo v Sovetskoy Armii i Flote, 1918–1961*, Moscow, 1964) claims
    that Stalin based his charges "on faked evidence from repressed military
    men" (pp. 299–300). On the basis of the Petrov account Conquest
    concludes that the forged German documents were not produced, and
    were used merely to give "the limited Stalin-Yezhov circle a proper
    sense of outrage and urgency." On the face of it the argument that over
    and above official orders the NKVD needed any special stimulus to
    pursue its task of extorting confessions cannot be taken seriously. The
    record of the March 1938 trial shows that not even the NKVD could
    extract convincing evidence of the alleged conspiracy from the "repressed
    military men" in its torture chambers. Under these circumstances it is
    most unlikely that Stalin would have scrapped the forged German docu-
    ments, which *were* convincing, and which the NKVD had taken such pains
    to procure. Since official documents dealing with the affair have not
    been made available (and have probably been destroyed), scraps of
    hearsay evidence produced by contemporary Soviet sources must be set
    against the testimony of responsible Western sources reporting on these
    events at the time. For this reason it is logical to assume with the U.S.
    military attaché, Colonel Faymonville, that the *raison d'être* of the
    June 1–4 conference was the crisis created by the reintroduction of
    political commissars and "dual command." It is also probable that
    Stalin used the occasion to raise the conspiracy charge against Tukha-
    chevsky, basing his accusations on both the forged German documents
    and the internal evidence extracted by the NKVD from "repressed
    military men."

31. Quoted from *Le Nouvel Observateur*, no. 109 (December 14–20, 1966),
    p. 16. With reference to "the enemies of the people" denounced in
    1918, Anfilov explained that "Stalin thus designated a certain number
    of former General Staff and line officers who were serving the Soviet
    honorably" at that time. In regard to Stalin's intervention in Tsaritsyn
    and his opposition to the former tsarist "military specialists," Erickson
    writes: "Stalin lashed out repeatedly and insolently over the ex-officers.
    Running what amounted to a private war in Tsaritsyn in the company
    of Voroshilov, Stalin embodied the opposition at the front . . . Trotsky
    on 5th October . . . managed to obtain the recall of Stalin, at the
    same time threatening Voroshilov and Minin with court-martial unless
    they followed regular procedure over reconnaissance and battle-reports"
    (*Soviet High Command*, pp. 39–40).

32. Ilya Ehrenburg, *Memoirs: 1921–1941* (Cleveland and New York, 1963),
    pp. 426–27.

33. Krivitsky, *I Was Stalin's Agent*, p. 254. See also Erickson, *Soviet High
    Command*, p. 736, n. 42.

34. See *Foreign Relations . . . Soviet Union, 1933–1939*, pp. 377–78.

35. As quoted in *ibid.*, pp. 378–79.

36. Military Attaché, Moscow, U.S.S.R., report no. 875, June 17, 1937 (Record Group 165/MID, File 2037-1833, National Archives, Washington, D.C.).

37. For a review of the arguments pro and con, see Conquest, *The Great Terror,* pp. 223–24.

38. Viktor Savostyanov, in an article on Yuborevich in T. K. Gladkov, ed., *Geroy Grazhdanskoy Voyny* (Moscow, 1963), p. 120. For other references to the "trial," see I. V. Dubinsky, *Naprekor Vetram* (Moscow, 1964), pp. 267–68, and Lev Nikulin, *Marshal Tukhachevsky* (Moscow, 1964), pp. 190–91. Nikulin's account of "the last days" of the marshal went through three different versions, all of them based on unreliable, secondhand German and English sources. (In addition to the work cited, Nikulin published a popular account in *Ogonëk,* no. 13, March 1963, and a lengthy serial version in *Oktyabr,* nos. 2, 3, 4, and 5, 1963.)

39. Quoted in Henderson dispatch (unpublished), no. 598, September 30, 1937 (file no. 861.20/429, National Archives, Washington, D.C.).

40. *Foreign Relations . . . Soviet Union, 1933–1939,* p. 385 and n. 30.

41. Davies, *Mission to Moscow,* pp. 191–92.

42. *Ibid.,* p. 194.

43. *Ibid.,* p. 201.

44. *Ibid.,* p. 192. (Coulondre is one of the "two very well-informed ambassadors" referred to; see also the reference on p. 194 quoted above.)

45. *Foreign Relations . . . Soviet Union, 1933–1939,* p. 386.

46. *Ibid.,* p. 385.

47. Robert Coulondre, *De Staline à Hitler, Souvenirs de deux ambassades, 1936–1939* (Paris, 1950), p. 83. Daladier, of course, had received this false report from Blum, who in turn got it from Benes, who had it from NKVD channels via Berlin, Paris, and Stalin, thus completing the vicious circle of disinformation.

48. *Ibid.,* p. 83.

49. *Foreign Relations . . . Soviet Union, 1933–1939,* p. 378.

50. E. L. Woodward and Rohan Butler, eds., *British Documents on Foreign Policy, 1919–1939* (London, 1949), 3rd series, I, 306. Max Beloff (*The Foreign Policy of Soviet Russia, 1929–1941* [London, 1949], II, 127) observes that J. A. Spender, "in his able defence of British policy in the Munich crisis," *Between Two Wars* (London, 1943), makes much of the point of Soviet military weakness resulting from the purge.

51. *Documents on German Foreign Policy, 1918–1945: From the Archives of the German Foreign Ministry* (Washington, 1949, and continuing), series D, II, 363.

52. Davies, *Mission to Moscow,* p. 481.

53. *Ibid.,* p. 280.

54. *Ibid.,* p. 203.

55. Beloff, *The Foreign Policy of Soviet Russia,* II, 121, n. 6.

56. Davies, *Mission to Moscow,* p. 290.

57. Beloff, in *The Foreign Policy of Soviet Russia,* II, 126.

58. Coulondre, *De Staline à Hitler,* p. 136.

59. See Léon Noël, *L'aggression allemande contre la Pologne* (Paris, 1946), pp. 200–201. See also Edward Benes, *Memoirs of Dr. Edward Benes* (London, 1954), *passim.*

60. Jane Degras, ed., *Soviet Documents on Foreign Policy* (London, 1953), III, 279.

61. Beloff, in *The Foreign Policy of Soviet Russia,* II, 130, n. 2.

62. Degras, *Soviet Documents on Foreign Policy,* III, 289.

63. *Ibid.,* pp. 289–90.

64. Erickson, *Soviet High Command,* p. 741, n. 47.

65. Coulondre, *De Staline à Hitler,* p. 157.

66. Degras, *Soviet Documents on Foreign Policy,* III, 303.

67. Quoted in L. B. Namier, *Europe in Decay* (London, 1950), pp. 163–64.

68. Coulondre, *De Staline à Hitler,* pp. 156–57.

69. Kennan, *Russia and the West,* pp. 312–13.

70. Erickson, *Soviet High Command,* p. 504.

71. Quoted in U.S. Embassy, France, dispatch no. 1267, November 23, 1937 (File 861.00/11705, National Archives, Washington, D.C.).
72. A. Agricola (Bauermeister), "Die Sowietunion auf dem Wege zum Bonapartismus," *Deutsche Wehr*, no. 44 (October 27, 1938). See also his *Der Rote Marschal Tukhachevskys Aufstieg und Fall* (Berlin, 1939). Boris Souvarine notes that "At the time a few serious Soviet specialists had taken due note of this article" ("L'affaire Toukhatchevski," in *Le Contrat Social* [Paris], III, no. 4 [July 1959], 209).
73. Blackstock, *The Strategy of Subversion* (Chicago, 1964), pp. 145–46.
74. Quoted in *Le Nouvel Observateur*, no. 109 (December 14–20, 1966), p. 17.
75. For a remarkably frank account of the situation at the front after the German attack, see A. V. Gorbatov, *Years Off My Life, The Memoirs of General of the Soviet Army A. V. Gorbatov* (London, 1964). For a Soviet "revisionist" view of Stalin's role at the time, see *A. M. Nekrich, 1941, 22 iynia* (Moscow, 1965). (A complete translation is included in Vladimir Petrov, *"June 22, 1941"; Soviet Historians and the Military* [Columbia, S.C., 1968].)
76. Richard H. Ullman, "The Davies Mission and United States–Soviet Relations," *World Politics* (January 1957), 220, 239.

Chapter 19 / Intelligence Operations and the Road to War

1. Conversation with the author in connection with a study, "Indications of Soviet Plans and Intentions in German-Soviet Relations, 1939–1941," Intelligence Research Project No. 3492, Intelligence Division, WDGS, November 26, 1946 (declassified, September 9, 1948).
2. Bruce Page, David Leitch, and Phillip Knightley, *The Philby Conspiracy* (New York, 1968), pp. 117–19.
3. Alexander Orlov, *Handbook of Intelligence and Guerrilla Warfare* (Ann Arbor, Mich., 1963), p. 61.
4. Page, *et al., The Philby Conspiracy*, p. 290.
5. David J. Dallin, *Soviet Espionage* (New Haven, 1955), pp. 462–63; Sanche de Gramont, *The Secret War* (New York, 1962), pp. 107–23; and an unpublished paper by Louis R. Sadler, "The Influence of Soviet Espionage Directed Against American Science," University of South Carolina Department of History, 1967.
6. In this regard see Page, *et al., The Philby Conspiracy*, pp. 117–19.
7. See, for example, the speech by the KGB Chairman Yu. V. Andrepov, *Pravda*, December 21, 1967, and that of his deputy, L. I. Pankratov, *Trud*, December 19, 1967.
8. For illustrations of such penetration, see Orlov, *Handbook of Intelligence and Guerrilla Warfare*, and Walter Krivitsky, *I Was Stalin's Agent* (London, 1939), *passim*.
9. John Erickson, *The Soviet High Command* (London, 1962), pp. 364–65; 386–87; 394–95.
10. Herbert von Dirksen, *Moscow, Tokyo, London* (Norman, Okla., 1952), p. 81.
11. Beatrice Farnsworth, *William C. Bullitt and the Soviet Union* (Bloomington, Ind., 1967), pp. 132–34.
12. Henry L. Roberts, "Maxim Litvinov," in Gordon A. Craig and Felix Gilbert, eds., *The Diplomats, 1919–1939* (Princeton, 1953), p. 373.
13. Farnsworth, *Bullitt and the Soviet Union*, p. 36 and n. 77 which cites a letter from Kennan.
14. *Ibid.*, pp. 136–37.
15. Prentiss B. Gilbert to Cordell Hull, August 14, 1936, National Archives file no. 761.62/389. Sometime in July and again in early August "an excellent source" reported to Ferdinand L. Mayer, the American chargé d'affaires in Berlin, "his belief in strong efforts being made here to improve German-Russian relations," and that negotiations to this end

"are going on both in Moscow and here." Mayer forwarded this information to the Department of State and to his friend Arthur Bliss Lane, the U.S. Minister to the Baltic States in Riga, Latvia. Lane in turn reported that the Estonian minister of foreign affairs, Akel, who had recently served as Estonian envoy to Germany, had received the same impression, "not only from sources in the German Government but from the Soviet Ambassador in Berlin as well." (Mayer to Lane, August 8, 1936, and Lane to Mayer, September 21, 1936, in the Arthur Bliss Lane Collection, Yale University New Haven.)

16. U.S. Army, Interrogation Report, No. 5818, October 17, 1945, cited in Intelligence Research Project No. 3492, "Indications of Soviet Plans and Intentions in German-Soviet Relations, 1939–1941," November 26, 1946, pp. 4–5, Intelligence Division, WDGS, Washington, D.C. (declassified). See also Gustav Hilger and Alfred G. Meyer, *The Incompatible Allies* (New York, 1953), pp. 306–7. In these passages of his memoirs Hilger omits any observations on the political-ideological motives which prompted Stalin to sign the Nazi-Soviet pact. This omission may have been due to the promptings of E. H. Carr, to whom Hilger sent an early draft of his manuscript, after which Carr rushed to press his *German-Soviet Relations Between the Two World Wars, 1919–1939* (Baltimore, 1951). Carr takes the view that the Kremlin was motivated solely by considerations of national security, a view which has since become the standard "line" followed by Soviet historians.

17. Robert C. Tucker and Stephen F. Cohen, *The Great Purge Trial* (New York, 1965), p. xxxvi.

18. Erickson, *Soviet High Command, passim.*

19. Even Alexander Orlov, the former NKVD chief during the civil war in Spain, accepted the conspiracy charges. See his article, "The Sensational Secret Behind the Damnation of Stalin," *Life*, April 23, 1956.

20. Eduard Benes, *Memoirs of Dr. Eduard Benes* (London, 1954), p. 20 and n. 8, p. 47.

21. *Foreign Relations of the United States, The Soviet Union, 1933–1939* (Washington, D.C., 1952), p. 385.

22. Quoted in a U.S. Embassy, France, Dispatch No. 1267, November 23, 1937 (National Archives File No. 861.00/11705, Washington, D.C.).

23. Quoted in Joseph E. Davies, *Mission to Moscow* (New York, 1941), p. 203.

24. *Documents on British Foreign Policy, 1919–1939* (London, 1949), 3rd series, I, 306–7.

25. Jane Degras, ed., *Soviet Documents on Foreign Policy* (London, 1953), III, 289–90.

DRAMATIS PERSONAE

A selected list of agents, both Soviet and émigré, connected with the Trust and General Kutyepov's operations.

ADERKASS, A. von. A member of one of General Kutyepov's combat teams which entered the U.S.S.R. in August 1927. Turned state's evidence against his companions, Samoilov and Stroevoi, and was sentenced to ten years' solitary confinement at the trial of the "five monarchist terrorists" in September.

ANISIMOV, A. A. Leader of one of General Kutyepov's combat teams which entered the U.S.S.R. in September 1928. Having broken his leg, he committed suicide to save his companions, Volkov and Voinov, who returned safely in early October.

ARAPOV. Soviet alias of a former tsarist officer and nephew of General Wrangel, who became a Trust representative in Berlin.

ARTAMONOV, Yuri A. (alias Lipsky). A Russian émigré who worked for British intelligence in Reval, Estonia, and a boyhood friend of the Trust agent Yakushev. Used the alias Lipsky as a Trust representative in Warsaw beginning in 1923.

ARTUZOV. Soviet alias of A. A. Slutsky (*q.v.*), an OGPU commissar during the Trust operation.

BALMASSOV, Aleksandr B. A member (with Solsky) of one of General Kutyepov's combat teams which entered the U.S.S.R. in August 1927 and was captured. Executed after the show trial of "five monarchist terrorists" in September 1927.

BASKAKOV (alias Kuzen). A Moscow policeman and bona fide member of the Trust who discovered it was an OGPU provocation and lost his life during its collapse in April 1927.

BIRK, Roman Gustavovich. Nephew of Estonian Ambassador Ado Birk and press attaché in Moscow. Worked as a double agent for the OGPU, handling liaison and communications for the Trust.

BOBADILLA, Pepita (Mrs. Sidney REILLY). A Latin-American actress who unknowingly became Reilly's second wife (a bigamous marriage approved by British intelligence) in 1924, and tried in vain to investigate his disappearance into the U.S.S.R. through Trust channels in 1925. Still living in obscurity in London in 1966.

BOYCE, Commander Ernest. The British intelligence agent who developed the first contacts with the Trust (1921–22) and who in later correspondence with Sidney Reilly urged him to work with the Trust, thus leading to his entrapment.

BUNAKOV, Nikolai Nikolayevich. A Russian émigré agent of British intelligence in Helsinki who turned double agent of the OGPU and figured in the entrapment of Sidney Reilly.

BURTSEV, V. L. Paris émigré intellectual and journalist who figured in the entrapment of both Boris Savinkov and Sidney Reilly.

CHEBISHEV, Nikolai. The minister of internal affairs with General Wrangel's forces in Yugoslavia, and one of the first to denounce Yakushev as an OGPU agent and the Trust as a provocation.

DICKHOFF-DEHRENTHAL. The confidential secretary and trusted lieutenant of the terrorist Boris Savinkov, who returned to the U.S.S.R. with him in 1925. Presumably a double agent of the OGPU. His wife was Savinkov's mistress.

DOLGORUKOV, Pavel Dimitrievich, Prince. One of General Kutyepov's agents who went into the U.S.S.R. for a week under Trust auspices in 1924 and returned again in 1926. Executed by the OGPU in June 1927.

DOVGALEVSKY, V. The Soviet ambassador in Paris at the time of the kidnaping of General Kutyepov in January 1930.

DRIMMER, V. T. The Polish military attaché in Reval, Estonia, who was closely involved in the entire development of the Trust operation.

DZERZHINSKY, Feliks Edmundovich. Head of the combined Soviet security police and intelligence agency from 1922 until his death in 1926, when he was succeeded by Menzhinsky. The agency was known as the Cheka, from the Russian initials of its title (All-Russian Extraordinary Commission for Combating Counterrevolution and Sabotage), and its agents as Chekists; renamed the GPU in 1922 and the OGPU in 1923; abolished and reorganized as the NKVD in 1934, after the death of Menzhinsky, when Yagoda became head of the agency. The headquarters, on what was formerly Lubyanka Square in Moscow, is still often called the Lubyanka, although the square has been renamed Dzerzhinsky Square. The Trust operation was directly supervised by Dzerzhinsky in its early stages.

ELVENGREN, Georgi Yevgenevich (alias Georgiev, Yurievsky, and Pavel Jordan). An anti-Soviet agent and terrorist who worked with Savinkov, Reilly, and General Kutyepov in a number of operations. Entered the U.S.S.R. in the summer of 1926, was captured and executed in June 1927.

FOSS, Klavdi A. Secretary of the émigré military organization, the ROVS. Head of "the Inner Line," a special counterintelligence agency under General Kutyepov, in 1927, with the tasks of eliminating security risks and *agents provocateurs* from his Combat Corps.

HELFAND, Lev B. An OGPU agent who as second secretary of the Soviet embassy in Paris presumably organized the kidnaping of General Kutyepov in January 1930, assisted by the local "resident" or station chief, Volovich (alias Yanovich), both of whom left Paris shortly after the event.

KARINSKY. One of General Kutyepov's agents who worked within the Leningrad branch of the Trust and escaped when it collapsed in 1927.

KHOLMSEN. Émigré general in General Kutyepov's organization who handled liaison with the Trust.

KLIMOVICH, General Yevgeni E. Former tsarist police director and head of General Wrangel's counterintelligence and security service who regarded the Trust as an OGPU provocation.

KOLESNIKOV, Viktor Stanislavovich (alias KIAKOVSKY or KOSINOV; family name Stetskevich). An OGPU commissar who with Artuzov (Slutsky) and Pillar supervised the Trust operation. Accidentally murdered by a religious fanatic in Mongolia in 1932.

KOVERDA, Boris. The sixteen-year-old émigré who assassinated Voikov, the Soviet ambassador to Poland, in June 1927, touching off an international crisis. (Not a member of General Kutyepov's Combat Corps.)

KUTYEPOV, General Aleksandr Pavlovich. Deputy commander of the émigré military forces in Gallipoli and Yugoslavia. Moved to Paris in the summer of 1923 and was put in charge of covert operations ("political work") by Grand Duke Nikolai in March 1924. Director of combat teams sent into the U.S.S.R. and, after the death of Wrangel in 1928, of all émigré military forces. Kidnaped by the OGPU in January 1930.

LAMPE, Colonel, later General (f.n.u.) von. General Wrangel's representative in Berlin who warned Paris émigré circles (Generals Kholmsen and Miller) after his first contacts with the Trust that it was a provocation.

LANGOVOY, General Aleksandr Alekseyevich (alias Denisov). A Trust military figure selected for liaison work with youth groups in Berlin and the "Eurasian Movement." Survived the purges and died in Moscow in 1964.

LARIONOV, Captain Viktor A. One of two known survivors of General Kutyepov's Combat Corps who led a three-man terrorist raid into the U.S.S.R. and bombed the Leningrad Central Party Club in June 1927. His companions, Monomakhov and Solovyev, were lost in later raids.

MARKOV, Nikolai Yevgenevich. An "Old Guard" émigré leader of the Supreme Monarchist Council (the VMC) in the early days of the Trust in Berlin.

MELGUNOV, Sergei Petrovich. Socialist Revolutionary émigré, historian and editor of the newspaper *Borba za Rossiu (The Struggle for Russia)*. While involved in an OGPU provocation, the "Second Trust," Melgunov simulta-

taneously directed an anti-Soviet underground inside the
U.S.S.R. during the period 1927–29.

MENZHINSKY, Vyacheslav Rudolfovich. Under Dzerzhinsky,
deputy chief of the OGPU and head of the agency from
1926 until his death in 1934, when he was succeeded by
Yagoda. Helped direct the Trust operation from the outset in 1921–22.

MILLER, General Yevgeni Karlovich. After the kidnaping of
General Kutyepov in 1930, the head of the émigré mili-
tary forces (ROVS), until he himself was kidnaped by the
OGPU in September 1937.

MONOMAKHOV, Vladimir. One of General Kutyepov's agents
who took part in Captain Larionov's raid on the Leningrad Party Club in June 1927. Returned on a terrorist
mission in July 1928 with Georgi Radkovich and bombed
the Lubyanka headquarters of the OGPU; escaped to the
suburbs, but died of injuries incurred in the explosion.

NIKOLAI NIKOLAYEVICH, Grand Duke. Former commander in
chief of the tsarist armies and later the leader of the
Russian émigrés in Paris. Died in January 1929, leaving
General Kutyepov the undisputed leader of émigré political as well as military affairs.

NOBEL, Gustav. Émigré industrialist and leader of *Torgprom,*
an anti-Soviet commercial and industrial association in
Paris which financed covert operations against the
U.S.S.R.

ORLOV, Vladimir. A notorious double or triple agent in Berlin;
a forgery expert who aided the anti-Soviet operations of
Elvengren, Reilly, and Savinkov.

PAVLOVSKY, Sergei. One of Boris Savinkov's most trusted agents
inside the U.S.S.R., who was broken by the OGPU and
used to lure Savinkov back into Russia.

PETERS, Georgi N. (alias Vosnessensky). An agent of General
Kutyepov's Combat Corps who accompanied Maria
Zakharchenko and Edward Staunitz on a terrorist raid
into the U.S.S.R. in early June 1927, during which all
three were killed.

PILLAR von Pilhau, Roman Aleksandrovich. An OGPU commissar who with Artuzov and Kiakovsky (Kolesnikov)
ran the Trust operation and who also took part in the
entrapment of Savinkov and Reilly.

PLEVITSKAYA, Nadezhda. Famous émigré singer, OGPU agent, and wife of General Skoblin, with whom she was involved in the kidnaping of General Miller in September 1937. Sentenced to twenty years' imprisonment at hard labor by a French court in 1938, she died in the Rennes prison for women in 1944.

POPOV, Colonel A. N. Former tsarist army colonel and OGPU agent, who conferred with General Kutyepov in Berlin shortly before the latter was kidnaped in Paris in January 1930.

POTAPOV, Nikolai Mikhailovich. A former lieutenant general recruited by the OGPU to play the role of chief of staff of the Trust, and to handle liaison with émigré military leaders. Survived the purges, taught military history at the Frunze Academy in Moscow, and died in 1946.

RADKOVICH, Georgi Nikolayevich. One of General Kutyepov's intelligence agents who with his common-law wife, Maria Zakharchenko, worked for more than three years inside the Trust organization in Moscow until its collapse in 1927. Returned in July 1928 on a terrorist mission with Monomakhov and exploded a bomb in the Lubyanka headquarters of the OGPU, but was himself killed by the explosion.

REILLY, Sidney George. "Britain's master spy," who collaborated with and financially supported Elvengren and the terrorist Boris Savinkov during several years of anti-Soviet operations. Lured back into the U.S.S.R. through Trust channels and executed in November 1925.

REILLY, Mrs. Sidney George. See Bobadilla, Pepita.

ROBERTI, N. A. de. Former tsarist colonel and OGPU agent who met General Kutyepov in Berlin shortly before the kidnaping in Paris, January 1930.

ROSENSTRÖM, Captain (f.n.u.). A Finnish intelligence officer of the Second Division who regularly assisted General Kutyepov's agents and other illegal border-crossers into the U.S.S.R.

SAMOILOV, Vasily Aleksandrovich. A Latvian intelligence agent in 1925. Later joined General Kutyepov's Combat Corps and entered the U.S.S.R. in August 1927 with a combat team. Captured and sentenced to death at the show trial of the "five monarchist terrorists" in September.

SAVINKOV, Boris Viktor. A Socialist Revolutionary (SR) terrorist who planned the assassination of several tsarist officials and later operated against the U.S.S.R. with support from Sidney Reilly and various Western intelligence agencies. Returned to the U.S.S.R., played a stellar role in a famous show trial, and was imprisoned in the VIP quarters of the Lubyanka, where he committed suicide (or was killed) in 1924.

SHCHELGACHEV, Captain Vsyevolod Ivanovich. An émigré officer who represented General Wrangel in Reval, and who also collaborated with British intelligence.

SHIRINSKY-SHIKHMATOV, Prince Yuri Aleksevich. A prominent émigré figure in Berlin, the ideologist of the Supreme Monarchist Council (VMC), which had early links with the Moscow Trust organization. His son Kyril represented the Trust at first in Berlin, later in Paris.

SHORIN, Aleksandr A. One of General Kutyepov's agents who worked inside the Leningrad branch of the Trust and escaped when it collapsed. Returned to the U.S.S.R. on a terrorist mission (with Solovyev) in August 1927. Tried and executed in September.

SHULGIN, Vasily Vitalevich. Prominent civilian associate of General Wrangel in Yugoslavia who made an extended trip into the U.S.S.R. (December 1925–February 1926), under Trust auspices, and wrote a sensational account *(Three Cities)* of his journey. Totally deceived by the OGPU.

SKOBLIN, General Nikolai Vladimirovich. Talented White Russian officer (a major general in command of the Kornilov Division at age 29), who married the famous singer Nadezhda Plevitskaya, an OGPU agent. Prominent in Paris émigré military circles from 1928 to 1936. A double agent of both the OGPU and the Nazi SD, through which he planted disinformation about the alleged Tukhachevsky conspiracy. Helped organize the kidnaping of General Miller, with whom he vanished in September 1937.

SLUTSKY, Abram A. (alias ARTUZOV). Chief of the counterintelligence branch of the OGPU during the Trust operation, 1922–27, and one of its managers (with Pillar and Kiakovsky-Kolesnikov). As chief of the INU (the Foreign Operations department of the NKVD) in the mid-1930's, he directed a number of assassinations and the kidnaping of General Miller. Resigned in protest against the purges and was liquidated.

SOLOVYEV, Sergei. One of General Kutyepov's agents who took part in Captain Larionov's raid on the Leningrad Party Club in June 1927. Returned to the U.S.S.R. on a terrorist mission with Shorin in August 1927, and was tried and executed in September.

SOLSKY, Aleksandr A. One of General Kutyepov's agents who entered the U.S.S.R. on a mission with Balmassov in August 1927. Tried and executed in September.

STAUNITZ, Edward Ottovich. (Family name Upenish; aliases: Savelev, Selyaninov, Staunitz, and Opperput). An OGPU agent who with Yakushev was a principal leader of the Trust. In charge of finances and black-market operations. His defection caused the collapse of the organization. Returned to the U.S.S.R. on a terrorist mission with Maria Zakharchenko and Georgi Peters (Vosnessensky), during which all three were killed in June 1927.

STROEVOI, Nikolai Pavlovich. A Latvian intelligence agent who joined General Kutyepov's Combat Corps and entered the U.S.S.R. on a mission in July 1927. Tried and executed in September.

SUSSALIN, Colonel Ivan Mikhailovich. One of General Kutyepov's agents who entered the U.S.S.R. through Trust channels, disappeared in Moscow, and was listed as executed by the OGPU in June 1927.

TICKSTON, Paul. A British (?) agent and representative of *Torgprom,* a "commercial and industrial association" in Paris used to finance anti-Soviet operations of Elvengren, Savinkov, and Reilly.

VOIKOV, Pavel I. One of the "executioners" of the Tsar and the royal family during the Russian Revolution. While serving as Soviet ambassador to Poland was assassinated by the sixteen-year-old émigré Boris Koverda in June 1927, an act which precipitated an international crisis.

VOINOV, S. S. A surviving member of the Anisimov mission, which penetrated into the U.S.S.R. for General Kutyepov in September–October 1928.

VOLKOV, V. J. A survivor of the Anisimov mission, which penetrated the U.S.S.R. in September–October 1928.

VOLOVICH, Vladimir B. (alias Yanovich). The OGPU "resident" or station chief in Paris in January 1930, who with

Helfand presumably organized the kidnaping of General
Kutyepov. Both left Paris shortly after the event.

WRANGEL, General Piotr Nikolayevich. The ablest of the White
Russian leaders during the Civil War, and later commander of the émigré forces in Yugoslavia, assisted by
his deputy, General Kutyepov. Died in Brussels in April
1928, leaving Kutyepov in command of the ROVS, the
émigré military force.

YAGODA, Genrikh Grigoryevich. Deputy chief of the OGPU
under Menzhinsky (1924–34). After 1934 chief of the
organization, renamed the NKVD, and organizer of the
Great Purges. Replaced by Yezhov in September 1936
and executed along with Bukharin and Rykov after a
show trial in March 1938.

YAKUSHEV, Aleksandr Aleksandrovich (alias Fedorov). A
Soviet engineer and "monarchist" who belonged to an
antiregime underground organization, the MOCR, which
was converted into the Trust. Became an OGPU agent
and political leader of the Trust, and made several liaison
trips abroad. Returned to civilian life after collapse of the
operation in 1927 and died in 1936.

ZABELIN, Vladimir. Soviet naval lieutenant. A member of the
Leningrad branch of the Trust who decided to withdraw
and was murdered by his companions.

ZAITSOV, Colonel A. A. General Kutyepov's deputy for intelligence and covert operations against the U.S.S.R.

ZAKHARCHENKO, Maria Vladislavovna (alias Schultz or Krash-
notonov). General Kutyepov's top intelligence agent who
with her husband, Georgi Radkovich, worked inside the
Trust in Moscow for over three years. Returned in June
1927 on a terrorist mission with Staunitz and Peters
(alias Vosnessensky), during which all three were killed.

ZAYONCHOVSKY, General A. M. (alias Boyar Vasily or Verkhovsky). Original leader of the antiregime "Monarchist
Union" (MOCR) in Moscow in 1921. Forced to work
for the OGPU when the MOCR was converted to the Trust.
Died in 1927 before the collapse of the organization.

ZUBOV, Aleksei. A Red Army officer assigned by the OGPU to
work as an agent within the Trust. Lost his life during the
collapse of the organization in 1927, and was decorated
posthumously with the Order of the Red Banner.

INDEX